Geography of Production and Economic Integration

The question of where economic activity will locate in the future is an important issue in present-day economics. In all societies, each market-oriented firm must make decisions about what to produce, for whom, how and where, while taking into consideration varying levels of economic integration caused by factors such as discriminatory trade deals and the growing importance of regionalisation in the world economy.

The traditional neo-classical model of international trade was updated during the 1980s with 'new trade theory' and subsequently by the geography of production in the1990s. This has deepened our understanding of the basis for, and effect of, specific locations of industries on trade and vice versa. At the heart of this development are market imperfections such as transport costs, imperfect competition, economics of scale, product differentiation and sunk costs. Although this new spatial economics is in its pioneering phase, it is nonetheless a formidable task to formalise it because of a mix of numerous market imperfections, historical accidents and chances that shape the geography of production. This book discusses the way in which economic integration and preferential trade agreements reinforce or alter the existing location of industries. Using a conceptual approach with real-life examples, the author seeks to clarify and explain the key tendencies and influences of the relationship between spatial distribution of production and economic integration.

Geography of Production and Economic Integration will help to develop the understanding of this highly topical subject for students, specialists and policy-makers.

Miroslav N. Jovanović is Associate Economic Affairs Officer in the Trade Division of the United Nations Economic Commission for Europe in Geneva. He is the author and editor of several Routledge books, including *International Economic Integration* and *European Economic Integration*.

Routledge Studies in the Modern World Economy

Geography of Production and Economic Integration

Miroslav N. Jovanović

London and New York

First published 2001
by Routledge
2 Park Square, Milton Park, Abingdon, Oxon, OX14 4RN

Simultaneously published in the USA and Canada
by Routledge
270 Madison Ave, New York NY 10016

Routledge is an imprint of the Taylor & Francis Group

Transferred to Digital Printing 2005

© 2001 Miroslav Jovanović

Typeset in Goudy by
Prepress Projects Ltd, Perth, Scotland

British Library Cataloguing in Publication Data
A catalogue record for this book is available
from the British Library

Library of Congress Cataloging in Publication Data
Jovanović, Miroslav N., 1957–
  Geography of production and economic integration / Miroslav N.
Jovanović
    p. cm. – (Routledge studies in the modern world economy ; 28)
  Includes bibliographical references and index.
    1. Economic geography. 2. Production (Economic theory). 3. Industrial
location. 4. International economic integration. I. Title. II. Series.

  HF1025 .J66 2001
  338.6´042–dc21   00-062738

  ISBN 0-415-23816-1

Printed and bound by Antony Rowe Ltd, Eastbourne

Својим синовима, Јовану и Николи

Στους υιούς μου, Γιάννη και Νικόλαο

Ai miei figli, Jovan e Nikola

To my sons, Jovan and Nikola

Who has put wisdom in the mind?
Or who has given understanding to the heart?

Job 38:36

Contents

Figures

Tables

Preface

I was very busy during the mid-1990s. During that period I wrote two books for Routledge: *European Economic Integration* (1997) and the second edition of *International Economic Integration* (1998). In addition, I edited, for the same publisher, a four-volume anthology entitled *International Economic Integration: Critical Perspectives on the World Economy* (1998). Towards the end of 1997 I decided to cut down on my writing and to devote time elsewhere.[1] But, around Christmas, Professor Bertram Schefold (Frankfurt) invited me to present a paper on the topic of economic integration and location of industries to a graduate summer school organised by Academia Europea (Bolzano) (Bressanone/Brixen, Italy, 31 August to 10 September 1998). I accepted with delight, thinking that it would take me only a short time to draft the paper. I was wrong.

I was so fascinated by the subject that my intellectual voyage continued. The present book is the result of the initial disturbance that created a bifurcation point in the location of my non-ergodic research interests. I apologise to the reader for the previous unintelligible sentence. It is a direct consequence of the 'professional deformation' that I experienced while analysing spatial economics and the geography of production. However, if the curious academic traveller reads the chapter on theory, the sentence that makes little sense now will be perfectly clear. At least that is my hope.

This book is organised as follows. The introduction (Chapter 1) spells out the basic issues that are considered throughout the book. Chapter 2 discusses a variety of key theoretical ideas regarding geography of production and international economic integration. Particular attention is devoted to the reasons why national and international firms choose specific locations and why clusters and entire industries develop in certain areas. The role of history and expectations is considered. Numerous examples from real life, including some that are the result of chance or accident, are provided to support the analysis. There are also several examples of how wars crucially influence the national geography of production. In essence, international economic integration and the resulting reduction in trade costs can affect the spatial distribution of economic activity in three ways,

---

1 'And further, by these, my son, be admonished: of making many books *there is* no end; and much study *is* weariness of the flesh' (Ecclesiastes 12:12).

depending on functional intra-industry production links, mobility of factors of production and public policy: an industry may spread, it may agglomerate, or the regional industrial structure may stagnate and polarise such that advanced regions develop high value-added activities and experience low unemployment while backward regions are left with low value-added economic activities and high unemployment.

Classic spatial economics was preoccupied by the geometrical shape of market areas in an idealised landscape or the ideal production site for given resources and markets. This ignored the crucial effect of market structure on the location of production. Chapter 3 identifies the extent and significance of market structure on spatial economics within a group of integrated countries. The chapter examines how firms compete, produce in an efficient way, innovate and specialise. The competition policy of the European Union is based on strict rules. Its impact on the spatial distribution of economic activity is discussed within the framework of non-tariff barriers, restriction of competition, monopolies and public subsidies.

Chapter 4 is devoted to industrial policy and its effect on the location of firms and industries. As such, it is closely entwined with the preceding chapter on market structure and competition policy. The chapter passes judgements on various rationales and instruments for intervention. In reviewing industrial policy in the European Union, this chapter includes a survey of the evolution of this policy; examines how the policy supports the creation, development, use and spread of new technology in the manufacturing sector; considers the role of powerful rent seekers; and analyses the involvement of the European Union in the services sector.

Chapter 5 discusses the geography of foreign direct investment. The importance of foreign direct investment and the trans-border business activities of transnational corporations, and the variety of forms these take, as well as their extent, are examined and supported by substantial statistical material from the European Union. The overused and confusing term 'globalisation' is considered and the determinants, advantages and dangers of transnational corporations locating and operating in a country or group of integrated countries are discussed.

Regional policy of the European Union is explored in Chapter 6. This policy affects around half of the 377 million citizens of the European Union and has a strong daily impact on tens of millions of them. Regional policy will become increasingly important as a result of two crucial developments. The first is Economic and Monetary Union. The participating member countries will no longer be able deal with national economic problems by manipulating policy instruments such as interest rate, the national debt or exchange rates. Potential national balance of payments disequilibria will become regional disequilibria once there is Economic and Monetary Union. Hence, one of the policy instruments to deal with such problems is regional policy. The second development is the enlargement of the EU to include Eastern European countries, which will introduce significant regional disparities. The chapter identifies and evaluates various justifications and instruments for intervention in regional matters. Regional discrepancies within the European Union, policy intervention and gaps in development in some candidate countries are discussed at length. It is concluded that, whereas member states are abandoning regional policy, the European Union is increasingly interfering in regional affairs.

Chapter 7 concludes the book by reasoning that the analysis of the interaction between international economic integration and geography of production is more suggestive than conclusive. Thus, it leaves the subject open to future analysis. In spite of this, certain lines and policy implications are obvious. Economic integration has an impact on the change in the geography of production (agglomeration, dispersion or a combination of the two). This influence is slow and depends on factor mobility, intra- and inter-industry production links and public policy.

The extensive bibliography at the end of the book may serve as a departure point to a curious student or researcher into the demanding, expanding, surprising and academically rewarding world of the geography of production and economic integration.

I hope that the book will be of interest to economists specialising in spatial economics, economic geography, location theory, international economics, economic integration, business studies, foreign investment and European studies. However, I would not regret it if it provokes curiosity in those whose principal interests lie elsewhere.

Acknowledgements

My involvement in the field of spatial economics and economic integration began at the end of 1997 following Professor Bertram Schefold's invitation to present a paper on the subject at a graduate summer school organised by Academia Europea. It extended and built on the already existing personal base of accumulated insight and research experience in economic integration. Over the years I benefited from discussions with and intellectual capital of many friends and colleagues. There are, however, several to whom I owe special gratitude for various types of assistance that resulted in this volume.

Un ringraziamento particolare va a Marina Rossi per il suo valido contributo, mai richiesto ma sempre presente. Lisa Borgatti gave detailed and useful comments on specific chapters. The same holds for Birgit Hegge and Antonio Majocchi. I am also grateful to Iain Begg, Ron Boschma, Evgenia Fainberg, Mariaelena Giorcelli, Bernd Hayo, Richard G. Lipsey, Robert LoBue, Marinette Payot, Andre Sapir, Bertram Schefold, Dusan Sidjanski, Gabriele Tondl, Marinko Veković and Tony Venables for their kind advice and assistance.

Statistical and legal material from the European Union, as well as explanations and updates, were kindly and swiftly provided by Axel Behrens, Hans-Peter Bucher, Kris Dekeyser, Céline Gauer, Francis Lefort, Nives Navarro-Blanco, Paolo Passerini, Sebastian Reinecke, Silke Stapel, Franca Stighezza and Carol van Mechelen. Cristina Giordano and the staff at the United Nations Library in Geneva supplied me with numerous sources. Slobodan Gatarić continued to solve PC-related problems, while Jovan Jovanović assisted in scanning, conversion and adjustment of images. I was delighted by Helen MacDonald's editing of my text. Finally, Andreja Živković, Robert Langham and Alan Jarvis of Routledge encouraged this project from the outset. Heidi Bagtazo was always helpful and efficient in handling everything before and after the manuscript reached Routledge.

Apart from the graduate summer school at the Seminary of Bressanone, where one can find peace and tranquillity, some of the content of this book has been presented at Idaho State University in Pocatello, the University of Geneva, the European summer school in Spetsae (Greece), at the University of Reutlingen (Germany) and at Johannes Kepler University in Linz. I benefited greatly from stimulating discussions with colleagues and students.

I am sincerely grateful to all those mentioned above. The usual disclaimer, however, applies here: it is I who am responsible for all shortcomings and mistakes. In addition, the views expressed are my own and have nothing to do with the organisation in which I work.

Miroslav N. Jovanović
Geneva and Bressanone,
January 2001

Abbreviations

CMEA	Council for Mutual Economic Assistance (Comecon)
DTI	Department of Trade and Industry
EFTA	European Free Trade Association
EIB	European Investment Bank
EMU	European Monetary Union
ERDF	European Regional Development Fund
EU	European Union
FDI	foreign direct investment
FIRA	Foreign Investment Review Agency
GATT	General Agreement on Tariffs and Trade
GDP	gross domestic product
GNP	gross national product
IIT	intra-industry trade
IMF	International Monetary Fund
MAI	Multilateral Agreement on Investment
MITI	Ministry of International Trade and Industry
NAFTA	North American Free Trade Agreement
NGO	non-governmental organisation
NTB	non-tariff barrier
OECD	Organization for Economic Cooperation and Development
PPS	purchasing power standard
PSI	production specialisation index
R&D	research and development
SITC	Standard International Trade Classification
SME	small and medium-sized enterprise
TNC	transnational corporation
TRIM	trade-related investment measure
TSI	trade specialisation index
US	United States
VAT	value-added tax
VCR	videocassette recorder
WTO	World Trade Organization

1 Introduction

One of the most important questions in economics is where economic activity will locate in the future. The purpose of this book is to contribute to the discussion on the way in which economic integration and preferential trade agreements (reduction or elimination of trade barriers within a group of countries) reinforce or alter the existing geography of production (location of industries). The approach taken in this book is conceptual, as the objective is to clarify and explain key tendencies rather than to provide definite answers to the issue of the relation and influence between spatial distribution of production and economic integration.

The subject of this book is relevant for three reasons. First, all societies and market-oriented firms must decide what, for whom, how and where to produce. Second, almost every country in the world is involved in some form of economic integration (discriminatory trade deals). These two issues must be considered together. Third, and equally relevant, is the growing importance of regionalisation of the world economy. This is exemplified in the inability of 135 member countries of the World Trade Organization to agree even on the agenda for the 'Millennium Round' of the global trade negotiations that took place on 30 November 1999 in Seattle. Well-organised and vociferous worldwide protests by farmers, environmentalists, opponents of genetically modified food and big business, labour unions and animal right activists made the job even more difficult. Therefore, the creation of integrated global economic policies appears to be a very hard task for quite some time to come. It seems that the regional approach to economic problems will call the tune at least in the medium term.

In this situation, the crucial questions for research are the following:

- Where will economic activity locate in the future?
- Does international economic integration encourage agglomeration, clustering, adjoint locations of linked productions, 'thick' market effects and spatial concentration of industries? Or, conversely, does agglomeration encourage economic integration?
- Does this cause convergence or divergence in the geography of production in the participating countries?
- Does this induce convergence or divergence in income in the participating countries?

- How do these forces interact?
- What is the role of public policy (intervention)?
- What will be the properties of economic adjustment (reallocation of resources) to the new situation?
- Where will be the new business 'hotspots' be?
- Who will benefit from these developments?

The spatial location of a firm is an issue only in an imperfect market. In an ideal market, for example one in which there are no transport costs (so that location makes no difference), the decision as to where to locate production would be easy. With no market imperfections, firms may be divided into units of any size and operate in all locations without any cost disadvantage.

The traditional neo-classical model of international trade was upgraded during the 1980s with 'new trade theory' and, subsequently, during the 1990s, by the geography of production (new spatial economics). These new theories deepened and extended the scope of our understanding of the basis for and effect of specific locations of industries on trade and vice versa. At the heart of the new extension of our knowledge are market imperfections such as transport costs, imperfect competition, economies of scale, product differentiation and sunk costs. Nonetheless, the new spatial economics is still in its pioneering phase. It is still a formidable task to formalise a mix of numerous market imperfections that shape the geography of production. One additional imperfection is economic integration. The issue at stake is whether, how and where increased specialisation, due to integration, alters the existing and future geography of production.

A reduction in trade costs should, theoretically, bring benefits through an increase in the scale of a country's specialisation. Neo-classical theory predicts that national specialisation will be reflected in differences in comparative advantage. Countries trade in order to take advantage of their differences. The 'new economic geography' and the 'new trade' theories argue that countries specialise and trade according to their economies of scale in production even if the countries are the same size and identical in terms of factors affecting trade.

Also of interest to the 'new school' is the impact of economies of scale on geographical agglomeration of production. The specialisation process (reallocation of resources) is associated with adjustment costs that need to be taken into consideration when ascertaining the net effect. These costs are lower in the case of intra-industry trade than inter-industry trade. The two 'new economic theories' study production linkages. They show that, depending on the strength of the functional production linkages, regional, national or international geography of production may change in response to the alteration in trade costs. This change in costs of trade may lead to changes in marketing, transport and communication technology, as well as in bilateral, regional or international reductions in trade barriers.

The study of the geography of production involves determining where specific goods or services are produced relative to the production of other goods or services. The subject is important because the geographical distribution of production throughout the world is not uniform. For example, the need to utilise specific technologies that depend on economies of scale and strong internal production links encourages clustering in 'central' areas where the costs of accessing large pools of information, suppliers and consumers (external economies of scale) are low. In this case, it is unlikely that development will be promoted in peripheral regions where trade costs are higher and where there is a lack of external economies of scale, resulting in the so-called 'distance fine'. This fine increases the costs of production and the cost of trade and hence reduces the competitiveness of a firm's regional output. Fortunately, there are positive factors, for example new transport and communications technology, that can reduce the size of the 'fine'. Trade liberalisation also eases the problem of trading across national frontiers.

Underdeveloped regions worry that high value-added economic activity will concentrate in the core regions. Prosperous regions worry that economic activity will move to other regions where wages are lower. In summary, all regions are anxious that competition will assault the established geography of production from all sides.

International economic integration and reduction in trade costs has three basic effects on the spatial distribution of economic activity depending on the functional intra-industry production links, the mobility of factors of production and public policy: an industry may either spread or agglomerate or the regional economic structure may stagnate and polarise in such a way that advanced regions develop high value-added activities and experience low unemployment, while backward regions are left with low value-added economic activities and high unemployment.

Policy-makers in countries that advocate trade liberalisation and economic integration are often faced with the argument that such policies will provoke a large-scale, unwanted and harmful (to some segments of business and labour) geographical reallocation of national or regional industries. For example, faced with a possible increase in the number of Eastern European countries in the EU, regions with a high proportion of 'sensitive' industries are concerned that their economic activities will be threatened by lower nominal labour costs in the East. Similar anxiety can be found in those Central and East European countries whose economies are in transition and which are negotiating to become full members of the EU. Some in these countries fear that their fragile industries will not be able to withstand competition from other EU countries in their home market and that their higher value-added output will not necessarily satisfy the demand criteria of the markets of other EU states.

Although regional specialisation results in obvious and real gains, asymmetric realignments may cause some problems: one region may experience monetary contraction, while another experiences monetary expansion. In the case of the EU countries, this is relevant not only because of the deepening of integration (the Single European Market and Economic and Monetary Union, EMU), but also because of the imminent increase in size of the EU with the inclusion of Eastern European countries. Without clear and strong policy instruments (strongly linked to fiscal and competition policy tools in the short term) the smooth operation of the Single European Market and the EMU may be in jeopardy.

This introduction sheds light on the continuing importance of research efforts, public debate and the search for appropriate policy to face the challenges of spatial distribution of economic activity and economic integration. Let us now consider the theories underlying choice of location by national and international firms, clusters, the effects of history and expectations, and the impact of and relation with international economic integration.

2 Theoretical considerations

2.1 Introduction

The purpose of this chapter is to provide an overview of the theoretical foundations of the field of spatial economics and its impact on and relation with international economic integration. It considers the factors and conditions that influence this decision of where to locate a business and the effect (if any) of economic integration on changes in the geography of production.

The chapter is structured as follows. Section 2.2 discusses the theoretical considerations underlying the location of economic activities. Special attention is devoted to the geographical origin, ownership and control of business assets. Section 2.3 considers the origin and operation of clusters of related and competing firms. The role of history and expectations is the subject of section 2.4. Wars can crucially influence the national geography of production. This is exemplified in section 2.5. The impact of international economic integration on the location of firms and industries is presented in section 2.6. The ideal partners for a customs union, free trade areas and the distribution of costs and benefits are covered in sections 2.7, 2.8 and 2.9 respectively. Following the conclusion, Appendix 1 recounts how the geographical location of some firms and industries has arisen by chance, while Appendix 2 lists clusters in Italy and Germany.

2.2 Theory of industrial location

Background

Spatial economics is found as a sub-branch of a number of branches of learning within the field of economics, albeit with varying degrees of rigour. Contributions to the study of spatial economics are to be found in a wide range of disciplines, including microeconomics, planning, development, economic geography, regional science, urban economics, location theory, industrial organisation, international trade,[1] foreign investment, economics of transport, business economics, innovation studies, public finance, price theory, competition (imperfect), labour economics, environment economics and resource economics. The common research denominator in all these fields is spatial dimension as an opportunity, as a medium for interactions and as a limitation. As a multidisciplinary research field, spatial economics integrates these previously separate research fields. This is in line with the new trend in science, in which various research methods are merged.

Progress in technology and moves towards a liberal economic policy create new challenges for theorists, policy-makers and business executives. As a number of economic activities became 'footloose', i.e. not reliant on a specific location, and highly mobile, one of the most taxing issues is the location or relocation of firms.

The geographical location of a firm is an issue only in a market with imperfections. In a ideal market, for example one in which there are no transport costs (so that the location makes no difference), the decision as to where to locate production would be easy. With no market imperfections, firms may be divided into units of any size and operate in all locations without any cost disadvantage. When considering possible locations for its business in an imperfect market, a firm may:

- prefer a least-cost geographical location for production and ignore the demand side of the function; or
- emphasise demand/revenue and neglect everything else.

In practice, neither of these options necessarily yields the maximum profit. Therefore, when deciding on a suitable location for its business, a firm must consider both options simultaneously. Firms attempt to maximise profit and minimise operating costs and any 'penalty' associated with different geographical locations.

Factors determining the location or relocation of firms and, hence, production geography include:

- availability, substitutability and prices of inputs (raw materials, energy, labour);
- cost of market access (trade costs);
- demand (size and consumer preferences);
- returns to scale;
- input–output production links
- competition and market structure;
- location decisions of other competing or supplying firms;
- earlier sunk costs in other locations (not yet depreciated);
- externalities;
- technology and the speed of its change;
- local R&D resources and capabilities;
- brain drain;
- utility costs;
- infrastructure;
- government policy ([dis]incentives: taxes, subsidies, public procurement);
- transport cost of inputs and output;
- cost of the project;
- availability of investment funds;
- retirement patterns.

This is a complex and risky task, and it comes as no surprise that national or regional production geography changes slowly, with or without economic integration.

Regions and intervention

A region may be more easily discerned than defined. The definition of a region varies depending on the context. As a geographical phenomenon, a region is easily distinguished from other regions. However, the concept of 'region' also has political, governmental and administrative facets, as well as an ethnic and social aspect characterised by human and cultural features. A region is also an economic concept characterised by various economic factors, their combinations and mobility. In economic terms a region can be defined as a geographical area that consists of adjoining units with similar incomes and greater interdependence of incomes than between similar geographical areas (Bird, 1972: 272). A region of a country or an economic union may be thought of as an open economy.

Controversy regarding the 'region problem' remains. However, several observations may provide some insight into the issue:

- Different regions may grow at unequal rates for long periods of time, resulting in government intervention aimed at reducing this problem.
- Intervention may also aim to equalise consumption or gross domestic product (GDP) per capita among different regions.
- A government may be interested in attaining relatively equal access of the population to an adequate level of public goods and services.
- Public authorities are also interested in having a spatially stable distribution of economic activities and population in order to avoid negative externalities.

The neo-classical or convergence school of thought takes no account of economies of scale and argues that the 'regional problem' and the location of economic activity are not problems at all. This school of thought holds that free trade and unimpeded factor movement would result in a uniform geographical distribution of people, skills and economic activity, equalising factor earnings and living standards in all regions. Poorer regions would converge on richer ones. Apart from transport costs, it should not matter where a tradable good or service is produced. Hence, the location of production (spatial distribution of output or production geography) is no more than an operational detail as transport and communication costs decrease with time.[2] Peripheral countries and regions should benefit from liberalisation of trade and integration in terms of an increased inflow of goods and services and from the development of new industries. At the extreme, there will be complete equalisation of factor prices.

The prevailing liberal (non-intervention) attitude in the field of regional policy in the market economies had some credence until the economic crisis of the 1930s. With free trade and perfect allocation of resources,[3] regional policy intervention is not necessary. Such a 'classical' or convergence approach was not borne out by time. Even *laissez-faire* governments may consider it beneficial to intervene in the economy as the adjustment process may take too long to be politically acceptable.

The 'new' spatial economics (geography of production) focuses on increasing structural disparities rather than equalisation among regions and countries. It takes into account market imperfections and cumulative causation effects and shows how new assumptions, integration and trade liberalisation may increase geographical concentration of industries in the core countries and regions rather than decrease it. Imperfect markets with economies of scale, entry barriers,[4] constrained mobility of factors or externalities may increase the attractiveness of already advanced areas, reinforce their absolute advantages and widen regional gaps, rather than reduce them. However, structural disparity among the regions does not necessarily mean that there is an income disparity. If each region specialises in a different output activity, economic structure changes but incomes in all the regions may both grow and remain similar.

The inclusion of transport costs and market imperfections (economies of scale and other externalities) in theoretical considerations expanded the classical concept and moved it closer to reality. Given that concentration is the most striking feature of the geography of production, there exists a clear evidence of some kind of increasing returns to scale (Krugman, 1992: 5). New technologies in some industries may overcome some of the obstacles to the spread of production, but not to any great extent. Hence, the pattern of regional specialisation and trade can be arbitrary, and potential gains from specialisation and trade are likely to be ambiguous.[5]

Even in a perfectly homogeneous world, production activities would tend to cluster as a result of economies of scale and varying resource endowment. In these circumstances, government intervention (industrial, competition, trade and regional policies) is generally directed towards an increase in the national or regional production potentials and capabilities through a (supposedly) more efficient allocation of resources from the national standpoint.[6] The objective of such intervention is to influence the geographical distribution of economic activity and to create wealth to ameliorate and eventually eliminate the 'regional problem'. If policies matter, then one would expect to find an abrupt change in production activities when crossing frontiers at which policies change.

Governments intervene in regional matters for at least the following three reasons:

- *Equity*: this is a strong social motive prompted by public pressure on the government to try to achieve a 'proper' balance and an 'orderly' geographical distribution of national wealth among different regions.
- *Efficiency*: this is a desire to employ, sustain and increase national economic potentials and capabilities.
- *Strategic behaviour*: this gives public authorities the chance to shape comparative advantages and influence the output potentials and capabilities of the country.

Intervention in the form of a regional policy is not a simple task as technology, competition and demography change constantly. In spite of intervention in regional affairs over the past decades, in the 1990s many EU member countries exhibited a trend towards abandoning or reducing intervention in regional matters. However, at EU level, enthusiasm for intervention in regional affairs remained.

Theories of location

The study of the location of production (spatial economics) has a long if somehow meagre history (Krugman, 1998a: 7). The problem was noted, for example, by Ohlin (1933: 589), who wrote that 'the theory of international trade is nothing but *internationale Standortslehre*' (teaching about international location). In the same vein, Isard (1956: 207) wrote that 'location cannot be explained without at the same time accounting for trade and trade cannot be explained without the simultaneous determination of locations… trade and location are the two sides of the same coin'.

Let us now turn to the principal theoretical considerations about the location of a firm. We shall first look into the issue without paying attention to the origin and ownership of the firm. Second, the issue of ownership and control is included in consideration in order to get the full picture.

National firms

Adam Smith and David Ricardo referred to the geography of production and spatial economics in an indirect way. A country specialises in the production of a good for which it has an absolute advantage in production. Hence, according to Smith, an absolute advantage determines the geographical location of production. Ricardo's argument is similar, but in his model a country specialises in the production of goods for which it has a *relative* advantage in production.

In addition to these classical models, the standard *Heckscher–Ohlin* model holds that the location of production is determined by national endowment of the factors of production. A country produces and exports goods for which it has a relative abundance of the factors of production in comparison with factors of production for other goods. Conversely, a country will import goods whose production requires factors that are scarce in the national economy. Ohlin (1933: 133), in considering 'localisation' of industry in one or a few countries, argued that 'it must be shown that costs of production on the basis of existing factor prices are lower than in other countries: certain factors are cheaper here than abroad, which accounts for that condition'. This model elegantly assumes that there are no specific factors and that production functions are identical in all countries. As such, it does not provide a complete answer to the issue of the location of production because it cannot explain intra-industry trade. Although the importance of endowment of factors of production in the location of production and some processing of primary resources is indisputable, this approach cannot explain the location of footloose industry, nor does this model consider market structure, demand conditions and trade costs. In addition, the Heckscher–Ohlin theory does not explain the location of industry in regions with a high mobility of factors (such as the US) or in countries with a broadly similar endowment of factors (France and Germany).[7] A common feature of standard trade theories is that they consider states but completely ignore firms or the distribution of economic activity within a country. This gap is filled by spatial economics

A common starting point in urban (spatial) theory is the land rent and land use model formulated by von Thünen (1826). This model is primarily concerned with the location of agricultural production. The model assumes a given isolated city (one consuming centre) and surrounding agricultural hinterland, as well as homogeneous land surface. Land rents are highest in the city. From there, they steadily decline to zero at the outermost limit of cultivation. Under the above assumptions the model explains the kind of crop that would be grown at places at different distances from the market. In other words, farmers decide on the type of production by taking into account land rent and cost of transportation. As transport costs and yields differ among crops, the result is a spontaneous development of concentric circles of production around the city. Land is allocated to different crops in a (optimal) way that minimises the production and transport costs of different crops. This early model, however, does not consider the role played by economies of scale.

The problem in von Thünen's model is determining which crop to produce in a given location. In contrast, Weber's (1909) model of an optimal plant site specifies which branch of industry is being considered and the problem is to determine the geographical location for production. Weber's model takes the geographical location of markets, raw materials and population as given. An individual producer tries to minimise the combined costs of production and delivery. The assumption is that there can be only one location for production. When the production costs are independent of location, the location problem relates to the minimisation of transport costs for inputs and output.[8] This is the key condition in the decision-making process about the location of a firm according to Weber. Geographical remoteness is used by some to explain why peripheral regions are marginalised in economic and certain social terms. However, in the case of many industries this is a weak reason. Innovations in transport and communication technologies mean that these costs are rarely the most important determinant in the location of business. Hence, a peripheral location is not an insurmountable obstacle for a number of businesses, as demonstrated by the examples of Japan, Australia or New Zealand. Moses (1958) extended Weber's work and integrated location theory with theory of production. This allowed the relation between substitution of inputs and geographical location of a firm to be investigated.

Christaller (1933) sought to clarify and explain the rationale underlying the number, sizes and spatial distribution of cities. His analysis is based on the idea of market threshold and transport distance. He put forward the idea that cities form a 'hierarchy of central places'. This hinges on the supposition that larger cities can sustain a wider variety of activities relative to smaller (low order) cities and villages. Such uneven distribution of production arises from economies of scale. In spite of obvious value for the analysis of urban growth and distribution of services, this rigid application of the impact of market size neglects the impact of unequal distribution of natural resources, progress in technology and negative externalities that come from agglomeration.

Developing the central-place theory further, Lösch (1940) started with a useful, but most unrealistic, assumption that the spatial distribution of raw materials and population is completely uniform. An efficient pattern of central places would have the shape of nested hexagonal (honeycomb) market areas with no empty corners. This means that certain economic activities can be carried out only at a restricted number of locations. It was subsequently demonstrated that there is a wide range of geographical configurations of firms. Spatial arrangements that satisfy the equilibrium condition include squares, rectangles and regular and irregular hexagons (Eaton and Lipsey, 1976: 91). Even though based on unrealistic assumptions, the model of central places should not be completely disregarded. A coherent general equilibrium model found some justification for the central-place theory (Krugman, 1993a: 298).

Central-place theory reveals the factors that need to be examined during the process of deciding the location of an industry or a firm. These factors are sources of supply, intersections of traffic routes and the centre of gravity.[9] In order to reduce the inaccuracy of such a 'technical' process (suitable for centrally planned systems) one needs to consider additional elements that operate in a market-based economy. They include the actions of other functionally related firms, competitors, consumers and government policies.

Perroux (1950; 1955; 1961) introduced the intuitive concept of 'growth poles' in spatial economics. The idea was discussed in the context of controversy between balanced and unbalanced regional growth during the 1950s. Geographical agglomeration, significant production linkages (with the key industry) and substantial human resources are necessary for the growth of a pole. A firm is located in a space surrounded by poles. Each pole exerts both centrifugal and centripetal forces. Hence, each pole has its zone of influence (it attracts and repulses firms) and interacts with other poles. If, however, a particular pole does not have some degree of flexibility and adaptability to new technologies and changes in the market, it will stagnate and decline. For instance, during the 1960s the French government chose eight urban areas and bolstered their growth in the hope that this policy would counteract the growth of Paris. However, the policy of geographical concentration of investments was diluted over time as it was beset with political problems. Many other national 'areas' exerted pressure to be included in the group of geographical poles selected for special treatment. The evaluation of the policy of geographical growth poles is fraught with difficulties as the policy was not vigorously implemented in practice.

Arthur (1989; 1990a; 1994a,b) argued that models of production geography should give weight to differences in factor allocation, transport costs, rents and competition. In this case, the pattern of production locations is an equilibrium outcome. Hence, history has no place in these models: the location of firms is fixed and predictable (Arthur, 1994a: 49–50). However, if one takes increasing returns and multiple equilibria into consideration, the new model has four properties that cause serious difficulties in analysis and policy-making. These features are (Arthur, 1989: 116–17):

- *Non-predictability*: ex ante knowledge of firms' preferences and the potential of new technologies may not be sufficient to predict the 'market outcome'.
- *Potential inefficiency*: increasing returns may promote the development of technology with inferior long-term utility.[10]
- *Inflexibility*: once an outcome such as a dominant technology begins to emerge it becomes 'locked in' and persists for a long period of time.[11]
- *Non-ergodicity*:[12] small, unpredictable, random and arbitrary events (chances and accidents) and economies of scale in a non-ergodic system may irreversibly determine the final outcome as they are neither normalised, nor averaged away, nor forgotten by the dynamics of the system.

This model takes account of history, but the dynamics of the system, increasing returns, multiple equilibria and non-dependencies place theoretical and practical limits on the degree of certitude with which the future spatial location of an industry can be predicted.

When agglomeration forces based on increasing returns are unbounded, an industry will be monopolised by a single geographical location. Which region wins depends on its geographical attractiveness and to some extent historical accident, in particular the early preferences of the first entrants. If, however, the agglomeration forces that result from increasing returns are bounded, then various regions may share the industry in the same way as if agglomeration economies were absent (Arthur, 1990b: 249). Places containing a large number of firms in one industry cast an 'agglomeration shadow' in which little or no settlement takes place. This results in separation of an industry. In bounded agglomeration economies, neighbouring locations cannot share the industry, but sufficiently separated regions can. Bounded agglomeration economies caused separation and dispersion. Again, 'which locations gain the industry and which become orphaned is a matter of historical accident' (Arthur, 1990b: 247).

According to Fujita *et al.* (1999: 131), cities exist because firms locate at a cusp in the market potential function produced by a concentration of other firms. Cities form because a growing and spreading agricultural population makes it beneficial for producers to form new cities. The size of cities differs (there is a hierarchy) because of differences in industrial externalities and transport costs. Finally, natural advantages (i.e. the existence of harbours) help as they create natural cusps in market potential. In addition, according to Arthur (1994b: 109), the development of cities cannot be explained by economic determinants alone; chance events must also be taken into account. Cities emerged in areas where immigrants with particular skills settled, where politicians decided to build railways and canals and where trains stopped for the night.

Why are cities (clusters) different sizes? Henderson (1974) argued that there is a trade-off between economies of agglomeration of industries specific to that city and general diseconomies (negative externalities) such as costs related to commuting and high rents which (apart from pollution) do not depend on the structure of the local industry. The optimum city size depends on the maximum welfare of participants in the economy. It makes little sense for industries with no overlap (e.g. steel production and publishing) to locate in the same city. Cities need to specialise in one or a few industries with related external economies. These external economies, however, vary a great deal across industries. Because of strong links internal to the industry, a financial centre may do best if it includes virtually all financial institutions. This is not true for the textile or food industry. Hence, the optimum size of a city depends on its role (Fujita *et al.*, 1999: 20).

The literature on the geographical location of firms is obsessed with the geometric shape of market areas in an idealised landscape or with the optimum production site given resources and markets. It ignores the crucial issue of market structure. According to Krugman (1992: 5), this is 'doing things in the wrong order, worrying about the details of a secondary problem before making progress in the main issue'. This is one of the reasons for devoting a special chapter in this book to the issue of market structure.

International firms

Spatial economics usually ignores the issue of ownership and control of a firm because it implicitly assumes that these do not matter or supposes that all assets are domestically owned. Transnational corporations (TNCs) increase mobility of capital, expand availability of information and new products, change competition structure, alter substitution of labour for capital and have different locational considerations than a comparable national firm engaged in the same type and scale of activity. There is a tendency for strictly national firms to expand where they already are, while TNCs locate where they think they may profit from access to the largest and growing market, favourable costs of labour, transport and/or taxes and subsidies. TNCs have 'organisational capital', i.e. a common set of rules, practices, routines and values, that enable them to overcome various barriers while operating in different geographical, social, legal and other environments.

There are at least seven basic theories as to why firms engage in trans-border business activities and become TNCs.[13] First, the motivation to control foreign firms may come not from the need to employ assets in a prudent way in foreign markets, but rather from the need to remove competition from other enterprises. Hymer (1976) advocated such a *market power* approach by TNCs. Reuber (1973: 133–4), in a similar vein, argued that long-term strategic factors for foreign direct investment (FDI) include the desire to eliminate competitors from foreign markets, to be within a protected foreign market, to secure a low-cost source of supply and to lock the target country to a specific technology for a long time. Such a longer-term strategic view overshadows possible short-term variations in the profitability of FDI. The problem with this argument is that most TNCs (in terms of numbers) are small or medium sized. In 1999, there were around 63,000 parent firms with around 690,000 foreign affiliates (UNCTAD, 2000: 9). This shows that not all TNCs are monopolists or oligopolists at home and are trying to exercise that power abroad. If there is strong competition in the market for differentiated goods and services and an easy substitution is possible (perfumes, soaps, watches, clothing, vehicles, passenger air transport on certain lines, to mention just a few examples), then the market power argument for the transnationalisation of business is weakened.

Second, while the market power model excludes potential rivals from competition, the *internalisation* theory holds that an arm's-length relation among individual firms is in some cases less efficient (e.g. trade in technology) than an intra-firm cooperative association. Profits may be maximised by means of an efficient and friendly intra-firm trade in intermediaries that eliminates sometimes excessive transaction costs (middlemen, exchange rate risk, infringement of intellectual property rights, bargaining costs) when the business is conducted through the market. In these circumstances a hierarchical organisation (an enterprise) may better reward parties in the longer term, as well as curbing bargaining and incentives to cheat, than markets and external contractors. Payments of around 80 per cent of fees and royalties for technology 'take place between parent firms and their foreign affiliates' (UNCTAD, 1997: 20). This is an indication that TNCs play a key role in disseminating technology around the world (at least where they operate).

While Hymer conceives of TNCs as vehicles for reaping monopoly profits and for the internalisation of pecuniary externalities, the internalisation model views TNCs as a mode of business organisation that reduces transaction costs and internalises non-pecuniary externalities. This model of FDI may be convincing in some cases, but it does not explain the structure and location of all FDI flows, since in addition to the internalisation possibilities there ought to be ownership-specific and locational advantages for FDI.

Third, the *eclectic paradigm* (Dunning, 1988a: 42–5; 1999: 1–3) explained the geographical location of the production of goods and services (trans-border business activities of TNCs) as a mix and interaction of three independent factors:

- In order to locate production abroad and be successful, a TNC must have or control internationally mobile income-generating *ownership*-specific (O) advantages, assets or skills. These firm-specific advantages include tangible and intangible advantages such as better technology, brand name, access to wide markets, monopoly, competence of managers, etc., that are superior to the ones that are available to local firms (including other TNCs) in the potential target country.
- *Locational* (L) (non-mobile) advantages refer to the comparative or location-specific advantages of the target country. They refer both to the geographical distribution of resources and to those created by the government.[14]
- There must be opportunities for the *internalisation* (I) of ownership-specific advantages (management and quality control, protection of property rights, avoidance of uncertainty of buyers, etc.). It should be in the interest of the firm to transfer these advantages abroad within its own organisation rather

than sell the right to use these advantages to other firms located in the country of intended production. Fixed exchange rates or a single international currency provide a degree of stability necessary for longer-term business planning with a high degree of confidence.

The eclectic paradigm claims that the exact mix of the OLI factors facing each potential investor depends on the specific context. If a firm possesses/controls ownership-specific advantages, then it may use licensing to penetrate foreign markets. If such an enterprise has both ownership-specific and internalisation advantages, it may use exports as a means of entering foreign markets. Only when a firm is able to take *simultaneous* advantage of OLI advantages will it employ FDI as a means of locating and operating in foreign markets. This model, however, does not apply to diversified and vertically integrated TNCs (Caves, 1996: 5).

Fourth, the *product cycle* model reasons that mature (and, perhaps, environmentally unsound) lines of production of goods (there is no explicit reference to services) will be passed on to the developing countries (Vernon, 1966; Posner, 1961). Such geographical reallocation of production depends greatly on low factor costs. This argument as the major explanation for the location of business abroad cannot pass the test of recent developments. There is a heavy concentration of FDI in developed countries, whereas the majority of developing countries are relatively neglected in FDI flows. In addition, countries are now beginning to invest overseas at a much earlier stage of their development than ever before. The newly industrialised countries and many other developing countries are investing abroad. In many cases these investments are in the developed world. Such developments may be prompted by the desire:

- to be present in the developed countries' markets (closer to the customers);
- to be near the source and cluster of the major technological developments in manufacturing, distribution and management (to have a foreign 'listening and learning post');
- to participate in R&D programmes;
- to avoid the dangers of protectionism in target countries;
- to win public contracts;
- to exploit the strength of host country's domestic currency.

Fifth is the *follow my leader* thesis. Oligopolists are risk minimisers. They want to protect their own market position and avoid destructive competition and therefore try to minimise risk and follow each other into new (foreign) markets (Knickerboker, 1973: 100). A study of timing of FDI by the US TNCs in manufacturing seems to support this proposition. Japanese TNCs involved in car manufacturing and consumer electronics were 'following their domestic leader' and located their manufacturing facilities in the EU and US during the 1980s and 1990s. In addition, the mergers and acquisitions 'mania' of the 1990s in the EU and US shows how asset seeking by one TNC may be followed by others.

Sixth, the competitive international industry model for the location of business abroad refers to oligopolistic competition and rivalry within the same industry. This is basically *exchange of threats* (tit for tat strategy) to business moves by foreign rivals (Graham, 1978). Large firms keep an eye on the actions of their rivals, i.e. they act strategically (pay attention to the likely reaction of their competitors to their own actions). What Standard Oil does in Europe, Shell will (try to) do in the US. Competition is not 'cut-throat', but rather is 'stable' among several oligopolies. Other examples of this rivalistic trend include FDI in the manufacturing of cars and tyres or supply of services such as hotels and advertising. Small and medium-sized enterprises (SMEs) such as petrol stations in the middle of nowhere may act independently, but SMEs in a cluster keep a vigilant eye on the actions of their competitors.

Seventh is the *diversification of portfolios* model of foreign investment (Brainard and Tobin, 1992). This approach considers uncertainty. Fluctuations in the rates of return on capital invested in various countries introduce an element of risk. This inconvenience may be reduced by a diversification of portfolios.

In addition to the seven basic theories of why firms locate abroad, two other dimensions are relevant for coming to grips with the issue. Kravis and Lipsey (1982: 222) argued that *cost minimisation* determines the location of foreign affiliates of TNCs. However, the importance of this determinant varies from industry to industry. While Yamawaki (1993: 19–20) does not dispute the importance of a relative difference in factor costs, he argues that the *availability of technology* in the target country is an additional and equally important factor in the location of Japanese FDI in the EU. A Japanese TNC operating in a particular industry will decide to locate in the EU country that has a certain advantage over other EU countries in the same industry. Japanese TNCs prefer Britain for the production of cars and electric/electronic equipment, Germany for precision instruments and machinery and Belgium for stone, glass and clay products, while TNCs in the chemicals industry prefer Germany, the Netherlands, Spain and France (Yamawaki, 1993).

No single theory can completely account for the trans-border investment activities of firms. However, taken together, these theories may provide useful elements for the understanding of the issue.

Conclusion

The geography of production (spatial economics) has been neglected by mainstream economic theory not because this research field is uninteresting but because the issues have traditionally been regarded as intractable. Ricardo's comparative advantage model provided insufficient answers to the problem. New research 'tools' such as increasing returns, production linkages (presence of intermediate goods), multiple equilibria (with centrifugal and centripetal forces) and imperfect competition were introduced to the field of the geography of production in the early 1990s. These tools helped to explain why firms form clusters. Such new developments did not mean the birth of a new subject. Economic geography (spatial economics) has always been important. Although ever-increasing demand for quantitative severity is making analysis harder, the introduction of new analytical tools has helped economic geography find its proper place in the mainstream economics and become a hot research topic.

2.3 Clusters

Urbanisation is an important feature of modern society. One of the reasons for this is that the share of labour in agriculture is declining relative to capital. Footloose industries are less dependent on natural resource than other types of manufacturing and service industries. They may sometimes place more emphasis on proximity to final markets, which contributes further to the urbanisation trend. Another incentive to urbanisation is the dependency of many manufacturing and service operations on access to public services, especially in countries that are known for intervention. For these reasons, lobbyists cluster in politically significant cities such as Brussels or Washington, DC, because this is where decisions are made and subsidies distributed.

In the dim and distant past the creation of wealth largely depended on the local availability of natural resources. However, as the economy evolved, wealth creation came to depend more on physical assets (mainly equipment and finance). The prosperity of the modern economy depends not only on the physical, but also, and increasingly, on intangible assets such as knowledge,[15] information-processing capacity and organisation capabilities.

In the past, a mix of geographical, economic and historical factors shaped the industrial development and location of firms, industries and cities. Many of these factors were quite accidental. The most attractive geographical locations for setting up cities, industries and businesses included:

- crossroads;
- mouth of a river;
- safe natural harbours;[16]
- defendable hilltops;
- places with ample fresh water;
- rich soil;
- dry cool highlands (free of malaria-carrying mosquitoes).

In general, these locations can be internationally linked either by a reduction in transport costs or by agglomeration economies (increasing returns in spatial form)[17] that include a large market. A country that has a growth-friendly population distribution is the US. Some three-quarters of the US population lives in the 100-km-wide coastal belt that includes the Great Lakes and the St. Lawrence Seaway.

During past centuries, colonial powers obtained natural resources from their colonies. In many cases they prevented the development of manufacturing industry in the colonised countries in order to secure those 'outer markets' for the exports of the manufactured goods from the colonial master. Thus, local competition was eliminated and any development of manufacturing activity that did take place was usually in port cities and was limited to primary processing.

Previously the location of a firm was influenced both by its share of immobile local resources and by flows of mobile factors.[18] Once a business activity develops in an area, provided the economic system is flexible, the area attracts (by gravity) other business activities to the region. This model of uneven development is based on the possibility of meaningful multiple equilibria in the presence of external economies. The point is evident: with external economies, the return to resources in any particular industrial activity is higher when more resources are committed to it (Krugman, 1991: 651). Modern firms are characterised by a high degree of mobility in their search for profitable opportunities, and this mobility extends not only to the region or country but internationally. In the case of a footloose firm, the advantages of one location over another depend more on artificial factors than allocation of natural resources.

The probability of the location of an industry resulting from a historical accident is shown in highly stylised, graphical form in Figure 2.1 (Arthur, 1994b: 107–9). If the distribution of potential locations of an industry is convex (Figure 2.1a), with a single minimum and a corresponding single outcome, the location is not influenced by historical chance. This type of distribution is exemplified by the mining and steel-making industries, which are normally located close to their source of raw materials. If, however, the distribution is concave (Figure 2.1b), with two minima, then there are two potential outcomes, each resulting in a different location, and the outcome may depend on the historical chance. Hence, multiple equilibria make policy analysis conceptually difficult. This type of distribution is exemplified by corner shops, bakeries and petrol stations. However, firms in most industries need to be close to each other (i.e. they tend to agglomerate and create towns and cities) not only to be close to common supplies of inputs, but also to foster competition and to facilitate exchange of information, which can be hampered if firms are spatially dispersed.

A concentration of functionally related business activity within a relatively small area (agglomeration; 'thick' market effects; benefits of co-location; and non-ergodicity) provides firms with collective gains that would not be available to

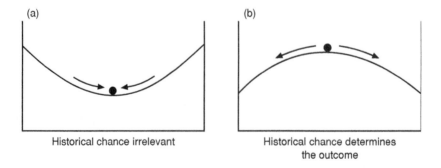

(a)   (b)

Historical chance irrelevant   Historical chance determines
                                            the outcome

Figure 2.1 Concave (a) and convex (b) distributions of potential industry locations.

them if they operated in a remote place. These shared benefits or externalities are different from those that are created within and available to a single firm. In essence, clusters create economies that are external to individual firms but internal to a network of firms in a cluster. Hence, a great deal of an individual firm's competitive advantage is outside it but inside the location where it operates.

A cluster is a large group or a critical mass of functionally related firms in a specific geographical location. This functional relation among the firms may be downstream (clients), horizontal (competitors) and/or through the circulation of the accumulated knowledge by the means of turnover of personnel.

A firm locates in an area where there are firms in the same or related industry (a cluster) because:

- it has production links with other firms;
- it may benefit from the already existing pool of suppliers;
- there are services such as finance, information, consulting and maintenance in the area;
- there may be a pool of trained and experienced labour;
- the cost of transport may be reduced;
- there may be a concentration of consumers (proximity to the major growing markets is often the most important reason for the selection of a particular location);
- they may jointly negotiate contracts with transporters and organise export promotion boards and so on.

Manchester (England) in the nineteenth century provides an example of a cluster specialising in textile manufacturing. Subsequently, firms involved in the manufacturing of looms and their repair or the provision of bleaching, dying and finishing facilities also located there. In the course of time, the town set up a technical college to train people for the manufacture of machinery, textile design and other skills related to the local industry. All this was supported by marketing organisations such as the Cotton Exchange (Smith, 1981: 60–1). A similar story can be told about Reutlingen in Germany. However, even new industries follow the 'old rule' of geographical concentration (clustering). That is why there is a Silicon Valley in California or Route 128 in Boston (because the best universities are nearby).

A more recent example of clustering can be found in the town of Sialkot in Pakistan. This town is the world's major exporter of surgical instruments and hand-sewn footballs. The success of this, as well as of all other, clusters is based on two factors: a demand-driven approach and competition based on collective efficiency (Schmitz, 1998: 6). An example of a joint action can be found in the surgical instruments manufacturing cluster in Tuttlingen, Germany. Firms in the cluster produced joint publications on various topics of common interest including booklets on the quality requirements of the surgical instruments industry, how to use the instruments correctly and a list and profile of firms in Tuttlingen that produce surgical instruments (which is distributed to customers visiting the city).

Technical advances in transportation, information technology and the organisation of production and distribution reduce production time and costs. They 'do away' with distance. 'Globalisation' (integrated international production) enables production and ownership to be separated. This makes it difficult for established locations to hang on to income-generating activities. At the same time, strong centripetal forces means that some locations remain 'sticky places in slippery space' (Markusen, 1996a: 293). Spatial barriers to the location of businesses are becoming less important, but capital is more sensitive to the choice of location.

Until the 1960s it seemed to be more efficient to move people to jobs by migration. However, the footloose nature of many modern industries supports production in relatively small and flexible units. Hence, there is an arbitrary and uncertain element (multiple equilibria) in the location of firms that have footloose industrial character. Locations that are close to consumers mean savings in the transport costs of final output, whereas other locations may result in savings in the cost of production. Because of the costs of inputs, economies of scale and forwarding outlays, one business may favour peripheral locations while another may prefer locations nearer to the consumers.

In a simple model, the allocation of manufacturing between two regions sets the difference in real wages between them. Consider the situation depicted in Figure 2.2. The horizontal axis represents the share of manufacturing workers residing in region 1 and the vertical axis shows the percentage difference in real wages between the two regions. The figure shows how transport costs influence the relation between regional manufacturing population and real wages. Transport

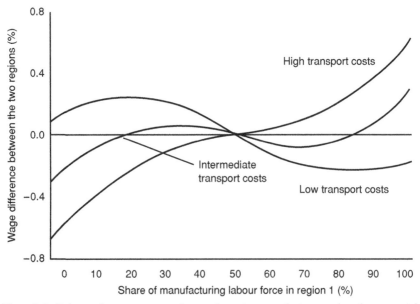

Figure 2.2 Relation between regional manufacturing populations and real wages with varying transport costs.

costs are taken to represent all costs of doing business across geographical space. When transport costs are high there is little interregional trade. Regional wages depend mainly on the local conditions in the labour market. If there is an increase in the regional labour supply, competition reduces wages. When transport costs are low, there is a large volume of interregional trade. A firm can have superior market access if it is located in a region with a higher concentration of workers (consumers). It can also afford to pay higher wages. These higher wages increase the purchasing power as the workers have a better access to consumer goods. As the number of residents/workers increase in the region, real wages increase in the same direction. At intermediate transport costs, there is equilibrium between centrifugal and centripetal forces (Krugman, 1999: 95).

Figure 2.3 shows the situation in which the workers move to the region that offers higher real wages as measured by the share of manufacturing labour force in region 1. A set of equilibria depends on transport costs. Solid lines specify stable equilibria while broken lines show unstable equilibria. If an economy starts out with high transport costs, then there is an even distribution of manufacturing between regions 1 and 2 (point A). Suppose that there is then a reduction in transport costs and that the economy reaches point B. At this point the process of manufacturing concentrating in one region begins. The economy would spontaneously organise itself into core–periphery geography (Krugman, 1999: 96). A relatively high interregional labour mobility is the feature of the US economy, but not within the EU. However, 'agglomeration can be generated equally well by an interplay between the location decisions of firms in industries that are linked

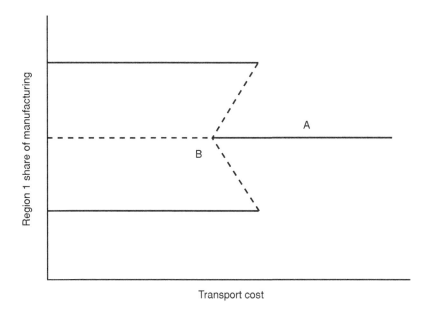

Figure 2.3 Transport costs and equilibria.

through an input–output structure. Thus, even without labour mobility, there may be forces leading to agglomeration of activity at particular locations in an integrating region' (Venables, 1996a: 356).

A promising point of departure for more advanced analysis of clusters is to consider two basic forces that influence the spatial concentration of firms. These are:

- *Centripetal forces* promote agglomeration. They concentrate production and employment in specific geographical areas. These 'snowball' forces include external economies, forward and backward linkages in production, trade costs, increasing returns in transportation, concentration of firms and consumers, spread of information, as well as a robust labour market (especially for certain skills so that employers can find workers and workers can find jobs). Centripetal forces push the production system towards equilibrium.
- *Centrifugal forces* push the other way and test whether the equilibrium is stable. These forces discourage further geographical concentration of business. They favour a geographical spread of firms and include factor immobility, relative land rents, competition for factors and consumers, commuting costs, pollution, congestion, sewage and waste disposal.

The final result depends on the balance between these two forces, barriers to the reallocation of resources (factor mobility) and public policy. In essence, three outcomes are possible. First, economic activity may spread so that each region specialises in a particular activity. This type of clustering is not the same as polarisation, as is exemplified in North America. The US economy is less geographically polarised than Europe. Second, activity may agglomerate in core regions, leaving others without production potentials and without people. Finally, a long-term polarisation may split the country or economic grouping into advanced regions where incomes are high and unemployment low and depressed regions with low income and high unemployment (Braunerhjelm *et al.*, 2000: 29–30).

Agglomeration in general and spatial clustering of firms and industries in particular are motivated by efficiency considerations. They are based on economies of scale in production and transportation, as well as transaction costs. For example, the Massachusetts General Hospital in Boston is among the largest in the world in terms of the R&D funds it receives. Industrial managers come to the R&D department of the hospital because all the specialists and all the required knowledge is 'within 20 minutes walking' (Lambooy, 1997: 298).

Marshall (1890) considered the issue of why it is beneficial for producers from the same industry to be located together. He offered three basic reasons why producers concentrate (to form a cluster). These are:

- *Knowledge spillovers*: proximity eases spread of information.
- Advantages of '*thick markets*' *for specialised skills*: firms may easily find the necessary labour and workers are promoted quickly or can readily change jobs if the current employer does poorly. There is no need to create the human capital from scratch. In addition, tacit knowledge is difficult to transfer without labour mobility.

- Backward and forward *linkages* associated with large markets: links may clarify and explain a part of the concentration story only if there are economies of scale. Otherwise, a firm would set up a separate production unit to serve each distinct market. A concentrated industry provides a market for specialised local suppliers of components, as well as private and public suppliers of various services (institutional thickness).

These economies, external to individual firms in a cluster, are essential but not sufficient to explain the strength of firms in a cluster. Conscientiously pursued joint action and horizontal and vertical cooperation by firms in a cluster (sharing equipment, developing a new product, various consortia) enhance collective efficiency and improve the competitive advantage of the participating firms. When there is a problem of a market failure, it can be resolved by government intervention and/or by private self-help (as was the case in Sialkot) (Schmitz, 1999: 468–70).[19]

There are, however, additional reasons for the spatial clustering of firms. They include the following:

- If competition and technology change, the past arm's-length and hierarchical organisation of a firm can be replaced by a flexible network of business organisation in a cluster.
- The labour markets of two unrelated industries may be complementary, e.g. one industry (metal or car assembly) may employ predominantly men, while other(s), e.g. textiles, may employ predominantly women.
- The presence of one firm/industry creates a direct or indirect market for another firm/industry.
- Two industries use a common resource.
- One industry's output is used exclusively as another industry's input (tyres and cars).
- Firms use common services (marketing, storage, accounting, repair, transport).
- Firms use a common social infrastructure (schools, health, roads).

Because of a relatively large concentration of consumers and economies of scale, agglomeration can bring certain economic advantages through interrelationship of functionally connected as well as competing businesses. Competition forces firms to employ state-of-the-art technology; hence, there are no low-technology industries, only low-technology firms within them.

Clustering of firms that sell identical goods (competitors) was thought to be welfare wasteful from a social standpoint (Hotelling, 1929: 53). However, clustering of firms often occurs in response to consumers' desire to make comparisons between goods (e.g. in shopping centres). Consumers usually visit more than one shop before making a major purchase. Department stores often insist that shopping centres make some space available to small shoe and clothes retailers. This is to reassure clients that the goods they sell are competitive (i.e. that a minimum differentiation exists) in comparison with those offered by other retailers. Clustering of *identical* firms can serve a socially useful purpose as it results in lower transportation costs (Eaton and Lipsey, 1979: 422–3). The same holds for clustering of *heterogeneous* firms. A rational consumer would connect purchasing activities such as search, purchase and transport. Multipurpose shopping assists in the lowering of shopping costs (Eaton and Lipsey, 1982: 58).

Similar firms are likely to seek similar if not identical features in the geographical location of their business. In this case, the outcome may be a cluster. For example, the US film industry started a century ago in California, around Los Angeles. The firms involved in film-making were similar and favoured locational features such as dry weather and excellent daylight conditions. Although modern filming and lighting technology does not depend on natural light at all, the clustering of film and entertainment industry in California has continued. Homogeneous initial needs of firms created the film cluster rather than input–output production relations. Hence, functional production links and agglomeration economies are not a necessary condition to create a cluster.

The existence of a good university or a research institute is not enough in itself to guarantee the overall economic success of an area. During the period of central planning in the former Soviet Union, Akademgorodok (near Novosibirsk) was essentially a town of research institutes financed by the Soviet Academy of Sciences. It has remained isolated as it has not developed functional links with industries. During the centrally planned period, Soviet enterprises depended primarily on ministries and the central plan.

The cluster of high-technology firms around Cambridge, England, tells a different story. The common tacit code of behaviour among the high-technology firms in the region includes trust and cooperation. The cluster is based on two local 'collective agents': Cambridge University and consulting firms in R&D. In contrast to most other British universities, which have formally regulated links with industry, Cambridge has rather liberal rules governing such links. In fact, faculty members are allowed to work part-time in the private sector. All this has had a strong and positive spillover effect on the regional cluster of high-technology firms. Hence, there are economies that are external to individual firms but internal to a network of firms in the cluster.

Sophia-Antipolis was developed in vacant space at the end of 1960s in the south of France. It did not develop around an established university as in the case of Cambridge. A great deal of effort, including the establishment of the University of Nice in 1986, was necessary to create links among the high-technology firms in the Sophia-Antipolis cluster.

2.4 History and expectations

Background

The Heckscher–Ohlin theory cannot explain why an industry locates in a region with high mobility of factors (e.g. the US) or in one country with much the same share of production factors as another (e.g. France rather than Germany). Patterns of regional specialisation and location of firms and industries are often created by a historical accident. Ohin noted that 'Chance plays a significant part in determining the localisation of industry… A different distribution of inventions would have caused a different localisation' (Ohlin, 1933: 137). More recently Krugman (1992: 9) wrote: 'I at least am convinced that there is a strong arbitrary, accidental component to international specialisation; but not everyone agrees, and the limitations of the data make a decisive test difficult'.

Once a business is established at a specific geographical location, it is then 'locked in' through learning, circular causation and cumulative causation effects (for examples see Appendix 1). In this sense '…history matters in a way that it does not in neo-classical theory…' (Eaton and Lipsey, 1997: xxv). Two questions are relevant here:

- Are there inherent differences among locations that create predestination for certain activities?
- How can a small historical accident, a chance (something that is beyond the prior knowledge of an investor), alter the economic fate of an industry, region or a country?

Meaningful multiple equilibria exist when firms make independent profit-maximising decisions about output, prices and location. The question is which equilibrium gets established? On the one hand, there is a belief that the choice is basically resolved by history. Past events set preconditions that move the economy from one steady state to another. This reasoning of the traditional literature argues that history matters because of increasing returns and lumpiness (inseparability) and activity-specific knowledge and capital goods (Eaton and Lipsey, 1997: x–xi). The same reasoning is behind promotional campaigns or 'location tournaments' (David, 1984) between countries to attract international footloose capital (TNCs). The idea is that, once an activity is established in a location, it perpetuates itself and related businesses gravitate towards it. However, 'this self-reinforcing aspect of foreign investment begins to operate only after a certain development threshold has been reached' (Wheeler and Mody, 1992: 71).

There is, on the other hand, a view that the choice of equilibrium is determined by expectations. This observation is based on the belief 'that there is a decisive element of self-fulfilling prophecy' (Krugman, 1991: 652). Let us consider both views in turn.

History and clustering

The non-linear probability theory can predict with some certitude the behaviour of systems subject to increasing returns. Suppose that balls of different colour are placed in turn on a table. The probability that the next ball will have a specific colour depends on the proportion of the existing balls of that colour on the table. Increasing returns occur when a red ball is more likely to be added when there is already a high proportion of red balls (Arthur, 1990a: 98). Equilibrium depends on the initial point and later arrivals. Hence, history as a series of (random) arrivals sets the final result.

The national rate of growth of capital stock (without FDI and foreign loans) depends on home savings and investment. Suppose that one region/country initially accumulates more capital than another. Subsequently, both regions grow, but the one with more capital grows faster than the one with less capital. As manufacturing capital grows, the relative prices of manufacturing goods fall. After a certain period of time, there comes a point at which the lagging region's industry cannot compete internationally and it begins to shrink. Once this process begins the new theory of trade and strategic industrial policy suggests that nothing can stop agglomeration for a long time. Economies of scale may drive prices down in the capital-abundant region and at the same time the lagging region's manufacturing industry disappears. In this model, relatively small beginnings can have large and irreversible consequences for the manufacturing structure of a country, its trade and the competitiveness of its output (Krugman, 1990a: 99–100).

The dynamics of capital accumulation makes the region that starts with a higher capital stock than the other regions end up with a dominant industrial position. If this is reinforced by a learning process and cumulative causation (strong internal production links where extension of one activity increases the profitability of others), then the existing pattern of comparative advantage is reinforced over time even if the overall structure of the economy has changed. This process-dependent development adds new layers of firms and industries to the inherited production structure. If output is concentrated within a relatively small area, firms can benefit from economies of scale and linkages (growth of one activity increases the profitability of other). If this area is close to a larger market, there are additional benefits in the form of lowered trade (including transport) costs. Hence, the current state of the economy determines its future shape.

Investment decisions and the trade policy of a country at the present time will have an impact on the shape of the national economy in the future. For example, at the end of the nineteenth century Argentina and Sweden were similar, relatively backward farming-based economies. At about that time, Argentina invested in the education of lawyers and priests, whereas Sweden invested in the education of engineers. The impact of such choices, coupled with other economic policies, on the material standard of living in the two countries is obvious.

Once the structure of an economy becomes unsustainable, there are certain critical branching points (bifurcations) at which the qualitative behaviour of the economy changes. New production geography either evolves or is triggered. This history-dependent development can follow different paths, hence it is unpredictable. A long period of stability is broken up by an event of change (equilibrium is punctuated). For example, nearly all large cities are ports. However, New York and Boston stopped being primarily harbour cities a long time ago. Examples of punctuated equilibrium are to be found elsewhere too. In biology, for instance, many species (crocodiles, crabs, turtles or monotreme animals) remain stagnant for a very long period of time. However, there are crucial, relatively brief and unpredictable moments (bifurcations) when new species arrive and old ones disappear. The reasons for this include a change in climate as a result of volcanic activity or a meteor, as resulted in the extinction of dinosaurs 64 million years ago (the burning meteor started fires that destroyed forests, while smoke covered the atmosphere, preventing the penetration of heat from the Sun leading to part of the Earth becoming frozen).

More than a century ago Alfred Marshall spelled out the idea of 'backward-looking dynamics' or external economies (in the modern jargon). According to his analysis, factors of production migrate towards those industries in which they earn the highest current rate of return. If there are several meaningful equilibria in which the returns would be equalised, then the initial conditions determine the outcome. History matters together with factor endowment, tastes and technology (Krugman, 1991: 653–4).

Marshall (1890: 332) also described the concentration of specialised industries in particular localities in the following way: 'When an industry has once chosen a locality for itself, it is likely to stay there long: so great are the advantages which people following the same skilled trade get from near neighbourhood to one another… if one man starts a new idea it is taken up by others and combined with suggestions of their own; and thus becomes the source of yet more new ideas'. Contemporary jargon calls this process externalities of innovation.[20]

Somewhat similar 'first mover advantages' (to borrow a term from analysis of competition) may be found in biology as many bits and pieces of the past can be found long after their functions were lost. For example:

> Embryonic birds and mammals still have gill arches, which have been useless for 400 million years. Why are the vestiges not eliminated by natural selection? The usual answer is that baupläne and the vestiges are developed early in the embryo and hence are more difficult to modify than features that develop later. The genetic programmes controlling embryonic development were formed in the early days and have been frozen ever since.
>
> (Auyang, 1998: 195)

A similar example in humans is the appendix. However, a question immediately comes to mind: why can newly created adaptive features not also be frozen?

Positive feedback economics may also find parallels in non-linear physics. For example, ferromagnetic materials consist of mutually reinforcing elements. Small perturbations, at critical times, influence which outcome is selected (bifurcation), and the chosen outcome may have higher energy (that is, be less favourable) than other possible end states (Arthur, 1990a: 99).

One of the chief causes for the localisation of industries can be found in the physical conditions in an area. Production of metals tends to cluster either near mines or close to sources of cheap energy. First-rate grit (for grindstones) was found near Sheffield, England, which therefore developed a cluster for the manufacturing of cutlery as well. Another reason for the localisation of production has been the support of a court. In the Middle Ages, many European rulers constantly changed their residences (partly for sanitary reasons). They frequently invited artisans from afar and settled them in a group near the royal court. Once the court left, if the town survived, it in many cases continued the development of a specialised industry (Marshall, 1890: 329–30).

Thus, cities often began to develop around royal courts and bishops' sees (where there was a concentration of consumers). Later, the administrative, defence and educational dimensions of towns and cities reinforced their function as consumers, but industrial production also started evolving. Today, many cities produce more value added than they consume.

There is also a view that:

> Clusters often emerge and begin to grow naturally. Government policy had little to do with the beginning of Silicon Valley or the concentration of mechanical firms around Modena, Italy. Once a cluster begins to form, however, government at all levels can play a role in reinforcing it. Perhaps the most beneficial way is through investments to create specialised factors, such as university technical institutes, training centres, data banks, and specialised infrastructure.
>
> (Porter, 1990a: 655)

In fact, many governments impede the development of clusters by enforcing regional policy that subsidises firms to locate in an area without the supporting infrastructure. It comes as no surprise that firms located in such areas demand subsidies to continue operations in the future. However, universities have always been established in cities where potential students can easily assemble. It is only relatively recently that universities have been established in rural areas.

Governments and large TNCs often have nothing to do with the establishment of clusters (Silicon Valley, clusters in Italy, City of London financial district), but they may easily support their growth through the provision of education, infrastructure, tax policy,[21] as well as through sponsoring of R&D. Funds-hungry governments can increase taxes on firms in a cluster (up to a certain extent) without provoking a flight of firms from the cluster. However, such a policy may be unfavourable towards future investment and development of the cluster.

Firms cluster together in order to benefit, among other reasons, from the availability of a close network of suppliers. They usually cluster in locations with large local demand. This demand will be large in the areas where most producers chose to locate (a process of circular interdependence or cumulative causation). 'There is a degree of indeterminacy in the location of activities – firms locate where they do because of the presence of other firms, not because of underlying characteristics of the location' (Venables, 1996b: 57).[22] For example, there are around 600 tanneries in Arzignano, Vicenza, Italy, most of which employ just a few dozen workers. The region, however, produces 40 per cent of Europe's leather supply. Firms in the area around Vicenza not only soak, dye, stretch, stamp, cut and ship material used for Gucci handbags, Louis Vuitton luggage, Nike sneakers and BMW car seats, but they also produce gold chains, clothing and machine tools, many of them for export. The major disadvantage of an SME is often not in its 'smallness', but rather its isolation. Clusters may overcome this problem. Papageorgiou (1979) demonstrated that agglomerated firms can achieve higher aggregate profit and lower prices per unit of output as well as facing increased demand than more dispersed firms.

Should one, in such an indeterminate situation, search elsewhere for answers to the questions on the geography of production? Should it be outside economics? Should it be in non-linear dynamics (popularly known as chaos theory), which examines unstable behaviour with multiple dynamic equilibria, bifurcations and extreme sensitivity to initial conditions; or in self-organisation (spontaneous appearance of order),[23] so common in complex systems; or in evolutionary biology (evolution and hybridisation);[24] or elsewhere? 'Organisms are vulnerable, but they are not passive; they dig holes, build dams, modify the environment, and create their own niches of survival. Thus organisms and their environment interact, and together they form an ecological system that is better treated as a whole' (Auyang, 1998: 61). Similarly, the effects of externalisation are also pronounced in economics. Consumers' tastes and private and public institutions interact, evolve and alter over time. Consumers, for example, in similar situations make different choices (think of the diversity of breakfast cereals, painkillers, cigarettes, chocolate bars, T-shirts, shoes, cars or bicycles available). Hence, complex systems keep on moving from one pseudo-stable situation to another.

The principal reason for the success of clusters of related firms in northern Italy ('Padania') is their extreme degree of specialisation and the fact that most businesses are family-run. Relatives support each other in the business, so there is no need for supervision, skills are relentlessly upgraded and there are ample opportunities for invention. Common values and local consensus is preserved. This reduces the possibility for business sclerosis, so common in large, vertically organised firms. For example, in Lumezzane (near Brescia), which produces two-thirds of the national output of bottle openers, one family business specialises in the production of screws, while another has expertise in covers, etc. A similar situation occurs in Cadore, near Austria, with the production of spectacles. In general, company strategy is friendly with fast changes, customised products and niche marketing. A summary of properties of such industrial districts would include (Garofoli, 1991a: 52):

- a high level of division of labour between the firms and close input–output relations;
- a high level of specialisation, which stimulates accumulation of knowledge and introduction of new technologies;
- a high level of skills of workers as a result of a very long-term accumulation of knowledge at a local level;
- a large number of local competitors, which leads to the adoption of 'trial and error' behaviour and fast imitation by others;
- efficient local informal (and formal) system for the exchange of information;
- an increased emphasis on face-to-face relationships.

The following could also be added:

- entrepreneurs;
- innovators;

- financial institutions with venture capital;
- demanding clients.

With the exception of a few global TV stations such as the BBC or CNN and newspapers such as *The International Herald Tribune* or electronic media, one may easily find that most of the stories that the editors still publish or broadcast are indeed local. Proximity of firms in the same industry increases both the visibility of the course of action of competitors and the speed of the spread of information. 'Popular luncheon spots are patronised by executives from several companies, who eye each other and trade the latest gossip. Information flows with enormous speed' (Porter, 1990a: 120). This 'cafeteria effect' overcomes geographical barriers to information flow and creates incentives for other firms in the cluster to make similar improvements. It also offers a partial confirmation that there is a spatial limit to knowledge spillovers.

High-speed dissemination of information is one of the major strengths of clusters. Entrepreneurs often prefer to enter or stay in a cluster even if they may be able to obtain a higher return on their innovation elsewhere. The reason for this is that the firms in a cluster are not only providers of information but also recipients (Schmitz, 1999: 475). In fields in which technology changes often, personal contact may be a better means of communication than less timely sources such as professional journals, fairs and conferences. 'Human capital accumulation is a *social* activity, involving *groups* of people in a way that has no counterpart in the accumulation of physical capital' (Lucas, 1988: 19). This all supports progress in technology (creation of knowledge).

Personal contacts and informality are essential for the exchange of tacit knowledge.

> *Tacit knowledge*, as opposed to *information*, … can only be transmitted informally, and typically demands direct and repeated contact. The role of tacit knowledge … is presumably the greatest during the early stages of the industry life cycle, before product standards have been established and a dominant design has emerged.
>
> (Audretsch, 1998: 23)

> Companies that have gone furthest towards linking their global operations electronically report an increase, not a decline in the face-to-face contact needed to keep the firms running well: with old methods of command in ruins, the social glue of personal relations matters more than ever.
>
> (*The Economist*, 30 July 1994: 11).

Such a durable social network, informality in contacts and local embeddedness are essential to identify user requirements, proper installation, operation and service of the product.[25]

The growing importance of intangible assets, particularly intellectual capital, increases the importance of knowledge externalities (spillovers) and frequent face-to-face contacts among the relevant players. It is important to exchange uncodifiable knowledge, to become involved in interactive learning, to provide feedback and suggestions and to have a dialogue about risk and the changing situation in the market and technology. 'Knowledge is the most important resource and learning is the most important process' (Pinch and Henry, 1999: 820). Knowledge externalities are one of the key reasons for the existence and success of clusters. Hence, clusters may also be seen as networks for information gathering and fact processing.

> Almost every internationally successful Italian industry has several if not hundreds of domestic competitors. Frequently, they are all located in one or two towns... Where domestic rivalry is absent Italian firms rarely succeed internationally.
>
> (Porter, 1990a: 447).

The existence of competitors in the vicinity serves a useful business and social purpose. If one imagines a cluster in the shape of an input–output matrix for information, then the direct and indirect functional relations are 'diffused' through rows and columns. Competition increases productivity, which is the key ingredient of prosperity. Firms do not chase every chance to ruin rivals. This is contrary to the standard story in every introductory economic textbook.[26] Every firm in a cluster perceives its survival, growth and success in terms of collective growth. These firms learn and prosper collectively. The learning process in a cluster is not only interactive, but also cumulative as it persists over time (once it exists it does not cease to exist; experience and discovery build on experience and discovery). Turnover of labour, technical staff and management among these firms reinforces the transfer of tacit knowledge, cross-fertilising research, collective learning process and regional competitive advantage.

The underlying general operations within a cluster can be seen from another example. 'New York City's garment district, financial district, diamond district, advertising district and many more are as much intellectual centres as Columbia or New York University. The specific ideas exchanged in these centres differ, of course, from those exchanged in academic circles, but the process is much the same. To an outsider, it even *looks* the same: 'a collection of people in similar activities, each emphasising his own originality and uniqueness' (Lucas, 1988: 38). Continuous and straight dealings among players can pass on and exchange tacit and accumulated knowledge among players. Social closeness in such cases may be equally as relevant, if not more relevant than, the geographical proximity. However, established locations can be vulnerable to 'technological lock-in' in certain cases. Some industrial regions become victims of their own success because they become complacent and lose their competitive and innovative capacity. For example, the German Ruhr region was led into the 'trap of rigid specialization' (Grabher, 1993: 275). New ideas may need new space. 'When IBM developed its own personal computer, the company located its fledgling PC capacity in Boca Raton, Florida, way outside of the manufacturing agglomeration in the North-east Corridor' (Audretsch, 1998: 24). This is an example of a bifurcation point.

Expectations

Resources move gradually from one location and/or industry to another in response to differences in current earnings. If this shift is only gradual, then there must be certain barriers that increase the cost of the move. If there are costs, then the owners of resources would be interested in the expected returns in the future, rather than the current returns. However, the future returns also depend on the decisions of owners of other factors and their expectations about future earnings. For instance, when a new technology is introduced, multiple equilibria cause expectations of potential action from competitors. In this model, expectations (rather than history) determine the future shape of the economy.

A river may over centuries bolster its bed and reinforce the work of natural forces over time. However, a strong earthquake (a bifurcation point) may instantaneously ruin such a long history. This is what happened to mechanical cash registers, which were made obsolete by digital ones. Subsequently, optical scanners that read bar codes replaced digital cash registers. Those changes were all based on totally different technologies. Other examples may be found in the disappearance, almost overnight, of the market for film cameras after the appearance of video cameras; in the downshift in the market for mechanical watches after the invention of digital and quartz ones; in the replacement of dot matrix printers by laser printers; and in fibreoptics, which evolved independently of the telecommunication technology. A good encyclopaedia has always been a must for parents who want their children to be well educated. But *Encyclopaedia Britannica* has been replaced by Microsoft's cheap CD-ROM encyclopaedia *Encarta*, first produced in 1993, putting many door-to-door salesmen out of a job. Similarly, Amazon is taking business from real-world booksellers. Innovation is threatening firms from every side; hence, being a key player is not a state but a process.

The basic structure of the economy in general, and the costs of adjustment in particular, influence the balance between and relative importance of history and expectations (Krugman, 1991: 666). Worlds where history matters (a) and the one with expectations (b) are different from each other and they are also different from the standard textbook competitive situation (c). However, are there circumstances in which both (a) and (b) are relevant?

Imagine a simple model of an economy with only one factor, L (labour), that produces two goods: C (a good produced with constant returns) and E (a good that is subject to an externality). Suppose that the economy starts with some initial allocation of L between the two industries and that L moves towards the industry that offers the higher wage. If the wage in industry E is initially higher than the wage in industry C, then the economy will end up specialising in E.[27] This is how history determines both the starting conditions and the final outcome. The problem with such reasoning is that it implies that labour can move costlessly between the two industries. In the real world, such moves are possible, but only at a certain cost. Once these costs are introduced, inter-sectoral labour mobility becomes an investment decision for a worker that depends not only on the ongoing difference in wages, but also on the expected future wage rates. The expected wage rate of a worker also depends on the decisions of other workers. If everyone expects that the majority of workers will move from C to E in the future, industry E will be more appealing, even if there are no immediate effects on wages between the two industries. Expectations bring a dynamic element into the model.[28]

As products mature, the production cycle could make some previously unattractive locations for business interesting for consideration. Following invention, innovation is the process by which inventions are put into commercial use, while technology transfer is the process by which 'old' products in location A are transformed into 'new' goods in location B. An increase in the number of new goods in the north usually creates demand all around the world. Hence, relative prices of northern goods rise in relation to the prices of southern commodities. It is profitable to invest in the north, so capital moves there from the south. Similarly, technology transfer shifts at least a part of demand towards goods produced in the south. This catch-up by the south makes a certain amount of capital move there, so the relative income of southern workers increases. However, this process may 'hurt' the technical leader, causing the northern countries to continuously research and adapt in order to maintain their real incomes (Krugman, 1990a).

A clear example of how expectations shape the future national geography of production can be found if one considers the case of debt in the developing countries.[29] Back in the 1980s, these countries found themselves unable to repay the huge debts they owed to the big international banks. If they had all defaulted at the same time, the global economic system would have been damaged or even sunk. The US Secretary of the Treasury, Nicholas Brady, developed a scheme for refinancing this debt, with the International Monetary Fund (IMF) playing the role of the financial policeman by linking lines of credit to painful austerity programmes. This was taken to be a victory for the IMF and international institutions. It could have been, but only in the short term.

During the 1970s, the world saw a massive increase in the price of oil and other internationally traded commodities. The conventional wisdom (expectation) was that commodity prices would only go higher. The Club of Rome and other similar observers of history pointed out that the world was running out of scarce resources. The world was compared to a space ship: resources were being exhausted by growing populations and intensified industrial use. It followed that the price of commodities such as oil, copper and wheat could only increase. If this were the case, a rational expectation was that the best business to invest in was in commodities. Correct?

The primary producers of commodities were developing countries that lacked manufacturing capability but controlled the natural resources so much in demand throughout the industrial world. Any sane investor in the 1970s knew that investing in industries that purchased raw materials was stupid, while investing in production of raw materials was smart. So everyone, particularly the international banking community and the World Bank, began investing billions of dollars in ventures designed to produce raw materials in developing countries such as Mexico to Nigeria to the Philippines. As the crucial commodity of oil was expected to cost 40, 50 or even 100 US dollars a barrel in the future, the cost of production was not a critical element in decision-making. The price was going up and it was important to get in early in this business. All of the technocrats simply knew this and the entire international economic system became skewed towards investing and lending to commodity producers in the developing countries.

As a consequence of the above process, the inevitable happened. It emerged that, although the world may have finite resources of oil or copper, there were huge untapped reserves of progress in technology (which saves resources). When these megaprojects in the developing world started operating, the price of commodities collapsed. When prices fell below the cost of production, projects went bankrupt because they became unsustainable. The outcome was the debt crisis. Nicholas Brady and the IMF stepped in to repair the damage. The debt crisis arose because belief in commodity scarcity led to an avalanche of investment decisions. This created a long-term capital shortage that has left a legacy of misery. The simplistic projection of a future in which commodity producers would dominate industrial commodity consumers was not only rendered false by the collapse in commodity prices but was rendered irrelevant by another phenomenon in the early 1980s. It is related to Microsoft and similar companies that came out of nowhere.

Microsoft and numerous other software and related companies that emerged during the 1980s altered the equation that had obsessed the World Bank and most other serious economic thinkers. The emergence of computing technologies and 'brain imports' in the US meant that it was possible to increase economic growth without having a similar increase in commodity consumption. Microsoft and creators of ideas, after all, produce wealth without consuming commodities in proportion to growth.

The extraordinary growth of the US economy has many causes. There is no doubt that the persistent growth of productivity in the US is due to the improvement in efficiency introduced by computing (and 'brain imports'). Even Federal Reserve Chairman, Alan Greenspan, has acknowledged this, while also acknowledging that it is hard to calculate the impact. This much is apparent. At a time when productivity should be falling, inflation and interest rates soaring and the economy moving towards recession, growth in productivity (driven by the effects of computing as well as new ideas) is running at unprecedented levels.

At the beginning of the 1980s, Japan produced cars and cameras that were smaller, cheaper and better quality than those made in the US. Twenty years on, the ability to produce cars, copiers and cameras is much less interesting than the ability to write software. Production has shifted in a way that is almost beyond recognition. The hardware that runs a web server is much less valuable than the intangible intellectual property that resides on the server. Japanese industrial targeting may have been superior during the era of fax machines, but the US liberal (unplanned) economic system and alert financial markets that force firms to adjust rapidly to shifting markets and changing technology are more becoming to the age of the Internet (Krugman, 2000: 174). To put it succinctly, the Japanese bet on hardware, while the Americans bet on software. The decoupling of value from physical production, its shift to intellectual production, is a millennial shift whose full impact will not become apparent for many generations.

The firms that will define the next twenty years of economic history and production geography are probably completely unknown to anyone today. Uncertainty is very high and the way forward is not always clear. It is therefore almost impossible to predict with any degree of confidence where the world's economy is going.

2.5 War and location of firms

Unexpected political events (chances, accidents) such as wars cannot be predicted by everyone with a high degree of certitude. Nonetheless, wars decisively influence the development, expansion, location, dislocation and spread of certain industries. There are numerous examples that support such arguments. For instance, as a latecomer in the colonial era and because of post-war(s) external sanctions, Germany had the 'incentive' (was forced) to produce various chemicals as substitutes for natural inputs that were not available either from its colonies or through 'normal' trade. Self-sufficiency has often been of vital national importance. Success was remarkable as the country developed world-leading chemical and related industries such as pumps, sophisticated precision measurement and control instruments. Here are some other examples of countries benefiting from wars.

- After the First World War there was a recession in Seattle, Washington. The economy of the region at that time was based on fishing, timber and ship/boat building. At about the same time, demand for aircraft (which then were made of wood) started to emerge. In the Seattle area were many unemployed boat-builders and other inputs. The workers had the skills needed to make wooden boats and could easily make a fully covered boat (the body of an aeroplane). They also knew how to fix a propeller. These skills led eventually to the emergence of Boeing. The US was the first country to take advantage of airmail on a large scale, to make large purchases of military aircraft and to demand fast travel, which in turn provided the domestic aircraft producers with early advantages and enabled them to lower production and learning costs per aircraft compared with foreign competitors.
- The first commercially successful motor scooter, the Vespa, was produced by the Italian company Piaggio in 1946, although the idea for it was conceived during the Second World War.[30] During the war, Piaggio, at Pontedera, near Pisa, made aircraft engines. After RAF bombing destroyed the factories, warehouses and roads at the site, it became difficult and tiring to get around the site on foot. The company owner, Enrico Piaggio, asked one of his engineers, Corradino d'Ascanio, to come up with a simple and economical two-wheel personal vehicle. d'Ascanio built the prototype using his imagination, the leftovers from small two-tact motors used to start the aircraft

engines, aircraft wheels (note the shape of wheels on a Vespa when you next see one) and whatever else he could find in the warehouse (or what remained from it), such as metal sheets. It also incorporated a shield on each side to protect the rider's legs from injury. The prototype was ready within a few weeks and once in production, the Vespa became an immediate hit. It was extremely popular and fashionable in the1950s and 1960s and was rediscovered by another generation in the 1990s because of increasing traffic congestion in the cities.

- The chemical and other heavy industries in Switzerland benefited from the two world wars. This was partly because German industries did not have access to the international market and Swiss entrepreneurs filled the gap where they could, partly because of an inflow of funds and skills and partly because German patents were declared invalid by the Allies.

- During the Second World War, Caterpillar, a US machinery manufacturer, expanded overseas in order to service machines used by the US Army. After the war, the machinery that remained abroad still had to be serviced. Hence, Caterpillar became an international company on a larger scale. Similarly, during the Second World War Coca-Cola was supplied to the US Army to keep up the morale of the soldiers and it remained abroad after the war ended. And Mars Bars were distributed to the armed forces all around the world during the war.[31]

- Military bases, military academies and weapons laboratories explain the fast post-Second World War growth of US cities such as Albuquerque, Santa Fe, San Diego and Colorado Springs. Defence plants contributed to a large extent to the growth of the areas such as Los Angeles, Seattle and Silicon Valley.

- Sialkot is a provincial town in the Punjab, Pakistan. During the period of British rule, a century ago, it contained a military garrison and a mission hospital. These created a demand for repair and, later, production of surgical instruments, tennis rackets and footballs. The area had for several centuries produced swords and daggers. As military technology advanced and the market for swords declined, medical advances resulted in an increased demand for surgical instruments, such as scalpels, from the local hospital. The Second World War, not surprisingly, further increased demand for surgical instruments. Technology and experts were brought from Britain to support production of those goods. Currently, a core of around 300 family-run firms (almost all with fewer than twenty employees) in Sialkot produce a range of 2,000 surgical instruments. These firms are, along with firms in Germany, the major world exporters of surgical instruments. As Sialkot has no airport and as it is located over 1,500 km from the nearest sea port, a private self-help action created the Sialkot Dry Port Trust, which brought 'the port to Sialkot'. The Trust offers a range of collective services, such as customs clearance, warehousing and transport. The success of this, as well as all other clusters, is based on two factors: a demand-driven approach and competition based on collective efficiency. However, not everything is rosy in Sialkot. The infrastructure is still somewhat undeveloped: the power supply is inadequate, communications are poor and roads are covered with ankle-deep mud during the monsoon season. Health and safety standards are inadequate and child labour is a serious problem in Sialkot's football-making industry (Nadvi, 1998).

- Italian companies such as Alfa Romeo, Ferrari and Lancia dominated the motor racing market in the period immediately after the Second World War. Soon, however, a cluster of a number of small firms around Oxford, England, became dominant world players. Several accidental events were responsible for this. First, there was a huge surplus of abandoned airfields in southern England after the war. Second, Mercedes withdrew form motor car sport in 1955 after an accident in Le Mans in which 183 spectators were either killed or injured. This left a gap for the British racing car builders. Third, large and vertically integrated manufacturers such as Ferrari and Porsche built cars for their own racing teams, whereas the British sold cars to anyone who wanted to buy them. Although the British cars were not winning races, they dominated the starting grids in terms of sheer numbers. A fourth influencing factor was the ban on cigarette advertising on TV in Britain in 1965. Tobacco companies turned to motor racing sponsorship and supplied vast sums of money in return for having their logos on the racing cars. Pinch and Henry (1999) argue that the success of the British constructors was influenced by accidents only to a small extent. Other, more important reasons, such as accumulated knowledge, its circulation through companies by the means of a transfer of personnel, as well as skilled labour, are the origins of the British success. The British have a tradition of expertise in engines and lubricants, aerodynamics and composite materials. In particular, the national aerospace industry was bigger and more sophisticated after the war than that in Italy. This could, according to Pinch and Henry, probably have resulted in an offshoot racing car industry even without the Mercedes crash and or sponsorship from cigarette manufacturers.

2.6 Impact of integration

Gains

Economic integration can increase the average welfare of the consumers in the countries involved in many different direct and indirect ways. The problem is that the benefits accrue in relatively small instalments and only in the medium and long term. Some of those gains include:

- secure access to the market of partner countries;
- increased investment opportunities as expectations may be established with an increased degree of security;
- improved efficiency in the use of resources;
- elimination of trade barriers, which reduces cost of trade;
- increased competition on the internal market, which exerts downward pressure on prices;

- facilitation of exchange of technical information;
- increased competition, which forces firms to implement new ideas and technologies;
- more opportunity to exploit and benefit from economies of scale;
- potential for coordination of certain economic policies;
- improved bargaining position with external partners;
- stimulation of research and innovation as a result of tougher competition in the larger market and the opportunity to share fixed costs in such a market environment;
- a wider range of goods and services for consumers, and hence more choice and utility;
- reduction in X-inefficiency, which moves the production activities of firms closer to best business practice.

However, one must always remember that international economic integration is never more than a useful *supporting* tool to sound domestic macro- and microeconomic policies and that it cannot act as their replacement. If these domestic policies are not healthy, integration cannot be their substitute.

Reallocation of resources and adjustment costs

Economic integration increases individuals' welfare through increases in product variety and consumption. The neo-classical model assumes that adjustment of production (shifts from unprofitable into profitable activities) is instantaneous and costless. This is a significant weakness of the model. The immediate effects of external shocks such as changes in technology, trade liberalisation and economic integration are increases in efficiency and income. Increased employment comes later. Adjusting to such shocks may require both time and government intervention. Gains from shifts in production and trade as a consequence of integration should be offset by the cost of adjustment in order to determine the net welfare effects of integration.

Adjustment costs (the social price of change) may be quite high in uncompetitive economies. Think of the 'pain' and length of time needed for the transition economies of Central and Eastern Europe to change to a market-type economic system. However, countries' failure to engage in external trade for a long time can become an additional obstacle to adjustment. Adjustment costs are borne both by individuals and by society. Private adjustment costs include a reduction in wages, losses in the value of housing and a depreciation of the value of firms' capital. Social costs include lost output from unemployed capital and labour.

Common external protection may discriminate against imports from outside countries in such a way that these external economies may adjust more swiftly than would otherwise be the case. To circumvent common external protection, the governments of excluded countries may respond by, among other things, shaping their geography of production and utilising their comparative advantage in high-level manufacturing to gain a competitive edge in advanced products and export them to the integrated group of countries. Dynamic models are not as straightforward as classical models of trade and investment, but they are much closer to real life.

Experience in the EU, the European Free Trade Association (EFTA) and successive rounds of tariff reductions under the General Agreement on Tariffs and Trade (GATT) has shown that geographical and industrial adjustment takes place relatively slowly but smoothly over a long period of time. In the case of the EU, the adjustment costs were much smaller than expected so that the elimination of tariffs was able to proceed at a faster pace than anticipated in the Treaty of Rome. Adjustments took place within industries, rather than between them. The disastrous scenario of firms going out of business in their own country on a large scale has never materialised. The reason for this, and for the mitigation of adjustment costs, may be found in increased capital mobility and flexible rates of exchange, although the relatively high growth rates and near full employment of the 1960s helped the adjustment process. One should not neglect the importance of having selective and achievable strategic goals. For example, the shipbuilding industry in Britain and Spain declined because it failed to specialise in the same way as the Finnish industry (in icebreakers), it was not able to match the production costs in Korea and it lacked the potential for diversification that existed in Japan. But this is the story of one and only one industry. One should never generalise the situation in the whole economy based on a single industry case study.

There is no gain without pain. If the pressure and adjustment costs that result from relaxation of trade restrictions do not hurt, then they probably produce no benefit either. The 'compulsory' reallocation of resources is a source of gains. The adjustment cost is a finite, one-off investment. The gains accruing from improved resource allocation are ongoing. Thus, there are reasons to believe that the 'pain' is much exaggerated (Curzon Price, 1987: 16). Trade liberalisation accelerates competition in participating countries. For this reason, the expectation that international economic integration is beneficial in the long term can be accepted with considerable confidence. Economic adjustment and changes in the geography of production are essential for countries that want continued economic growth in the face of fast-changing technology and markets when all decisions are high-risk ones. It is necessary to learn how to live with change in order to reap gains from such a strategy.

Adjustment costs associated with shifts in economic activities include a need for a reallocation of labour. Jobs will be lost in some business activities and geographical areas, while they will be created in others. Structural funds for social, regional and industrial issues can act as built-in stabilisers that help the initial losers to recover.

An economic policy of non-interference with market forces has obvious advantages because competition and efficiency are stimulated, consumers' tastes are satisfied and there is a reduction in the costs of government administration and intervention. On the other hand, government intervention may be necessary because markets are imperfect, firms seldom take into account the social costs of production (externalities) and adjustment and market forces may increase inequality through the regional distribution of income. However, intervention intended to ease the pain of adjustment can evolve into deeply rooted protectionism that eventually increases costs for everybody. Hence, neither a pure market system nor excessive government intervention can account for all the private and social costs and benefits of adjustment. While intervention may solve major economic issues, market forces may be more successful in fine-tuning the economy.

A country's comparative advantage and geography of production are dynamic concepts. They shift over time. Countries cannot be certain that their current production advantages will remain unchanged in the future. International economic integration may be a reliable way for a country to secure wide markets for home goods/services and to obtain sources of supply in the future. Geographical proximity of the partner countries ensures that gains from trade, specialisation and a wider choice of goods are not wasted on transport costs.

Clusters

The production geography of the US is particularly interesting for exploration as it is a country without important internal borders and is so large that it may serve as an example for economic comparison with an integrated Europe. Even a superficial look at the US production geography reveals a high degree of concentration of industries. For example, the following industrial clusters come to mind:

- aviation around Seattle;
- finance on Wall Street;
- insurance in Hartford (Connecticut);
- electronics in the Silicon Valley and Boston's Route 128;
- advertising on Madison Avenue in New York City;
- optics-related industries in Rochester (New York);
- cars around Detroit;
- medical equipment in Minneapolis;
- paints and coatings in Cleveland (Ohio);
- entertainment in California;
- office furniture in western Michigan;
- orthopaedic devices in Warsaw (Indiana);
- hosiery and home furnishings in North Carolina;
- carpets in Dalton (Georgia);
- wine in California;
- shoes in Massachusetts;
- gambling in Las Vegas and Atlantic City.

In Europe, production of knives is clustered in Solingen, watches in Geneva and the Swiss Jura, financial services in London, fashion garments and motorcycles in northern Italy, carpets in Kortrijk (Belgium), pleasure in Paris and sex/prostitution[32] in Amsterdam, although the European car industry has never formed a cluster similar to that in Detroit. A selection of clusters in Italy and Germany is given in Appendix 2. Once the concentration of businesses becomes too high, there may be negative externalities for work and private life such as pollution, sewage and waste disposal problems, congestion and increase in the price of land and rents. This may have an impact on the spread and decentralisation of businesses and their shift to other regions as firms may wish to leave the 'threatened' regions. However, the EU has on average a much less concentrated manufacturing geography and much more segmented markets than the US because of various non-tariff barriers that increase trade costs. The goal of the Single Market Programme (1985–92) was to eliminate all barriers to internal trade. If this succeeds, EU industries and the geography of production should resemble those in the US. This is not to say that the EU will ever become a homogeneous market like the US. In the US, most things and ways of doing things (culture) are alike throughout the country (e.g. food, habits, services, how towns and villages look). In contrast, in the EU, citizens of different countries exhibit distinct national consumer preferences, e.g. for food and drink. This will persist. In addition, the EU countries have different national policies regarding health, safety, social issues and worker representation.

The Single Market Programme of the EU (integration deepening) provided opportunities for production to concentrate in select hotspots, as well as for rationalisation of business operations. Amiti (1998; 1999) found evidence that this occurred in some manufacturing industries, e.g. industrial chemicals, petroleum, textiles, plastics, iron and steel, machinery and transport equipment. These are all industries that are subject to economies of scale and that have a high proportion of intermediate inputs in final production. Hence, this provides some support for the new theory of spatial economics. In the period 1976–89 geographical concentration increased in thirty out of sixty-five industries examined, concentration fell in twelve industries (the biggest fall was in the manufacturing of concrete for construction), while there was no significant change in the geographical concentration in other industries (Amiti, 1999: 580). Midelfart-Knarvik *et al.* (2000: 30) found that 'between 1970/73 and 1994/97, the general trend towards spatial dispersion is reflected in 29 out of 36 industries' and that there is an 'impression of a spreading out of European manufacturing activity'. On the other hand, a study by the European Commission observed that an 'examination of data offers mixed evidence for the contention that the single market is leading to a geographical concentration' (European Commission, 1998: 67) and that there is 'little evidence of concentration occurring in the EC' (European Commission, 1998: 69). Hence, this topic needs further research.

One result of fragmentation of production in various EU countries was a replication of various group functions. The principal impact of the Single European Market on TNCs located in the EU was increased competition. TNCs were forced to coordinate production in their subsidiaries in order to profit from economies of scale. Horizontally integrated TNCs such as 3M responded to the deepening of integration in the EU by specialisation of production in their plants. Post-it notes are made in its UK plant, while Scotch tape is produced in Germany. Previously,

3M produced a wide range of 'sticky' goods in each country in order to serve predominantly the local market. Vertically integrated TNCs such as Ford responded to the new opportunities by vertical specialisation. Differentials and gearboxes are produced in France, while engines are made in Spain. A further restructuring of the company, announced in 2000, ended production in Belarus, Poland and Portugal and concentrated output in Germany, Spain and Belgium.[33] In addition, there emerged a special kind of relation among the competing firms. The removal of non-tariff barriers on internal trade and liberalisation of public procurement 'forced' inter-firm specialisation in similar goods. For example, ICI (Britain) specialised in marine, decorative and industrial paints, while BASF (Germany) specialised in automobile paints (Dunning, 1994a: 296–7).

In spite of the potential for concentration of production provided by the Single European Market, the Japanese (and the US) car-producing TNCs continue to distribute production throughout the EU, rather than concentrate production to achieve economies of scale (Ando, 1998: 23). Although the Japanese set up car assembly plants in Britain, they also developed new production activities elsewhere in the EU (e.g. the Toyota plant in France).

Production geography with trade barriers

International economic integration may influence the geography of production in several ways. Three are most obvious. They were neglected in earlier analysis because of non-linear analytical complications that arise from externalities and they deal with trade costs (Fujita *et al.*, 1999: 251):

- When transport costs and barriers are high (i.e. autarky), a country is likely to have the manufacturing capacity to supply its local consumers.
- When transport and trade costs are low or non-existent (i.e. free trade), the world gets 'smaller' and markets larger, forward and backward linkages (presence of tradable intermediate goods) dominate and footloose manufacturing industries are able to agglomerate in a single country or location (as in America). There is no need for producers and consumers to be in the vicinity as trade is costless. Firms move to the lowest cost locations.
- At an intermediate level of transport costs, concentration becomes both possible and necessary. The costs of production may differ among countries depending on country size (market) and economies of scale. Firms in a smaller or peripheral country that produce tradable goods depend more on foreign trade than firms in larger countries. Therefore, if trade is liberalised, firms from the small country may gain more than firms from the large countries. However, firms from the large country may exploit economies of scale and have lower costs of production and prices of output than the firms in a small country. Once trade is liberalised and trade costs fall, firms from the large country may capture a large part of the small country's market. There then comes a period of adjustment. Certain firms may relocate in search of low-cost immobile factors (land, labour) and larger markets. In small countries

such as Austria, Switzerland or Luxembourg, firms may successfully adjust and penetrate niche markets in a large country.[34] Although the national production geography (distribution of industries) is altered, this does not mean that there is going to be a divergence in national per-capita income. Each country may have a cluster of industries that supplies the entire integrated market. However, this case brings with it a range of stable and unstable equilibria (as in Europe).

Figure 2.4 presents this process graphically. With no trade costs, firms spread in search of low-cost immobile factors. With prohibitive trade costs, firms are forced to produce locally. If trade costs fall below the prohibitive level, the circular causation is instigated and some firms relocate in search of bigger markets (Baldwin, 1997: 53).

Suppose that transport costs in the real world tend to decline over time. This has been a relatively reasonable assumption since the time of Ricardo. One may observe a trend in the narrowing of the income gap between the advanced countries (north) and certain developing countries (south). 'Declining trade costs first produce, then dissolve, the global inequality of nations' (Fujita *et al.*, 1999: 260). The problem is that industrialisation and economic development is not a uniform process. It takes place in a series of waves. Labour-intensive industries are the first to leave industrialised country because of high wages. The less labour-intensive industries move later but possibly faster than the earlier movers. Usually, upstream

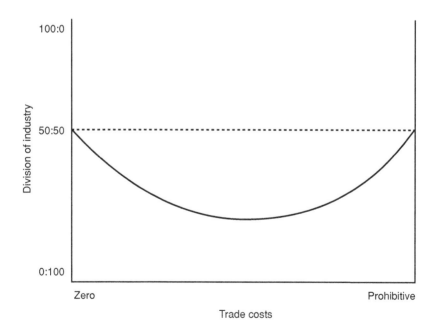

Figure 2.4 The U-shaped relation between concentration and openness.

industries move first and create potentials for forward and backward production links in the target country, which facilitates entry of firms from other downstream industries.

Production geography and reduction of trade barriers

There is a force that may assist lagging regions in an integrated area. Suppose that the initial elimination of barriers to the movement of goods, services and factors in a common market spurs an inflow of factors to already industrialised areas, which benefit from economies of scale and various externalities. If all barriers to internal trade and factor movements are eliminated or become insignificant, firms may benefit from economies of scale and externalities in other (less advanced or peripheral) regions where the variable costs of production are potentially lower than in the centre of the manufacturing or service activity (Krugman and Venables, 1990: 74; Venables, 1998: 3). In this case, the less developed region or a country that is part of a common market is likely to benefit on two accounts:

- it attracts firms that benefit from economies of scale;
- the former regional production structure that was typified by a lack of open competition is altered.

Kim (1995: 882–6) confirmed that this occurred in the case of the manufacturing industry in the US during the period 1860–1987. Industry specialisation increased substantially just before the turn of the twentieth century. At about the same time, the US was developing its transport and communication network with the aim of becoming a fully integrated economy. During the inter-war years, the level of regional specialisation 'flattened out', then fell substantially and continuously between the 1930s and 1987. Economic integration made the US regions less specialised today than they were in 1860. This trend of dispersion of industries and increasing homogeneity in the US continued throughout the 1990s (Midelfart-Knarvik *et al.*, 2000: 44). As we shall see later, economic integration in the EU made the industrial structure in the member countries more specialised and less similar.

In theory, economic integration may, but will not necessarily, bring greater benefits to the regions/countries whose development lags behind that of the centre of economic activity. However, if production linkages (forward and backward) are strong (so that production is indivisible) and internal to an industry, such as in the case of the chemicals industry or financial services, and imperfect competition prevails, economic integration would tend to trigger agglomeration (clustering). If those linkages are not limited to a relatively narrow industry group but are strong *across* industries and sectors, integration would tend to produce agglomeration in particular areas. If labour is not mobile, the whole process would tend to open up new and widen existing regional wage differentials (Venables, 1996b). Although this may result in deindustrialisation in the peripheral regions, it does not mean that integration is not desirable. For instance, education and regional policies increased the attractiveness of Spain as a location for various manufacturing industries from the EU and elsewhere. This was particularly obvious following Spain's entry into the EU in 1986. Integration of Mexico with the US shifted many manufacturing industries from the area of Mexico City northwards, along the border with the US. This took place not only because there was a growing demand in the US, but also because of the general trade liberalisation policy in Mexico. Once the economy turns outwards, internal production linkages weaken and firms have fewer incentives to stay in the congested hub.

If the cost of trade is high, industries tend to disperse. When this cost is reduced, agglomeration can occur as demand in distant places can be met by exports. When this cost of trade approaches zero (as is the case for computer software written in, say, Bangalore, India, and in industries that use the Internet), footloose production may be dispersed and located according to the availability of the specific resource inputs. Globalisation of certain industries (integrated international production) reduces the importance of physical proximity between various production units, as well as between producers and consumers. However, in industries that have strong internal links, such as ones based on new knowledge (innovation activities are still highly clustered in the world),[35] financial services or chemicals, there is a strong propensity to cluster in spite of 'globalisation' of other businesses.

In the EU, intensification of economic integration through the elimination of non-tariff barriers (NTBs) during the introduction of the Single European Market, reduction in the costs of transportation and economic and monetary union (EMU) may weaken motives for regional and national self-sufficiency. However, integration may also stimulate agglomeration and worsen the core–periphery discrepancy. Production in the EU may resemble that in the US, where industrial output (both in manufacturing and in services) is concentrated in distinct geographical locations. Hence, if this does in fact occur in the future, internal EU trade among its member countries will no longer be intra-industry but rather inter-industry in nature. Further reduction of trade costs in the EU may lead to further concentration of production, which is subject to the economies of scale in the already existing core locations, while periphery locations may come to specialise in manufacturing production that does not depend on economies of scale. This provides support to the arguments of the new economic geography and trade theories (Brülhart and Torstensson, 1996; Amiti, 1999).

Statistical evidence supports the assumption of a negative relationship between intra-industry trade and industries that are characterised by economies of scale. However, this tendency was reversed in the 1980s and became hump (∩) shaped in peripheral regions of the EU (Brülhart and Torstensson, 1996: 17–18). Certain regions may be losers for a (transitory) period of time, even though the group as a whole may be a net welfare gainer. But if changing structure of regional employment has impact on wages, then there comes a point where peripheral areas may become interesting to certain industries and may attract them. The incentive may be unimpeded access to the entire EU market and lower labour costs. These industries need not necessarily be those that are scale sensitive, because industries that are subject to large increasing returns to scale are usually already well established in the core geographical locations of the EU. Such a U-shaped relation between agglomeration and economic integration may partly explain why Spain attracted a relatively large number of foreign investors. This kind of reasoning and regional compensation funds may help to convince adversely affected peripheral regions to put up with the hardship that may temporarily follow trade liberalisation and economic integration (Puga and Venables, 1997: 364). Similar arguments may be used both in the current EU(15) member countries and in the new candidate countries from Central and Eastern Europe.

If indigenous entrepreneurs are flexible, then the regional geography of production can be altered within a large integrated area without substantial external assistance or even without a separate regional currency. A clear example is the conversion of New England's production geography from the production of shoes and textile in the 1960s (coupled with relatively high unemployment) to an economy based on 'high technology' and low unemployment in the 1980s.

Centripetal forces may explain relatively low indices of intra-industry trade (agglomeration, clustering) in industries subject to high economies of scale. Conversely, relatively high indices of intra-industry trade (in 'labour-intensive' industries) may suggest the spread of industries. In the case of the EU, Brülhart (1998a: 340–1) suggested that in the period 1980–90:

- there was no further concentration of already clustered industries that are subject to increasing returns in the central regions;
- there was further concentration of textile-related industries at the periphery;
- there were certain indicators of the spread of 'high-technology' industries towards the periphery.

Others, however, argue that the outcome may be the reverse of that just described and that an active regional policy is necessary, particularly where there is EMU. The outflow of emigrants would discourage entry of new businesses into such a region. This trend would further weaken the economic position of the region in question. Nonetheless, such a vicious circle has not come about in the EU. Although there are severe problems finding relevant data, particularly regarding the 1950s and 1960s, one may uncover certain leanings. What seems likely to have occurred in the EU is that regional disparities gradually reduced until the early 1970s. This was followed by a decade-long period of widening regional gaps and a mixture of stabilisation and widening of regional gaps between member countries ever since. It is not yet clear what prompted the halt in the convergence process after the 1970s. This does not mean that specific regions are irrevocably consigned to a specific position in the regional rank order. There is evidence that there is quite a lot of change in regional rank (Armstrong and de Kervenoael, 1997: 41; Midelfart-Knarvik *et al.*, 2000).[36]

The vast majority of EU countries 'experienced a growing difference between their industrial structure and that of their EU partners' (Midelfart-Knarvik *et al.*, 2000: 9). These growing divergences in the geography of national production may be the consequence of two factors. One is historical and arises because countries initially have industries that grow at different rates. Hence, a country with a high proportion of high-growth industries becomes increasingly more specialised than the rest of the group. The other factor is 'differential change', i.e. a move from one type of production to another. Midelfart-Knarvik *et al.* (2000: 6) found that over 80 per cent of the change in the EU during the period 1980–97 was due to 'differential change', while the rest could be attributed to the amplification of initial differences. The most striking feature of this process was a change in the industrial structure of Ireland and Finland. New high-technology industries and those subject to increasing returns to scale were established in these two countries.

The impact of integration on individual industries can also be looked at in the following way. Midelfart-Knarvik *et al.* (2000: 19–22) divided industries into five groups and observed their concentration in the periods 1970–73 and 1990–97. The results of the analysis were as follows:

- *Concentrated industries that remained concentrated over time*: motor vehicles, aircrafts, electrical apparatus, chemical and petroleum products. These are the industries with high increasing returns to scale, which depend on high/medium technology and have a high share of inputs from their own industrial group. In this group, Germany reinforced its position in motor vehicles, to the detriment of Britain and France. In the aircraft industry, Britain, France and Germany remained dominant. However, there was a slight reduction in the market shares held by Britain and Sweden, while Belgium, France and Spain achieved slight increases. Britain, Germany and France remained dominant in chemicals, but Britain's share of the petroleum and coal industry fell.

- *Concentrated industries that became less concentrated*: beverages, tobacco, office and computing machinery, machinery and equipment, and professional instruments. This group of industries relies more on inter-industry rather than intra-industry linkages, relatively high labour skills, but lower returns to scale than the previous group. Spread of these industries was pronounced in the period 1991–97. Germany saw a reduction in its dominance in this group. The same trend was also noted for Britain and France. Ireland and Finland gained the most in this industrial group. However, Austria, Italy, Portugal, Spain and Sweden also gained.

- *Dispersed industries that became more concentrated*: textiles, apparel, leather products, furniture and transport equipment. Relatively low technology in this group has low returns to scale, and requirements regarding the qualifications of the workforce are also low. Britain, France and Germany saw their shares in this group fall, while the share of the southern EU countries grew. In the transport equipment industry, however, Germany increased its share by 10 per cent, while Britain and Spain had a combined decrease of 7 per cent.

- *Dispersed industries that remained spread*: food, wood products, paper and products, printing and publishing, metal products, non-metallic minerals, and shipbuilding. There were no obvious changes in these groups. National differences in tastes and culture are behind the reasons for most industries in this group.

- *Residual group*: footwear, industrial chemicals, drugs and medicines, petroleum refineries, rubber and plastic products, pottery and china, glass and products, iron and steel, non-ferrous metals, railroad equipment and other manufacturing. This averagely concentrated group did not change much. The only significant change was in drugs and medicines, which became less concentrated. Production spread from Germany and Italy to Britain, Denmark, Ireland and Sweden.

The change in the production structure in the EU was to some degree reflected in the change in the structure of EU trade. Trade data support the finding that there was a decrease in specialisation during the 1970s. The picture is, however, mixed from the beginning of the 1980s. The increase in specialisation revealed by the production data is not reflected in the change in the structure of trade. The main reason for the faulty discrepancy is the growing volume of intra-industry trade (Midelfart-Knarvik *et al.*, 2000: 12). In addition, trade data may not be a suitable substitute for production records. The structure of trade may change as a response to changing demand without any change in production. If there is a change in domestic tastes, then domestic producers may sell goods on the home market rather than expend extra efforts on selling abroad. This would result in a change in the structure and volume of trade without change in the composition of the domestic output.

Compared with the pre-Single Market Programme, the EU 'problem regions' saw an improved economic performance in the period following the completion of the Single Market. This improvement was obvious in terms of growth in both employment rates and gross value added (European Commission, 1997a: 5). Concerns that the Single Market Programme would lead to a concentration of economic activity in the 'core' EU countries proved to be unfounded. There has been only limited spread of economic activity to the 'peripheral' EU countries that enjoy certain cost advantages (European Commission, 1998: 145). This is consistent with the view that as costs of trade fall for products of certain industries, the periphery may became more attractive for investment as the returns on the capital are greater. However, this development in the EU may also be the consequence of the impact of regional aid (European Commission, 1997a: 34).

One of the outcomes of the Single European Market was that some clusters of firms and industries in the EU became somewhat more visible. A relatively high geographical concentration of related firms in relatively small areas eased exchange of information. As a result, the areas with the highest rate of job creation are Frankfurt, London and Paris. However, the problem is that regions outside a large metropolitan area remain 'poor'. Success, like many other things, also appears to cluster.

The entry of the Central and East European countries whose economies are in the middle of a long transition process need not worry the southern EU countries for at least another decade. The most developed of the 'new democracies' still lag behind the 'poorest' EU countries (Portugal and Greece) in economic terms. The southern EU countries have nothing to fear in the medium term from the accession of select transition countries and the potential 'exodus' of jobs to Central and Eastern Europe because of lower wages there.[37] Firms who are looking for low-cost production may find China and India superior long-term choices than the transition countries in Europe. If relatively low wages were the sole determining factor for the location of production, then the EU would be flooded with cheap goods from these countries. Factors such as productivity, the capital stock and stability are often more decisive than differences in nominal wages. The southern EU countries are ahead of the transition countries in those matters. It is often forgotten that trade only alters the structure of employment among different industries and overall standard of living, i.e. the kind of jobs available, rather than the actual availability of jobs.

A similar debate on trade liberalisation with Mexico and the creation of the North American Free Trade Agreement (NAFTA) took place in the US in the early 1990s. In spite of strong opposition to the free trade agreement between the US and Mexico by US presidential candidate, Ross Perot, and a loss of jobs in the American economy (described by him as the 'giant sucking sound' of jobs moving south),[38] only 117,000 Americans applied for the benefits offered to workers displaced by the free trade agreement. Compared with the 1.5 million who lose their jobs each year as a result of factory closures, slack demand and corporate restructuring,[39] the cost of adjustment to the agreement by the US does not seem too high. Free trade might have destroyed some jobs in the American textile industry, which is 'labour intensive', but it created new ones in electronics and aeronautics.

The problem with such debates about the employment effect of trade liberalisation (in countries with developed and stable economies) is that they are based on 'a fallacy of composition, that the effect of productivity increase *in a given industry* on the number of jobs *in that industry* is very different from the effect of a productivity increase *in the economy as a whole* on the *total* number of jobs' (Krugman, 1998b: 16–17). The negative impact of jobs going 'south' on a large scale has not materialised in practice, and the net effect on the US job market might even have been positive.

The most important argument about the employment impact of the Eastern enlargement of the EU has, unfortunately, not yet made its way into the public consciousness. It has also wrongfooted some academic debates. The Eastern enlargement may have the effect of creating new jobs or keep the existing 'higher-quality' jobs in the EU. Isolated and highly publicised stories about the closure of a firm as a result of the expansion of the EU are not typical of the whole EU economy. Those stories need to be seen in the context of the big picture. With the advent of EMU in the majority of the EU countries, the average unemployment rate over the coming years will be what the European Central Bank wants it to be. The bank may pay little or no regard to the situation in the EU trade balance with the acceding transition countries.

Another advantage of the Mediterranean region of the EU is found in the economies of scale. This region of the EU is characterised by a high number of SMEs. These firms have the opportunity to grow efficiently in the single market of the EU and to take advantages of economies of scale. Large European firms have already taken most of the advantages that accrue from economies of scale. Hence, SMEs and countries in which they prevail have long-term potential for greater gains from the Single Market Programme.

2.7 'Optimum' partners for a customs union

International economic integration has been exercised in all parts of the world. There is hardly any country that is not touched by this process. However, since the Second World War many of these attempts have failed or achieved very little. The reasons for this include:

- overdependence on trade with countries outside the group (as is the case for all schemes that integrate developing countries);
- an internal market that is too small to support more than a modest degree of industrialisation (the Central American Common Market);
- high costs of transportation and poor communications (the Latin American Free Trade Association; schemes in Africa);
- a central planning system of economic integration, as in the case in the Council for Mutual Economic Assistance (CMEA), which ignored market signals and prevented spontaneous fine-tuning of the economy.

A large volume of trade between countries is a condition that may induce countries to contemplate integration. If trade is of minor importance for country A, this country may not have a serious economic interest in entering a discriminatory trade arrangement with another country. The US and Canada entered into a free trade deal with Mexico (NAFTA) primarily for political reasons. The Eastern enlargement of the EU is also primarily motivated by political considerations. Although it is obvious what the EU may contribute to the transition countries in Central and Eastern Europe in economic terms, it is much less obvious what these countries may contribute to the EU.

Common and widely used technical standards in areas of transport, telecommunications, data processing and electronics produce a relatively efficient operation of international grids without any form of economic integration. So, if this operates smoothly, the potential partner countries may look for some other economic fields that may operate as well but which require preferential trade or some other type of formal international economic integration arrangement.

Consider two countries, A and B. Country A is large and country B is small. Assume next that country A is diversified in production. If both countries are at the same level of economic development as measured by income per capita, then it is likely that the structure of imports of country B consists of a larger number of items than the structure of imports in country A. Country A may satisfy most or all of its demands from domestic sources, and this may influence its terms of trade.

These assumptions hinge on the existence of important economies of scale that permit firms in the larger country to have lower costs of production. Country B has to accept the world market prices (country A's) for all goods and services other than those in which it efficiently specialises. Country A sets most of the international prices. If small country B wants to sell a standardised good in country A's market, then country B has to accept country A's domestic price less the tariff and other costs of trade. Hence, large country A's tariff may bring greater welfare cost to small country B than are the benefits from country B's own tariff on imports.

In Figure 2.5, QQ′ illustrates country B's linear production possibility frontier. The price line coincides with the production possibility frontier in autarky. With the indifference curve I, home production and consumption is at point C. If the price line moves to P_1 because of trade, then the corner solution results. Country B becomes completely specialised in the production of good Y at point Q. With the indifference curve I′ consumption is at point C_1, that is the point where the indifference curve is tangential to the price line. If the price line changes so that production and consumption points meet, the result is offer curve QCB for country B with a kink. The construction of the offer curve for country A is similar, but the production possibility frontier for this country is shifted outwards from QQ′ and it also has a different (flatter) slope.

Consider the situation in Figure 2.6 with trade in two commodities X and Y and two countries, A and B, where country A is large and country B is small. OA represents big country A's offer curve, while OB represents small country B's offer curve. The offer curves for both countries are constructed in the manner described in Figure 2.5. The longer linear portion of OA relative to OB is due to the longer production possibility frontier of big country A. The equilibrium point between the two offer curves is where they intersect, point E. Between the origin of the Figure 2.6 and the equilibrium point may be pencilled in the equilibrium price line. The equilibrium point is on the straight portion of country A's offer curve. The price line coincides with offer curve OA. The small country B must accept

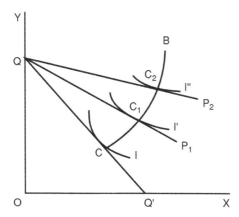

Figure 2.5 Offer curve in country B with a linear production possibility frontier.

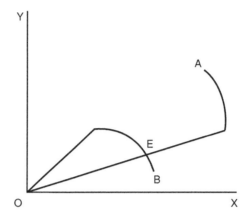

Figure 2.6 Terms of trade between a big and a small country.

country A's price if it wants to trade. The small country cannot change this situation in any way. If one keeps in mind that the offer curves are concave towards the import axis, one finds that the geography of production at price line OE is as follows:

• country B is specialised in good Y and imports good X;
• country A produces both goods and is indifferent to trade.

Imagine now a world with many countries in which a large country A and a small country B form a customs union. An increase in country B's demand for country A's good may be relatively easily satisfied by country A, either from stocks or from a marginal increase in the use of existing resources. An increase in country A's demand for country B's product may not be satisfied immediately if country B does not have free capacity or stocks. Country B's capacity may be limited by non-specialised, short production runs. If some reallocation of resources in the economies of these two countries is necessary, the assumption is that, because of its less specialised technologies, the rate of transformation in country B is smaller than in country A. Hence, country B can more easily shift its resources and direct them to the production aimed at country A's market than the other way around. If small country B cannot reallocate resources towards the production of goods that are in demand in country A, then trade cannot take place between these two countries unless country A transfers a part of its income to country B which the recipient country then spends on imports from country A.

To operate in a large market, a small country should undertake substantial investment in production and marketing. Failure in the customs union market for a small country will mean the loss of most of its external market. Investment expenses will not be recovered. The failure of a large country's exports to a small country's market will mean relatively smaller losses than those experienced by a small country in the same situation. The creation of a customs union in such a situation may be a much riskier enterprise for the small country than for the large country, although there is potential for a larger marginal gain.

Government intervention in the form of subsidies is often needed for the start and operation of some industries in rough times. When a small country subsidises an economic activity, it most often has exports in mind. When a large country subsidises home production it has in mind import substitution and employment. On these grounds, part of the small country's exports may be subject to countervailing duties by country A. Owing to the asymmetric size of their markets, the large country may not regard the opening of the small country's market as an 'adequate economic compensation' for the opening of its own larger market. If there are many countries, and if country B trades heavily with country A, then trade relations with the external world for country B are almost bilateral. The trade relations of country A may be more evenly distributed among various countries. On these grounds, country A would request further concessions from country B.

A sad example of 'integration' between a big and a small country is the US annexation of Hawaii. It all started with sugar. Very sweetly. Sugar was grown in Hawaii and exported to California as early as 1827. Exports grew continuously. Hawaii initiated a treaty on reciprocal trade with the US in 1848. The treaty was signed in 1855, but the US Senate did not ratify it. The same happened with another treaty of 1867. Finally, a new treaty of 1875 was signed and approved by the US Senate. It provided reciprocal duty-free trade. The treaty was supposed to be an economic success for Hawaii, in particular, for its exports of sugar. In 1890, the US passed a Tariff Bill that removed US duties on sugar from all other countries. Thus, Hawaii lost its privileged position in the US market. In this situation, annexation could have been the solution for Hawaii. In addition, Hawaii had political problems. The taxation system was inequitable and the government was not fully representing the will of the people. Various machinations, including a small revolution, ensued, with the objective of annexation. However, these efforts failed. Nevertheless, by a resolution of the US Congress in 1898, Hawaii became part of the US. The Hawaiians were, however, given no vote in the matter. This change caused little disturbance in Hawaii. After all, this country was so dependent on the US that annexation seemed to be the best way to have continued free access to the US market (Wilkinson, 1985). This unpleasant example belongs to the past century. Following the break-up of the former Soviet Union (1992), some newly independent states (Belarus) found it hard for both internal and external matters to 'go it alone' and are exploring ways to re-establish the broken ties with Russia.

The position of small countries in negotiations about economic integration is weak, but it is not hopeless. Of course, factors other than the relative size of countries influence negotiations. If it has a choice, then a small country has some negotiating power. This country may look for partners elsewhere and/or leave the integration deal if it thinks that the arrangement with the large country will bring losses. If a small country has a genuine resource, a strategic geographical location and/or if it specialises in certain production niches (Austria, Belgium, the

Netherlands, Switzerland[40]) then it may influence negotiations and its terms of trade with a large country. Economic integration reduces the importance of the size of the domestic market. As such, it is more favourable to relatively small countries that lack access to the larger market. Hence, small countries can benefit more from integration than large ones. This is true not only of the production side because of economies of scale, but also on the consumption side because of the relatively larger change in relative prices and because of the increased variety of the available goods and services. The small Benelux and Scandinavian countries, as well as Greece and Portugal, found sound economic grounds for integration with the rest of the EU. Canada and Mexico have done the same in integration with the US.

In an analysis of the 1986 enlargement of the EU (a large partner) when Spain and Portugal (small partners) joined the group, Casella (1996) found that the smaller EU member countries could gain more than the large EU countries. After 1986, France and Britain lost export market shares in Spain and Portugal to smaller EU countries. However, such a theoretical expectation was not confirmed in the case of Germany and in particular Italy (in fact, Italy increased exports). A continued empirical examination of the issue is necessary to draw more reliable conclusions regarding the problem. However, it is clear from the theory and data that larger countries do not gain asymmetrically more from integration (or an enlargement of the existing group) than smaller countries.

The greater the similarity between the countries that contemplate integration, the easier the negotiations and the smoother the adjustment and operation of the final arrangement. Optimum partners for negotiations about the creation of a customs union are those of equal economic size, such as France, Germany and possibly Italy were at the time of the establishment of the European Economic Community (1957). This condition of optimum partnership (political conditions aside) does not offer any country the chance to blackmail other countries on economic grounds and creates a more egalitarian relationship. Integration of partners of unequal size such as Switzerland and Liechtenstein, Belgium and Luxembourg or any enlargement of the EU made the smaller country accept *acquis helvétique*, *acquis belge* or *acquis communautaire* (around 90,000 pages of EU legislation in the year 2000), respectively, in full. Major negotiations were about the length of the transition period, not about the substance of the *acquis*.

The (intra-industry) adjustment to the new circumstances is easier and smoother in countries that are similar in terms of income levels and factors of production. Inter-industry adjustment in different economies is relatively hard. The existence, however, of relatively small and 'backward' countries in the EU is evidence that there are various possibilities for countries to participate in international economic integration.

Medium-size countries such as Canada (wheat), Saudi Arabia (oil) and Brazil (coffee) may influence the price of their primary products. Although income elasticities of demand for manufactured goods (traded on the oligopolistic markets of developed countries) are relatively high, the elasticities for primary goods (traded on competitive markets) are relatively low. Hence, smaller countries which are major exporters of primary goods generally have weaker bargaining positions than countries whose products are sold in oligopolistic markets.

The removal of tariffs on trade among countries may have substantive effects only if the integrated countries have or can create a base for the production of various goods and services that are in demand in the partner countries. This is of particular importance for developing countries. These countries have relatively low levels of income, many of them have a similar geography of production (often goods and services for subsistence which do not enter into international trade) and frequently production and export is concentrated on one or a few commodities. These countries do not have much to integrate in such a situation. The economic structure of such countries often does not permit them to trade even on a modest scale. The volume of internal trade within the groups that integrate developing countries seldom exceeds 10 per cent of total trade, (notable exceptions are MERCOSUR and ASEAN) as is obvious from Table 2.1. These countries compete on the same international markets with primary goods and do not have many goods and services to offer each other. As such, the developing countries have a structural bias against trade and, hence, benefit less from integration.

Reallocation of home resources in these countries, including upgrading of human capital, together with the discovery and commercial use of raw materials coupled with foreign aid and loans, may help developing countries to produce differentiated output and offer a variety of goods and services to partners in trade. A simple liberalisation of trade alone, within a group of developing countries, as the neo-classical school suggests, has not been enough. A more interventionist approach in the shaping of comparative advantage, imports of technology and capital from outside the group will be needed.

A necessary condition for successful international economic integration is a certain minimal level of economic development. It is assumed that an increase in development of developing countries will lead to an increase in product variety in the national output mix. This may give an impetus to trade. The minimum level of economic development depends on the ambitions of the countries involved. Do these countries want to form a customs union to increase their bargaining power or do they wish to use it as a means to increase or foster economic prosperity? The latter requires a higher level of economic development than the former.

The actual timing of integration plays an important role. During periods of economic prosperity it is easier to find gains for the participants than during a recession. Prosperity makes negotiations easier because every participant may expect to gain. Very high rates of growth, however, are not necessarily ideal for international economic integration. On the one hand, entry into a customs union introduces changes that do not necessarily have to be efficient because there is not sufficient capacity in the economy to accept them. The economy may be 'overheated' and integration may increase production (marginally), but it may also increase inflation. On the other hand, during a recession economic integration may mitigate the effects of economic crisis.

International economic integration is not suitable for all countries at all times.

Table 2.1 Intra-group exports of select integration groups as a percentage share of total exports

Group	1970	1975	1980	1985	1990	1995	1996	1997	1998
APEC[a]	55.7	53.4	54.5	65.9	65.6	69.2	69.7	69.3	67.1
EFTA(4)[b]	1.5	1.4	1.1	1.0	0.8	0.7	0.8	0.8	0.9
EU(12)[c]	53.2	52.2	55.7	54.4	60.6	57.5	56.5	50.9	52.1
EU(15)[c]	59.5	57.7	60.8	59.2	65.9	62.4	61.4	55.7	57.2
NAFTA[d]	36.0	34.6	33.6	43.9	41.4	46.2	47.6	49.1	51.7
Andean Pact	1.8	3.7	3.8	3.2	4.1	12.1	10.7	10.3	11.9
CACM[e]	26.0	23.4	24.4	14.4	15.4	17.0	18.9	15.5	14.5
CARICOM[f]	4.2	4.8	5.3	6.3	8.1	4.6	13.3	13.5	15.7
LAIA[g]	9.9	13.5	13.7	8.4	10.9	16.8	16.6	17.2	16.8
MERCOSUR[h]	9.4	8.5	11.6	5.5	8.9	20.3	22.7	24.8	25.1
OECS[i]	-	0.5	8.8	6.4	8.2	11.7	9.0	9.7	10.6
CEPGL[j]	0.4	0.3	0.1	0.8	0.5	0.5	0.5	0.4	0.6
COMESA[k]	12.5	9.9	8.4	5.1	7.9	9.0	10.2	10.0	10.8
ECCAS[l]	2.4	2.3	1.4	2.1	2.1	2.0	2.2	2.0	2.4
ECOWAS[m]	2.9	4.2	10.1	5.2	7.8	9.3	8.8	9.0	10.8
MRU[n]	0.2	0.4	0.8	0.4	0.0	0.1	0.2	0.4	0.4
SADC[o]	4.6	1.5	0.3	0.9	2.6	9.7	10.0	9.7	9.9
UDEAC[p]	4.9	2.7	1.6	1.9	2.3	2.2	2.3	2.1	2.6
UEMOA[q]	6.4	12.6	9.9	8.7	12.0	9.7	9.5	11.3	11.0
UMA[r]	1.4	1.0	0.3	1.0	2.9	3.7	3.4	2.6	2.6
ASEAN[s]	23.2	16.6	17.2	18.6	18.9	24.2	24.1	23.5	20.2
Bangkok Agreement	1.5	1.4	2.2	2.4	1.8	2.4	2.3	2.2	2.7

ECO[t]	4.2	4.9	6.3	9.9	3.2	8.0	7.1	7.6	8.3
GCC[u]	6.0	3.3	3.0	4.9	8.0	6.0	4.5	4.4	4.1
SAARC[v]	3.7	5.1	4.8	4.5	3.2	4.4	4.3	4.0	5.3

[a] Asia Pacific Economic Co-operation.
[b] European Free Trade Association.
[c] European Union.
[d] North American Free Trade Area.
[e] Central American Common Market.
[f] Caribbean Community.
[g] Latin American Integration Association.
[h] Southern Cone Common Market.
[i] Organization of Eastern Caribbean States.
[j] Economic Community of the Great Lakes Countries.
[k] Common Market for Eastern and Southern Africa.
[l] Economic Community of Central African States.
[m] Economic Community of West African States.
[n] Mano River Union.
[o] Southern African Development Community.
[p] Central African Customs and Economic Union.
[q] West African Economic and Monetary Union.
[r] Arab Maghreb Union.
[s] Association of South-East Asian Nations.
[t] Economic Cooperation Organization.
[u] Gulf Co-operation Council.
[v] South Asian Association for Regional Cooperation.

Source: UNCTAD (2000).

Certain types of integration are more attractive than others to different countries. There are, however, several conditions for the success of integration. They include:

- relatively large size of the group;
- level of protection (tariffs and NTBs) before and after integration;
- geographical proximity of countries;
- stage of development;
- market structure;
- achievement of the dynamic effects;
- distribution of costs and benefits;
- system for the settlement of disputes.

The potential partners for integration should check if they meet these conditions or if they can achieve them by means of international economic integration.

2.8 Free trade area

Both free trade areas (or, better, preferential trade areas) and customs unions yield similar results for an economy and the integrated group and differ only in detail. Free trade areas tend to result in more trade creation and less trade diversion than a tariff-averaging customs union. This detail has often been forgotten in discussions about international economic integration (Curzon Price, 1997: 182). A tariff-averaging customs union increases the level of protection of those countries that previously did not have tariffs or whose tariffs were below the level of the common external tariff, as was the case when relatively liberal-trading EFTA countries joined the EU. As such, free trade areas place a much lower cost on third countries than tariff-averaging customs unions.

If one assumes that the level of the common external tariff is equal to the lowest tariff of a member country in a customs union, then there is no theoretical difference between a free trade area and a customs union. The effects of both types of integration arrangements are identical. Of course, countries in a free trade area still take part in international negotiations about trade and tariffs on their own behalf, whereas countries in a customs union negotiate as a single unit. As there is no common commercial policy relative to third countries in a free trade area, countries (such as Canada or Switzerland) that value their sovereignty highly have the formal chance to go it alone in trade matters. Free trade areas in practice usually include manufactured goods but exclude agricultural ones. This is because many countries want to preserve independence in national agricultural policies. The wisdom (depending on values and priorities) of this policy choice is quite another matter.

Rules of origin are the basis of a free trade agreement. These rules prevent geographical trade deflection. This effect of free trade area refers to the import of goods from third countries into the area by country A (which has a relatively lower tariff than the partner country B) in order to re-export the goods in question to country B. These speculations depend not only on the difference in the level of tariffs, but also on transport, storage and insurance costs, as well as on the quality (perishability) of goods. Without rules of origin in a free trade area, only the lowest tariffs will be effective. Trade deflection problems do not exist in customs unions because of the existence of the common external tariff.

The proliferation of discriminatory, i.e. geographically preferential, trading agreements increased the importance of the rules of origin. Foreign exporters seek to avoid the payment of customs duties, while the protection-seeking domestic competitors endeavour to prevent them from avoiding those requirements. Rules of origin are required especially in free trade areas in order to determine which goods are entitled to enjoy those trade preferences. Apart from tariff discrimination, other purposes of rules of origin include the determination of eligibility for quota and informing consumers that have a preference for goods of a certain geographical origin. There are four different methods for the determination of these rules (Palmeter, 1993):

- *Substantial transformation*: geographical origin is determined by the country in which the good underwent the last substantial transformation (the one that gave the good a new name, a new character and a new use). Critics say that this is an imprecise and subjective method.
- *Change in the tariff heading*: even if the good made/assembled in country A has imported components, that good can be regarded by foreign countries as a good that originated in country A if that was sufficient to change the tariff classification of the imported materials. Opponents of this system say that the flaw is that the existing tariff schedules were not designed to determine the origin of the goods and that the system may be abused by strong industrial lobbies.
- *Value-added method*: a certain minimum added value must be incorporated in the good in country A in order to enable foreigners to regard the good as originating in country A. The trouble is that the method depends on controversial accounting systems and even a slight change in the exchange rate may produce a different result. The minimum area content requirement can be also criticised on the grounds that it shifts the production factor mix away from the optimum, it reduces rationalisation in production and can reinforce market rigidities.
- *Specified technological processes*: a good must pass through a certain technological transformation in country A in order to be regarded by foreign countries as having been produced in county A. The problems here are that technology changes rapidly and that it is impossible to draft and keep updated records on processes for all goods that enter into international trade.

The trade-diverting effects of the rules of origin could be mitigated by the elimination of quotas and multilateral tariff reductions.

The Kyoto Customs Convention (1973) states that, unless a good is wholly produced in a country, what determines the geographical origin of a good is the country where the 'last' substantial process took place. Packaging and dilution with water do not change the essential features of a good, so they are not taken as important elements that change the origin of goods.

Rules of origin can be restrictive or liberal. If the required value added within the area is, for example, 90 per cent, then very few commodities would qualify for duty-free treatment. Liberal rules of origin require that only a minor part of the value of goods should be added within the area. Commonly, rules of origin require that 50 per cent of value added should be within the area in order that goods receive a tariff-free status (for example, EFTA, Canada–US Free Trade Agreement). In the case of the NAFTA, Mexico and Canada were in favour of relatively liberal rules of origin because of the positive impact of such rules on the Japanese FDI in the two countries and the potential exports of goods to the US. Initially, the required local content of goods for liberal treatment in the NAFTA was 50 per cent, but that will gradually increase to and stay at 62.5 per cent from the year 2002.

An important issue is the basis for the application of, for example, a 50 per cent value-added rule. The choice is between the application of this rule to direct manufacturing costs or to invoice values that include overheads. Consider the following example. The direct cost of manufacturing good X in country A is $75, while overheads and profits are $25, making a total invoice value of $100. For good X to be exported without tariffs to the free trade area partner country B, the 50 per cent direct cost rule allows $37.50 worth of imported components, while the 50 per cent of invoice value rule allows $50 worth. The former rule offers a higher protection against the use of out-of-area inputs than does the latter rule. The Canada–United States Free Trade Agreement uses the direct cost rule (as does the free trade deal between Australia and New Zealand). However, the EFTA uses the invoice value rule (Lipsey and York, 1988: 31–3).

Rules of origin can be criticised on the grounds that they are open to much abuse (for example, a simple change of packing), that they can be avoided by unscrupulous traders (for example, fake origin statements and marks on the goods) or that the costs of monitoring the system are too high. The experience of the British Imperial preference scheme offered evidence that the operation of the system may be smooth. But in this case the parties were geographically separated, whereas it would be difficult to prevent smuggling along a reasonably open continuous land frontier (Curzon Price, 1987: 22–3).

Free trade in manufactured goods between the EU and EFTA countries operated easily. This was due to similar and low tariff rates between the parties. Nonetheless, the rules of origin were quite costly to implement. The cost of formalities to determine the origin of a good was between 3 and 5 per cent of the value of shipment. Many exporters did not find it worthwhile making use of the origin rules at all and opted for paying tariffs on their exports (Herin, 1986: 16). Elsewhere, certificates of origin may be abused. For example, according to the *European Voice*, the volume of Israeli orange juice imported into the EU at preferential rates was three times this country's production capacity.[41]

Hitherto, the analysis has dealt with tariffs on final goods. If tariffs are introduced on raw materials and semi-manufactured goods, and if one supposes that production functions are identical in all members of a free trade area, all other things being equal, production will be located in the member country that has the lowest tariffs on inputs. Such a situation results in the creation of 'tariff factories', which distort investment decisions and introduce geographical deflection in production. Once established, the producers would resist liberalisation of trade. All this increases both the prices paid by consumers and the possibility of retaliation from abroad. A solution to the problem may be found in liberal rules of origin that encourage trade creation and reduce misallocation of resources rather than in restrictive rules which generate trade diversion.

2.9 Distribution of costs and benefits

The welfare of the participating countries may change following economic integration. Market forces will not necessarily result in politically acceptable changes in the geographical, industrial or social distribution of the costs and benefits of integration. Some member countries may reap more benefits than others. This is similar to the problem of income distribution in a single country between owners of assets, industries, classes, regions, gender and so on. The most efficient producers in some member countries may increase sales, employ more factors, introduce large-scale production and generate government revenue. Other countries in the group purchase from their partners, who may not be the most efficient suppliers in the world but who are protected by the common external tariff in a customs union. These importing countries lose tariff revenue and they pay a higher price for the goods that their partners produce less efficiently than third-country suppliers. These countries, whose destiny would be to lose in integration without being compensated in any way, would never enter into this arrangement. Although the establishment of a customs union can make some countries worse off than before, compensation of losers by gainers may ensure that everybody is better off. For a successful integration scheme, member countries must remain satisfied, at least in the medium term, with the distribution of the costs and benefits.

There are three possible theoretical cases of geographical distribution of costs and benefits in a customs union:

- All countries in a customs union reap equal benefits which accrue from integration.
- All countries gain from a customs union, but benefits are distributed disproportionately.
- Some countries gain, while others lose.

If the criterion for the distribution of benefits in a customs union is equality of income per capita, then there are various options. In the first case above no action is required because everybody increases their income in proportion. The second case is harder. Is compensation necessary? Countries may wish to assess before the creation of a customs union whether some of them might gain more than others, and under which conditions. In the third case, if gains are larger than losses, compensation is necessary in order to convince the losers to take part or continue in a customs union. It is important to remember that just because one country's gains from integration this does not mean that other countries in the arrangement will lose out to a similar extent. The question is 'up to what point should one compensate?' Should one compensate only up to the point where losses are removed and give the rest of the benefits to the gainers? Should one compensate only up to the point where one may convince the losers to participate?

If a move (integration) increases welfare then those who gain from this move may compensate those who lose. This is the compensation test. The second, the bribery test, is one in which the potential losers remain better off by bribing the potential gainers not to make the move. If the gainers are allowed to make the change, the move will take place, unless the potential losers are able to persuade the potential gainers to stay where they are. Any change which passes the compensation test increases the size of the economic pie. If these moves are continuous, the pie grows continuously. With compensation, it is unlikely that a player's share will always go on falling. On the other hand, changes that do not pass the compensation test reduce the size of the economic pie, so in the long term everyone is worse off.

Compensation to the losers may be *ex ante* or *ex post*. In the former case, the unequal results of international economic integration for the member countries are foreseen in advance, while the latter method of compensation is necessary if compensation is to be in full. There is always a danger of systematic losses. The losers may blame integration for their troubles and seek compensation. The successful entrepreneurs may be discouraged from continued participation lines as endless transfers to the losers may tax their fortunes.

Compensation to the losers may be paid in different ways. It may be a mere transfer of funds. If unconditional, this transfer may destroy the recipient's incentives to adjust. Alternatively, compensation may take the form of development of infrastructure, education and training of labour and marketing studies that promote a local spirit of enterprise and a learning culture.

One criterion for fiscal compensation that is often put forward in the case of integration arrangements among the developing countries is the loss of customs revenue as a result of the creation of a customs union and the purchase of goods from the partner countries. Direct transfers of funds from supplier countries' treasuries to buyer countries' budgets may solve this problem. A country that receives full compensation for customs revenue losses has the same level of government proceeds that it had before integration. This country can shift its resources to the profitable production of goods that are in demand in partner countries and achieve production gains. However, full and exclusively fiscal compensation is not generally accepted as the sole means of compensation to countries that 'appear to lose' in any type of international economic integration.

If FDI is a possibility, the welfare and gains accruing to a country can be divided into on two components: 'national' welfare, which accrues to national factors of production, and 'domestic' welfare, which accrues to national and foreign-owned or controlled assets (Bhagwati and Tironi, 1980). A question often asked in Latin America during the 1970s and 1980s was 'who gains and how from economic integration?' There was concern that foreign TNCs were the major beneficiaries of integration to the detriment of the countries in the region (Vaitsos, 1978; UNCTAD, 1983).

Proceeds from the common external tariff should belong to the customs union. The level of proceeds depends not only on the volume and value of external trade, the relative size of the common external tariffs and the type of traded goods, but also on the preferential trade arrangements of the customs union with external countries and groups. The distribution of these proceeds may be a complex problem. Countries that trade with many partners and which obtain a significant part of their revenue from tariff proceeds do not have the right to dispose of these funds freely in the customs union framework. This was the situation in Britain before it joined the EU in 1973. In the developing countries, tariff revenues are an important element of public finances. If integration reduces them to any great extent, then there may be internal pressures to increase the level of common external tariff. In any case, there are several ways of distributing common proceeds. The revenue may be spent on the common activities of the customs union, distributed to the member countries, given to third countries as a compensation for trade diversion, saved as a reserve or any combination of these.

Manipulating the level of the common external tariff may also be of interest. It may be set as the average rate of tariffs of the customs union member countries before integration. However, to eliminate some internal monopolies, a customs union may set the common external tariff at a lower level in order to allow a certain degree of foreign competition. If the level of the common external tariff does not reduce trade with the rest of the world, then there will be no trade diversion.

The system for the distribution of costs and benefits of integration is often controversial. One must, however, remember that economic integration is not about clear balances and *juste retour* from the common budget, but rather about the enhancement of opportunities for business and growth in the group in the medium and longer term. However, some politicians do not readily accept the argument that integration is not a zero sum game.

A reduction in the level of the common external tariff and NTBs may be not only the most elegant but also the least harmful way of compensating those who are felt to be losers (consumers, external countries) from trade diversion in a customs union. If fiscal transfers are required between countries in a common market or economic union, these transfers may be implemented through regional, social and cohesion policies. Economics is the academic field which (among other things) studies the reasons for differences in efficiency among various agents. The distribution of the results among (un)equal players is a matter to be studied in politics.

2.10 Conclusion

In an age of 'globalisation' of business, one would expect the importance of the location of a firm to be diminishing. Some argue that the issue of distance is a dead duck. However, local proximity (clusters) of firms that produce similar, competing and/or related products together with supporting institutions still matters. Economies of scale, activity-specific backward and forward linkages (indivisible production), accumulated knowledge, innovation, existence of sophisticated customers and a fall in transportation costs all play a role in the 'protection' of clusters. 'Global' competitiveness often depends on highly concentrated 'local' knowledge, capabilities and a common tacit code of behaviour which can be found in a geographical concentration (a cluster) of firms.

The problem of regional (in)equalities is of great concern in all economic unions. Member countries are reluctant to lag behind their partners for any length of time, especially in monetary unions in which there are no balance of payments disequilibria but rather regional disparities. Depressed regions/countries can no longer resort to devaluation or capital controls as there is a single currency (in Europe the euro), while advanced regions/countries may not always be willing to finance regional disequilibria without proof that a structural adjustment is taking place in the assisted region.

Regarding the industrial structure of the EU, Midelfart-Knarvik *et al.* (2000: 46–7) concluded that from the early 1980s the EU countries became more specialised than before. This confirms the expectations of the standard, neo-classical and new theories of economic integration. However, a new pattern of industrial production is emerging in the EU. The major features of this divergence in the geography of industrial production in the EU countries are as follows:

- The process was slow and did not result in great adjustment costs. There was no clear effect of the Single Market Programme on the reallocation of manufacturing production and specialisation.
- During the 1970s the geography of production in the EU countries tended towards the EU average, whereas from the early 1980s it diverged from the EU average. This is an indicator of increased national specialisation in the EU. The most remarkable national change in the geography of production was the spread of relatively high-technology and high-skill industries to Ireland and Finland.
- The availability of highly skilled and educated workers is becoming an increasingly important determinant in industrial location. National economic policies concerning investment, industrial change, R&D, mobility of people and knowledge, investment in human capital (education) that develops and extends skills, experience and organisational competencies of the most important factor is crucial for the efficiency side of the economy; regional and social issues also play a role.
- Not all industries react in the same way to economic integration. Some of them concentrate, while others spread (repudiating the neo-classical theory that all industries will be affected in the same way). Several forces, therefore, drive such changes in the structure of production. Strong functional intra-industry linkages (high share of intermediate goods from the same industry and/or the need for a large pool of highly skilled labour and researchers)

stimulate agglomeration. Where these functional linkages are weak there is incentive to spread production.

- Although 'economic integration' has made the US geography of industrial production more homogeneous (less specialised) since the 1940s, integration in the EU has resulted in a growing disparity (increasing specialisation) in manufacturing production. This trend in both areas, although slow, shows signs of abating. The forces that drive this process are still unknown.
- The tendency to concentrate in the central locations is more pronounced in the case of industries with many intermediate inputs.
- Large returns to scale are becoming less important as centripetal (agglomeration) forces.

In the end, one may conclude that the analysis of spatial economics and economic integration depends on particular assumptions. It is often a study of individual cases. Even so, many useful things can be learned from exceptional cases. The examination of the issue is still highly suggestive (in particular how a historical accident may shape the production geography) rather than convincing and conclusive. No coherent theory of the subject is yet in sight. However, there are various approaches that contribute to the raising of new questions and understanding of the issue. This leaves the topic subject of further theoretical and empirical analysis.[42]

Appendix 1

Relatively modest initial differences between countries or humble beginnings of an industry or a firm in a region can have irreversible effects for a specific location or a region. The choice between two or more identical potential locations may be decided by chance. Hence, it is not possible to predict where a cluster will emerge. However, once the industry starts developing, the process of circular interdependence or cumulative causation takes effect and may be self-perpetuating for a long time even if the structure of the economy changes. For example, there are interesting stories of why certain firms/industries find themselves located where they are today.

- For centuries Basle was an important trading and banking city because of its favourable geographical position (the Rhine is navigable from Basle). This encouraged trade and later production specialisation in the textile industry. In neighbouring France, the National Patent Law of 1844 protected materials, not the process of production. Hence, a patent of 1859 gave the inventor of the red textile dye fuchsine a virtual monopoly to produce it in the country. However, a few months later another Frenchman invented a completely different method of producing the same dye. As the law prohibited him from producing this dye in France, even though domestic demand was greater than supply, he moved to Switzerland, where there were no patent laws. He chose Basle as his location because it was a trading and banking centre, electricity and salt were available in the vicinity, one could 'safely' unload arsenic in the Rhine, transport and forwarding infrastructure was readily available and it was the location of the oldest Swiss university, founded in 1460. Physician and alchemist Paracelsus (1493–1541), an early proponent of homeopathy, was a teacher at Basle University and studied the links between medicine and chemistry, which led to many advances in medicine. Hence, Basle was an obvious choice for a new industry. At the same time, in France, the producer (monopolist) of the dye, mollycoddled by the system, did not invest further in R&D or improvements in production, while the competitive market structure in Switzerland resulted in increased efficiency of production. The price of the dye in Switzerland was less than a half that in France, leading to a significant amount of smuggling into France. This French monopoly subsequently collapsed (Weder, 1995). A pharmaceutical industry emerged, almost by chance, around 1880, when the curative effects of dyes were observed. The Swiss dye industry could not compete with its German counterpart on the scale of output or access to raw inputs and so the Swiss specialised in the high value-added market segments of medicines, pesticides, herbicides, perfumes and flavourings. Highly sophisticated medical and health care equipment industries followed and expanded throughout the country. Strong incentives came from an inflow of skills and invalidation of German patents by the Allies following the two world wars, as well as from the government's education policy and support for R&D. As a relatively small country, Switzerland had to export from the outset. It became specialised and highly competitive in an industry that is not based on natural resources.

- Geneva goldsmiths and jewellers towards the end of Middle Ages were famous for their skill, knowledge of precious metals and the splendour of their products. They were 'expected' to jump on the bandwagon of the new industry of watch-making that emerged in France, Flanders, England and Germany around 1500. However, until the occurrence of two chance events the Genevans were so prosperous that they were uninterested in the emerging industry. The first event was Jean Calvin's edict against luxury, pleasure, elegant clothing and 'useless jewellery' in 1541. This limited the activities of the Geneva jewellers and goldsmiths and twenty-five years later almost put an end to their craft completely when their activities were even more restricted. Second, at about the same time, the prosecuted Protestant Huguenots from France and Flanders found sanctuary in Switzerland (Basle, Geneva and Zurich). Some of these refugees brought with them watch-making knowledge. One of them was Charles Cusin, who settled in Geneva in 1574. As watches performed a 'useful' function, their production was not prohibited and the Geneva jewellers and goldsmiths learned how to make quality, stylish and durable watches to provide them with a new source of income. In 1601, by which time the number of watch-makers had increased, they organised themselves in a guild. Most of the output was sold outside the country as only a few Swiss could afford such watches. Nonetheless, production flourished and the city became congested with watch-makers. It was increasingly difficult and time-consuming to become licensed as a master watch-maker, so that many apprentices moved to other locations. They mostly clustered in the Swiss Jura (Nyon, Neuchâtel, La Chaux-de-Fonds, Bienne and Basle). Unlike in Geneva, relaxed regulations permitted production of parts to be subcontracted to peasants in the mountains, who had limited sources of income, especially during the long winter months. These watches were, of course, less sophisticated and cheaper than the ones produced in Geneva, but they established a place in the market. In spite of changes in time measurement technology and hard times during the 1970s and 1980s, the Geneva and Jura watch-making clusters survived and they retained the 'global' dominance (Bumbacher, 1995).

- The chocolate manufacturer Nestlé was established in Vevey (Switzerland) because the town has a stream that could be used to turn a mill-wheel (with a hammer). The mill-wheel was used to crack cocoa nuts to make cocoa powder and, hence, chocolate. Although chocolate is no longer produced in Vevey, Nestlé still has its headquarters there.

- In Carrara, Italy, where there are marble quarries, craftsmen still carve marble as they have done for centuries, even though much of the stone is now imported.

- Once coal replaced wood as the source of energy and waterpower was replaced by steam, many cities emerged close to coal mines. The most obvious examples may be found in England, north-east France, Belgium and the Ruhr district in Germany. Aluminium production consumes an enormous amount of electricity. In the US aluminium production is concentrated in the state of Washington because that is where electricity is cheapest.

- In Italy, ski boot design and manufacturing developed from the walking shoes industry. Expansion of the industry received a large boost from the Winter Olympics of 1956 (which were held in Cortina). In addition, the small Italian firms were able to make plastic ski boots that were superior to those made in the US, and later expanded into the area of after-ski footwear. The Italians invented moon boots, which became popular worldwide, leading to an increase in the footwear cluster around Veneto.[43] Products change continually, stimulated by highly sophisticated demand conditions in the Italian market. Thus, investment is aimed not at increased production, but rather an increase in the quality and sophistication of the end product. In Italy, this applies not only to footwear.[44]

- Sassuolo, near Bologna, Italy, is, perhaps, the world leader in the production of ceramic tiles. Pot-making started there in the thirteenth century, and the manufacture of ceramic tiles for street names and house numbers began in the nineteenth century. Immediately after the Second World War, there were only a few ceramic tile producers in the area. However, post-war reconstruction created a explosion in demand for all building materials, including ceramic tiles. Tiles became popular in the Mediterranean area because they are cool in warm weather, because wood was scarce and expensive, and because Italians prefer natural materials to vinyl and carpeting. The principal raw material was kaolin (white) clay. Although red clay was abundant in the region, white clay had to be imported from Britain. The kilns and presses required were imported (mainly from Germany) in the1950s and 1960s. In the mid-1960s, local entrepreneurs learned how to modify the imported equipment to make use of the regionally available red clay with the result that, by the 1970s, Sassuolo tile manufacturers had become very competitive suppliers of kilns and presses and began to export them. By the 1980s, the Italian tile market had become saturated and the manufacturers were encouraged to export ceramic tiles all over the world. They were successful because they responded quickly to changes in fashion and other demand conditions, which gave them the competitive edge (Porter, 1990a: 210–25).

- Perhaps the highest concentration of dance clubs in Europe is in the Italian resort of Rimini. This led to the establishment of firms that produce disco equipment.

- Although German car manufacturer BMW has not inconsiderable experience in producing motorcycles, when it came to the making of moto-cross engines, the Germans turned to the Italians firms clustered in Noale (Veneto) and around Bologna (Emilia Romagna).

- An important hub for translations from and to many languages can be found in Modena. This area has for some time been renowned for the production and export of various types of agricultural machinery. Because of the requirement to produce instruction manuals in various languages, translations services developed in Modena and, once established, continued to grow.

- With the proviso that the profitability is not adversely affected, personal factors (i.e. whims) can play a role in the location of production. For example, car-making factories were established in Detroit and Oxford because they were each the birthplace of the founder of a major car manufacturer (Ford and Morris respectively). Incidentally, Bill Gates, the founder and chairman of Microsoft, was born in Seattle. Nowadays, golf-addicted entrepreneurs and business executives search for locations for their business that are close to good golfing facilities.

- Stalin, like the Russian tsars, admired classical ballet. Hence, the central plan allocated the 'necessary' resources for the education and training of ballet dancers and their teachers. The Russians still excel in the education and supply of highest quality dancers of classical ballet.

- Genoa and Venice were the first financial centres in the modern sense. In the Middle Ages a considerable share of trade between Europe and Asia passed through these two busy ports. Along with merchandise from various countries came their coins and bills. Venice was the first city to issue government bonds. Amsterdam dominated the financial business in the seventeenth century, developing the first stock market. Owing to the British Empire and the volume of commerce, London became the financial capital of the world in the nineteenth century. New York took that central place in the twentieth century because of the rate of growth and size of the US economy. Nonetheless, London and New York are still the most attractive places for financial business. Many clients and supporting services (security lawyers) are located there. Will the growth of e-business dilute centralisation of such a 'footloose' industry in the future? Many clients are not in London and New York, rents are high in those two cities and many prefer to live in less stressful places.

- Swiss producers took the lead in tunnelling equipment and services because of the need to tunnel during road and rail construction in the country. Similarly, US firms lead the manufacturing of rotary drilling equipment for the exploration of oil and gas, which started in Texas.
- International economic integration may alter the location of firms. For example, trade liberalisation in Mexico and economic integration with the US prompted an expansion of manufacturing production in northern Mexico and a decline of the Mexico City manufacturing belt.
- Policy changes, such as the passage of anti-union statutes in the southern states of the US, compelled some manufacturing firms to leave the northern part of the country. This process was supported by another unrelated event: the advent of air conditioning. This innovation made the south more attractive to live and work in than the north.
- The development of a telemarketing cluster in Omaha, Nebraska, is linked with the location of the Strategic Air Command of the US Air Force there. The first fibreoptic telecommunication cables in the US were installed in that Command. Such a demanding client forced the local phone company to develop extraordinary services. Other factors, although less important, for the development of the telemarketing cluster include location in the central time zone and an easily understandable local accent (Porter, 1998a: 84).
- St. Martin's Court is a short street near the English National Opera in London. The street is full of sellers of second-hand books and prints. Potential customers go there because they expect to find a number of shops with a wide range of second-hand books, while shop owners locate there because they expect to welcome a large stream of clients. A similar reasoning explains the cluster of theatres around Leicester Square and of restaurants in Soho.

Krugman (1996a) drew an interesting analogy between clusters and the natural evolution process:

> The general attitude of evolutionary theorists seems to be that nature can often find surprising pathways to places you would have thought unreachable by small steps; that over a few hundred thousand generations a slightly light-sensitive patch of skin can become an eye that appears to be perfectly designed.
> Imagine a group of frogs sitting at the edge of a circular pond, from which a snake may emerge … and that the snake will grab and eat the nearest frog. Where will the frog sit? … if there are two groups of frogs around the pool, each group has an equal chance of being targeted, and so does each frog within each group – which means that the chance of being eaten is less if you are a frog in the larger group. Thus if you are a frog trying to maxim your choice of survival, you will want to be a part of the larger group; and the equilibrium must involve clumping of all the frogs as close together as possible. Does this remind you on the principle of agglomeration?
>
> (Krugman, 1996a)

Unlike changes in biology, real-world entrepreneurs are smart and often radically change their behaviour within a short period of time in response to opportunities for business.

Appendix 2

Italy is an often-quoted example of a country with distinct manufacturing clusters. A select group of those clusters includes the following (numbers in parentheses are the number of firms):[45]

- motorcycles in Bologna [2,370];
- electronics, mainly alarms for cars, in Varese [100];
- jewellery in Valenza Po [1,400] (Alessandria), Vicenza [1,100] and Arezzo [1,300] (Florence);
- spectacles in Cadore [930] (Belluno);
- textile and clothing in Sempione [3,900] (Varese);
- textile around lake Como, Prato [8,481] (Florence), Olgiatese [2,614] (Varese), Biella [1,300] (Piedmont) and Valdagno (Pisa);
- clothing in Val Vibrata [1,150] (Pescara), Empoli (Florence) and Treviso
- female underwear in Castel Goffredo [280] (Mantua);
- silk in Comasco [2,600] (Como);
- wool in Biella;
- knitwear in Carpi [2,054] (Modena);
- shoes in Fermo, Montegranaro, Porto Santelpidio, Sanbenedetto, San Benedetto del Trono (Ancona), Lucca, Santa Croce Sull'Arno [1,749] (Pisa), Ascoli [3,100]; and Riviera del Brenta [886] (Padua);
- sports footwear in Montebelluna [623] (Treviso) and Asolo (Treviso);
- tannery in Arzignano [600] (Vicenza) and Solofra (Naples);
- ceramic tiles in Sassuolo [199] (Bologna);
- marble in Apuo-Versiliese [1,161] (Carrara);
- taps and valves in Alto Cusio [300] (Novara);
- furniture in Brianza Comasca Milanese [6,500) (Milan), Cantù [7,200] (Milan), Alto Livenza [2,000] (Udine), Poggibonsi [1,294] (Siena) and Bovolone-Cerea [3,000] (Verona);
- kitchens in Pesaro [1,200];
- chairs and tables in Udine [1,200];
- wood machinery in Rimini [1,345];
- agricultural machinery in Modena [100];
- foodstuffs in Parma [215];
- saucepans and valves in Lumezzane [1,008] (Brescia);
- packaging machinery in Bologna;
- musical instruments in Castelfidardo [400] (Ancona).

Clusters in Germany

Clusters are also common in Germany:

- steel in Dortmund, Essen and Düsseldorf;
- locksmith's products in Velbert;
- cutlery in Solingen;
- surgical instruments in Tuttlingen;
- chemicals in Leverkusen, Frankfurt and Ludwigshafen;
- jewellery in Pforzheim;
- cars in Stuttgart, Munich, Ingolstadt, Neckarsulm and Regensburg;
- machine tools in Stuttgart;
- pens and pencils in Nuremberg;
- printing presses in Heidelberg, Würzburg and Offenbach;
- optics in Wetzlar;
- toolmaking in Remscheid.

Notes

1 Trade theory has not come to grips with multiactivity firm and multiplant production as was the case with the theory of industrial organisation.
2 Trade costs decline over time because of (a) innovation and (b) as volume of trade increases, there is a decrease in unit costs.
3 The tacit assumption is that there are no transport and adjustment costs.
4 Entry barriers include sunk costs, product differentiation, R&D, regulation (product quality), marketing, predatory pricing, as well as trade, competition and industrial policies.
5 The interested reader is invited to consult Brülhart (1998b) for a brief survey of theoretical strands.
6 A strategic industrial (and trade) policy is based on a number of assumptions that include non-retaliation by the foreign partners and next to perfect information and forecast.
7 The fact that a large part of trade among developed countries is of an intra-industry nature may lead to the conclusion that the Heckscher–Ohlin (factor proportions) theory of trade is not valid. Intra-industry trade is not based on differences in factor endowments among countries. Countries tend to specialise and export goods that are demanded by the majority of domestic consumers. It is this demand that stimulates production, rather than domestic factor endowment. Countries have a competitive edge in the production of these goods and thus gain an advantage in foreign markets, whereas they import goods demanded by a minority of the home population (Linder, 1961). The US, Japan and Germany have the greatest comparative advantage in goods for which their home market is relatively big. These are standardised goods for mass consumption.
8 In the case with one market and two deposits of resources, the optimal firm location would fall inside the triangular area that links these three different spots.
9 Paris and Madrid have relatively central geographical locations in France and Spain respectively.
10 Positive feedback economics may also find parallels in non-linear physics. For example, ferromagnetic materials consist of mutually reinforcing elements. Small perturbations, at critical times, influence which outcome is selected (bifurcation point), and the chosen outcome may have higher energy (that is, be less favourable) than other possible end states (Arthur, 1990a: 99).

11 The American nuclear industry is dominated by light-water reactors as such reactors were used to propel the first nuclear submarine in 1954. The engineering literature asserts, however, that a gas-cooled reactor would have been a better choice (Arthur, 1989: 126). If, as is claimed, it is true that Betamax is a technically superior system for videorecorders than VHS, which won the market race, then the market choice did not represent the best outcome. Similar arguments could be used for the triumph of DOS over Macintosh during the mid-1980s.

12 An ergodic system (e.g. a pendulum) is one that always returns to its original state no matter what disturbances occur between the starting and ending points.

13 In an early study, Weber (1909) offered two basic reasons why firms 'go abroad' to produce. The primary reason is lower labour and transport costs, while of secondary importance is the benefit of large-scale production.

14 For example, governments may, over time, introduce policy that results in a change in the availability, quality and cost of domestic factors. The disposable tools of this policy include training of labour and education of management, R&D, science, transport and communication infrastructure and tax policies.

15 It is difficult to trace knowledge flows, because they are invisible and do not leave a paper trail by which they can be measured and tracked. Hence, a theorist may assume anything about them (Krugman, 1992: 53–4). Some evidence, such as quotations in professional journals may, however, be found.

16 Landlocked countries such as Chad, Mali and Niger have a geographical disadvantage that increases the cost of trade. However, Austria, Switzerland and Luxembourg show that the situation for landlocked countries is not hopeless.

17 The question with agglomeration economies is 'which geographical spot is going to dominate in production?' The difficulty in analysing agglomeration is that it introduces multiple equilibria.

18 Relevant factors that influence the tendency of agglomerate include the availability of raw materials, energy, labour and capital, while for consumers they include the availability of jobs and education, as well as climate and surroundings.

19 Relations between firms in a cluster may take different forms. Take a look, for example, at shoe-producing clusters in Italy and Mexico. While cooperation is more common in Italy, market rules prevail in Mexico.

20 Because of the ready availability of wood, Sweden developed an important pulp and paper industry. Strong links with suppliers contributed to the replication of the success in the manufacture of machinery that processes wood and pulp and to make and dry paper.

21 A brief survey reveals that fiscal incentives are of relatively little importance in choosing business location even though business executives often lobby hard for them. This is understandable because firms naturally welcome direct or indirect subsidies even if they do not affect location decisions to a significant degree (Wasylenko, 1991). Foreign investors typically prefer a high-quality infrastructure over tax incentives. Transfer pricing and tax deductions in the home country provide other ways to minimise the tax burden on profit (Wheeler and Mody, 1992: 71–2).

22 'Japanese business firms operating in Germany are inexplicably attracted to Düsseldorf rather than Frankfurt' (Beckmann, 1999: 61).

23 Have you ever noticed that, when an audience applauds after an opera or concert, the clapping, after a short time, develops the same tempo even though there is no conductor. Such self-organisation happens when many initially uncorrelated actions lock into each other's rhythm and create a strong collective group.

24 Despite the difficulties of applying biological analogies to social phenomena, they have been widely used in the analysis of firms. Examples include the 'life cycle' theory of the firm, 'viability' of the firm and 'homeostasis' (the tendency of a system to return to its initial equilibrium) (Penrose, 1952).

25 Personal contacts, proximity and a trusted partner are emphasised by Gordon and McCann (2000: 520), Sternberg and Tamásy (1999: 374), Porter and Sölvell (1998: 445–6) and Kleinknecht and ter Wengel (1998: 645–6), but were well known also to Perroux (1955: 317; 1961: 152).

26 Even though Siemens is a dominant firm in the Munich high-technology cluster, it does not threaten or absorb SMEs in the cluster, but rather develops ties with SMEs that are characterised by collaboration (Sternberg and Tamásy, 1999: 375).

27 This is a very special case indeed, as real-life problems that come with decreasing marginal productivity of labour were left out of the picture.

28 This model of specialisation is linear. The reader who is interested in the more complicated specialisation paths such as S-shaped and spiral ones is invited to consult Krugman (1991).

29 'IMF's Camdessus misses the point', Stratfor, 15 November 1999.

30 The first of many attempts to produce a small, economical runaround vehicle early in the twentieth century resulted in the Auto-Ped. Introduced in New York in 1915, this looked like child's scooter: it had no seat and a platform for the rider to stand on. A two-horsepower motor gave the Auto-Ped a maximum speed of 55 km/h.

31 In an attempt to eliminate textile waste during the Second World War, the US government reduced by one-tenth the amount of fabric allowed for women's swimwear. The chain of events that resulted in the ever-reducing quantity of material necessary for the bikini was set in motion.

32 This has always been an urban 'activity' because cities 'sell' anonymity and limited tolerance.

33 *The Financial Times*, 13 May 2000: 1.

34 Casella (1996) discusses the case of reallocation of resources and gains from an enlargement of a trade bloc in small and large countries that already belong to that bloc. She showed that smaller EU countries gained more from the entry of Spain and Portugal into the EU than the large EU countries.

35 The group of countries that generate the greatest number of innovations has been relatively small and stable over time (Jovanović, 1998a: 52).

36 The economic history of integrated states such as the US shows that integration is associated with regional convergence, which predominates over economic divergence in the long term. This process is rather slow, around 2 per cent a year, but it is sustained over a long period of time (Barro and Sala-i-Martin, 1991: 154). This conclusion has been confirmed by the literature; however, a poor region can expect the gap between its initial level of income and the aggregate to be reduced by only 30–40 per cent at most (Canova and Marcet, 1995: 1, 24). However, Armstrong (1995: 149) found that the convergence rate between 1970 and 1990 was only 1 per cent a year, which is half the rate estimated by Barro and Sala-i-Martin. In any case, regional policies based on pure transfers of funds do not work unless linked with structural changes.

37 With 18 million EU citizens out of work in 2000, the sensitivity of the issue does not come as a surprise.

38 *The Economist*, 18 September 1993: 51.

39 *The Economist*, 5 July 1997: 17.

40 Swiss companies accounted for a third of the world's production of textile machinery in 1997 (*The Financial Times*, 26 February 1998: 8).

41 *European Voice*, 20 November 1997: 7.

42 The public policy and administrative areas on which the authorities collect statistics do not usually correspond exactly to clusters. This is why it is difficult to determine the exact economic significance of clusters with a high degree of reliability.

43 Ski boots are made in Montebelluna whereas sports footwear is made in Riviera del Brenta.

44 Italians generally have more sophisticated taste and spend more on stylish clothes and shoes than the citizens of any other nation.
45 The list is based on data for 1996; where available, the number of related firms in the cluster is given in square brackets; and a bigger city in the vicinity or province is given in round brackets.

3 Market structure and geography of production

3.1 Introduction

The classical theory of international economic integration (customs unions) assumed that the static effects of resource reallocation occurred in a timeless framework. If one wants to move this theory towards reality, one must consider dynamic, i.e. restructuring, effects. These restructuring effects have often a spatial dimension. It is generally accepted that markets are imperfect. Externalities such as economies of scale and product differentiation (goods are very close, but not perfect substitutes for each other) introduce imperfections in competition in the market. When a market has such a structure, regionalism/integration may find its justification. The rationale is that integration extends the market, hence there are potentials for the reduction in the market power of firms. This can have a positive impact on competition, productivity and innovation, reduce prices and, hence, increase welfare on average.

The old, static, neo-classical rules of economics require significant modification. Information technology, the rapid pace of innovation and fast-changing technology generally characterise the current economy. A fast information flow has reduced many of the past barriers to business. In addition, innovative activity has significantly changed the extent and character of the modern economy. The Middle Ages in Europe (the fifth to fifteenth centuries) offered only a few important inventions, such as horseshoes, the horse collar (i.e. one that did not half-throttle the animal as soon as it started to pull with any significant force), windmills, the fork and underwear. The only constant feature in the modern dynamic economy is an ever-accelerating pace of innovation, in particular the improvement and reduction in cost of already existing goods and services.

Instead of considering only trade in commodities, dynamic models analyse resource allocation across time and space. The static effects of integration on the geography of production have their most obvious and profound influence in the period immediately before and following the creation of, for example, a free trade area or a customs union. Gradually, after several years of adjustment in the geography of production and consumption, the dynamic effects increase in importance and become dominant. These effects push technological constraints away from the origin and provide the group with an additional integration-induced 'growth bonus'.

Production and trade flows do not remain constant over time and space. They evolve and alter over time. Changes in the equilibrium points in the standard partial equilibrium model are presented as instantaneous moves. However, such shifts may not always be possible. Delays in reaction on the part of countries and consumers in a customs union could be caused by their recourse to stocks or to other barriers such as sunk costs. Hence, they do not immediately need to purchase those goods whose price has decreased as a consequence of integration or to alter the geography of production. They also may have some contractual commitments that cannot be abandoned overnight without a penalty. Finally, buyers may not be aware of all the changes.

Until the nineteenth century state intervention was negligible; markets remained disconnected geographically and in terms of production because of imperfect information and relatively high costs of trade. The Internet has eliminated the constraint of the lack of timely information. A time lapse between the implementation of a policy change (integration) and its favourable effects may include an initial period of economic deterioration in certain industries which may be followed by improvements due to the J-curve effect.

This chapter considers competition policy. Competition policy has important strands that include monopoly; other types of market structure, conduct and performance; innovation; specialisation; and returns to scale. Their source, importance and interrelations are related to efficiency in production and have an impact on the location of production. Competition policy in the EU is presented in terms of NTBs, deals among firms that restrict competition, abuse of the dominant position on the market and state aids. Finally, the concluding part speculates about the need for and possibility of introducing multilateral rules for competition.

3.2 Competition, efficiency and location

Background

The early literature about the geographical location of firms was obsessed with the geometrical shape of market areas in an idealised landscape or with the ideal production site, given resources and markets. It ignored the crucial issue of market structure. This was like putting the cart before the horse or 'doing things in the wrong order, worrying about the details of a secondary problem before making progress in the main issue' (Krugman, 1992: 5).

One of the most important functions of competition is the exchange of information. In theory, free market competition provides everyone with the widest opportunities for business and produces the best sectoral and geographical allocation of resources. By so doing, competition both improves efficiency in the use of factors because of their constant reallocation and, something which is often forgotten, introduces a permanent instability into the system. This conclusion has been accepted by neo-classical economic theory as a truth. It has provided the intellectual backing for competition (anti-trust) policy. However, while competition may create lucrative opportunities and gains, it may also be the source of problems and concerns such as risk and uncertainty. The objective of this policy is that markets attain and maintain the flexibility needed to promote initiative, innovation and constant improvement in allocation of resources. The final goal is, of course, to maintain and raise living standards. Hence, what matters in theory is how to play the competition game, rather than who wins or loses. In practice, however, politicians, members of the public, firms and lobbies are quite concerned about the winners.

Competition policy is a combination of two irreconcilable forces. On the one hand, there is an argument for the (geographical) concentration of business, which rationalises production and enables economies of scale. On the other hand, there is a case for an anti-trust policy,[1] which prevents monopolisation, protects individual freedom and rights and, through increased competition, increases welfare. The challenge for governments is to achieve a balance between these two tendencies. They need to keep the best parts of each of the two opposing tendencies, profit from the harmonious equilibrium between the two and employ competition policy as a tool to increase the standard of living.

The concept of 'competitiveness' was criticised by Krugman as redundant and dangerous.[2] This criticism is based on the close relation between productivity and competitiveness. In spite of the fact that world trade is larger than ever before in absolute terms, the US exports 'only' around 10 per cent of its gross national product (GNP). 'The growth rate of living standards essentially equals the growth rate of domestic productivity – not productivity relative to competitors, but simply domestic productivity' (Krugman, 1996b: 9). As for the danger in using the term 'competitiveness', former US President Bill Clinton stated that each nation is 'like a big corporation competing in the global marketplace'. This is the same as saying that the US and Japan are competitors in the same way as Coca-Cola competes with Pepsi (Krugman, 1996b: 4). Firms are rivals over a limited pool of potential profits. Period. What distinguishes states from firms is that one firm may absorb another, which is not possible in normal circumstances in the case of states. In addition, states may introduce protectionist measures (international disintegration). Such an option is not open to firms. Countries are not firms. They cannot be driven out of all businesses. However, countries can be driven out of some lines of business, which may have permanent effects on trade and the geography of production. States produce goods that compete with each other but, more importantly, states are each other's export markets and suppliers of useful things. David Ricardo taught us in 1817 that international trade is *not* about competition but rather about mutually beneficial exchange. The purpose of trade is imports, not exports. Imports give a country the opportunity to get what it wants. Exporting is a toll that a country must 'suffer' in order to pay for its imports (Krugman, 1996b: 120). Hence, the gain is not in the goods given or sold, but rather in the ones that are received or imported. Ricardo's ideas were as much misunderstood two centuries ago as they are today.

Strong equilibrating forces ensure that a country can sell goods (have a 'competitive' output) in world markets. David Hume pointed out 200 years ago that in the case of the gold standard a country that imports more that it exports experiences a drain of gold and a fall in the money supply. Prices and wages fall, and as a result goods and labour in that country become cheap so that they become attractive to foreign buyers. Thus, the deficit in trade is corrected. In the modern world, with no gold standard, deficits are usually corrected not by the depreciation of prices and wages, but rather through the depreciation of national currencies (Krugman, 1996b: 89–90).

New policy approaches to competitiveness take a pragmatic view. They have three basic elements (Jacquemin and Pench, 1997: 8–12):

- an emphasis on the efficient use and accumulation of factors as determinants of long-term economic performance;
- recognition of the importance of the international dimension of economic performance;
- an appreciation of the relevance of social cohesion (unemployment benefits, pensions, health insurance, labour market regulations), which provides opportunities for trust, cooperation and stability that are not available in more divided societies.

Regional integration widens markets for the participating countries, hence one of its first dynamic effects is in the field of competition. Competition encourages firms to perform profitably in open markets. Thus, the EU has its own rules for market behaviour. They refer to the restriction of competition, abuse of the dominant position and state aids. The Single Market Programme, completed at the end of 1992, increased the importance of the competition policy.

Monopoly

In a perfectly competitive market, the marginal revenue (MR) curve of a firm is a straight line (Figure 3.1). No firm can influence the market price. Each firm is a price taker.[3] Hence, the MR curve of every firm equals the market price. In a simple model with linear demand, cost and revenue curves, the MR curve passes through the horizontal axis OQ (representing the quantity produced) at point E. At this point, MR is zero. To the left of E on the horizontal axis, MR is positive and in moving from O to E total revenue increases. To the right of E on the same axis, MR is negative, and in moving from E to Q total revenue decreases. At E, total revenue is maximum.

The market structure of a monopolistic industry is at the opposite extreme from perfect competition. Entry into such an industry is costly, risky and time-consuming, although potentially highly profitable in the short and medium term. Whereas in a state of perfect competition no firm has any power whatsoever over the market price, a monopoly (exclusive) supplier has the power to influence the market price of a good or a service if there are no substitutes. To counter such behaviour, governments may choose to intervene and prevent/rectify such non-competitive behaviour. This can be done by regulation of the behaviour of

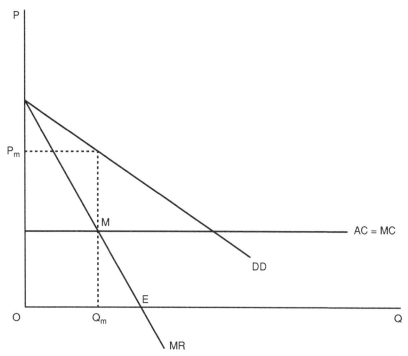

Figure 3.1 Welfare effects of a monopoly.

monopolies and/or by liberalisation of imports.[4] A monopolist which wanted to maximise total revenue would never supply a quantity bigger than OE.

With constant returns to scale, average costs are constant, hence the average cost (AC) curve is horizontal. The consequence of this simplification is that marginal costs (MC) equal AC. This enables the point to be found at which profit is at its maximum if demand curve is DD. It is maximised at point M, where MR=MC. At that point, a monopolist produces OQ_m and charges price OP_m. The quantity produced is smaller and the price charged by the monopoly is higher than in the case of perfect competition.

This is an obvious, although very simple, example of how a monopoly (or a cartel) undermines the welfare of consumers and allocates resources in a suboptimal way from a social standpoint. In addition, if left alone, there is no pressure on the monopoly to do anything about the situation. Such a safe and secure life does not encourage the monopoly to innovate and increase efficiency as would be the case with free competition. A secure life could make a monopoly innovation-shy in the longer term. However, in the short term the opposite may occur. If a firm thinks that an innovation may bring it a monopoly power, in the short term, such a firm would be tempted to venture into a process that may lead to innovation. If successful, this may bring inertia, less flexibility and reluctance to adjust in the longer term. However, such rigidities can be found not only on the part of firms. Labour, in particular labour unions, may pose obstacles and slow down the innovation process. Machines, it can be argued, may destroy jobs. If, however, this were ever true, it may be correct only in the short term. The response of the Luddites in the early nineteenth century to the introduction of looms and jennies was to destroy them.

Technological progress, increased productivity and alternative sources of employment, often requiring a superior skills profile, more than compensate for any supposed short-term social loss. Only those who are reluctant to adjust to the new situation suffer. Although technology has advanced rapidly in recent centuries, unemployment has not risen with it. Increases in productivity, output and job openings have risen together over the long term.

If a monopoly exists, one should not rush to the conclusion that its presence *per se* leads to economic inefficiency. It is possible that in industries with high entry barriers, sunk costs and economies of scale (for example, the aerospace industry), a single efficient producer may sell the good or a service at a lower price than would be charged by many inefficient producers in the same industry. In such cases it may not be astute to break up a concentrated industry. The authorities would be better taxing the excessive profits of firms in such industries and/or making sure that they are reinvested. If the market grows sufficiently, then the authorities need to encourage other, potentially efficient and profitable, producers to enter the same kind of business.

Policies intended to increase competitiveness sometimes produce unexpected results. During the 1950s, the US government wanted to break up large and powerful corporations. One such corporation was AT&T. Little attention was paid during the debate to the place of Bell Labs and the fact that it had played the major part in innovation in telecommunications over the preceding century. Deregulation of the industry prohibited the US telephone operating companies from making phones or switching equipment. As a result, US exports grew moderately, while imports exploded (Lipsey, 1992a: 295).

The decision of the US Court in 2000 that Microsoft should be split into two companies, provoked by the company's dominance of the software market, is another case that has generated a lot of hot air. The split would create one company to develop and produce the operating system and the other the application packages. The real outcome could be the creation of two monopolies instead of one! At the heart of the debate is the issue of capacity to innovate. There was a risk that Microsoft would limit the ability of third parties to innovate. The problem with splitting the company is that numerous operating systems and applications may emerge. However, the potential for customer confusion that could result may be exaggerated, as there is a strong commercial incentive to maintain compatibility. In addition, Microsoft was charged with exhibiting monopolistic behaviour such as operating exclusion contracts and increasing sales by increasing the prices of older versions of software after the launch of a new version.

From these examples stem convincing arguments in favour of a competition policy. The intention of this policy is to improve efficiency in the use of factors with the objective of increasing welfare. However, in a real market situation that is full of imperfections (economies of scale, externalities, sunk costs, innovation, product differentiation, asymmetric information, etc.) one may easily find arguments in favour of a certain concentration of production (mergers, clusters) and protection of intellectual property rights.

It is sometimes argued that it is quite costly to trade intangible technology assets at arm's length because 'it is a combination of skills, equipment and organisation embodied in people and institutions as much as in machinery and equipment' (Sharp and Pavitt, 1993: 147). If an inventor fears that his patent rights[5] are not sufficiently protected (enforcement, length of the patent right, level of penalties), he will keep the innovation secret or be disinclined to participate in R&D in the future. A part of the innovation process may lean towards outcomes that may not be easily imitated. A conflict between static and dynamic efficiency in production, as well as between the welfare of producers and consumers, is obvious. As technology becomes older and is no longer at the core of the business activities of the innovator, it becomes more likely that the innovator will disseminate the technology through licensing.

The appropriation of returns from innovation is not a major problem if the innovator is a non-profit institution such as a research institute, university or a government. Non-profit-making innovators are most likely to make their findings public and, in fact, may be disseminated immediately. It is estimated that around half of total investment in R&D is financed by the business community and between a half and two-thirds of R&D is carried out by private firms (Dosi, 1988: 1123–4). The problem of appropriation arises when there is a conflict between public interest in the spread of information and knowledge and private interest in holding and employing that knowledge for lucrative purposes. If private knowledge acquired through risky investment of resources is not protected, at least for some period of time, there will be no incentive to generate innovations that drive efficiency and, hence, contribute to future growth.

An analysis by Levin *et al.* (1987) of alternative ways of protecting the competitive (monopolistic) advantages of new and improved processes and products found that patents are the least effective means for appropriating returns. Lead time over competitors, a fast-track learning curve (unit costs of production fall as output increases over time) and sales/service effort were regarded by the surveyed firms as providing better returns than patents. Firms may sometimes refrain from patenting products or processes to avoid revealing the facts or details of innovation because of the possible disclosure of information to competitors and imitators. At the same time, firms have every incentive to advertise the benefits of new or improved products and disseminate them to consumers. Therefore, secrecy about innovation is both difficult and undesirable. It may be better to be anxious about the creation of future business secrets than to worry about the protection of the existing ones.

Additional profits can accrue from the production of complementary assets. Therefore, not only innovation and manufacturing (technological leadership), but also, and equally important, distribution and aftersales service (commercial leadership) are of great advantage in capturing markets and profits.[6] In the fields of cameras, audio and video goods (and some segments of the car market) Japanese companies have virtually ousted most of their international competitors and changed the international geography of production in these industries[7] through an uninterrupted tide of technical improvements and distribution/service network.

The benefits of increased competition will materialise only if firms compete and do not collude to avoid competition. Competition stimulates innovation. It may, in turn, bring new technologies with large sunk costs, geographical concentration of production and other entry barriers. If this is the case, then neither unfettered markets nor monopolies (oligopolies) need to be left alone. Otherwise, consumer welfare would be distorted and allocation of resources may take place in a suboptimal way from a social standpoint. Hence, there is a need for a competition policy not only in the market of a single country, but also in a much larger area. This area is generally limited by the geographical space where economic cycles are in step. The rule of law, based in part on economic theory, may modify market distortions both in single countries and in integration groups.

Concept

One of the most obvious initial effects of international economic integration is the improvement in efficiency in the use of factors due to increased competition in the geographically enlarged market. In this context, competitiveness of firms has two aspects: national and international. In both cases, a competitive *firm* is one that is able to make a profit without being protected and/or subsidised. This means that the output of a firm (goods and/or services) is in demand and is produced at the right time, in the right quantity and quality, as well as being superior to the output of most of its competitors. The goods and services of a *country* are internationally competitive if they are able to withstand free and fair competition on the world market while, at the same time, the country's inhabitants maintain and increase their standard of living on average and in the long term.

There are three concepts related to competitiveness:

- *Cost competitiveness* addresses the difference (i.e. profit) between the price at which a good is sold and the cost of its production. If a firm is able to reduce the costs of production by reducing input prices, innovation and/or organising production and marketing in a more efficient way that is not available to its competitors, it may improve its relative profit margin.
- A firm has a *price-competitive* product if it matches other firms' products in all characteristics, including price. This type of competitiveness can be improved if the firm unilaterally reduces the price of its good (other things being equal) and/or upgrades its attributes and provides a better service.
- *Relative profitability* exists when there is the possibility of geographical price discrimination (e.g. between domestic and foreign markets). The different profit margins in these markets indicate relative profitability.

The measurement of the competitiveness of an integrated group of countries includes the intra-group trade ratio (intra-group export/intra-group import) and extra-group trade ratio (extra-group export/extra-group import). In addition, the competitiveness of an integrated *country's* economic sector (or industries within it) may be measured in the following two ways.

- *Trade specialisation index* (TSI). This provides details about the integrated country *j*'s specialisation in exports in relation to other partner countries in the group. If this index for good *i* is greater than 1, country *j* is specialised in export of good *i* within the group. TSI (eqn 3.1) reveals country *j*'s comparative advantage within the group. The conceptual problem with this approach is that the structure of exports may vary because of a change in domestic consumption that may not alter either the volume or the composition of domestic output.

$$\text{TSI} = \frac{\dfrac{X_{i,j}}{X_{\text{ind},j}}}{\dfrac{X_{i,g}}{X_{\text{ind},g}}} \tag{3.1}$$

where:

$X_{i,j}$ = export of *good i* from country *j* to the partner countries in the integration group;

$X_{\text{ind},j}$ = total *industry* exports to the group from country *j*;

$X_{i,g}$ = intra-group exports of *good i*;

$X_{\text{ind},g}$ = total *industry* exports within the group.

- *Production specialisation index* (PSI). This is identical to the TSI, except that export (X) variables are replaced by production (P) ones. PSI shows where country *j* is more specialised in production than its integration partners. This index reveals country *j*'s production advantage as well as its domestic consumption pattern. Interpretation of both the TSI and the PSI may be distorted if the production and export of good *i* in country *j* is protected/ subsidised. The revealed 'advantage' would be misleading, as in the case of exports of farm goods from the EU because of the Common Agricultural Policy.

Goods that are produced and traded by a country may be categorised by their economic idiosyncrasies. There are five, sometimes overlapping, types of goods (Audretsch, 1993: 94–5):

- Ricardo goods have a high natural resource content. These commodities include minerals, fuels, wood, paper, fibres and food.
- Product-cycle goods include those that rely on high technology and where information serves as a crucial input.[8] This group includes chemicals, pharmaceuticals, plastics, dyes, fertilisers, explosives, machinery, aircraft and instruments.

- R&D-intensive goods include industries where R&D expenditure is at least 5 per cent of the sales value. These are pharmaceuticals, office machinery, aircraft and telecom goods.
- High-advertising goods are the ones where advertising expenditures are at least 5 per cent of the sales value. These include drinks, cereals, soaps, perfumes and watches.
- Goods that are produced by high-concentration industries include tobacco, liquid fuels, edible oils, tubes, home appliances, motor vehicles and railway equipment.

Audretsch (1993: 95–6) made a geographical comparison of these five types of goods. The comparison was for the period 1975–83 among the rich Western countries (mainly the OECD), poor Western countries (mainly the south European countries) and then the centrally planned countries of Central and Eastern Europe. The findings were as follows:

- In 1975, Western countries had a comparative disadvantage in the Ricardo goods while the other two groups had a comparative advantage. By 1983, Central and East European countries, together with the rich Western countries, were exhibiting a comparative disadvantage in Ricardo goods, reflecting their inability to compete with resource-rich developing countries.
- The rich Western countries have a constant comparative advantage in product-cycle, R&D-intensive and advertising-intensive goods over the other two groups of countries.
- Rich Western, as well as Central and East European, countries have a competitive advantage in highly concentrated industries over the poor Western nations.

Whereas competition in goods is more or less global, competition in many services is localised. A large part of competitive activity in manufactured goods has a price component; competition in many services has, predominantly, a non-price dimension. Reputation and past experience of services often play a crucial role in choosing a supplier for a certain type of service. Local providers of some services, as well as those with a good (international) reputation have a specific market power. Local market influence on producers of goods is in most cases non-existent as goods may be (easily) traded across space. Because the service industries are generally subjected to a lower degree of competitiveness than the manufacturing industries, and as a result of legislation designed to consumers, administrative regulation in the services sector is quite high.

The competitiveness of a country's goods and services may be increased through depreciation of a home currency and/or by a reduction in wages. The simplest way to increase competitiveness, however, is to increase productivity. Developing, intermediate and advanced countries trade more or less successfully all over the world, but their standard of living depends on their productivity. However, the ability to trade depends only on the ability to produce something that is wanted, while the rate of exchange ensures that exports can be sold. This was the message of David Ricardo in the early nineteenth century and is as important (and as little understood) today as it was in Ricardo's time (Lipsey, 1993: 21).

The new theory of trade and strategic industrial policy (initiated in the early 1980s) argues that, with imperfect competition, there are no unique solutions to economic problems.[9] The outcome depends on assumptions about the conduct of economic agents. There is a strong possibility that in a situation of imperfect competition firms are able to make above-average profits (rents). Intervention in trade, competition and industry may, under certain conditions, geographically redistribute these rents in favour of domestic firms. This shift is the main feature of strategic trade policy. Hence, there is an assumption about the 'strategic interdependence' among firms. This means that profits of one firm are directly affected by the individual strategy choices of other firms and such a relation is understood by the firms (Brander, 1995: 1397). The strategic trade policy of beggar-thy-neighbour ('war' over economic rents) does not occur in the situation of either pure monopoly or perfect competition. This policy may look like a zero-sum game, where everybody loses in the long term through a chain of retaliations and counter-retaliations. However, 'countries that would otherwise compete with each other at the level of strategic policy have an incentive to make agreements that would ameliorate or prevent such rivalries' (Brander, 1995: 1447–8).

There is, potentially, at least one good reason for intervention.[10] With externalities, spillovers and geographical clustering of production, governments may find reasons to protect some growing, often high-technology industries that depend on economies of scale. These are the industries for which accumulated knowledge is the prime source of competitiveness and whose expenditure on R&D, and employment of engineers and scientists is (well) above the average for the economy. Sunk costs and R&D may be funded by governments, as the positive effects of introducing new technology are felt throughout the economy and beyond the confines of the firm that introduces it. The whole world may benefit, in some cases, from new technology whose development was supported by government intervention. For example, spaceships had to be equipped with computers. They needed to be small and light. A spillover from the development of this kind of equipment was the creation of personal computers. Therefore, the new theory goes, with externalities and under certain dubious conditions (no retaliation, well-informed governments[11]), intervention may be a positive-sum game where everyone potentially gains in the long run. Critics of the new theory have not been able to prove is wrong, but argue that it is not necessarily correct. In fact, what is not understood is that the new theory provides only a programme for research, rather than a prescription for policy (Krugman, 1993a: 164).

Market structure

A market for a good or a service is said to be contestable if there is a smooth entry and exit route for a firm. The number of firms in the market should be 'sufficient' to prevent a single firm or group of firms from increasing prices and making rents (super-normal profits). Relative ease of entering the business would prevent the incumbent firms from charging exorbitant prices. The opportunity of making high rents would immediately attract new entrants. Geographical extensions of the market (economic integration) reinforce potentials for pro-competition market behaviour.

Imagine a situation with two identical countries A and B, one good X and no trade. Assume also a monopoly in country A, and free competition in country B in the market for the same good. One can reasonably expect that prices for good X are lower in country B. If one now introduces free trade between the two countries, country B would export good X to country A. This example shows that a pure difference in market structure between the countries may explain the geographical location of production and trade, even though the countries may have identical production technologies and factor endowments. This crucial aspect has been overlooked by the classical theory of spatial economics.

Competition policies may be classified according to the structure–conduct–performance (SCP) paradigm. The thrust of the SCP paradigm is that performance in a defined market depends on the interaction between the structure of the market and the conduct of buyers and sellers in it.

- *Structure* refers to the organisation of production and distribution, i.e. which enterprises are permitted to enter into which business activities. It determines the number and size of buyers and sellers; product differentiation; and relationships (horizontal and vertical integration) between buyers and sellers.
- *Conduct* describes how firms behave in their business. This refers to the competitive strategy of suppliers such as (predatory) pricing, innovation, advertising and investment.
- *Performance* refers to the goals of economic organisation such as efficiency, technological progress, availability of goods and full employment of resources.

The most common indicator of market structure or the degree of competition is the proportion of industry output, sales, investment or employment attributable to a subset (usually three to ten) of all firms in the industry. It shows the force of the competitive pressure on the incumbents. If this ratio is relatively high, then it illustrates that market power is concentrated in relatively few firms.

It is, however, important to be cautious when dealing with these ratios. While an employment concentration ratio may show a monopoly situation, a sales concentration ratio may not. Competitiveness is linked not only to market shares, but, as a dynamic phenomenon, to the relative growth of productivity, innovation, R&D, size and quality of the capital stock, mobility of resources, operational control, success in shifting out of declining lines of business, education of management, training of labour, incentives and so on. Therefore, there is no need to fear that a jobs exodus from the EU to the transition countries of Central and Eastern Europe or to the south Mediterranean countries (because of the relatively low labour costs there) would change the entire production geography and undermine the global competitiveness of the economies of the EU. If it were true, the EU would be flooded by goods from those countries, and this is not the case in spite of the liberal trading regime for manufactured goods with these countries. Many factors other than relative labour costs influence competitiveness. In most of the 'other factors' (mentioned above) the EU fares much better than its competitors from the other two regions. A very similar situation exists in the trade relation between the US and Mexico. These ratios do, however, provide a useful, if second-best, barometer of the oligopolistic restriction of competition.

The Hirschman–Herfindahl index (HHI) is an alternative and more complete measure of market structure than the concentration ratio. It is being increasingly used in the public fight against oligopolies.

$$\text{HHI} = \sum_i S_i^2 \times 100 \qquad\qquad (3.2)$$

The HHI (eqn 3.2) is the sum of squared market shares of each firm in the defined market. It is between 0 and 100. The index is 100 when there is a monopoly, while it is relatively small in competitive industries. The HHI takes accounts of all firms (i.e. both their absolute number and relative difference in size) in the defined market, whereas the concentration ratio accounts only for a select number of firms in the same market. Antitrust lawyers still place much weight on the HHI. However, economists are increasingly sceptical about its value. Although some economists use the HHI as an initial screening tool, it is more useful to consider how easy it is for new and efficient firms to enter the target market. New firms are attracted to enter an industry by the potential for new profit lures. Estimates of the ease and likelihood of new firms entering an industry are inevitably highly speculative.

Integration may provoke several scenarios regarding market structure. On the one hand, an increase in industrial concentration may arise from firms' decision to take advantage of economies of scale and intra-industry production linkages. Economies of scope[12] may also increase geographical concentration because they favour diversified firms which are often large. On the other hand, smaller firms may benefit, as in Japan or in Germany, because they may be included in the network of large ones. In addition, reduced trade costs make it easier for smaller firms to penetrate into the markets of partner countries. This may reduce concentration.

Firms compete through product differentiation, innovation, quality, R&D, advertising and special close links with suppliers, clients and various institutions, as well as on price. The exceptions are, of course, raw materials and certain standardised semi-finished goods. In spite of trendy talk about the 'global economy' and the diminishing role played by specific geographical locations for business, competitive advantages are often heavily local. These gains come from the clustering of highly specialised knowledge and skills and the existence of rivals, sophisticated customers and institutions in a specific geographical area (Porter, 1998b). Even though many of these advantages are external to individual firms, they are internal to the cluster in which they locate their operations.

Major changes in the capacity of a firm that are linked to high sunk costs do not happen frequently. It is, however, more difficult to test the impact of non-price rivalry such as competitors' R&D, innovation, design activities and non-technical matters such as management and marketing than their prices. It also takes longer to retaliate in these areas than to change prices (Schmalensee, 1988: 670).

Innovation

The process of technological change is driven by several factors. They include the existence of unexploited lucrative opportunities for the solution of problems such as the transformation of electricity into sound or light into electricity. Second, it is stimulated by changes in government regulation such as changes in technical and safety standards (including concerns about the environment) and trade policy. Third is the change in prices (relative scarcity) of raw materials, energy, labour or transport and communication. Fourth, supplying clients with the toughest demands may set in motion the innovation process. Search for a challenge and rivalry, rather than staying away from them inspires innovation. The same holds for regular contacts with research centres. Fifth is a change in consumers' needs. Increases in income and decreased working time increase the demand for leisure and entertainment. At the same time, more stressful work takes its toll on workers' health, increasing demand for medical and rehabilitation services.

The innovation process has four distinct, but inter-related phases:

- invention (discovery of something new which can 'work');
- innovation (translation of invention into commercial use);
- spread (diffusion in the market);
- absorption (learning from clients and conversion into a public good).

If, because of a change in circumstances (e.g. integration), firms innovate (i.e. realise their technological and organisational potentials and capabilities to develop, produce and sell goods and services) and introduce new technologies and new goods/services in order to maintain or improve their market position, then efficiency overall may increase. From a given set of resources one may expect to achieve more and/or better-quality output. This directly increases national welfare on average. In fact, for a small or medium-sized country integration enables economic development and progress at a lower cost than does autarky. There is, however, an opposing force. When there are market imperfections, such as economies of scale and externalities, firms make rents.[13] Free competition leads to concentration and agglomeration, which may reduce competition in the future. The new theory of trade and strategic industrial policy holds that there may be fierce competition even among a few firms. Examples include the aircraft industry, the long-distance telephone call market and the Japanese market for electronic goods (largely confined to half a dozen domestic conglomerates). Technical innovations prompt legal innovations. Telephone business, for example, was for a very long time considered to be a 'natural monopoly'. Nowadays, it is a highly competitive industry.

Innovation changes the mix of factors that are used in the production and/or consumption of goods and services. Usually, an innovation brings a reduction in the quantity of factors needed to produce a good or service, as shown by an arrow in Figure 3.2. This makes output cheaper and, consequently, more competitive. Suppose that the production of a good requires two factors, f_1 and f_2. If production requires, per unit of output, OA of factor f_1 and OB of factor f_2, then the resource required to produce the good is represented by rectangle OACB. Innovation normally reduces the area of rectangle OACB (note the direction of the arrow). If, however, one factor, such as oil or some other raw material, suddenly becomes scarce, innovation may reduce the consumption of that factor but disproportionally increase (at least temporarily) the requirement for the other factor. Hence, in such a special case, the area of the rectangle OACB may increase as the result of innovation.

Economic integration opens up the markets of the integrated countries to local firms. It is reasonable to expect competition to have a positive effect on innovation, but what are the effects of such a process in the long term?

- If innovation *spreads* geographically, and if it increases competition, then competition and innovation reinforce each other.
- If, however, innovation becomes *centralised* over time and space because it is costly and risky so that it can be undertaken only by a few large firms, then

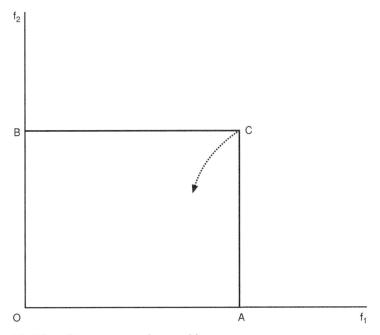

Figure 3.2 Effect of innovation on the use of factors.

geographical extension of markets would have a positive effect on innovation only in the short term.

It is therefore necessary to ensure that immediate positive effects continue in the long term (Geroski, 1988: 377–9). In order to maintain the 'necessary' level of competition within the integrated area, the countries involved may decide to reduce the level of common external tariff and NTBs.

The impact of competition is not restricted to prices and costs. Competition also yields other favourable effects. It stimulates technical progress, widens consumer choice, improves the quality of goods and services and rationalises the organisation of firms. It is important to remember that firms seldom lose out to competitors because their product is overpriced or because their production capacity is insufficient; rather, they lose because they fail to develop new products and production processes as well or as quickly as their competitors (Lipsey, 1993: 13). If a firm does not make its own product obsolete through innovation, some other entrepreneur will. The 'prospect theory' of psychology explains that the individuals are more hurt by a loss than they are encouraged by gains of equal size, i.e. fear of loss is often more powerful than the expectation of gain.

The innovation process is sometimes accidental but always uncertain and risky. For example, in 1970, Spencer Silver, a research chemist at 3M, was working in the area of adhesive technology. His goal was to produce the strongest glue on the market and his reputation was ruined when he developed a product that was quite the opposite. He did, however, discover that his new glue could be used again and did not leave any traces on the surface to which it was applied. He tried for a decade to find an application for his glue, but there was no interest at 3M. However, Silver had a friend, Arthur Fry, who was a singer in his local church choir. Every Sunday he inserted slips of paper into his hymnbook to mark the pages of the hymns to be sung during the service. And every Sunday the slips would fall out as he opened the book. Fry remembered Silver's 'futile' invention and applied it to the slips of paper, which stayed in place. A year later, in 1981, 3M started producing now omnipresent Post-it notes (Hillman and Gibbs, 1998: 183).

As a result of innovation, techniques used in the production process change constantly. But innovation changes not only the method of production of goods and services, but also our values and the way we live. For example, Hollywood films changed how we lived and worked, how we saw the world, even how young people courted (in cars, away from the eyes of parents and chaperones). These changes can be minor or revolutionary. Lipsey (1993: 3–4) described four levels of innovation:

- *Incremental innovation*: a series of changes, each small, but with a large cumulative effect.
- *Radical innovations*: major but discontinuous changes such as the development of a new material (e.g. plastic), a new source of power or new products (aircraft, computer or laser).

- *Changes in the technology system:* changes that affect an economic sector and industries within it, such as the changes that occurred in the chemical and related industries in the nineteenth century.
- *Technological revolution:* innovations that change the whole technoeconomic paradigm.[14]

Innovation is an important economic driver. It will be the basis of competition in the future and will continue to affect the location of production. In the field of personal computers, for example, the greatest competition is no longer between assembly companies such as Compaq, IBM, and Toshiba but between companies operating in the area of added value, such as microprocessors, dominated by Intel, and operating software, where Microsoft, through its Windows program, reigns supreme. Market advantage for critical elements of the system is often held in the form of intellectual property (Borrus and Zysman, 1997; Zysman and Schwartz, 1998: 409).

There is, however, no simple answer to the question of whether international economic integration (extension of the market) stimulates or prevents innovation. There are two opposing views. First, a monopoly organisation has a secure market for its output. It can anticipate reaping normal or supra-normal profits (rents) from any innovation. It is therefore easier for such a firm to innovate than one that does not have such market security. On the other hand, with no competitive pressure, a monopolist company may not feel the need to innovate. The sense of long-term stability fosters a conservative way of thinking that may restrict innovative activity. Monopolists may not wish to 'rock the boat' and can prevent or delay the implementation innovations of their own production or developed by others.

The huge increases in income and living standards that have been seen over the past 250 years, particularly in the West, are the consequence of several factors. At the end of the seventeenth century there was a strong convergence between the theoretical understanding of science and the application of that knowledge. A critical mass of knowledge in the fields of mathematics and mechanics was accumulated and applied to the understanding of atmospheric pressure and the invention of the steam engine. This provided the foundation for a technological revolution that resulted in a 150-year period of radical innovation in the areas of transport (rail and water), textiles, mining, tools, metallurgy and food processing.

Most inventions originated in a small group of countries, and this group has remained relatively stable over time. There is a clear geographical localisation of innovation activities. During the Industrial Revolution, Britain led the way, joined by Germany, the US, France, Switzerland and Sweden in the second half of the nineteenth century. Membership of this select group of countries has been stable for over a century. The only major newcomer to the group was Japan just after Second World War, although a few newly industrialised countries, such as South Korea and Taiwan, may shortly join this still exclusive club.[15]

Why is this? What happened in these (Western) countries at the end of the seventeenth century and was allowed to continue undisturbed? Why did it not happen before? What prevented the Islamic world from continuing its innovative course after the thirteenth century or what prevented China from doing so after the fifteenth century? Evidence to support theories about these issues is still imperfect and highly controversial. Nonetheless, several overlapping factors may, in combination, provide a partial explanation.

- Willingness and readiness to accept and live with the change (*values*) are one element. Continuous change and adaptation is essential to make a population and state wealthier. However, this 'greed' needs to be coupled with investments and displacement of the mentality of self-sufficiency.
- *Politics* steps in when there is resistance to change. All societies have tried to resist change at one time or another, but this is inevitably self-damaging and in vain. For example, ancient China looked with suspicion at new ideas introduced by foreigners. Indeed, the country's rulers often banned such innovations. In Florence, in 1299, bankers were forbidden from using Arabic numbers. And in Danzig (Gdansk) in 1579, the City Council ordered the inventor of the ribbon loom to be drowned.
- In the successful countries, *institutions* that provided a favourable environment for innovation and growth were created. In Britain, for example, the Magna Carta of 1215 gave subjects the right to their own property. They were protected from the Crown, which until then had been entitled to seize property at random. In contrast, arbitrary confiscation continued to be common in the Moslem world and in Asia. In the West, rulers quickly learned that a tax on property was more profitable than random confiscation as tax proceeds continue to accrue indefinitely. The outcome was a social system that promoted innovation and growth more than any previous system. In modern times it has almost eliminated the gap between frontline science and applied technology.
- The size of the *local market* (remember that integration increases the size of the market),[16] competition and supply of skills are important ingredients in the complex links between technological opportunities and entrepreneurial decisions. R&D plays a crucial role in the innovation process as it sustains a supply of knowledge.
- Another possible explanation for the relative constancy of countries that innovate most is that innovation reflects the *cumulative* and inter-related nature of acquired knowledge. Once it exists, knowledge does not cease to exist, and discovery builds on discovery. Innovation also reflects a change in technological capabilities and economic incentives.[17] It is related not only to the creation and absorption of new knowledge, but also to its adaptation and extension within an innovation-friendly environment. Taken together, this provides strong grounds for the creation of dynamic comparative advantages, certain irreversibilities[18] and economic growth[19] of firms and nations as success breeds the potential for further success. The higher the level of accumulation of knowledge and capital stock, the greater are the benefits of technological progress[20] and vice versa. The law of diminishing returns does not apply to

the accumulation of knowledge (Lipsey, 1994). This is also reflected in the export performance of those countries, as well as in differences in labour productivity. Innovation is concentrated in a few firms in industries with high entry barriers such as aerospace, chemicals, automobiles, electric and electronic industries, while it is spread among many firms in machinery and the production of instruments (Dosi *et al.*, 1990).

Empirical studies show that monopolisation or concentration is not the main reason for innovation. Cumulative (clustered) knowledge made Germany excel in the fields of chemicals and high-quality engineering, Britain in pop music and publishing, Italy in fashion and design and the US in computers, software and cinema. But innovation is also to be found in industries that are less concentrated and where there are no significant barriers to entry. New entrants may have greater motivation to test and develop new products and technologies than well-established firms.

In many industrialised countries, the average size of firms is becoming smaller, not bigger. This reflects increased demand for more custom-made goods, produced in smaller batches, utilising production factors that can be readily switched to various alternative uses. But this is only on average. The industries with the most advanced technology are often the most geographically concentrated, highly profitable and the largest. Modern technology is increasing the importance of capital, especially human capital.[21] Krugman (1996a: 13–14) found statistical evidence from the US economy that the 'really high value-added' industries (in relation to the number of employees) are cigarette manufacturing and petrol refining, whereas the so-called 'high-technology industries' such as aircraft and electronics turned out to be roughly around average. However, one has to remember that high-technology industries have important externalities and linkages for the whole economy, although the number of computers a nation has is somewhat less important than how and for what purpose they are used, for example playing Tetris or Solitaire or organising inventories and production. Another problem is that most computers are used in the services sector (finance, accounting and health care) where it is hard to measure output.

It is one thing to invent or discover new or improved goods or services (product differentiation) and/or uncover a new way to produce or market already existing goods and services and quite another to exploit that success commercially. The electric dynamo was invented in 1881, but it took firms four decades to reorganise plants to take advantage of the flexibility in production offered by electric power. The basic videocassette recorder (VCR) technology was the result of the invention by Ampex in the US in the 1950s. Philips, a Dutch company, produced the first VCR aimed at the consumer market in 1971, several years before Sony introduced its Betamax model. Soon after, other Japanese manufacturers entered the market. and before long Japanese companies came to dominate the international market for (home) video equipment. To avoid a repeat experience, Philips took a different tack after inventing compact discs and developed the final technology jointly with Sony. Hence, the geography of innovation and the geography of production need not coincide. The microprocessor was invented in 1971, but firms are still learning how to make best use of it.

In a similar vein, commercial jet technology was a British invention. Rolls-Royce was the first producer. This led to the production of the first jet transport aircraft. Later, the US took the lead (with Boeing and McDonnell-Douglas), which was, subsequently, seriously challenged by the European Airbus (a consortium of government-supported British, German, French and Spanish firms). Government support of the Airbus provoked a sharp reaction from the US (which ignored the fact that US aircraft producers were generously subsidised through defence contracts). This led to the GATT Agreement on Trade in Civil Aircraft (1979). While 'supporting' the civil aircraft programmes, the signatories 'shall seek to avoid adverse effects on trade in civil aircraft' (Article 6.1). This is a statement that offers a number of different interpretations.[22] As such, it was insufficient to calm down tensions in aircraft trade. A Bilateral Agreement (1992) between the US and the EU was supposed to introduce a framework for all government 'involvement' in the development of commercial aircraft with 100 seats or more. However, it did not take account of past damage. The deal did not eliminate, but merely constrained, subsidies (for innovation and R&D). It set quantitative limits on both direct and indirect (military) subsidies for the development of new aircraft. The permitted limit for the direct subsidy for the development cost of a new aircraft was set at 33 per cent. Identifiable benefits from indirect subsidies were limited to 4 per cent of each firm's annual sales (Tyson, 1992: 207).

A positive effect on innovation (creation of technology) in the EU was expected to come from the completion of the Single Market Programme. A deepened regional market would stimulate competition and provide an incentive to innovation that would further promote competition for the benefit of the consumers. If corrective measures (in support of trade, competition or industrial policy) were added, they would not necessarily violate a liberal trading system in the long term. They would simply add an adjustment mechanism to the already highly imperfect and suboptimal market situation.

Perfect competition eliminates inefficient firms from a market but at the same time rewards the efficient ones; Schumpeter called this process 'creative destruction'. If inter-country factor mobility is allowed for, the supply of factors (labour, capital, land, technology, organisation and entrepreneurship) increases. Competition probably operates best when a firm believes that it is in a process that is leading it towards becoming a monopolist (at best) or an oligopolist (at least). However, consumers may suffer in a monopolistic or oligopolistic industry structure. This can be redressed somewhat if oligopolistic firms introduce the most efficient innovations as rapidly as perfectly competitive firms would and if governments prevent such a market structure from behaving in a non-competitive way.

Small open economies inevitable have to rely on various foreign technologies. Such countries often do not have the necessary resources to develop basic technologies for all lines of production. If this situation is regarded as detrimental, then economic integration may increase the pool of resources (human, technological and financial) for innovation and the development of new technologies, products and inputs, which may mitigate the potential disadvantage of smallness and isolation. Such pooling started in the EU in the mid-1980s with a series of R&D programmes.

In a relatively well-integrated area such as the EU, one would expect the prices of similar goods in different countries to be similar, owing to competition and trade. The stronger the competition and the larger the volume of trade, other things being equal, the smaller the price variation. Pre-tax prices of the same good would be expected to vary only as a result of differences in the cost of transportation, handling, insurance and, to some extent, marketing between countries. However, this expectation is not borne out in reality. The EU was aware of the barriers to competition other than tariffs and quotas (NTBs), so it created the Single European Market.

Various regional factors prevent full equalisation of prices. Some geographical areas may have small markets for certain goods and services (for example, parasols in Finland and antifreeze in Greece). So, in order to do business there, firms may price their goods relatively higher. Or, for example, differences in taste or special requirements regarding the basic ingredients of a product (for instance, chocolate) may cause the price of a good to vary. And, if there are local substitutes, foreign suppliers may modify the price of their goods. Some goods (such as wine) may be regarded as luxuries in one country and taxed accordingly but regarded as basic necessities in another country. This widens the price gap for the same good in different countries, and sometimes even in different regions of the same country. In a perfectly competitive market (with free entry and exit) for a good, free competition ensures equality of prices and drives profits to zero. In imperfectly competitive markets there is scope for price variation and, therefore, for profits.

The problem of innovation and new technology not resulting in an obvious and measurable increase in output is known as the 'productivity paradox'. Some argue that there is no technological revolution and that computers are not productive: a personal computer that is 100 times more powerful than one made 10 years ago is not proportionately more productive. Others argue that decades must pass before the fruits of technological breakthroughs can be discerned. Yet others insist that there are benefits, but that standard statistical tools are inadequate to measure them. This is most obvious in the services sector. How can the output of a bank be measured? Has the economy become so complex and fast-changing[23] that it has become unmeasurable? If that is so, it is harder and harder to regulate it, and to tax it.

Specialisation and returns to scale

From the vantage point of production, it might be expected that economies of scale would require some level of standardisation that would restrict product variety and consumer choice. Standards are technical regulations that specify the characteristics of goods. They can be quite different in different countries. It can be a difficult to harmonise them in an integrated area for trade and competition purposes. For example, it took eleven years for the EU to agree on the technical standards for mineral water. This and other examples from the 1970s are clear proof that such an approach will never result in a genuine single market in the EU. Hence, the EU opted for the mutual recognition of national standards in the short and medium term. The EU strategy for the longer term is an evolutionary convergence of minimum standards towards best practice rules. This places traders in different countries on an equal footing and eliminates the disadvantages to some of them that accrue from NTBs.

Trade in general, and intra-industry trade in particular, could increase product variety in countries compared with autarky. Product differentiation could reduce export opportunities for small open economies such as Austria, Belgium or Switzerland. These countries have little influence on foreign tastes and tend to enjoy comparative advantages in semimanufactured goods (Gleiser *et al.*, 1980: 521).

In the field of consumer durable goods, for example, the market in the US and Japan, is dominated by one or two brands and the manufacturers are able to take advantage of economies of scale. In the EU the situation is quite different. Almost every country has a its own producer of consumer durables, but the American and Japanese formula for the geographical distribution of production cannot easily be replicated because of diverse and deeply rooted national preferences. While Britons like to load their washing machines from the front, the French prefer to do so from the top. The Dutch prefer high-powered machines which can spin most of the moisture out of the washing, whereas the Italians prefer low spin speeds and allow the southern sun to do the drying. This situation affects the geography of production and protects against competition from third-country suppliers, but also restricts competition from within the EU, as each producer is prevented from following a pan-European production strategy. However, in the case of some other, relatively new, goods consumers' preferences are identical in different countries. It is likely that French cheese producers are going to look for the same qualities in a mobile phone, photocopier or a fax machine as do Italian wine exporters. Thus, common accounting, company or banking laws could be quite useful in the EU.

If in the EU harmonisation of standards means that they continue to rise, the overall level of regulation and costs of production will increase and south European and the acceding Central European countries will find it increasingly difficult to withstand international competition and will grow at a slower pace than the rest of the EU. As growth falls, protectionism increases. Alternatively, if, for example, some types of labour regulation are allowed to vary in member states and the framework of mutual recognition is maintained, then the northern EU countries could abolish some laws and the southern and Central European countries would grow rapidly. EU growth would continue at a substantial rate, which would permit the implementation of a liberal trade policy. The ultimate irony is that only the latter course would allow northern EU countries to pay high wages and sustain a heavy social expenditure (Curzon Price, 1991: 124).

Although the Single Market Programme (1985–92) removed many NTBs to internal trade in the EU, others still persist and make the single internal market imperfect. Before the Single Market, the major obstacles to internal trade included physical border controls, technical barriers (standards and product/service regulations), public procurement, different intellectual and industrial property laws, state aids and fiscal barriers, as well as obstacles to the mobility of labour and capital. The Single Market Programme made a distinction between what had to be harmonised and what could be left to mutual recognition. While EU standards are being developed, the guiding principle should be mutual recognition of national standards. EU standards are being developed on a large scale, around 1,000 a year. However, too many national regulations are still being produced, making it as hard as ever to reach a truly homogeneous single market (Curzon Price, 1996).

Various attempts to harmonise diverse goods at EU level created a public furore in some countries. Examples include the fuss about prawn cocktail crisps in Britain; the permissible level of bacteria in cheese in France;[24] small apples in Denmark; the use of other than durum (hard) wheat for pasta in Italy; the application of other than the *Reinheitsgebot* (of 1516) purity rule for brewing beer in Germany; and the removal of the tilde (~) from computer keyboards in Spain. Each year every EU country produces thousands of new regulations on new technologies and products. Every one that relates to the smooth operation of the internal market must be submitted to the European Commission. As each one carries a possible seed of conflict, it must be treated with caution, and, following implementation, monitored constantly and carefully otherwise the genuine Single European Market may disappear. Thus, Decision 3052/95 (adopted in 1995 and implemented in 1997) provides an improved procedure to deal with the remaining obstacles to the free movement of goods in the single market. The Decision obliges member states to notify the Commission of individual measures preventing the free movement of a model, type or category of a product that has been made or sold legally in another country.[25] The purpose of the measure is to encourage member states to think twice before making any exception to the EU system of mutual recognition.[26]

The neo-classical theory of international trade argues that countries should specialise in the production of those goods for which they have a comparative advantage. Modern theories question this line of reasoning: the international geography of production, specialisation and trade are affected by other factors as well. Economies of scale stimulate specialisation in production for a narrow market niche but on a wide international market. This may entail only the reallocation of resources within a single industry or sometimes within a single company. Modern footloose industries are not linked to any particular geographical region by inputs such as iron ore or copper. Thus, a country's comparative advantage can be created by deliberate actions of firms, banks and/or governments.

Returns to scale have not been thoroughly studied in the theory of economic integration because it is difficult to model them. Therefore, one should be very careful about using classical theory either to describe what is likely to happen in a customs union or as a guide to policies that will ensure that such a union or other type of integration fulfils its expectations. It is also important to bear in mind that a substantial part of production is linked with economies of scope[27] rather than scale. While economies of scale imply a certain level of standardisation in tastes and production, economies of scope deal with the diversity in tastes, products and processes. Economies of scope allow firms such as Benetton to respond swiftly to changes in the supply of inputs and shifts in demand because they come from the common control of distinct, but inter-related production activities. For example, the same kind of fabric and sewing machines can be used in the production of various goods. Similarly, the same type of aircraft can be used for cargo and for passenger transport.

Intra-industry trade

Although increased competition offers potential gains from both more efficient industrial and geographical allocation of resources in production and increased consumption, there is no guarantee that these gains will be achieved in practice. If a government takes this view and believes that domestic production will be wiped out by foreign competition, then it may pursue a policy of protection on the grounds that it is better to produce something inefficiently at home than to produce nothing at all. This disastrous scenario has not been borne out in reality. The very existence of the EU, which has continued to expand in size, as well as in depth, is the best example of a positive scenario. Most firms in the EU countries have not been put out of business because of competition from firms in partner countries. Instead, many of them have continuously increased their business. They have specialised in lines of production that satisfy distinct demand segments throughout the EU. This fact cannot be explained by the classical theories. The 'awkward fact' is that trade takes place in differentiated products (Eaton and Lipsey, 1997: 228–9). Strong advertising campaigns create awareness about 'differences' among what are basically very similar and easily substitutable goods (for instance, cars, printers, fax and photocopying machines, T-shirts, skis, soaps, toothpastes, TV sets, audio- and videorecorders and cassettes, painkillers, breakfast cereals, refrigerators, trainers, cigarettes or bicycles). This phenomenon is known in theory as intra-industry trade[28] Generally, product differentiation tends to dominate product specialisation in the internal trade of the EU.

There are also other examples that support the thesis of a smooth intra-industry adjustment in trade and geography of production. Successive rounds of negotiations within the GATT reduced tariffs. The ensuing intra-industry adjustments in trade and specialisation among developed countries were relatively smooth. Contrary to the expectation of the factor endowment theory, intra-industry adjustment prevailed and carried fewer costs than would have been the case with inter-industry adjustment. If it is feared that foreigners will eliminate domestic firms through competition, exchange rates can act as an important safety valve to prevent this happening and ease the process of adjustment to the new situation.

Inter-industry trade between countries basically reflects differences in national factor endowment. This type of trade brings efficiency gains through resource allocation, as well as benefits that come from the supply of a new set of different products. Intra-industry trade, on the other hand, is associated with product differentiation. Consumers benefit from this type of trade through increased variety of closely substitutable goods and services, as well as through increased competition of products made with increasing returns of scale.

As incomes have risen, consumers are no longer satisfied with identical or standardised goods. They demand and pay for varieties of the same basic good, often tailored to their individual needs and tastes. The larger the variety of available goods and services, the smaller the importance of economies of scale. Intra-industry trade refers to trade in differentiated commodities. It happens when a country simultaneously exports and imports goods (final or semifinished) that are close substitutes in consumption. Differentiation of goods begins when various characteristics are added to the basic good or component, backed up by strong R&D and advertising campaigns. Thus, gains from trade in differentiated goods may arise through an increase in consumer choice (not necessarily through lower prices only).

The variety of goods produced in a country, the new theory suggests, is limited by the existence of scale economies in production. Thus, similar countries have an incentive to trade. Their trade may often be in goods that are produced with similar factor proportions. Such trade does not involve the major adjustment problems that are commonly found with more conventional trade patterns (Krugman, 1990a: 50–1). In fact, one of the most distinctive properties of the liberalisation of trade in the EU was an increase in intra-industry trade coupled with modest adjustment costs (Sapir, 1992: 1496–7).

At the heart of neo-classical international trade and customs union theory is the analysis of two goods only. Therefore, it cannot satisfactorily account for preference diversity and intra-industry trade. The neo-classical theory's 'clean' model of perfect competition is not applicable here. The potential for intra-industry trade increases with the level of economic development, similarity in preferences (tastes), openness to trade and geographical proximity, which reduces the costs of transport, marketing and aftersales service.

A significant portion of trade among developed countries is intra-industry. In this case, variety may be preferred to quantity, so that some proportion of trade is attributable not only to differences in factor endowment, but also to different national preferences (tastes). This is the case in the EU. The response of successful firms to such business challenges is to find a specialist market niche and to employ economies of scope, rather than scale.

In an 'early' example of intra-industry trade, Linder (1961: 102) noted that ships that brought European beer to Milwaukee took American beer back to Europe. Although without a formal theory, the examination of international trade flows by Grubel and Lloyd (1975) noted that an important part of these flows was within the same industry classification.

Finger (1975) believes that intra-industry trade is an anomaly due to the definition of new products and processes and statistical sorting of data. However, Loertscher and Wolter (1980: 286) demonstrated that intra-industry trade between countries is not a statistical fabrication but a real phenomenon. This type of trade between countries is likely to be strong if:

- they are both relatively highly developed;
- the difference in their level of development is small;
- they have large national markets;
- the barriers to trade are low;
- there is a high potential for product differentiation;
- entry in narrow product lines is obstructed by significant barriers (sunk costs);
- transaction costs are low.

Research shows that incentives to intra-industry trade are similar levels of per-capita income and country size, product differentiation, participation in regional integration schemes, common borders, as well as similar language and culture. Negative influences on this type of trade are exerted by standardisation (reduction in consumer choice), distance between countries (which increases the cost of information and services necessary for trade in differentiated goods) and trade barriers that reduce all trade flows (Balassa and Bauwens, 1988: 1436).

Intra-industry trade is relatively high among developed countries. It refers to trade within the same trade classification group. One may, therefore, wonder if intra-industry trade is a statistical aberration rather than an authentic phenomenon. In addition, it may be argued that two varieties of the same product are not always two distinct goods. The criteria for data aggregation in the Standard International Trade Classification (SITC) are similarity in inputs and substitutability in consumption. These criteria often contradict each other. Many of the three-digit groups in the SITC include heterogeneous commodities. For example, SITC 751 (office machines) includes typewriters, word-processing machines, cash registers and photocopying machines, whereas SITC 895 (office and stationery supplies) includes filing cabinets, paper clips, fountain pens, chalk and typewriter ribbons. On these grounds one could conclude that intra-industry trade is a pure statistical fabrication. However, this is not so in reality. If one studied trade groups with more than three digits, differences could and would appear. The index of intra-industry trade (IIT) in a country is represented by the ratio of the absolute difference between exports and imports in a trade classification group to the sum of exports and imports in the same classification group.

$$IIT = 1 - \frac{\left|X_j - M_j\right|}{X_j + M_j} \tag{3.3}$$

The IIT index (eqn 3.3) is high and is equal to 1 for complete intra-industry specialisation (a country imports and exports goods in a group in the same quantity). This is a sign of a geographical spread of an industry. The index is low and equals 0 for complete inter-industry specialisation. Such geographical concentration of production is usually the result of high entry barriers and economies of scale. In any case, intra-industry trade increases welfare because it extends the variety of available goods to the consumers. As there is no evidence of large adjustment costs to this type of trade, one may conclude that intra-industry trade makes everyone better off.

The *ex ante* expectation that trade liberalisation and integration could shift the IIT index closer to 1 (suggesting a geographical spread of production) in the case of developed countries has been investigated in numerous studies.[29] Among the EU countries, the IIT index was the highest in 1987 for France (0.83), Britain (0.77), Belgium (0.77), Germany (0.76) and the Netherlands (0.76) and lowest in Portugal (0.37) and Greece (0.31), implying that these two countries had a high inter-industry specialisation (European Economy, 1990: 40–1). Nonetheless, various statistical results regarding the significance of intra-industry trade may be called into doubt. For example, if there are strong centripetal (agglomeration) forces in high-technology or chemical industries because of economies of scale and production linkages, the IIT index should be low. However, 'average intra-EU IIT in high-tech products has been higher than the overall mean for most of our sample period, which indicates above average geographical dispersion of these sectors' (Brülhart, 1998a: 328–9). This is an indication that additional theoretical and empirical work needs to be done in this field (Brülhart, 1998b: 790).

Some goods belonging to the same classification group may be perfect substitutes and have identical end uses (e.g. plates). However, plates can be made of china, glass, paper, plastic, wood, metal or ceramic. Every type of this end product requires totally different and unrelated factor inputs and production technology. Other examples include tableware, furniture, clothing, etc. These differences among goods that enter a single SITC group may not be important for statistical records, but they are often of crucial importance to consumers. Demand for a variety of products increases with a rise in income. Higher income gives consumers the opportunity to express variety in taste through, for example, purchasing different styles of clothing. Economic integration may change consumers' preferences as the choice of goods available before the formation of a customs union or reduction in tariffs may be quite different.

Integration in the EU increased intra-industry trade within this group of countries, whereas integration in the former Council for Mutual Economic Assistance (CMEA) had as its consequence greater inter-industry trade (Drabek and Greenaway, 1984: 463–4). Preferences in the centrally planned economies are revealed through plan targets and are different from those in economies in which market forces demonstrate consumer preferences. In market economies, competition takes place among firms, whereas in centrally planned economies competition occurs among different plans offered to the central planning body. A free trade area between the US and Canada (1987) was not expected to alter crucially the pattern of trade between these two countries. One reason was that the last step in the reduction in tariffs agreed during the Tokyo Round of the GATT negotiations took place in 1987. After this reduction, trade between the US and Canada became largely free: 80 per cent of all trade was duty-free, while a further 15 per cent was subject to a tariff of 5 per cent or less. Another reason was that consumer tastes are more similar in North America than between countries in the EU.

The fact that a large part of trade among developed countries is intra-industry may lead to the conclusion that the Heckscher–Ohlin (factor proportions) theory of trade is not valid. Intra-industry trade is not based on differences in factor endowments among countries. Countries tend to specialise and export goods that are demanded by the majority of domestic consumers. It is this demand that induces production, rather than domestic factor endowment. Countries have a competitive edge in the production of these goods and thus gain an advantage in foreign markets, while they import goods demanded by a minority of the home population (Linder, 1961). The US, Japan and Germany have the greatest comparative advantage in goods for which their home market is relatively big. These are standardised goods for mass consumption. There is, however, one major exception. The major market for German dyes is the British textiles industry (and to a lesser extent that in the US). The German domestic market for dyestuffs is relatively small (Nelson, 1999: 12).

Verdoorn suggested that the principal difference in manufacturing between US and European firms is not so much the size of firm/plant as the length of the individual production run. The range of processes carried out in the same factory is much smaller in the US than in Europe (Hague, 1960: 346). Compared with plants in the same industry, production runs in the US are several times larger than in Europe, even where the plants are owned by the same TNC (Pratten, 1971: 195, 308–9; Pratten, 1988: 69–70). On the other hand, even in the most efficient developed countries, manufacturing is often carried out in factories of quite moderate size. Differences in plant productivity are best explained by (1) inappropriate labour relations, in particular where many thousands of workers need to be employed together; (2) inadequate level of technical training; and (3) an unsatisfactory incentives structure (Prais, 1981: 272 ff.). In support of one of these arguments (1), it has been found that the number of strikes increases exponentially with plant size (Geroski and Jacquemin, 1985: 174).

Because of a larger and more homogenised market, which required large production runs, labour productivity in the manufacturing industries in 1986 was some 50 per cent higher in the US than in Germany. This figure may overstate the difference in productivity between the two countries as it makes little allowance for the high quality of German manufactured products (Pratten, 1988: 126–7). For example, a preoccupation with large quantities of output and economies of scale rendered the taste of standard American chocolate, for a European, appalling.

Intra-industry trade may be described in terms of monopolistic competition and product differentiation. Perfect competition is not a realistic market structure, so perfect monopolistic competition is the most perfect market structure in a situation with differentiated goods (Lancaster, 1980). Armington's assumption states that products in the same industry, but from different countries, are imperfect substitutes (Armington, 1969: 160). In other words, buyers' preferences for different(iated) goods are independent. Armington's assumption, however, overestimated the degree of market power of a particular producer.

Three main findings stem from the data presented in Table 3.1. First, intra-industry trade is relatively high in the EU. Second, there was a convergence of

Table 3.1 Intra-industry trade within the EU by country, 1961–92[a]

Country	1961	1967	1972	1977	1985	1988	1990	1992
Belgium–Luxembourg	0.51	0.56	0.49	0.57	0.56	0.57	0.58	0.60
Denmark	0.30	0.37	0.41	0.44	0.42	0.44	0.43	0.47
France	0.60	0.69	0.67	0.71	0.68	0.67	0.67	0.72
Germany	0.47	0.56	0.57	0.57	0.60	0.59	0.61	0.68
Greece	0.02	0.06	0.08	0.10	0.15	0.15	0.16	0.15
Ireland	0.22	0.28	0.36	0.45	0.40	0.38	0.38	0.41
Italy	0.44	0.56	0.57	0.56	0.52	0.51	0.51	0.51
Netherlands	0.54	0.57	0.59	0.59	0.60	0.62	0.61	0.67
Portugal	0.04	0.10	0.13	0.14	0.24	0.25	0.30	0.31
Spain	0.10	0.16	0.29	0.38	0.47	0.56	0.57	0.60
UK	0.51	0.67	0.65	0.71	0.62	0.59	0.64	0.68
EU[b]	0.48	0.56	0.57	0.59	0.58	0.58	0.59	0.64

Source: Brülhart and Elliott (1999: p 108).
[a]Unadjusted Grubel–Lloyd indices calculated from SITC five-digit statistics from OECD, for SITC sections 5–8.
[b]Average of eleven countries, weighted by values of intra-EU manufactured imports and exports.

levels of intra-industry trade across countries between 1961 and 1990. The countries with the lowest initial levels of intra-industry experiences sharp increases over this period. Third, intra-industry trade in manufactured goods in the EU grew consistently in the 1960s and early 1970s and then stabilised, but it resumed its increasing trend between 1988 and 1992. However, it is important to bear in mind that the SITC was revised twice in this period, in 1978 and in 1988. Thus, it is not possible to conclude that the upward trend in intra-industry trade in the EU is slowing down. In addition, it appears that the Single Market Programme, contrary to the *ex ante* predictions, 'did not entail an increase in inter-industry specialisation' (Brülhart and Elliott, 1999: 106–9). It could be concluded that the increase in intra-industry trade in the EU is evidence that economic integration did not produce a geographical concentration of production in select EU regions or countries.

Further data show that between 1968 and 1990 specialisation increased in Denmark, Germany, Greece, Italy and the Netherlands. A significant increase was recorded in Belgium, Britain, France, Portugal and Spain between 1980 and 1990. Data indicate that there was either a fall in specialisation or no noteworthy change in Britain, Portugal and Spain between 1968 and 1990. The most likely explanation is that, before joining the EU, these countries had relatively high trade barriers that protected production for which there was no national comparative advantage. Entry into the EU eliminated administrative trade barriers and reduced trade costs. However, in all countries, specialisation increased over the period 1980–90.

> So with integration, specialisation may initially fall during structural adjustment and then increase. This would explain why Spain, Portugal, and the UK, which were all late joiners to the EU, show a fall in specialisation when comparing 1968–1990, and an upward trend starting in the late 1970s and early 1980s.
>
> (Amiti, 1999: 579)

Each country's geography of production became different from the rest in the group. Although this reallocation of resources has obvious benefits that come from specialisation, the snag is that specialised countries may react in a different way to asymmetric shocks and require diverse policy instruments to counter them. Therefore, in the light of the EMU and Eastern enlargement, there is a strong need for the creation of EU policy tools to counter such obstacles to the smooth operation of the Single European Market.

Instead of taking goods themselves as the basis for analysis, 'address models' of goods differentiation take characteristics that are embodied in commodities as their starting point (Lipsey, 1987a). A computer is a good that can be considered as a collection of different attributes, such as memory, speed, printing, graphics and the like. Figure 3.3 illustrates two characteristics of a set of goods (computers).

Each good (computer) A, B and C, has a certain combination of characteristic S (speed) and characteristic M (memory). Each good is defined by its location in

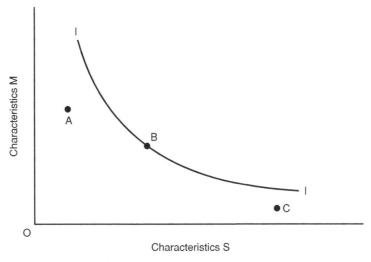

Figure 3.3 Characteristics of computers.

the continuous space of characteristics, hence it has a certain 'address'. Consumer preferences are defined by characteristics, not goods. Some consumers prefer memory over speed, whereas others prefer the opposite. Under the assumption that all three goods in Figure 3.3 have the same price, let a consumer have tastes embodied in the indifference curve II. This consumer maximises utility by purchasing good B. Each good in this model has close and distant neighbours. There are many goods and many consumers. Every consumer attempts to attain his or her highest indifference curve. This gives rise to intra-industry trade. Address models of localised (monopolistic) competition can be an important factor in explaining intra-industry trade and, hence, contribute to the explanation of the location of production.

All general explanations of trade in differentiated goods refer only to final goods traded among developed countries. In addition, intra-industry trade is affected by imperfect product markets (monopolisation) and consumer demand for a variety of goods. Economies of scale can be another important factor in explaining trade in differentiated goods. Countries with a similar endowment of factors will still trade. Imperfect information about goods on the part of consumers might have had an impact on intra-industry trade in the past, but this aspect is rapidly diminishing as the Internet, global advertising and other methods of disseminating information worldwide gain importance.

The Heckscher–Ohlin theory gives students the impression that the factor proportions theory of trade is orthodox. Linder's theory tends to be less rigorous and thus has not made the same impression on students. Nonetheless, Leamer (1984) found evidence which supports the classical theory, while Greenaway and Torstensson (2000) found that both factor proportions and economic geography variables appear to be important in determining trade within industries. Linder's research does not reject the factor proportion theory – rather it asserts that factor proportion is not the only cause of trade. One may conclude that the factor proportions theory determines geographical location of production (specialisation) and trade *among* different SITC classification groups, while economies of scale and diversity in tastes determine the geography of production and trade *within* SITC classification groups. As most changes in demand take place *within* certain clusters of goods, this is a sign that changes in technology are important driving forces of trade and (re)allocation of production.

3.3   European Union

Introduction

Competition policy is one of the foremost economic policies of the EU. It is also an area where centralisation of authority makes full sense. The European Commission has special responsibility for the proper operation of competition in the EU because it 'handles' a much larger number of firms than any member country. The Commission's approach to the policy is based on strict rules. Basic rules (including exceptions) in EU competition policy can be found in the Treaty of Rome and the rulings of the Court of Justice. In essence, there should be no barriers to internal trade and competition. Freedom of movement for goods, services, people and capital (four freedoms) are contained in Article 3 of the Treaty of Rome. The EU does not tolerate any discrimination on the grounds of nationality[30] (Article 12[31]). 'The internal market shall comprise an area without internal frontiers in which the free movement of goods, persons, services and capital is ensured' (Article 14[32]). This provision was intended to abolish NTBs on internal trade and ensure the most liberal competition rules for EU residents. Freedom of movement of goods is elaborated in Articles 23–31.[33] Free movement (and establishment) of persons, services and capital is regulated by Articles 39–60.[34] As for national tax provisions, they must not discriminate against goods that originate in other member states of the EU (Articles 90–93).[35] In addition, Article 157[36] requests both the EU and its member states to ensure the necessary conditions for competitiveness of the EU industry.

Competition rules are founded on the assumption that the concentration of (private) economic power within monopolies, oligopolies, cartels or other market structures that have similar negative effects on consumers need to be outlawed and/or regulated and monitored. Individual economic freedom needs to be fostered through the rules of market competition. The objective of this approach is to allocate factors among sectors and space according to the criteria of efficiency and, hence, contribute to an increase in the average standard of living.

In 1985, the EU accepted a technical blueprint, known as the Single Market Programme,[37] which outlined 282 measures for the attainment of the genuine Single European Market by the end of 1992. Its founding principle was the removal of NTBs to internal trade in the EU. The move from a fragmented to a genuinely integrated market can produce some of the most striking results of economic integration. The Single Market Programme was meant to increase competition and increase the competitiveness of EU goods and services compared with export from the US, Japan and the newly industrialised countries. The Programme removed border controls, introduced mutual recognition of standards, established a single licence and home country autonomy over financial services and opened national public procurement contracts to suppliers from other EU member countries.

The principal gains of the Single Market Programme come not from the reduction in the costs of internal EU trade, which is a result of the removal of NTBs, but rather from the longer-term dynamic benefits of increased competition on the expanded internal market. The anti-competitive market behaviour of various local monopolies is largely checked. Competition in the EU could, however, be furthered if EU internal liberalisation were coupled with external trade liberalisation. There are at least two arguments for additional external opening of the EU in order to deepen competition. First, intra-EU trade is mostly in differentiated products (intra-industry). Second, an element of intra-EU trade takes place between subsidiaries of a single TNC. Extra-EU competitive pressure is necessary to ease such an oligopolistic structure and increase the competitiveness of both traditional and new-growth industries (Jacquemin and Sapir, 1991).

Monetary union, which to date includes twelve out of fifteen EU member states, will help businesses to eliminate the risk and costs associated with currency fluctuations. The elimination of this distortion of competition, trade and investment will contribute to the reduction in intra-EU trade costs. The existence of the euro will guide the EU economy towards a greater price transparency that will ease and motivate expansion in intra-EU trade. The whole process will lead towards a downward convergence in prices.

Here we will concentrate on the rules that govern the actions of firms and governments to prevent them from reducing competition in the EU market and, hence, have an impact on production geography. Two articles of the Treaty of Rome govern the actions of *firms*. Article 81[38] refers to restrictions on competition, while Article 82[39] prohibits the abuse of a dominant position. *Governments* may also jeopardise the process of competition. This is the case with state aids (subsidies). Article 87[40] regulates this issue. The European Commission must be notified of all cases of aid above a certain level so that it can examine its legality and compatibility with the goals of the EU. In 1999, 1,201 new cases of breaches of competition regulations were referred to the European Commission, indicating that the Commission is quite active in this area.

In order to implement its duties as the guardian of the Treaty of Rome, the Council of Ministers issued Regulation 17/62 (1962). The European Commission has the right to request relevant information from all enterprises, their associations and member states. If the information is not provided, the Commission may impose a daily fine of up to €1,000 until the information is provided. The Commission is also empowered to investigate the case. This includes 'dawn raids' (unannounced early-morning visits) to the premises of the parties involved in a case.[41] An example occurred in 1995, when inspectors raided the offices of Volkswagen and Audi in Germany as well as the premises of their Italian distributor Autogerma. Inspectors may examine books, accounts and business records, take copies and ask questions, although the approval of the visited party is required as the investigators are not permitted to use force. As the information obtained may disclose business secrets, the Commission must use it exclusively for the purpose of the case in question. The 'dawn raids' on various VW premises found that the company was threatening to end contracts with fifty dealers who were selling to non-Italian residents, and in fact had already done so in twelve cases.

If an infringement of the rules is found, the Commission may fine the culpable party/parties. The maximum fine is 10 per cent of the total annual turnover of the enterprise concerned. When setting the fine, the Commission considers both the gravity and the duration of the violation of the Treaty of Rome. Aggravating circumstances include repeated infringements, refusal to cooperate and the role of the head of the company in the infringement. Attenuating conditions include a passive role in the infringement, cooperation in the proceedings and termination of the infringement following the intervention by the Commission. In 1998, the Commission fined VW €102m, the highest fine ever imposed on a single company. The size of the fine reflected the duration of the felony (which began in 1987 and continued until 1993 in spite of repeated warnings). A look at the fines imposed by the Commission shows that these have been increasing over time. The guilty parties may appeal against decisions of the Commission to the Court of First Instance. A further appeal may be brought before the Court of Justice.

Non-tariff barriers

The GATT was quite successful in achieving a continuous reduction in tariffs on industrial goods during the post-war period. Unfortunately, at the same time, NTBs have flourished and eroded the beneficial liberalising effects of tariff cuts. NTBs are all measures other than tariffs that influence international trade and hence affect the geography of production. Some of them are overt (quotas), while others fall into a grey area such as the application of technical standards or rules of origin. Although they are costlier in terms of resource efficiency and they do not create customs revenue, they have increased because the GATT does not permit a unilateral introduction of new tariffs, while at the same time domestic pressure groups may be quite successful in eliciting protection. NTBs are strongest in the 'sensitive' commodity groups; in fact, the use of NTBs may determine which commodity groups are sensitive. The implementation of the Treaty of Rome eliminated tariffs and quotas on internal trade in the EU in 1968. The elimination of NTBs, is the duty of the Single Market Programme.

Whereas tariffs, like transport costs, increase the price of good, NTBs act like import quotas but do not generate revenue for the government. Currently, NTBs present the most important and dangerous barriers to trade, fragmenting markets and production more severely than tariffs have ever done. Tariffs were, on average, reduced under the auspices of the GATT/WTO to relatively low levels, so that they now play a relatively minor role in the economic inefficiency of a country. Nonetheless, national administrations try to obtain short-term political gains through protectionism at the expense of long-term economic benefits. Hence, NTBs are and will be high on the agenda for all future international moves to liberalise trade.

Consideration of NTBs has always been difficult. One reason for this is the creativity of their instigators, but another, more important, reason is the lack of data. Administrations either do not record the use of NTBs, or do so only partly. It comes as no surprise that the reported impact of NTBs can lead to considerable underestimations. Our classification of NTBs is presented in Table 3.2.

The greatest criticism of NTBs is their lack of transparency. Hence, they are prone to abuse and need to be monitored closely, which increases firms' administrative costs. As an economic policy instrument, tariffs are a blunt weapon against which markets can defend themselves through adjustment measures. In contrast, NTBs circumvent market forces and, hence, introduce greater distortions and uncertainty and prevent efficient spatial and industrial allocation of resources specialisation.

Government at all levels (local, regional and central) is an important consumer of goods and services. It can use its procurement policies either to protect home business (SMEs in particular, as is the case in Germany) and employment or to influence the geography of production and support young industries during the first fragile steps in order to help the creation of a country's comparative advantage. *Public procurement* can also be employed as an instrument to implement regional policy and/or aid to the disadvantage of certain population groups (for instance women and minorities).

An open public procurement market in the EU is seen to be one of the major potential benefits that EU firms may exploit. The EU-wide competitive tendering directives require the publication of all tender notices above a certain (rather low)[42] financial threshold in the *Official Journal of the European Community*. The low threshold is intended to avoid understating the value of the contract in order to evade open tendering. Coupled with compliance with the EU technical standards and a reasonable time for the submission of the offer, together with transparent award criteria, this increases the fairness of the bidding and award procedure. The Commission may exclude foreign firms from the public procurement market if EU enterprises do not have reciprocal access to public contracts in the countries from which these firms originate. In spite of this, there is a chance of inertia (read 'buy domestic'). A public authority could subdivide a large public contract into a series of small ones and thus avoid the obligation to advertise and award the business locally.

The annual EU public procurement market is 14 per cent of the combined GDP of member countries, yet the value of public procurement contracts advertised in the *Official Journal of the European Community* is only 2 per cent of total GDP. Germany, Italy, the Netherlands and Austria are the main culprits in this area. In the EU, suppliers from other countries win, on average, 10 per cent of public procurement contracts; however, in Germany, which is the most restrictive country in this respect, other EU countries account for only 5 per cent of public contracts. The countries most receptive to foreign EU suppliers are the smaller countries,

Table 3.2 Non-tariff barriers

Major group	Type
1. Government involvement in international trade	Subsidies (production, exports, credit, R&D below the cost public services)
	Public procurement (local, regional, central)
	State monopoly trading
	Exchange rate restrictions
	Embargoes
	Tied aid
2. Customs and administrative entry procedures	Customs classification
	Customs valuation
	Monitoring measures (antidumping and countervailing duties)
	Rules of origin
	Consular formalities
	Trade licensing
	Deposits
	Calendar of import
	Administrative controls
3. Standards	Technical
	Health
	Environment ('green standards')
	Testing and certification
	Packing, labelling, weight
	Cultural
4. Others	Quotas (tariff-free ceilings)
	Local content and equity rules
	Tax remission rules
	Variable levies
	Bilateral agreements
	Buy domestic campaigns
	Voluntary export restriction agreements
	Self-limitation agreements
	Orderly marketing agreements
	Multifibre agreement
	Ambiguous laws
	Cartel practices
	Permissions to advertise

such as Ireland (32 per cent), Finland (28 per cent), Denmark (26 per cent) Greece (26 per cent) and Portugal (21 per cent).[43] These data would suggest that only those countries that lack indigenous industrial capacities of their own seem prepared to source outside their domestic economies.

Public procurement accounted for 11.5 per cent of the EU GDP or €721bn in 1994, equivalent to the combined Belgian, Danish and Spanish economies, or €2,000 per citizen. As a consequence of the Single Market Programme, the number of national tender notices published in the *Official Journal of the European Community* increased from around 12,000 in 1987 to 67,244 in 1997, 73,688 in 1998 and 80,383 in 1999.

Goods eligible for tariff and quota-free trade in all integration arrangements are those goods produced by countries within the group. The exceptions are the products that endanger public morality, public security and order, or human, animal or plant life or health. An important NTB can be found in the guise of *technical standards* (a set of specifications for the production and/or operation of a good). The intention of this hidden barrier to trade is in many cases to protect the national producer despite the long-term costs in the form of higher prices that come from lower economies of scale, poorer technical/energy efficiency and reduced competition.

One of the best-known examples of a NTB operating within an integrated group arose in Germany 1979. Germany banned the importation of a French fruit-based liqueur, Cassis de Dijon, on the grounds that liqueurs consumed in Germany should have an alcohol content of at least 25 per cent, and that of Cassis de Dijon was 5 per cent less than this. The case was considered by the EU Court of Justice, which ruled that the ban on liqueur imports was not legitimate. The implications of this ruling are of paramount importance: any goods legally produced and traded in one member country cannot be banned from importation in partner countries on the grounds that national standards differ. The ruling opened the way to competition in all goods manufactured in the EU, with the exception of goods that could jeopardise an important national interest. Where differences in national standards do exist, consumer protection is assured by the addition of a warning on the product. However, this ruling is not in itself sufficient to guarantee a uniform market throughout EU and a concomitant increase in competitiveness. To achieve a uniform market requires harmonisation, with all its attendant disadvantages of excess regulation, reduction in choice and the long time required for its implementation. The Cassis de Dijon case was cited as a precedent when the EU forced Germany in 1987 to open its market to beers from other EU countries despite the fact that some beers do not comply with the German beer purity law (*Reinheitsgebot*) of 1516, which specifies that beer must be composed only of water, barley, hops and yeast. This decision has not, as feared, endangered Germany's beer production. Many other national laws define, in particular countries, what, for example, can be sold as pasta, sausage or lemonade. In any case, since the Cassis de Dijon case in 1979, mutual recognition (and standardisation) has been the cornerstone of the Single European Market.

Another imaginative NTB is illustrated by the *Poitiers case*. In the early 1980s, the French government wanted to protect the home market from imports of Japanese VCRs. There was, however, no indigenous production of VCRs. The domestic manufacturer, Thomson, simply imported Japanese VCRs and distributed them under its own name. Just before Christmas 1982, the French government decreed that all Japanese VCRs should undergo a customs inspection in the town of Poitiers in order to ensure that they were accompanied by instruction manuals in French. Poitiers is in the centre of France, far from all main ports of entry for these goods; its customs post was staffed by only eight officers and was not well equipped. This decision increased costs (transport, insurance, interest, delays) and reduced the quantity of imported and sold VCRs to 3,000 units a month.

Such a measure might make some sense in a situation where a government wanted to restrain rising consumer expenditure that was causing a short-term drain on the balance of payments. In such instances, however, a more appropriate measure might be an excise duty or high sales tax. The moral of this tale is that the time to protect against the importation of goods whose efficient manufacturing depends on economies of scale and a steep learning curve is before external suppliers have captured most of the domestic market. The attention that this case attracted in the media was considerable, leaving the French government 'no other choice' than to revoke the measure. After Christmas, of course! A supplementary tax 'replaced' the Poitiers customs clearance procedure in January 1983.

Consider another example. In 1952, Japan, fearing that small Italian cars would make substantial inroads into their market, imposed a quota on the number of *Japanese cars* that could be imported into Italy. The quota allowed for the annual import of 2,800 passenger cars and 800 all-terrain vehicles directly from Japan. When the situation changed and the Japanese became highly competitive in the production of cars, this NTB rebounded on Japan.[44] Since 1987 the European Commission has refused to support Italy's attempts to use Article 134[45] to block indirect imports of Japanese cars through other EU countries. Hence, imports of Japanese cars have soared.[46] Other EU countries have annual 'caps' on the imports of Japanese cars. For example, the 'cap' for Japanese cars in the French market was around 3 per cent, while in Britain it is around 10 per cent of domestic sales. A tacit limit to the market share achieved by Japanese car producers in the German market was around 15 per cent. The result is a lose–lose situation. On the one hand, consumers lose as they have to pay more for both domestic and imported cars and, on the other hand, the geography of the EU car industry is postponing its inevitable structural adjustment and potentially losing its competitive edge relative to the Japanese. The governments of the EU countries simply bow to the short-term interests of powerful domestic manufacturing lobbies.

The EU and Japan concluded a 'car deal' in 1991. The EU offered the Japanese an increase in market share from 11 per cent in 1991 to 17 per cent (including Japanese cars manufactured in the EU) until 2000, when all quotas disappeared. Unfortunately, the parties placed different interpretations on the deal. The EU argued that the maximum number of Japanese cars either imported from Japan or produced in Japanese plants in the EU is based on forecasts of market growth and that, that if the market grows less than forecast, it had the right to renegotiate the deal. The Japanese interpretation of the deal was that the EU has committed itself not to restrict the sale of Japanese cars in the EU. In any case the accord shows that the EU is keen to increase competition and efficiency in the EU car industry. Another accord between the EU and Japan of 1995 is intended to simplify EU exports of cars and commercial vehicles to Japan through the mutual recognition of vehicle standards, as well as allowing Japanese inspectors (who issue certificates to imported cars) to work in Europe.

As stated above, all goods legally produced in the EU may be freely traded throughout the EU unless they endanger public morality or the life or health of humans, animals and plants. France used this so-called '*precautionary principle*' in

1999 to maintain its unilateral ban on the imports of beef from Britain. This was a direct challenge both to the principle of the free movement of goods and to the authority of the European Commission, which had lifted its ban (which had been in place for several years) on exports of British beef because of 'mad cow disease'. This principle touches on several sensitive and emotional issues (health, food safety) and can provoke fierce protests by consumers' groups. Although the precautionary principle is not (yet) enshrined in EU law, the political significance of this case is that the principle may be applied at any point. If the application of the principle were to proliferate to any great extent, this would signify the end of the Single European Market for the goods involved.[47]

There are many examples of NTBs arising from the application of standards, and this has a direct impact on the geography of production. Belgium allows margarine to be sold only in oval containers, while square ones are reserved for butter. The standard width of consumer durables in the EU countries is 60 centimetres, but in Switzerland is a few centimetres less. A bylaw of the City of London stipulates that in taxis gentlemen must be able to sit comfortably in an upright position with their hats on. While in Britain it is illegal for lifts to have a stop button, the same button is obligatory in Belgium. In the Netherlands beer can be sold only in returnable bottles, whereas the German standard for a beer container is non-returnable bottles. None of these technical specifications has a crucial impact on the protection of life and health. Their final effect is to reduce competition and increase price to the consumers. Trade policy is one detail that easily escapes the scrutiny of voters whereas small but well-organised manufacturing lobbies may wield a strong influence on government attitude in trade and industrial policy.

Harmonised standards are essential in some areas, such as safety, health and the environment, whereas mutual recognition (an agreement to acknowledge diversity) may be an interim solution for traded goods until harmonisation is implemented. In any case, a long-term advantage of harmonisation is that firms will have to comply with only one set of rules instead of up to fifteen different sets. This may increase the gains that can be achieved from economies of scale. However, this only makes sense when the market for a good or a service extends to more than one member state. For example, although consumer preferences for relatively new goods such as VCRs, fax and photocopying machines, CD-ROMs, computers, printers and mobile phones are similar throughout the EU, there are widespread differences in the markets for foodstuffs and beverages, with preferences often strictly local.[48] In such cases, a potential EU standard that does not embrace these distinctions may do more harm than good. The member states of the EU are, however, obliged to notify the Commission in advance about all draft regulations and standards. If the Commission or other member states find that a new standard contains elements of a barrier to trade, they may implement remedial action as allowed in Articles 28 or 94,[49] of the Treaty of Rome.

Liberalisation of trade and FDI with third countries potentially increases both trade with those countries and the share of foreign inputs in domestically produced 'hybrid' goods.[50] *Rules of origin* in general, and the minimum local content requirement in particular, are used as NTBs to prevent goods with a high external content from receiving preferential treatment in the internal trade of the EU. However, it is increasingly difficult to determine the 'nationality' of some goods, e.g. cars. Countries throughout the world are free to use rules of origin as policy measures, as they are not yet regulated by the WTO. As a result, practice varies considerably, causing difficulty for both producers and traders.

A UNCTC (1991a) survey of *trade-related investment measures* (TRIMs) found that local content requirements are more common than regulations regarding exports or employment. Although TRIMs exist in both developed and developing countries, they are more common in the developed world. They are usually concentrated in specific industries, such as the automotive, chemicals and computers industries. A study of 682 investment projects found that in 83 per cent TRIM requirements (such as local sourcing, exporting) would have been undertaken anyway, i.e. not only were TRIMs intruding in the mix of inputs in the production process, but they were also redundant.

EU rules of origin are based on Regulation 802/68, which states four criteria for the determination of the origin of a good, i.e. origin may lie in the country where:

- the last substantial operation was performed;
- the last 'economically justified' operation took place;
- the good was equipped for its purpose; or
- a new product is manufactured or where an important stage of manufacture takes place.

The WTO is intending to draft new standards for the determination of origin that will be universally applicable. Until it does so, the EU will continue to follow the Kyoto Convention, with one important difference. The EU will determine the origin of the good according to the country where the last 'economically justified' operation took place. This allows considerable scope for arbitrary interpretations of the origin rules and introduction of protection.

If a government observes that a good is or is likely to be imported into its country in large quantity, it may introduce an antidumping tariff. Foreign exporters can circumvent this barrier by changing the geography of production. For example, they may move the final, often screwdriver, stage of production to the tariff-imposing country. To counter this action, the home authorities may request that the goods produced domestically must have a certain local content in order to obtain preferential treatment. Once the original supplier of the good meets this requirement, the local authorities may go further, as was the case with the EU control of imports of Japanese integrated circuits (microchips). Chips that are only assembled in the EU do not qualify for domestic treatment. The EU rules of 1989 link the origin of microchips to the place where the diffusion process takes place. Assembly and testing come after the diffusion process and they add to the final value of the chip approximately as much as diffusion. There are two reasons for this decision by the Commission regarding rules of origin for integrated circuits. First, these rules demand that a part of the manufacturing process takes place in the EU. This requires an inflow of foreign investment and the creation of high-quality local jobs. Second, the intention was to support EU producers of microchips, some of whom carry out diffusion in the EU while assembly and testing takes place in non-EU countries where labour costs are lower. In this case, the EU defined the origin of the good as the place where the 'most' (rather than the 'last') substantial production process took place. Origin is determined by where R&D takes place and by the location of capital equipment used in the production of such goods, rather than by the place of transformation of goods. According to these rules, Ricoh photocopiers, which are made (well, assembled) in California, originate not in the US but rather in Japan because that is where essential parts such as drums, rollers, side plates and other working equipment originate. Having declared the origin of these machines to be Japan, the EU has an arsenal of NTBs to curtail imports of these goods from the US. This has provoked tensions in EU trade with the US.[51]

However, in the EU there is a so-called 'sunset' clause that applies to antidumping duties. Antidumping measures apply for 'only' five years unless there is a review in which dumping and injury are again established (Regulation 2026/97). There is no sunset provision in US antidumping laws, which can last almost indefinitely, as exemplified by the fact that they have been applied to Japanese colour TV sets for 30 years. In addition, the scope of the measures has been expanded to cover liquid crystal display, as well as projection television (Belderbos, 1997: 425).

A firm may avoid antidumping actions by changing production geography (relocating production). A new plant may be located either in a third country or in the country that has imposed antidumping duties (tariff jumping). However, the European Commission and the US Department of Commerce have the right to include third-country exports within the scope of an antidumping measure. For example, during the period 1989–90 nine Japanese fax plants were established in the EU even though there were no antidumping investigations. Some of these firms explicitly stated that fear of antidumping measures was their major reason for investing and location in the EU (Belderbos, 1997: 434–4). However, once established in the EU, these firms can sell at any price they want (below the production costs or below the prevailing prices on the local market). The penalty is that they are not allowed to discriminate or segment the market and may not follow predatory pricing policies.[52]

Yet another complication in the calculation of added value and the shares of different countries in the final origin of a good are presented by fluctuations in the rates of exchange. For example, what rate of exchange should be used to calculate added value: the rate prevailing on the date of importation of inputs or the rate on the date when the final good is exported into the EU? A case in point arose in the export of ballpoint pens (made from American components) from Switzerland to France in 1983. The EU Court of Justice decided in favour of the date of importation.

Controversies about origin were for a long time confined to trade in goods but are now relevant to trade in services too. What determines the 'nationality' of traded services? Many are based on wide international networks. Nonetheless, certain criteria are emerging. They include place of incorporation, location of headquarters, nationality of ownership and control, and the principal place of operation and intellectual input.

Rules of origin are responsible for many controversies, heated debates and tensions in international trade. In a supposedly 'globalised' international economy where TNCs are increasingly involved in foreign production, rules of origin make less and less sense. They are associated with distortions in investment decisions and reduction in international production and trade, and generally do more harm than good.

Non-tariff barriers contribute to the costs that accrue from the non-competitive segmentation of the market. They encourage import substitution and discourage rationalisation of investment. The anticipated benefits that would come from the elimination of NTBs include increased competition, with its concomitant effects of improved efficiency, increased economies of scale and a consequent reduction in unit costs of production for an enlarged market, as well as increased specialisation. The outcome of this process would be an increase in average living standard.

A study by Emerson *et al.* (1988) illustrated the possible benefits that could accrue, under certain conditions, from the completion of the Single Market Programme. The total EU gross domestic product in 1985 (the base year for most estimates) was €3,300bn for the twelve member states. The private and public sector firms in Emerson *et al.*'s study estimated the direct cost of frontier formalities to be 1.8 per cent of the value of goods traded in the EU, or around €9bn, and the cost identifiable barriers, such as technical regulations, to be 2 per cent total costs, or around €40bn. Liberalisation of public procurement would bring gains of €20bn, while liberalisation of the supply of financial services would save a further €20bn. Gains due to economies of scale would reduce costs by between 1 and 7 per cent, yielding an aggregate cost saving of €60bn. A downward convergence of presently disparate price levels could bring gains of about €40bn under the assumption of a much more competitive and integrated EU market. The estimate of gains offered by the surveyed companies ranged from €70bn, or 2.5 per cent of the EU GNP, to €190bn, or 6.5 per cent of the EU GNP. The same, one-off gains for the 1988 GNP would give a range of €175–255bn. At the time, these figures seemed likely to be underestimates as they excluded important dynamic effects on economic performance such as technological innovation and the introduction of new goods and services, which is difficult to predict. There was no widespread opposition to the completion of the Single European Market, because opponents to the plan could not offer an alternative strategy that would make up for the losses forgone from preserving the status quo.

The analysis of Emerson *et al.* was based, in part, on shaky assumptions. Hence, there were those who disagreed with their conclusions because of their *underestimation* of the effects of the Single Market Programme. Baldwin (1989) believed that one-off gains would be translated into a substantial 'medium-term growth bonus'. Others disputed Emerson *et al.*'s conclusions because they thought that the expected results were *overestimates* by a factor of two or three (Peck, 1989: 289). A communication from the European Commission provided an *ex post* assessment of the impact of the Single Market Programme (European Commission, 1997b: 5–6). Its findings included:

- solid evidence of the positive effects of the Single Market Programme;
- growing competition between firms in both manufacturing and services;
- an accelerated pace of industrial restructuring;
- a wider range of products and services available to public sector, industrial and domestic consumers at lower prices, particularly in newly liberalised services such as transport, financial services, telecommunications and broadcasting;
- faster and cheaper cross-frontier deliveries resulting from the absence of cross-border controls on goods;
- greater inter-state mobility of workers, as well as students and retired people;
- between 300,000 and 900,000 more new jobs created than would have been the case without the Programme;
- an extra increase in EU income of 1.1–1.5 per cent over the period 1987–93;
- inflation rates 1.0–1.5 per cent lower than would have been the case otherwise;
- an increase in economic convergence and cohesion between different EU regions;

The above quantitative findings are (for whatever reasons) more in accord with the expectations by Peck (1989) than in line with any other *ex ante* estimation. Several arguments that may be put forward to explain these results, including:

- Although the Single Market Programme was 'formally' implemented and the Single European Market introduced in 1993, the process of 'digestion' of all changes still needs additional time. In spite of the large wave of (defensive) mergers and acquisitions around 1990, the exploitation of new opportunities for output and business in an enlarged market (free of NTBs) needs more time. That is relevant both for the manufacturing sector end, even more important, for services.
- The reunification of Germany has affected the performance of the EU.

Evidence regarding the effects of integration, in particular the Single Market Programme, is sometimes conflicting. For example, Neven (1990) concluded that the Programme was relatively unimportant to the northern EU member countries since they have already exploited most of the potential for large-scale production. Alternatively, Smith and Venables (1988) and Cecchini/Emerson believed that the potentials for economies of scale were significant throughout the EU. This divergence shows that even now there is not a complete understanding of the determinants of trade and production patterns in the EU and suggests that the analyses of integration will remain speculative (Norman, 1990: 52).

Restriction of competition

It is increasingly risky and costly to develop a new good, service, technology or organisational competence. The same if often true of entering a new market. Thus, sharing costs and risk, as well as achieving economies of scale, is a major incentives for firms to form various types of partnership. Article 81[53] of the Treaty of Rome prohibits 'as incompatible with the common market' all explicit or implicit, as well as horizontal or vertical agreements (collusion) among firms that may have a negative impact on internal EU trade 'and which have as their object or effect the prevention, restriction or distortion of competition within the common market', unless authorised by the European Commission. Private practices that restrict competition according to this Article include:

- direct or indirect fixing of prices and other trading conditions;
- limitation or control of production, markets, technical development or investment;
- sharing of markets;
- application of dissimilar conditions to equivalent transactions with different clients;
- tying unconnected transactions into contracts;

It has been recognised for quite some time, at least in the smaller countries in Europe, that there is a need for some geographical concentration of business. Hence, Article 81(3)[54] states exemptions from the general EU rules of competition. Its application is often based on political compromises, hence the potential danger (uncertainty) that comes from the lack of transparency. An agreement, decision or practice may be declared as compatible with the common market if it contributes to an improvement in the production or distribution of goods, or to the promotion of economic or technical progress, 'while allowing consumers a fair share of the resulting benefit'. In addition, to be exempt from the rules of competition, the restrictive agreement must be necessary for the accomplishment of the desired business end (the appropriateness principle). If some kinds of business practice occur frequently and are compatible with the rules of competition, the Commission may grant a block exemption. For example, the Commission recognised the importance of cooperation for technical progress. The 1985, Regulation 418/85 granted a block exemption, until 1998 (extended until the end of 2000), to agreements among firms on joint R&D and joint exploitation of those results (manufacturing or licensing to third parties). The regulation includes a list of authorised and forbidden clauses in the agreement. The forthcoming new and revised block exemption will replace the existing system of specifically exempted 'white list' clauses by a general exemption. This would give a greater contractual freedom to the parties to such agreements. However, 'hardcore' restrictions (price fixing, output limitation or allocation of markets or customers) will remain prohibited. Other areas where block exemptions may be granted include SMEs, protection of the environment and employment and training.

Manufacturers in the EU constitute a powerful lobby with a large influence on economic policy, for example car producers have been exempt [Article 81(3) of the Treaty of Rome] from the full rigour of competition since 1985 (Regulation 123/85). The rationale put forward by the car lobby, and accepted by the Commission, was that cars are a unique type of consumer good: they are specialised items that require individual attention and aftersales service. Thus, cars are sold through tightly controlled exclusive dealerships and, as far as possible, serviced using only original spare parts (consumers benefit from the specialised knowledge of dealers, and service engineers, which should improve safety). In addition, producers control geographical market segmentation and regulate the quantity and prices of cars sold. Although there is little competition between retailers of the same type of the car, there is still solid competition among different producers of cars. Despite receiving such favour from the Commission, car manufacturers have failed to fulfil their part of the bargain, i.e. to allow consumers to shop around within the EU for the best deals. There are still significant differences in prices for the same type of a car among the member countries of the EU and guarantees are not honoured throughout the region. The consumers pay the cost of this uncompetitive behaviour in higher car prices and reduced choice.

For example, in 1995 prospective buyers from Austria flooded into Italy to buy cars because identical models were as much as 30 per cent cheaper there (partly due to the depreciation of the lira). The Italian car dealers refused to sell cars to non-nationals. In other countries, dealers also often refuse to sell cars to non-nationals or discourage them from purchasing cars by quoting excessively long delivery times, various surcharges or warnings that aftersales service would not be honoured abroad. In spite of all these problems, the block exemption was in 1995 extended for a further seven years (Regulation 1475/95). The new terms allow multidealership as a means of avoiding 'exclusive' dealership. However, this is a largely futile gesture as the second franchise has to be on different premises, under different management and in the form of a distinct legal entity. The Consumers' Association of the UK sent a protest to the European Commission signed by 20,000 people saying that they were being 'ripped off' by the dealers.[55] This is not easily ignored and, as the exemption has not brought tangible benefits to the consumers, there is a possibility that the Commission will seek a radical change in the car dealership regime once the current exemption expires in September 2002.

Although there has been some reduction in price differentials for the same model of car in the EU over the past decade, price differences remain and are not likely do disappear soon. The car market remains a 'black hole' in the Single European Market, which formally started in 1993. The 'normal' rules of competition do not apply in this important market. Although the gap has narrowed somewhat, it is still considerable, almost 20 per cent on average across the euro zone countries. For the best-selling models in the small and medium market segments price differentials can be as much as 33 per cent (VW Golf).[56]

A 1998 study of 53 homogeneous products in the euro area by Lehman Brothers found that, on average, prices varied among countries by 24 per cent. This is twice as much as in the US.[57] Prices will always differ by a margin that may include transport costs and difference in tax rates, but consumers tolerate small differences.

The single currency (the euro), as well as Internet shopping and the competition that it introduces, will lead to a convergence of prices, and those sellers that do not adjust will lose business. However, those that cater to the local market with specific regional tastes may not be affected to a large extent by increased competition.

Examples of uncompetitive behaviour may be found elsewhere. Fragrance producers have a similar right to license only upmarket shops to sell their products. And, after all, could or should competition laws force Burger King outlets to sell McDonald's hamburgers and vice versa?

The merger/acquisition control procedure of the EU has seven, often overlapping, steps. They are pre-notification discussions, notification, investigation, negotiation, decision, political evaluation and judicial scrutiny. The strength of the EU procedure in comparison with the past and with other jurisdictions is that it is:

- fast (the majority of cases are resolved within a month);
- flexible (pre-notification discussions resolve the question of the necessary background information for the decision);
- a 'one-stop shop' (the Commission is the single body in charge of receiving notifications, investigation and decision).

The European Commission may approve a merger, clear it with conditions or block it. Although the EU procedure is simple, it has one (at least) major weakness: its lack of transparency. The Commission has considerable discretionary room for manoeuvre in the decision-making process.[58]

Exemptions from the competition rules of the EU are possible under Article 81(3) of the Treaty of Rome. To obtain an exemption, the firms involved need to demonstrate that the benefits of the deal outweigh the anti-competitive effects. The firms need to prove to the Commission that the deal improves production and/or distribution of goods and that it promotes technological progress. In addition, a 'fair share' of the resulting benefits must be passed on to consumers. In the past, the procedure for clearance was quite long, typically taking up to two years to obtain an exception. However, since 1993, in the case of any deal (principally, but not exclusively, joint ventures) between firms that has implications for the structure of an industry, the parties must receive a consenting or a warning letter within two months of the mandatory notification of the Commission about such an agreement. The first examples included an approved joint venture between Olivetti and Canon (1992) for the development and production of printers and fax machines. The justification for this exception was the avoidance of duplication of development costs and the transfer of technology from Canon (Japan) to Olivetti (Italy). The joint venture by Asea Brown Bovery (ABB) for the development and production of high-performance batteries was also approved on the grounds that it brings innovation, reduces dependence on imported oil and, indirectly, improves the quality of life of consumers. In 1991, however, a merger between Aérospatiale and Alenia/de Havilland was prohibited on the grounds that the merged company would enjoy a dominant position in the worldwide market for medium-sized (40–59 seats) turbopropelled aeroplanes.

Competition rules apply not only to the written and enforceable deals among undertakings, but also to tacit ones such as concerted practices. The 'dyestuffs' case (1969) is an example of this. On three occasions in the 1960s (1964, 1965 and 1967), the biggest EU producers of aniline dyes increased their supply prices by identical margins with a time lag of only a few days. Professional organisations from the textile and leather industries complained to the Commission. The ten firms charged denied the existence of any gentlemen's agreement and argued that in a closely knit industry each producer follows the price leader. Nonetheless, the Commission had enough circumstantial evidence of collusion to find the parties involved guilty of price fixing and to fine them a total of €0.5mn. The firms involved in this case were BASF, Bayer, Hoechst and Cassella Farbwerke Mainkur (Germany); Francolor (France); ACNA (Italy); ICI (Britain); and Ciba, Sandoz and Geigy (Switzerland). The Court of Justice upheld the decision of the Commission on the grounds that the national markets for dyestuffs were fragmented and that synchronised price rises did not correspond to the normal conditions of the market. One of the important issues that came out of this anti-cartel case was that the Commission and Court applied the EU competition rules on an extraterritorial basis. British and Swiss enterprises were party to the gentlemen's agreement, and although at that time neither Britain nor Switzerland was a member of the EU the companies involved were fined for the non-competitive market behaviour. The principle that was established in this case was that each firm must independently determine its business policy in the common market.

EU competition legislation may be applied to firms that are located and/or do business anywhere in the world. Acceptance, adoption, implementation and enforcement of the EU competition rules is one of the key conditions that must be accepted by any country that wants to join the EU. In order to avoid a potential problem regarding competition in the EU market, two Swiss companies, Ciba-Geigy and Sandoz, requested that the European Commission 'clear' their domestic merger to form Novartis. The Commission considered over 100 affected markets. As this extraterritorial merger was predominantly of a complementary nature, it was approved in 1996. And in 1998, the Commission approved the merger of two Swiss banks, UBS and SBS. These cases provide further proof that there is a need for an internationally or, perhaps better to begin with, regionally accepted common set of minimum rules in the area of competition policy. These rules would oust, or reduce, the use of unilateral and extraterritorial competition policy instruments.

There was a big fuss in the EU about a purely American acquisition when Boeing bought McDonnell-Douglas in 1997.[59] Although the American authorities and the European Commission investigated the same market, they came to different conclusions. This was in spite of the bilateral European Commission/US Government Competition Agreement (signed in 1991, approved in 1995) to exchange information, coordinate procedures and consult on cases and remedies. The limits of bilateralism were exposed by this case. *The Economist* reported that there was 'the lethal cocktail of politics, national champions and defence interests'

(26 July 1997: 62). In addition, the two competition regimes have different economic rationales, different principles, legal forms and institutional contexts. They are not likely to see all cases in an identical way (Cini and McGowan, 1998: 207). Nonetheless, Boeing recognised the jurisdiction of the European Commission when it filed details of the merger. The European Commission accepted the deal subject to some minor concessions by Boeing. However, there are encouraging examples of cooperation between the EU and US authorities, such as a joint investigation of Microsoft in 1995.

Competition policy requires skilful handling in any scheme that integrates countries. Breaking up a price-fixing cartel is obviously a competition issue. However, deciding how many large chemical or car companies the EU should have is a political question which shapes the geography of production. There should be some control over mergers with an EU dimension. All industries in the EU use mergers and acquisitions in their business strategy. This was most pronounced in the second half of the 1980s when firms were faced with the possibility of a genuine Single European Market from the early 1990s.[60] One tool of the Programme was the elimination of unnecessary regulation (NTBs) that was splintering national markets for goods, services and factors in the EU. The business community responded to this challenge with mergers, acquisitions, strategic alliances, joint ventures and networking, all with the aim of consolidating their position in the new, frontier-free and highly competitive market. Such a business policy had an indirect positive effect on standardisation. The European Commission tolerated it because it believed that it would increase efficiency.

After a flurry of merger activity in the second half of 1980s, reaching a peak in 1989/90 (when much restructuring took place), concentration activity decelerated (Table 3.3). By late 1992, when the Single Market Programme was finally implemented, the business structure and operation had been shaken out. Unfortunately, the Commission does not publish data to enable Tables 3.3 and 3.4 to be updated.

Table 3.3 Mergers and majority acquisitions, 1987–93

Year	National mergers[a]	EU internal[b]	EU international[c]	International EU[d]	Outside EU[e]
1987/88	2,110	252	499	160	114
1988/98	3,187	761	659	447	310
1989/90	3,853	1,122	655	768	356
1990/91	3,638	947	550	729	376
1991/92	3,720	760	497	605	326
1992/93	3,004	634	537	656	381

[a]Deals among firms of the same country.
[b]Deals involving firms from at least two different member states of the EU.
[c]Deals in which EU firms acquire firms of non-EU origin.
[d]Deals in which the bidder is from outside of the EU and acquires one or several EU firms.
[e]Deals in which there was not any involvement of EU firms.

Source: *XXIIIrd Report on Competition Policy 1993*. Brussels: European Commission (1994).

Table 3.4 Mergers and majority acquisitions by major economic activities in the EU, 1987–93

Economic activity	1987/8	1988/9	1989/90	1990/1	1991/2	1992/3
Agriculture	16	22	45	45	37	22
Energy and water	53	77	75	88	102	81
Minerals and chemicals	215	452	594	589	489	452
Metal, engineering and cars	588	975	1,229	1,137	1,154	941
Manufacturing	560	1,090	1,307	1,306	1,230	1,061
Distribution and hotels	547	863	1,173	899	1,025	797
Transport and telecommunications	95	178	253	257	238	224
Banks, finance and insurance	748	1,046	1,309	1,194	968	918

Source: *XXIIIrd Report on Competition Policy 1993*. Brussels: European Commission (1994).

Most mergers and acquisitions occurred in the manufacturing industry and, especially, in paper manufacturing (Table 3.4), followed by the food and drink,[61] sugar-based production and chemicals industries. This is explained by the removal of NTBs in internal trade. The metal-based production industries (mechanical and electro-based engineering and vehicles) also experienced a relatively high level of concentration activity. Suppliers of public goods in these two industries concentrated with the intention of sharing R&D costs and thus withstanding potentially strong competition. Wholesale distributors reacted to the elimination of NTBs by concentration of their activities. The same was true for the providers of financial services.

The major motive for mergers and acquisitions throughout the period of observation was to strengthen market position, followed by the development of commercial activities (market expansion) and rationalisation of business (European Economy, 1994: 20). The objective was to prepare for intensive competition in the Single European Market. Companies in Britain, Germany[62] and France were the most favoured targets for intra-EU mergers. At the same time, firms from these three countries were the most active buyers of companies in the EU. Nonetheless, the EU concentration in manufacturing was still 12 per cent below that in the US in 1993 (European Economy, 1996: 119). Parent companies from Britain, Germany and France (the 'trio') were also active in purchasing non-EU firms. While British firms preferred to purchase companies in North America, German and French parent firms distributed their non-EU purchases evenly among North America, Western (non-EU) and Eastern Europe. As for non-EU acquirers of EU firms, North American buyers were most active in the EU 'trio', followed by Switzerland, Sweden and Japan.

A new trend in inter-firm relations that has emerged is that firms operating in the low- and medium-technology sectors use mergers and acquisitions in their business strategy, whereas those in high-technology industries employ cooperation and collaboration (joint ventures). This is a divergence from the historical pattern of inter-firm relations, as firms have traditionally tried to protect their knowledge and experience in manufacturing and marketing. The high costs of developing new and upgrading existing technologies has made it pragmatic to share the high costs of R&D.

In a competitive market, mergers and acquisitions are thought to bring at least two efficiency gains: a reduction in management costs and a reduction in transaction costs. These benefits need to be weighed against the possible costs that accrue from the potential inefficiencies that may be the consequence of concentration. If the expected efficiency gains are not realised and do not outweigh the disadvantages, the new merged enterprise may suffer as a result of differences in corporate cultures (in Germany engineers run firms, in Britain accountants, in Italy designers), inflexibility and poor coordination of business functions. A number of studies examining full legal mergers in various countries in the EU have found no evidence of substantial efficiency gains. Nor were economies of scale significant. Mergers had little or no effect on post-merger profitability. There was no significant difference in the returns per share three years after the merger.[63] The costs of changes in business organisation were often greater than the benefits claimed by the promoters of takeovers. The main reasons for these disappointments include the high prices paid for target firms, overestimation of the business potential of the acquired firm and mismanagement of the integration process with the acquired firm (Jacquemin, 1990a: 13–14; 1990b: 541; Jacquemin and Wright, 1993: 528). This is most obvious in the cases of mergers of firms in the production of steel or cars, as well as in airlines.

Despite promises of reduction in costs, economies of scale and the creation of 'champions' to counter foreign rivals, mergers were used as defensive business policy instruments. The rationale that led to the large wave of mergers in the US (and Britain) during the 1960s and 1970s proved to be unfounded. Instead of supporting adjustment, mergers obstructed it by protecting firms from competitive pressure. That was reflected in the relatively slow response of some US firms to oil crises and Japanese competition in certain industries. Firms in the EU would be wise to avoid any repetition of the US experience. The presence of Japanese TNCs with their advanced technology and business organisation in some lines of manufacturing industry in the EU may be the best motivation to the EU domestic firms to restructure their business and become more competitive.

In general, shareholders in acquired firms are likely to benefit from a merger, but investors in the acquiring firms are likely to lose out. There are also problems in creating a new management culture in the merged company, whereas cost savings and new economies of scale can be negligible. This does not mean that all mergers and acquisitions have been failures, but it does mean that all claims about the splendid future of the merged company need to be taken with a pinch of salt. Business gurus, management consultants and investment bankers have reached the same conclusion: less than half of all mergers add value in the medium term.[64] Thus, some conglomerates sell off parts of their business that are not at the core of their activity in order to raise money for acquisitions in their main business area and to make their operations simpler. Mergers and acquisitions are not necessarily wrong business strategies, but they are very risky.[65]

A tidal wave of mergers and acquisitions in the EU was prompted by the need to restructure segmented industries and liberalise capital markets (exploiting restructuring and financial know-how from the US), as well as by the Single European Market. The volume of mergers and acquisitions relative to start-up investments raises serious questions regarding competition (because of the reduction in the number of independent firms and an increase in the potential for collusion) in the Single European Market. Mergers and acquisitions are a global phenomenon. However, so is competition, so anxieties about the effect of the location and structure of merged businesses on competition is to some extent offset by the expansion of 'global' over regional or national competition, as well as by the fact that there has been some restructuring of business of the acquired firms (European Commission, 1998: 144–5).

One result of the numerous mergers and acquisitions is that the degree of concentration in the EU has risen compared with the pre-Single Market Programme era. That may *increase* price competition on the internal EU market and abroad through rationalisation of production and economies of scale. At the same time, an increased concentration of business may *restrict* competition. Therefore, the EU introduced an important legal instrument for the *ex ante* control of mergers in 1990.[66]

The EU needs a sound competition policy to prevent pan-EU oligopolies (corporate fortresses) replacing national ones and eliminating the competitive pressure that comes from open markets. Revised merger legislation (designed to simplify the regulatory burden on merging companies) that came into force in 1998 gives the European Commission a say in any merger with an EU dimension (smaller mergers are under the control of national authorities). This is the case if:

- annual worldwide turnover of the new (merged) company is above €2.5bn (the general threshold);
- in each of at least three member states the combined turnover of all of the companies concerned is above €100m;
- in each of these three member states the aggregate turnover of each of at least two companies involved is over €25m;
- the aggregate EU-wide turnover of at least two involved firms is more than €100m.

The decisive determinant according to these thresholds is *turnover*, not the country of domicile/nationality of the parent enterprise.[67] If the proposed merged company would occupy a dominant position that could restrict competition (the new firm could, for example, increase prices by 10 per cent without losing market share), the European Commission has the authority to stop the deal. However, the Commission has not so far blocked any deal that would result in the merged firm having a market share of less than 40 per cent. Thus, the purpose of the Merger Control Regulation is to prevent *ex ante* the creation of unwanted market behaviour that comes from the abuse of dominant position in the Single European Market, although the implementation of the policy has some arbitrary aspects such as estimating the market strength of potential entrants or remaining competitors, determining substitutes and defining the product or geographical market.

A number of firms do have as their aim worldwide market dominance and, as a result, merger and acquisition deals are getting bigger and more complex. This increases the workload on the Commission's limited resources to the possible detriment of the merits of the system: predictability and speed. That the system needs to be reformed is obvious, the question is should the time allowed for decisions be extended, thus compromising a basic tenet of the system, or should the Commission be empowered to handle only the biggest deals and leave the rest to the national courts (and 'punish' smaller merger deals with a set of national jurisdictions).

The European Commission's White Paper of April 1999, which applies mainly to Article 81 (restriction of competition), proposed abandoning any requirement on companies to seek prior authorisation. It will be up to firms themselves to assess whether their agreements fulfils the conditions laid down in the EU's competition law. This approach is expected to have several benefits. First, it will afford extra protection of the competition process and reduce the costs of notification. Secondly, the change will free up limited EU resources (around 150 officials) and make them available for swift pursuit of unlawful practices. Under the new system, national courts and national competition authorities would enforce the competition policy legislation together with the European Commission.

It has been argued that this proposal could reduce legal certainty and that competition policy would not be applied evenly throughout the EU. However, legal certainty would be maintained at a sufficient level by block exemption regulations and guidelines that allow companies to assess themselves the legality of their agreements. A system of exchange of information and of consultation between the Commission and the national competition authorities would ensure a consistent application of competition law. As far as national courts are concerned, the mechanism of preliminary reference to the Court of Justice will, in this area, as in many other areas of EU law, ensure consistency. If accepted by the Council, this change may be implemented in 2003. No changes in the existing control of mergers are planned.

Dominant position

If a firm has or achieves a dominant market position, it may significantly affect competition and geography of production. The dominant market position may be secured in several ways, including the following five:

- Firms may have innovative skills and competences not only in products (goods/ services), but also in management and firm-level planning. They may make risky investments in R&D, production and/or marketing that their competitors do not have the nerve for. Such first-mover advantages that are in line with the rules may result in dominance of the market and super-normal profits (Microsoft's MS-DOS and Windows, as well as Nintendo's Game Boy are obvious examples). The life cycle of products is shortening all the time, hence the importance of innovating. In fact, most firms compete by continually assuming quasi-monopolistic positions that are based on innovation of various kinds.[68] In spite of continuous innovations by Microsoft, the most valuable user assets (personal files) are transferable from one Microsoft system to another. Apple, a competitor, failed to realise this, allowing Microsoft to achieve a near-monopoly. The classical view that firms are only an input conversion mechanism does not reflect the contemporary world. In addition to their input conversion and value-adding functions, firms are also involved in learning-by-doing and innovation activities. Geographical concentration in industries with various entry barriers may occur as a direct consequence of a firm behaving efficiently. A policy that promotes R&D among firms in the EU may provide them with a better basis for oligopolistic competition at home and abroad and to face up to foreign rivals, mainly from Japan and the US.

- The dominant position in the market could be reached through mergers and acquisitions. This is typical in English-speaking countries.
- A firm may achieve or protect its dominant position through anti-competitive business practices. Examples of this include exclusive dealerships and predatory pricing. However, exclusive dealerships do not always reduce welfare, for example compared with the situation of free entry and exit among dealers/retailers, permanent and exclusive dealership (including aftersales service) might be a superior and welfare-increasing solution.
- The dominant position can be captured through a competitive and risky pricing policy. If economies of scale and learning result in a significant fall in prices as output increases over time, a risk-loving firm (for example, Texas Instruments in the 1960s and 1970s) may choose to set current prices on the basis of the expected (low) costs of production in the future or based on the average cost of production over the life cycle of the product.
- Yet another way in which firms come to dominate a market is through the granting of a licence by public authorities. Examples can be found in 'natural' monopolies such as public utilities (water, gas, electricity, rail transport, postal service and the local telephone service). In these industries, the minimum efficient scale is so large that a single firm is necessary to serve the entire national market.

From the outset one should be less concerned about the existence of a dominant firm (Microsoft) than about how the dominant firm 'plays the game'. Many people forget that Microsoft competes with Microsoft (Windows Millennium Edition competes with Windows 98, which competes with Windows 95). If the price of the new version is too high, consumers will stick to the old computer software. However, Microsoft may increase the price of the old versions when the new one is launched on the market in order to boost sales of the new version.

Article 82[69] of the Treaty of Rome refers to the issue of the dominant position in a market. It does not prohibit a dominant position (monopoly or monopsony) *ex ante*, but rather forbids the *abuse* of it. This Article has only an *ex post* effect. In order to determine whether an infringement of the EU market took place, the Commission looks at three factors:

- the existence of the dominant position;
- its abuse (in pricing or control of production, distribution or servicing);
- the negative effect on trade among the member countries.

Large firms are permitted by the Treaty of Rome to enjoy market dominance, but they are forbidden to exercise it. This is somewhat naive! Whoever yields the power will behave as a monopolist – the temptation is irresistible. In any case, the legal framework recognises that there is a need for some level of concentration[70] in some industries for reasons of efficiency. It is inevitable for the attainment of the efficient scale of production, in both home and foreign markets. Otherwise, protected and inefficient national firms, which have higher production costs than foreign competitors, would continue to impose welfare losses on consumers. That is why many/most European countries have relaxed their anti-trust policies. Otherwise, small domestic firms could be protected only at a high cost and with a diminution of production efficiency. Concentration (geographical agglomeration) of production is a potential barrier to foreign competition on the home market and a springboard for penetration into foreign markets.[71]

State aids

In the neo-classical economic model, perfect competition can be undermined by protection and subsidy. The distinction between the two distortions is subtle. On the one hand, tariff and non-tariff *protection* allow protected suppliers to charge higher prices in the local market than would be the case with free imports. Such protection provides an 'implicit subsidy' paid directly from consumers to producers. On the other hand, *subsidies* go to domestic producers not directly from consumers, but rather from taxpayers to the government and then to producers. The two types of 'support' have the same objective: to support to a certain national (inefficient) production geography as resources are kept in or shifted into import-substituting industries. Where they differ is in transparency and the method of supplying funds to the selected industries or firms within them.

Those that accept that the market functions efficiently use this argument as a case against subsidies (state aids). Although such an argument applies in many instances, there are others situations in which the neo-classical theory does not hold. In a situation with imperfections such as externalities (R&D or pollution), economies of scale, multiple equilibria, imperfect mobility of factors and sunk costs, intervention may be justified. Therefore, industrial and regional policies may be used as justifications for the existence of state aids.

A key element in the EU competition policy is a unique control of state aids. Subsidies may distort competition and efficient allocation of resources (geography of production). Article 87[72] of the Treaty of Rome recognises this issue and regulates it.[73] It prohibits any aid that distorts or threatens to distort competition among member countries. This means that Article 87 does not apply to aid given as support to firms or for the production of goods and services that do not enter intra-EU trade (local consumption), as well as aid for exports outside the EU (regulated by Article 132[74]). The European Commission accepted a transparent approach to subsidies and publishes *Surveys of State Aid in the EC*. It also expects its trading partners, particularly candidate countries, to follow suit.

There are, however, a few exceptions to the general rule of incompatibility of state aids. Article 87 states that aid that *is* compatible with the Treaty is of the kind given on a non-discriminatory basis to individuals for social purposes, as well as aid to regions affected by disasters. Aid that *can be* considered compatible with the Treaty is the kind given to projects that are in the EU's interest and aid for regional development in the 'areas where the standard of living is abnormally low' (for the purpose of social cohesion in the EU). The Council of Ministers (based on the proposal from the Commission) has the discretionary right to decide that other aid may be compatible with the EU rules. This includes aid to SMEs,[75] conservation of energy, protection of environment, promotion of national culture or alleviation of serious disturbances in a national economy. If an industry comes under competitive and/or restructuring pressure, the Commission considers the social and other impact of such an adjustment according to the Guidelines of 1979. The Commission may permit aid under conditions that are based on principles that include:

- *temporariness* (a clear time limit);
- *transparency* (the amount of aid has to be measurable);
- *selectivity* (aid is supposed to be given to firms and industries that have a reasonable chance of standing on their own after the restructuring period);
- *appropriateness* (aid has to match the basic needs of the assisted firm/industry to operate during the restructuring period,[76] after which the assisted firm/industry has to become economically viable on its own).

In order to ease the workload and concentrate on the large and potentially the most damaging cases, the Commission introduced a *de minimis* rule in 1992. According to this rule, governments are not required to notify the EC of aid that does not exceed €100,000 over a period of three years. The Commission holds that such aid does not distort competition. In addition, aid linked to environmental issues may be allowed if it enables an improvement in conditions beyond the required environmental standards. The Commission takes the same favourable view regarding aid to SMEs as long as they contribute to social stability and economic dynamism.

Article 87, as well as Court practice, provides the European Commission with a wide discretionary margin in the decision-making process. Nonetheless, the Commission employs two criteria:

- *Compensatory justification.* To 'clear' aid as compatible with the rules, aid has to conform with goals set out in Article 87 and it must be proven that, without state aid, free markets would not be capable of accomplishing the same end.
- *Transparency.* Each aid programme has to be justified and its effects measurable. Member states must notify the Commission about the form, volume, duration and objectives of aid.

If, two months after the notification, the Commission has not made an explicit decision, aid is regarded as tacitly accepted. The Commission may decide 'not to raise objections', which means that the application is preliminarily approved, but the Commission needs further information in order to reach a final decision. The Commission can open up the procedure (Article 88[77]) and ask the parties concerned to submit their comments. The Commission then makes a final decision on the compatibility of aid with the EU rules.

Article 87 does not define state aid. Nonetheless, the Commission and the Court of Justice interpret aid in a broad sense. They take it to mean any favour given by a government in a form that includes subsidies, special public guarantees, supply of goods or services at preferential conditions and favours regarding credit terms offered to one or more firms or their associates. Loans and guarantees given by the state or its agency do not necessarily constitute aid. The aid element exists only when such injections of funds are offered on conditions that are superior to the ones prevailing on the market.

Some governments still attempt to disguise industrial aid as regional aid. This is difficult to detect if the aided company makes a loss. R&D support can similarly be abused. 'Support' to the manufacturing and services sectors needs to be in the R&D stage otherwise foreign competitors, mainly from the US, would complain that EU subsidies are distorting international competition. Any EU member state can finance basic and applied research in the private sector according to agreed sliding scales.[78] The Commission's framework on state aid for R&D of 1995 outlines several criteria for the compatibility of such aid with the common market. They include the following:

- There is a distinction between 'industrial research' and 'pre-competitive development activity'. The closer to the marketplace for final goods, the more aid is likely to distort competition.
- State aid for R&D should create an incentive for the recipient firm to carry out R&D *in addition to* what it would undertake in the normal course of its business operation (now prove that!).
- Aid for 'industrial research' may be up to 50 per cent of the cost, whereas aid for 'pre-competitive development' may be up to 25 per cent of the cost. Nonetheless, there are special additional bonuses of 10 per cent for projects that involve SMEs, of 15 per cent if the project is a priority under the EU R&D programme and up to 10 per cent if R&D is undertaken in regions eligible for regional aid.
- Maximum aid for R&D in the EU (allowable under the GATT Agreement on Subsidies and Countervailing Measures) is 75 per cent for 'industrial research' and 50 per cent for 'pre-competitive development activity'.
- Member states have to notify the Commission about all individual aid packages for projects exceeding €25m where aid exceeds €5m.

The State-aid Department of the EU Commission has a staff of eighty officials responsible for monitoring state aid and carrying out other tasks in the field. They cannot be expected to examine every instance of state aid, especially as every region in each member country has staff (which often significantly outnumber the Commission's) to dispense aid. Therefore, the Commission's priority is to prevent the most anti-competition aid programmes.[79] The Commission has to make sure that aid is given to the most disadvantaged regions and that it is compatible with the Treaty rules. All these formidable issues linked to competition are increasingly becoming a paradise for lawyers.

The European Commission has approved aid for many purposes, usually when it serves the common interest of the EU. Such derogations from Article 87 include support to regional development, R&D, SMEs, training, savings in energy and protection of the environment. Table 3.5 provides data on annual averages and trends in the overall volume of state aid granted by the EU(15) member countries in the periods 1994–96 and 1996–98, as well as the distribution of aid per beneficiary. Although there was a predictable downward trend in the volume of granted aid during the period of observation, average annual aid remained massive, at over €93bn. Manufacturing industry, transport and agriculture were the principal beneficiaries of aid although it declined in absolute terms in all sectors with the exception of financial and other services and media and culture. Table 3.6 shows that there has been a gradual and continuous downward trend (which started in 1993) in the volume of state aid in the manufacturing industry. The same is true regarding the percentage value added in manufacturing and aid per person employed (Table 3.7). Over the period 1994–98, this was reduced by a third.

The data in Table 3.8 demonstrate that there were still large disparities in both overall per-capita national aid and per-capita aid in manufacturing in the period 1996–98. In terms of overall aid, the relative difference between the most interventionist country, Germany, and the most liberal, the UK, was 3:1. In terms of aid to manufacturing, the same ratio between the most interventionist, Italy, and least interventionist, Portugal, was 8:1.

The general downward trend in aid giving was almost entirely due to a continued decrease in handouts in Germany and Italy (Table 3.9). A decline in assistance offered in Germany reflects the fact that the restructuring process of the German manufacturing industry peaked after the reunification of the country in 1990. There was a slight increase in intervention per employee in Austria, Ireland, Denmark and Luxembourg, which were the most interventionist states in terms of assistance per employed person, whereas Portugal and Britain were the most

Table 3.5 Overall average annual national aid in the European Union, 1994–96 and 1996–98 (€m)

Beneficiary	1994–96	1996–98
Overall national aid, of which	104,215	93,127
Manufacturing sector	38,531	32,639
Agriculture	14,515	13,339
Fisheries	294	260[a]
Coal mining	9,079	7,227[b]
Transport	36,666	32,193[a]
Financial services	1,959	3,283
Tourism	316	229
Media and culture	636	748
Employment	1,104	1,416
Training	844	900
Other services	272	892

Source: *Eighth Survey on State aid in the European Union* (2000). Brussels: European Commission.
[a]1998 total partially estimated.
[b]1997 and 1998 data for French coal mining are not included.

Table 3.6 State aid to the manufacturing sector in the European Union, 1994–99: annual values in constant prices, 1997 (€m)

	1994	1995	1996	1997	1998
EU(15)	–	39,615	34,486	33,730	29,702
EU(12)	40,341	38,441	33,357	32,470	28,400

Source: *Eighth Survey on State Aid in the European Union* (2000). Brussels: European Commission.

Table 3.7 State aid to the manufacturing sector in the European Union: annual values, 1994–98[a]

	1994[b]	1995	1996	1997	1998
In per cent of value added	3.0	2.8	2.5	2.3	2.0
In € per person employed	1,357	1,298	1,182	1,151	1,007

Source: *Eighth Survey on State Aid in the European Union* (2000). Brussels: European Commission.
[a]At constant 1997 prices.
[b]Estimated EU(15).

liberal. Although public aid declined in general terms in the EU(15), it remained massive throughout the period 1995–98. This 'price' for maintaining a certain production geography was paid mostly through grants and tax exemptions.

A breakdown of aid according to sector and function (Table 3.10) reveals that regional objectives (57 per cent) were the major reason for distribution aid in the period 1996–98. This was followed by horizontal objectives. The highest priority was accorded to R&D (11 per cent), which shows the interest that the EU countries have in shaping future comparative advantage. The next highest priority area was SMEs, which received 9 per cent of aid.

A general downward trend in state aid reflects not only the application of competition rules in the EU, but also a reduction in public expenditure and budget discipline 'forced' by the Maastricht criteria for the EMU. Reduction in state aid is a pro-competition move in the EU. This is an encouraging trend as this type of assistance to businesses and regions is one of very few policy instruments available in the presence of EMU. Reliance on competition policy within the Single European Market will continue to stimulate market-led restructuring and more efficient allocation of resources (production geography). However, this has important policy implications for the Eastern enlargement of the EU. While the candidate countries would need substantial assistance to catch up with the ever-expanding *acquis communautaire*, budgetary restrictions would provoke internal political problems. One can already hear voices saying: 'Why should we subsidise the new member countries when we have unsettled domestic problems and when we make unprecedented efforts to reduce domestic expenditure still further because of the EMU?'.

Table 3.8 State aid per capita in the European Union: annual averages during the period 1996–98 in 1997 prices

Country	Overall amounts of state aid[a]		Of which aid to manufacturing		Population (millions)
	€m	€ per capita	€m	€ per capita	
Austria	1,186	147	495	61	8.07
Belgium	2,532	249	732	72	10.17
Denmark	1,356	257	712	135	5.27
Germany	26,808	327	11,463	140	81.96
Greece	1,306	125	616	59	10.49
Spain	4,709	120	1,800	46	39.30
Finland	500	97	391	76	5.13
France	13,887	237	4,481	77	58.49
Ireland	688	188	416	114	3.66
Italy	15,853	276	8,864	154	57.45
Luxembourg	78	188	48	114	0.42
Netherlands	1,963	126	629	40	15.57
Portugal	1,471	148	195	20	9.94
Sweden	1,570	178	344	39	8.84
United Kingdom	5,881	100	1,454	25	58.90
EU(15)	79,787	214	32,639	87	373.66

[a]Not including agriculture.

Table 3.9 State aid to the manufacturing sector in the European Union: annual averages, 1994–96 and 1996–98 (averages in 1997 prices)

Country	Per cent of value added		€ per person employed		€m	
	1994–96	1996–98	1994–96	1996–98	1994–96	1996–98
Austria	1.3	1.4	654	719	455	495
Belgium	2.5	1.9	1,376	1,093	931	732
Denmark	2.6	2.9	1,252	1,433	607	712
Germany	3.8	2.6	1,941	1,434	16,201	11,463
Old Länder	–	–	451	435	3,080	2,856
New Länder			8,783	6,021	13,121	8,607
Greece	4.8	4.9	925	997	592	616
Spain	2.3	2.1	769	691	1,883	1,800
Finland	1.6	1.6	928	959	366	391
France	1.7	2.0	895	1,131	3,607	4,481
Ireland	1.3	1.9	909	1,458	240	416
Italy	5.5	4.4	2,419	1,955	11,040	8,864
Luxembourg	2.2	2.3	1,400	1,476	46	48
Netherlands	1.1	1.1	702	735	602	629
Portugal	1.4	1.0	263	188	272	195
Sweden	0.8	0.8	421	441	330	344
United Kingdom	0.6	0.7	317	334	1,358	1,454
EU(15)	2.8	2.3	1,292	1,113	38,531	32,639

Source: *Eighth Survey on State Aid in the European Union* (2000). Brussels: European Commission.

Table 3.10 State aid to the manufacturing sector, 1996–98: breakdown of aid according to sector and function

Sectors/function	A	B	DK	D	GR	E	FIN	F	IRL	I	L	NL	P	S	UK	EU(15)
Horizontal objectives	69	54	90	27	2	33	72	52	40	23	33	82	65	44	39	35
R&D	30	16	24	10	0	10	36	27	5	3	7	20	6	10	11	11
Environment	10	1	33	1	0	1	1	1	0	0	4	10	0	14	0	2
SMEs	15	16	3	9	1	15	17	7	1	8	21	3	6	16	21	9
Trade	0	2	4	0	1	0	10	3	1	2	1	4	0	0	6	2
Energy saving	1	0	27	2	0	1	7	0	0	0	0	34	5	4	1	3
Other objectives (including rescue and restructuring)	12	20	0	5	0	6	1	13	33	10	0	11	48	0	0	8
Particular sectors	3	13	9	5	1	52	11	8	5	4	0	6	17	0	1	8
Shipbuilding	0	0	8	3	1	37	9	4	0	2	0	6	6	0	1	5
Other sectors	3	13	1	2	0	15	2	4	5	2	0	0	11	0	0	3
Regional objectives	29	33	1	68	97	15	17	40	55	72	67	12	18	56	60	57
Regions under 87(3)c	23	33	1	5	0	11	17	25	0	3	67	12	0	56	44	11
Regions under 87(3)a	6	0	0	63	97	4	0	15	55	69	0	0	18	0	16	46
Total	100	100	100	100	100	100	100	100	100	100	100	100	100	100	100	100

Source: *Eighth Survey on State Aid in the European Union* (2000). Brussels: European Commission.

3.4 Conclusions

Relatively small countries that are in the process of development employ industrial/ trade policies that may not always be competition-friendly. Relatively large and developed countries value competition quite highly. As agglomeration of business in some industries increases, there is a tendency to tighten anti-trust policy and maintain a certain level of competition in the internal market. Increased competition would, in most cases, without doubt, exert downward pressure on prices and costs. This outcome would enable economic growth with a reduced inflationary pressure. However, it is not clear how this would happen in practice. Competition may reduce the prices of goods and services or it may increase output but keep prices constant. In this case, a reduction in prices would be offset by an increase in demand. The most likely outcome in practice would be that competition would produce a blend of benefits that accrue from increase in output and decrease in prices.

The Single Market Programme enhanced the dynamic process of competition through an easing of market segmentation and, somewhat paradoxically, by increasing concentration in some businesses. This concentration permitted the employment of economies of scale and an increase in technical efficiency in production. In addition, it enhanced R&D through a joint sharing of high costs.

A change in global competition and the perception of a relative diminution of competitiveness in the EU at the turn of 1980s in comparison with the US in the computer and aerospace industries, Japan in cars and consumer electronics and certain developing countries in textiles and clothing, as well as a potential loss in a number of other industries, were among the driving forces that brought about the Single Market Programme. Businesses reacted to the Programme by consolidating, through mergers and acquisitions, as well as through joint ventures. An increase in internal EU competition through the elimination of internal barriers gave the EU the opportunity to benefit from the so far unexploited economies of scale that would, over time, reduce the costs of production and increase global competitiveness not only in manufacturing, but also in services. All of this would provide an additional boost to investment and the growth of the EU's economy. Hence, not only innovating firms and those that use state-of-the-art technologies, but also consumers are able to reap rewards in terms of opportunities provided by increased competition. The dynamic labour segment might gain from the integration process, as trade and competition would determine not if there were jobs, but what kind of jobs are available.

The ways forward in the short and medium term should rely on three ideas (Jacquemin and Pench, 1997: 38):

- developing key EU factors for the long-term growth and attraction and anchoring footloose economic activities;
- deepening of market integration;
- finding international points of reference (benchmarks) for comparison in order to determine the degree of success.

Binding multilateral competition rules would both do away with distortions in competition and promote an efficient allocation of resources on a global scale. These rules would restrain the behaviour of firms (in the same way that binding international trade rules curb the behaviour of governments). These rules would also prevent bilateral conflicts in competition matters. However, binding international competition rules will not be introduced in the near future. Almost a half of WTO member countries do not have competition laws, while other member countries have diverse competition values and apply competition laws in different ways (the US seldom allows exceptions, whereas they are quite common in the EU); yet another group of countries values its sovereignty so much that it is unwilling to accept another international bureaucratic superstructure. Because of its large and relatively closed economy, the US has been applying competition policy with a greater vigour than was the case with other developed countries with smaller and more open economies. A number of countries are opposed to a strong and vigilant supranational authority and dispute settlement system (as is the case in the EU and US) because it would prejudice their sovereignty. If a country suspects that the gist of its national competition model is not going to be adopted in the international arena, that country may wish to remove this issue from the list of its priorities. Even though they have limits (recall the Boeing/McDonnell Douglas case), bilateral agreements are a provisional reaction to and way out of the difficulties in competition matters. Although the speedy adoption of multilateral competition rules is unlikely for a host of reasons, the issue needs to be put on the international agenda for discussion.

Notes

1   Competition policy does not protect individual competitors, but rather the process of competition.
2   The interested reader is invited to consult Dunning (1995) and Krugman (1995) for further discussion.
3   Hayek criticised the neo-classical model, which is based on perfect competition, in the following way: 'But I must be content with thus briefly indicating the absurdity of the usual procedure of starting the analysis with a situation in which all the facts are supposed to be known. This is a state of affairs which economic theory curiously calls "perfect competition". It leaves no room whatever for the activity called competition, which is presumed to have already done its task' (Hayek, 1978: 182).
4   Liberalisation of imports has the strongest impact when exchange rates are stable. Volatility in the exchange rate market may loosen the grip of this policy instrument.
5   Patent rights exist to protect an individual's codifiable innovation and knowledge, whereas trademarks protect the reputation of a firm. Other knowledge that comes from learning through trial and error is largely unprotected because it may not be put into 'blueprints'.
6   The importance of aftersales service varies depending on the good. This service is non-existent for soaps and detergents but essential for printing presses or photocopiers.
7   Self-satisfaction and a lack of real local competition contributed to the German camera industry being driven out by the Japanese (Porter, 1990a: 169).
8   Timely, correct and cheap information is becoming a crucial input in the decision-making process. A banker who is handling large funds over his PC terminal is a long way from the British general, Sir Edward Pakenham, who lost the battle of New Orleans and his life on 8 January 1815, fifteen days after the Treaty of Gent ended the war but

several days before the frigate arrived at his headquarters with the news about the end of the war (Lipsey, 1992a: 288).

9 The neo-classical doctrine relies on an elegant, but unrealistic, assumption that markets are perfect. Without such a hypothesis, there is no case for the optimality in resource allocation.

10 If there is no retaliation, the 'optimal tariff' may be another reason for intervention. This is the case when a (large) country (or a group of countries) is strong enough to influence the world prices of the goods it trades. This country can reduce the world demand for the good in question by imposing or increasing tariffs. The price of the affected good falls, hence the tariff-imposing country tilts the terms of trade in its favour.

11 Because of asymmetric information, firms may have certain incentives to mislead the government.

12 Economies of scope are the outcome of the need for flexible (innovation-driven) methods of production. This is because the total production costs of manufacturing two separate goods may be higher than the costs of producing them together.

13 Rents are proceeds that are surplus to what is necessary to cover the costs of production and yield an average return on investment. They are due to barriers to entry such as large sunk costs, economies of scale, externalities, advertising, regulatory policies, distribution and service networks, asymmetric information, as well as consumer loyalty to a certain brand.

14 'Schumpeterians' point to five long waves in modern history: (1) 1780–1840, steam power drove the industrial revolution; (2) 1840–1890, the introduction of railways; (3) 1890–1930, the introduction and production of electric power; (4) 1930–1980, cheap oil and cars; and (5) information technology.

15 While R&D and innovation activities in the US are mainly led by the military and double-use industries where demand is limited, these activities are in other countries more consumer related, i.e. they are directed towards the development of goods and services for which demand exists everywhere. In addition, R&D is chiefly mission oriented towards big problems in countries such as the US, France and Britain. In countries such as Germany, Japan, Sweden or Switzerland, R&D is directed more towards the solution of practical problems.

16 Apart from the integration of separate markets, other supporting adjustment devices include deregulation and privatisation.

17 The era of imaginative individuals as major sources of innovation was the nineteenth century and earlier. To fly to the Moon involves the work of a large team of experts.

18 These irreversibilities include savings in factor (including energy) inputs per unit of output.

19 Economic growth may be propelled (among other elements) by the following three components (or by their combination): investment in capital and/or human resources, trade and technological change.

20 The time it takes for national income per capita to double in the early stages of industrialisation has fallen dramatically. In Britain it took around sixty years to do so after 1780, in Japan some thirty-five years after 1885, in Brazil eighteen years after 1961 and in China ten years after 1977. The main reason is technological progress. Countries are able to purchase foreign technology to make their home factors more productive.

There is also another dimension to new technology. While it was an increase in the physical capacity to influence the environment and to produce goods that brought about the industrial revolution in the nineteenth century, the current industrial revolution has a more qualitative dimension. A note of caution was exercised by Lipsey when he compared present-day England with that in the Elizabethan era: 'It took 400 years for England to develop from that stage to its present one. To do the same elsewhere in half of the time of 200 years would be a tremendous achievement; to aspire to do it in 25 or 50 years may be to court disaster' (Lipsey, 1992b: 755).

21   'The great majority of innovations did *not* come from formal R&D (even in organisations such as Du Pont ... which had strong in-house R&D facilities). Most ... came from production engineers, systems engineers, technicians, managers, maintenance personnel and of course production workers' (Freeman, 1994: 474).

22   International agreements are usually ambiguous. This allows diplomats to interpret them at home in their own favour. Conversely, constitutions and other domestic laws are (supposedly) clear. This is because domestic politicians want the voters to understand them in order to win their votes.

23   'The idea that we are living in an age of dramatic technological progress is mainly hype; the reality is that we live in a time when the fundamental things are actually not changing very rapidly at all. ... The slightly depressing truth is that technology has been letting us down lately' (Krugman, 1998b: 104). This may be the truth if one remembers the constant maintenance necessary for PCs. The only new good that altered life of the people on a larger scale during the 1990s was a mobile phone. The Internet is the only major service that has done the same in the same period. However, there is a continuous stream of small improvements in already existing goods.

24   *Lait cru* (unpasteurised milk) contains many bacteria. However, some (many) consumers prefer cheese made from such milk because of its special taste. For example, Camembert made from *lait cru* is dearer than other types of Camembert. If the EU bans unpasteurised cheeses, then jobs will be at risk and many consumers will be affected. There are many interests at stake. Unpasteurised cheese provoked an outbreak of food poisoning that claimed several victims in Switzerland. Such cheeses were banned for some time afterwards but slowly returned to the market.

25   If a country such as Germany sets higher standards than other EU countries, it could enforce those standards with trade restrictions. The purpose of Decision 3052/95 is to prevent such behaviour.

26   For a dissenting view about harmonisation the curious reader is invited to consult Krugman (1997: 120), who argues that 'the demand for harmonisation is by and large ill-founded both in economics and law; realistic political economy requires that we give it some credence, but not too much'.

27   A single firm can reduce average costs of production of two or more goods or services that share a common input without complete congestion. Identical technology can be employed for the production of differentiated output.

28   A large part of intra-industry trade is in parts and components.

29   The interested reader is invited to consult the surveys by Greenaway and Milner (1987) and Greenaway and Torstensson (1997).

30   This refers to the nationality that belongs to the EU.

31   Old Article 6.

32   Old Article 7*a*.

33   Old Articles 9–37. An exception to the general freedom of movement of goods is possible only in the case when such movement jeopardises public morality, security and the health of humans, animals or plants [Article 30 (Old Article 36)].

34   Old Articles 48–73.

35   Old Articles 95–99.

36   Old Article 130.

37   This Programme is also known as the White Paper, the Cockfield Report or the 1992 Programme.

38   Old Article 85.

39   Old Article 86.

40   Old Article 92.

41   There were ninety-one on-the-spot investigations including eighty-seven unannounced inspections in 1995 [European Commission (1996). *European Community Competition Policy*. Luxembourg: European Communities: 22]. There are no more recent official and publicly available data on this issue.

42 Public procurement contracts that surpass certain thresholds must be advertised in the *Official Journal* of the EU. The Directives operate within many different thresholds. For example, the threshold for public works is €5m, supply contracts for various goods and services have all different thresholds which are around €0.2m. There are, of course, loopholes. For example, certain public works may be split into a number of smaller ones that are below the limit. Another way of avoiding EU scrutiny is to underestimate the value of the procured goods and services. The supply of military goods is excluded from these rules.

43 *The Financial Times*, 10 May 2000: 2.

44 It was the US demand to exclude agriculture from the Agreement that resulted in the formation of the GATT. This resulted in a later backlash against the US in trade with the EU and Japan.

45 Old Article 115.

46 Between 1989 and 1991, the annual imports of Japanese cars into Italy more than doubled from 10,000 to 22,000 (*The Financial Times*, 5 August 1991).

47 There was little that the European Commission could do against the French unilateral action. This was not because of the fear of protests in France, but because it would take up to two years to settle the dispute in the European Court of Justice. 'If the Commission cannot bring the "offenders" into line fast, its confidence can be seriously damaged. Therefore, a change in the EU rules is necessary that would provide the Commission with the necessary instruments for a quick reaction' (*The European Voice*, 28 October 1999: 11).

48 In 1999, 54 per cent of all EU products followed EU standards, another 28 per cent followed international standards, while the remaining 18 per cent of products were covered by national standards. In 1987, the share of national standards was 72 per cent (Source: direct communication from the European Commission).

49 Old Articles 30 or 100 respectively.

50 An example is cars produced by Nissan in Britain. France limited imports of Japanese cars to 3 per cent of the domestic market and claimed that the Nissan Bluebird cars produced in Britain were Japanese in origin. An earlier informal guideline stated that Japanese cars produced in the EU would receive preferential (domestic) treatment in the EU market if local EU content was at least 60 per cent. In 1988, France asked that to receive national treatment (i.e. to be treated as goods produced domestically) the proportion of a good that must be of EU origin be increased to 80 per cent. Currently, in order to qualify for national treatment in the EU, the produced (assembled) cars must have 60 per cent of local (EU) content.

51 Canon invested over $100m and located a new production facility for photocopiers in the US, rather than build it in China or Malaysia where the production costs are lower. The reason was a special NAFTA rule of origin for copiers which requires 80 per cent of local value added (UNCTAD, 1999b: 15).

52 A comparative study of anti-dumping actions in the US, EU, Canada and Australia concluded that 90 per cent of imports that were unfairly priced according to anti-dumping rules would be found to be fairly priced under corresponding domestic rules of competition (UNCTAD, 1999b: 17).

53 Old Article 85.

54 Old Article 85(3).

55 *The Financial Times*, 12 May 2000: 1.

56 European Commission, 'Car prices in the European Union', 7 February 2000. As for other consumer goods, the greatest convergence in prices following the Single Market Programme was observed in highly traded goods, as well as in those that are more open to competition from non-EU producers. However, energy and construction are exceptions to such a trend. In general, a high degree of concentration in national markets is conducive to price disparity, whereas highly internationalised markets tend to ease price disparities (*European Economy*, 1996, pp. 134–9).

57 *The Economist*, 28 November 1998: 87.

58 A special and still unresolved issue refers to takeovers by foreign firms. If the foreign buyer comes from a country with relatively cheap capital (low rate of interest) relative to the country of the target firm, such an acquirer has an advantage over other potential buyers that have access to financial markets that charge higher interest rates. If the authorities in the country of the target firm want to retain domestic ownership of such a business, they could restrict takeovers by foreign firms and/or give subsidies to the domestic acquirers. A much more effective policy than such direct interference in business would be to keep the domestic macroeconomic policy in order and, hence, have a domestic capital market competitive with the international one.

59 At the beginning of 1997 Boeing's share of the world market by was 64 per cent, Airbus's was 30 per cent and McDonnell-Douglas's was 6 per cent. In Europe, the corresponding figures were Boeing 31 per cent, Airbus 37 per cent and McDonnell-Douglas 2 per cent (*Agence Europe*, 23 May 1997).

60 If to start a business requires overcoming substantial sunk costs, then mere deregulation (the Single Market Programme) may not be enough. Further measures (such as subsidies) may be necessary to provide an investment impetus to firms.

61 The degree of concentration was much lower in the food and drink than in the chemical industry. It was higher at the national than at the EU level because of the barriers to trade (European Communities, 1991: 227).

62 Privatisation in the former East Germany accounted for a part of the merger and acquisition activity in Germany.

63 This result was similar to the one reached in many studies on mergers in the US.

64 *The Economist*, 9 January 1999: 13.

65 Europe has forty battery producers compared with five in the US, fifty tractor makers while America has four and sixteen firms building railway engines, whereas the US has two (*The Economist*, 23 January 1999: 67). Some firms think that they may prosper better if they become huge through mergers and acquisitions.

66 Another important tool for the control of dominance in the EU market and for enhancing competition was the conclusion of the Uruguay Round in 1994. After ratification, this deal further liberalised international trade, increased competition and, hence, modified/limited the non-competitive behaviour of the concentrated EU industries.

67 These thresholds also apply to firms that originate outside the EU.

68 If competitive firms want to keep their lead, they need to follow developments not only in their own industry, but also in unrelated, but potentially competing, ones. Examples of 'learning-by-watching' may be found in the disappearance, almost overnight, of the market for cine cameras after the appearance of video cameras, the seismic shift in the market for mechanical watches after the invention of digital ones, and the move from dot matrix to laser printers or fibreoptics that evolved independently of the telecommunication technology.

69 Old Article 86.

70 The growing concentration of the semiconductor equipment and materials industries by a few Japanese enterprises created a strategic threat to both commercial and defence interests. For example, because of the concerns of the socialist members of the Japanese Parliament in 1983, the Ministry of International Trade and Industry (MITI) reportedly ordered Kyocera (a domestic manufacturer of high-technology ceramic products) not to take part in contracts to sell ceramic nose cones to the US Tomahawk missile programme (Graham and Krugman, 1995: 118). In another example, Nikon, one of only two Japanese suppliers of some kinds of semiconductor-producing machinery, withheld its latest models from foreign customers for up to two years after making them available to Japanese clients (Tyson, 1992: 146). The 'explanation' put forward was that the 'regular' customers needed to be served in a better way and before the others. The behaviour of IBM was similar. This firm has also refused to sell its components to other clients (Sharp and Pavitt, 1993: 144).

71 A refusal to supply goods or services was taken to be an infringement of Article 82. In the United Brands case (1976) the European Commission found that United Brands, the major supplier of (Chiquita) bananas to most of the EU countries, abused its dominant position by refusing to supply green bananas to Olesen, a Danish ripener and distributor. Although Olesen had taken part in an advertising operation with one of United Brands' competitors, the Court found that the reaction of United Brands to competitive threat was excessive and, hence, abusive. The discontinuance to supply bananas was a significant intrusion into the independence of small and medium-sized enterprises. United Brands was fined €1m by the Commission. The Court reduced the fine to €0.85m.

72 Old Article 92.

73 This Article, however, neither outlaws nor discourages state ownership of enterprises.

74 Old Article 112.

75 EU Guidelines for state aid for small and medium-sized enterprises (1992) state that these firms (defined as having fewer than fifty employees) may receive support of up to 15 per cent of investment cost. Enterprises with fifty to 250 employees may receive the same aid up to 7.5 per cent of their investment cost, while larger firms may get the same only in the assisted regions of the EU.

76 In the case of steel, shipbuilding or textiles, restructuring often means a reduction in production capacity.

77 Old Article 93.

78 A special type of public aid is in the form of public purchases. In Italy, for example, a law required that 30 per cent of contracts be awarded to firms based in the southern part of the country. The EU Court of Justice ruled in 1990 that such a law violated the public procurement directives. In other countries such as France or Germany there is no explicit buy-national law. Nonetheless, publicly owned enterprises (railways, PTT) are 'expected' to prefer home-made goods and services to foreign ones.

79 The biggest state-aid case that came before the Commission was the $9.4bn rescue package for Crédit Lyonnais, the French state-owned bank. It was approved in 1995 (*The Financial Times*, 27 July 1995: 13). The cost soared to $16.9bn in 1998 (*The Financial Times*, 7 May 1998: 2). One cannot avoid the impression that the approval by the Commission did not have political motivations. In addition, the Commission failed an important test. It should have requested a bigger reduction in the bank's business.

4 Industrial policy and production geography

4.1 Introduction

Explicit industrial policy as a part of overall economic policy did not attract the attention of research interests in the industrialised countries with market-based economies until the mid-1970s. This can be explained by the underlying economic developments. During the 1960s and early 1970s the industrialised countries experienced relatively fast economic growth with low rates of both inflation and unemployment. The prices of raw materials were stable and relatively low, while labour was able to move without major disturbances from agriculture to the manufacturing and services sectors. Excess demand for labour was met by a steady inflow of labour from abroad. This period was also characterised by sporadic government intervention to influence the national geography of production in the manufacturing and services sectors. Relatively free markets were operating smoothly without significant disruption. During this period, the GATT was active in the lowering of tariffs.

The 'golden 60s' were followed by a period whose principal characteristics were the result of a sharp increase in the price of oil in 1973. This triggered rises in inflation, unemployment and a deceleration in the rate of growth throughout the world. International competition increased sharply because suppliers were fighting in shrinking markets. It seemed that the free market system and the entrenched geography of production were not capable of coping satisfactorily with this situation. There developed an awareness of a need for alternative strategies (i.e. ones based on intervention in manufacturing, services and trade) to cope with the new situation. Industrial policy could be seen as a supply-side response to market imperfections. Discussion was less about the formation of capital and more about its sectoral, industrial and geographical allocation and use. It was also more about economic adjustment policy than industrial policy (a term disliked by both politicians and neo-classical economists). Nonetheless, the gloves were off in the debate about industrial policy in the developed market economies.

This chapter is structured as follows. Definitions of industrial policy, its rationale, intervention, instruments and selectivity are discussed in section 4.2. This is followed by a consideration of underlying principles of EU industrial policy, its evolution, importance and variety, technology policy and possible ways ahead. Additional analysis is devoted to the character and significance of services in general and in the EU in particular. The conclusion offers a list of forms and means that should be included in any self-respecting industrial policy.

4.2　Industrial policy issues

What is the meaning of an industrial policy?

An industry is usually taken to mean a group of firms that produce the same or similar kinds of good (or service) and which compete in the same market. The literature on modern industrial policy started its development in the early 1980s. There appeared various definitions of industrial policy. Before surveying a selection of them, it is helpful to recall the difference between competition and industrial policy. The former is directed towards the freeing of market forces, while the latter seeks to channel them (Geroski, 1987: 57). In addition, industrial policy may sometimes have strong anti-competitive results, such as the need for the functional and geographical concentration of business to achieve economies of scale.

Some definitions of industrial policy are specific and selective. Industrial policy can be defined as coordinated targeting. It is the selection of parts of the economy, such as firms, projects or industries, for special treatment (targeting), coupled with a coordinated government plan to influence industrial structure in defined ways (coordination) (Brander, 1987: 4). Industrial policy implies policies that relate to specific industries, such as the correction of restrictive business practices (Pinder, 1982: 44). Industrial policies can be those government policies that are intended to have a direct effect on a particular industry or firm (McFetridge, 1985: 1). Industrial policy is aimed at particular industries (and firms as their components) in order to reach ends that are perceived by the government to be beneficial for the country as a whole (Chang, 1994: 60). This definition does not, however, distinguish between the short- and long-term perspectives. Different policies need to be employed to achieve efficiency if the timescale changes.

Other definitions of industrial policy are broad, often overloaded, and include many areas of public policy. For example, 'industrial policy includes all government actions that affect industry such as domestic and foreign investment, innovation, external trade, regional and labour policies, environmental features and all other aspects' (Donges, 1980: 189). 'Industrial policy can be any government measure or set of measures used to promote or prevent structural change' (Curzon Price, 1981: 17). Industrial policy may mean all measures that improve the economy's supply potential: anything that will improve growth, productivity and competitiveness (Adams and Klein, 1983: 3). Another look at industrial policy can take it to mean a government policy action that is aimed at or motivated by problems within specific sectors. These 'problems' presumably occur in both declining and expanding (manufacturing or service) industries. The solutions to these problems are not necessarily sector specific, although that is a possibility (Tyson and Zysman, 1987a: 19). Initiation and coordination of government activities in order to influence and improve the productivity and competitiveness of particular industries or the whole economy is industrial policy (Johnson, 1984:

8). Industrial policy can be defined as the set of selective measures adopted by the state to alter industrial organisation (Blais, 1986: 4). Another definition states that its focus has been on the ideal relation between governments and markets. 'Industrial policy need not be equated with national planning. It is, rather, a formula for making the economy adaptable and dynamic' (Reich, 1982: 75, 79). 'The term industrial policy describes that group of policies whose explicit objective is to influence the operation of industry' (Sharp and Shepherd, 1987: 107). 'An industrial policy implies intervention by a government which seeks to promote particular industries in some way. This may be either to stimulate production and growth of an industry's size or to promote export sales' (Whalley, 1987: 84). This definition does not, however, include government influence on the decline of and exit from an industry. 'Industrial policy may be equated with intervention employed to cope with market failures or a price system that affects the allocation of resources' (Komiya, 1988: 4). 'All acts and policies of a government that relate to industry, constitute industrial policy' (Bayliss and El-Agraa, 1990: 137). Industrial policy is defined by the World Bank as 'government efforts to alter industrial structure to promote productivity-based growth' (World Bank, 1993: 304). It is not clear if this means that aid to ailing industries lies outside the scope of industrial policy. 'Industrial policy includes all actions that are taken to advance industrial development beyond what is allowed by the free market system' (Lall, 1994: 651). Industrial policy may also mean 'a set of public interventions through taxes, subsidies and regulations on domestic products or factors of production that attempt to modify the allocation of domestic resources that is the consequence of the free operation of market forces' (Gual, 1995: 9). To formulate a definition of industrial policy may be as difficult to describe as a Chinese dish. 'One US Supreme Court Justice tried to find a definition of pornography and said: "You know it when you see it, but you can't define it"; so it may be with industrial policy' (Audretsch, 1989: 10).

A critical definition of industrial policy states that it is 'the label used to describe a wide-ranging, ill-assorted collection of micro-based supply-side initiatives that are designed to improve market performance in a variety of mutually inconsistent ways. Intervention is typically demanded in cases with market failures and where major changes need to be effected quickly' (Geroski, 1989: 21).

Industrial policy may mean different things for various countries at different times. Developing countries look at industrial policy as a means of economic development. They may favour some industries over others. Once these countries become developed, industrial policy may be directed towards fostering free competition. In the former centrally planned economies, industrial policy meant planning and imposing production and investment targets in each sector and industry within it.

Industrialised countries have had implicit industrial policies for a long time. They are embodied in trade, competition, tax, R&D, standardisation, education, regional, public procurement and other policies that have derived effects on the industrial structure. This is due to the interdependence of economic policies within the economic system. Therefore, some countries have joint ministries of industry and international trade. This is the case, for instance, with the British Department of Trade and Industry (DTI) and the Japanese Ministry of International Trade and Industry (MITI), although there are differences in the powers and role in the economy between the two ministries.

In most developed countries the period after the Second World War was characterised by reductions in tariffs, as well as measures to prevent the demise of declining industries. However, governments' industrial policies may be a simple continuation of the old protectionism by more sophisticated means (Pinder *et al.*, 1979: 9). Governments' tax and transfer policies have their impact on demand, which affects the structure and location of manufacturing production. By direct production and supply of public goods, as well as through public procurement, governments influence, at least in part, the geography of production of their economies. Other government policies, such as foreign policy, have no direct effect on the size of the economic pie in their country. However, they can influence industrial structure, its geographical distribution and employment. This is the case when governments ban the export of (high-technology) goods abroad.

Three (non-mutually exclusive) broad types of industrial policy are macroeconomic, sectoral and microeconomic orientation. Macroeconomic orientation is least interventionist because it leaves the operation of industries and firms to market forces. Policy orientation simply improves the general economic climate for business. Sector-specific orientation becomes relevant when market failures affect certain industries. It tries to amend the particular market shortcoming. Microeconomic orientation of industrial policy may direct a government to act directly towards specific firms or industrial groups (Jacquemin, 1984: 4–5).

There are another three broad types of industrial policy: market oriented, interventionist or mixed. The first type (market oriented) fosters competition and free markets. The second (interventionist) policy may be conducted as in the centrally planned economies. In practice, industrial policy is most often a mixture of the first two. Most countries may be classified as 'massaged-market economies'.[1] The thing that most often differs between countries is not whether or not they intervene, but rather the degree and form of intervention in industry.

Industrial policy may be also be described as adjustment prone or adjustment averse. Adjustment-prone industrial policy stimulates adjustment of various industries to enter into new production, remain competitive or ease the exit from selected lines of production. Adjustment-averse industrial policy is the policy of protection, which impedes changes in an economy by preserving the status quo.

The level of industrial policy can be general or specific. The choice is between discrimination and non-discrimination. The degree of intervention should be as high as possible. This means that it needs to be general, i.e. available to every industry and enterprise. Once the policy is put in place, the market is perhaps the best tool to fine-tune the economy, to create and to exploit unforeseen opportunities, as well as to select the firms or industries that should take advantage of the employed policy instruments. Market forces may prevent players from the inefficient employment of resources. The policy should be tailored to suit local needs (industry or firm) in cases where there are no externalities. In addition, it should be used with care because governments are not infallible and may well make the wrong choice, as was the case with the French and British Concorde project.

Various economic policies have their impact on industrial policy. As seen in Chapter 2, they all have a strong spatial impact: not only trade policy, but also social, education, regional, energy, transport and other policy areas. Hence, most definitions of industrial policy include, at least implicitly, the need for a stable economic environment and coordination of various economic policies. Only then can specific targeting of industrial policy makes its full contribution to economic growth and improvement in productivity and competitiveness, the final objective being an increase in the standard of living. On such grounds, broad definitions of industrial policy may embrace all of these facets. Hence, industrial policy is an economic policy that shapes a country's comparative advantage. Its objective is to influence the change in national economic structure (reallocation of resources among sectors, industries, professions and regions) in order to enhance the creation and growth of national wealth, rather than to distribute it.

Rationale

The classical economic model based on free trade and perfect competition predicts that *laissez-faire* is universally beneficial and costless. However, the new theory of strategic[2] trade and industrial policy has shown that intervention can sometimes play a useful role in mitigating the shortcomings of market imperfections and can alter the national and international geography of production. In general, economic adjustment (industrial, sectoral, professional and geographical reallocation and use of resources) is prompted by an increase in GNP, as well as by changes in demand, technology, market structure, tastes, prices, foreign competition and marketing, all of which contribute to a potential loss (or increase) in current competitiveness. This adjustment is neither smooth nor easy nor costless nor fast, hence the need for an industrial policy.

Instead of relying on inherited and natural advantages, industrial policy may help in the conscious shaping of a country's comparative advantage through the supplies of trained labour and educated management with a specific profile (engineers vs. ethnographers), tax, infrastructure, public purchase and R&D policies. One thing, however, has to be clear from the outset. Both intervention (action) and *laissez-faire* (non-intervention) have an impact on the structure of industry and, hence, on the geography of production. The challenge for a government is to achieve the best balance between the two approaches. That is, however, not at all easy.

Countries in the EU and the US responded to the circumstances prevailing during the 1970s primarily by protectionism. Along with other industrialised countries, they realised that the solution to lagging productivity, recession, deteriorating export performance, increasing market penetration for manufacturing goods from developing countries and reallocation of some manufacturing activities outside the developed world may be found in policies that affect the structure and development of national industry. Nonetheless, inadequate economic performance is not a sufficient condition for the justification of industrial policy. The question is not whether the economy is operating (un)satisfactorily, but rather whether an industrial policy might have achieved a better result than a free market system (Adams, 1983: 405). Any policy has to be tested according to its gains and losses in a dynamic context.

Once free markets lose credibility as efficient conductors of an economy, the introduction of intervention (various economic policies) seems inevitable. The question then is 'How can the government intervene in the most efficient and least harmful way?'. The choice might be between leaving the economy to imperfect entrepreneurs and the possibly even greater riskier strategy of having it run by imperfect governments (Curzon Price, 1981: 20). However, there is no a priori reason why an economy run by imperfect governments should be at greater risk than one run by imperfect entrepreneurs. Both of these are second-best (suboptimal) solutions.

Risk-taking (entrepreneurship) has always been a significant engine of economic growth albeit the benefits achieved are accompanied by attendant dangers. And the costs of adjustment are borne principally by those that are weak or powerless. Thus, governments have often followed a defensive policy with the objective of securing employment in the short term and evading social tensions, at least during their term at the office. The socialisation of risk in the form of various economic policies may make life safer, but it also prevents both free operation of individual entrepreneurial activity and an even greater increase in the economic pie. This process may be seen as bowing to the public's desire to see a happy marriage between progress and stability (Blais, 1986: 41). Interestingly, however, in Britain rescuing a declining industry (coal) to protect jobs proved not to be the safe route to re-election for the government. Taxpayers and consumers are not unaware of the costs of such a rescue. However, in many countries strong trade unions in declining industries can still mobilise a strong lobbying influence. Those who have full confidence in the operation of a free market system say that the market would take care after itself. Why bother to change those things which will happen anyway? This school of thought fails to take account of a number of serious market imperfections.

The most influential reasons for intervention may be found in the loss of a competitive position, the management of expansion of new and the decline of old industries, the handling of industries subject to scale effects and externalities, and attracting footloose industries (Lipsey, 1987b: 117). Fostering strategic industries with strong forward and backward links to the rest of the economy can be a very attractive policy goal. These industries supply external or non-priced gains to the rest of the entire economy. Growing industries such as semiconductors, electronics or telecommunications have a much more profound spillover effect on the economy than do the furniture or clothing industries.

Technologies that are 'critical' for a large country's competitiveness and/or defence include those that deal with new materials, energy sources and environment; biotechnology and pharmacy; manufacturing, including production of tools; information gathering, communications, data processing and computers; and transportation and aeronautics, including navigation. Because of large sunk costs and economies of scale, small and medium-sized countries do not have the means, or indeed the necessity (if they can acquire them through trade), to develop all or most of those technologies and make them commercially viable. What these countries may do instead is to select a 'critical' mass of 'critical' technologies or parts of them (e.g. components, basic chemicals) and try to excel in those market niches, as is the case with Switzerland, Austria and the Benelux and Scandinavian countries.

Another classification of the reasons for an industrial policy groups them into three broad categories: respectable, false and non-economic (Curzon Price, 1990: 159–67).

Respectable arguments include *market failures* because, in practice, a perfect competition model does not always lead to a stable equilibrium. However, the problem is that a market failure such as wage rigidity or monopolies can frequently be traced to a previous intervention by the government. Another pretext for intervention is *domestic distortions*. A uniform rate of value-added tax (VAT) would have a neutral effect on the consumption of goods or services in a country, but a reduction in VAT on food, for example, may cause some resources to shift to that industry at a time when the telecommunication or data processing industries could have made better use of them. *Infant industries* provide good excuse for intervention, but the problem is that there are many old 'infants' that may never become self-sustaining. Is Airbus one of them? One can also build an intellectually respectable case for industrial policy based on *positive externalities* and spillover effects (Krugman, 1993a: 160–1).[3] These include benefits arising from the establishment of common technical standards for the production and/or operation of goods, e.g. in the telecommunications industry. However, mistakes can be costly if the wrong industry is targeted, e.g. computers in France, Concorde (Britain and France) and petrochemicals and aluminium in Japan before the first oil shock. The process may become overpoliticised and subject to strong lobbying as in the case of *public goods* that everyone wants and consumes, although these goods could be produced at a loss.

The first *false* argument in favour of intervention is the issue of *employment*. Employment subsidies used to prolong the life of jobs in declining sectors are often implemented at the expense of growing industries that may need them to expand operations and which could provide more and better jobs in the future. Likewise, proponents of the *balance of payments* argument for intervention tend to forget that resources that move into the protected industries may come from those industries with better export opportunities. Hence, a drop in imports may provoke a fall in exports.

Non-economic arguments may be quite strong. It is often hard to dispute the issue of *national security*. This is a political process that confounds the predictive abilities of an economist. The problem is that it may be pushed to the limit in the case of industries that can be labelled as essential for national defence. In general, 'smart bombs' and electronic and nuclear weapons counteract the national security argument for intervention. Long-term supply contracts from allies and stockpiling may be considered prior to intervention. *Social arguments* for intervention, focused on the redistribution rather than the creation of material wealth, such as regional development or the protection of environment and culture, may have some non-economic weight during any discussion about intervention.

The relative shares of the manufacturing industry and agriculture in GDP and employment have been declining continuously in industrialised countries over the past decades. In 1998, the GDP of the EU was accounted for predominantly by services (66 per cent), with the rest is distributed between manufacturing (31 per cent) and agriculture (3 per cent). Hence, the process of deindustrialisation leads countries to a post-industrial society. These countries are better called service rather than industrialised economies, because manufacturing industry is a statistically 'shrinking' sector in relation to services. It needs to be noted that some manufacturing jobs in developed countries have geographically relocated to the developing world.

One has to be very cautious with generalisations. Many services (around half) are directly linked to the manufacturing of goods, such as transport, finance, telecommunications and other business services including everything from cleaning offices to business consultancy and advertising. Such services are not directly aimed at individuals for their personal consumption. If they are included in manufacturing and agriculture, then the relative share of these sectors in the national economy is significantly increased. In fact, they are most intimately linked with each other. In regions with few services, manufacturing industry performs below its potential. Hence, the relation between manufacturing and services is not one way. New manufacturing technologies require new, better and/or more services, while services (such as R&D) may create new manufacturing technologies that may, in turn, create demand for services and so on. Profound changes in the structure of manufacturing and services have blurred the distinction between the two economic sectors.

A relative increase in the demand for services and growth in this sector was made possible by an increase in the productivity of the manufacturing sector. This has made more resources available for the services sector of the economy. Increased productivity results in a reduction in the price of manufactured goods, leading to an increase in disposable funds for the consumption of services. This makes industrial policy in manufacturing and services interesting for consideration.[4]

The importance of manufacturing has been studied by the MIT Commission on Industrial Policy. From a study the US the Commission drew the following conclusions (Dertouzos *et al.*, 1990: 39–42):

- In 1987 in the US, imports of goods and services were ten times higher than exports of services. It is necessary to manufacture and export goods in order to pay for imports. The more resources are reallocated to services, the lower the chance of balancing the balance of payments.
- Moving resources from the manufacturing industry into services causes a shift from a sector with relatively high productivity growth to one with lower growth.

- Almost all R&D is carried out in the manufacturing sector.
- National defence depends on the purchase of a great deal of manufactured goods. If a country starts to depend on foreign suppliers, national security may be placed in jeopardy.

Industrial policy issues

The role of the government

The standard comparative advantage and factor proportions theories of international trade may be satisfactory for the explanation of trade in primary goods. However, they are less satisfactory in explaining trade in industrial goods. Manufacturing can be seen as a collection of industries with no factor abundance base. On those grounds it is difficult to explain why the US exports computer software, why France exports perfumes while Japan exports copiers, cameras and VCRs, or why the Swiss export chocolate, chemicals and watches.

A country's comparative advantage not only depends on its geographical resource endowment, but is also shaped over time by the actions of both businesses and government. Government economic policies may affect comparative advantage over time by influencing the quantity and quality of labour, capital, incentives and technology. Comparative advantage in manufacturing industries is not an unchangeable condition of nature, but often the outcome of economic policies that affect incentives to save, invest, innovate, diffuse technology and acquire or 'import' human capital.

Until the 1970s market imperfections and multiple equilibria were at the margin of orthodox economic analysis, but these imperfections are at the heart of the analysis of the new theory of trade and industrial policy. A country's size, regional disequilibria, skill, mobility and unionisation of labour, R&D, sunk costs, economies of scale, competition and bankruptcy laws are just a few imperfections. To ignore them is to fail to realise that their effects can be mitigated by economic policy (Tyson, 1987: 67–71). In the field of manufacturing, a government has at its disposal several policy instruments. These include trade policy (tariffs, subsidies and NTBs) that may reduce competition and anti-trust policy that increases it; preferential tax treatment; non-commercial loans and loan guarantees as a support to risk capital; exports, insurance and other subsidies; public procurement; support for education and vocational retraining; assistance to workers to improve their professional and geographical mobility; and the provision of public or publicly financed R&D.

Free competition within an economic union brings costs of adjustment to which governments, voters and citizens are not indifferent. It is often forgotten that increased competition brings benefits in terms of economic restructuring. The costs of adjustment are often highly concentrated on the (vociferous) few and are usually temporary, whereas the benefits are dispersed over a long period of time and throughout the society, but in relatively small instalments to everyone. In the real, second best and imperfect world, there may be enough scope for both market mechanism and select intervention (economic policy).

The role of governments as organisers of national economies is coming under increasing inquiry. Governments can play at least four roles in the economic activity. They are:

- initiation;
- supervision;
- ownership of assets;
- arbitration.

The role of government as an organising force in a market economy is increasingly being re-examined. In spite of general agreement about the need to reduce the extent of public intervention in the allocation of resources in a national economy, it is a fact that the countries that have had the most impressive economic achievements during the past two decades are those whose governments exerted a strong and positive influence over all facets of commercial affairs (Dunning, 1994b: 1). However, the actions of governments, markets and firms are not substitutes for each other, but they do need to be mutually supportive. Instead of being obstacles, they need to be structured in such a way as to support and facilitate the actions of the others. This is a formidable task indeed.

A general reduction in tariffs and NTBs, as well as economic integration, may increase a country's market. However, free markets often fail to take a long-term view of society's needs when making structural adjustments. Such adjustment (the transfer of resources from declining to growing industries) is not necessarily a swift, cheap and smooth process. In addition, it is a risky operation, as the future of expanding industries is not secure in the long term. If (a big if) astute adjustment policies (intervention) can facilitate these shifts and the new use of resources by providing incentives and support to the private businesses to adjust to the new situation, then intervention may have a certain justification.

One can make predictions about the model of economic adjustment based on the characteristics of a country's financial system. First, if this system relies on capital markets that allocate resources by competitively established prices, the adjustment process is company-led. The allocation decisions are the responsibility of firms, as is the case in the US. Secondly, in a credit-based financial system where the government is administering prices, the adjustment process is state-led (such as the past experiences of Japan and France). Finally, in a credit-based system where price formation is dominated by banks, the adjustment process can be considered as negotiated. An example can be found in Germany (Zysman, 1983: 18).

A common view of the world holds that firms play Cournot–Nash games against all other players (each firm decides on a course of action, e.g. optimising output, on the assumption that the behaviour of the other firms remains constant), whereas governments play the Stackelberg game (the agent knows the reaction functions of all others) against firms and Cournot–Nash games against other governments (Brander and Spencer, 1985: 84). Unfortunately, these are all games that can produce relatively unstable equilibria and fluctuations in prices. In contrast, collusion among the players would lead to a relatively stable (Chamberlin) solution.

Justified intervention

The key question in the debate on industrial policy (the relationship of states and market) still remains: can imperfect governments make the shift of resources any better than imperfect markets? The answers is 'generally not', but this does not mean that market solutions are always superior to other ones. Just as the dangers of market failure are often exaggerated, so are the competencies of governments. Nonetheless, in some cases a government's intervention (policy) may fare better than a free market solution. Here are some examples of situations in which intervention may be justified.

First, the time horizon in which private markets operate is relatively short. They may not foresee countries' long-term needs in the face of changing circumstances, capabilities and opportunities with a high degree of accuracy. Japanese manufacturing is financed to a large extent by bank credits, whereas US industry uses this source of finance to a much lesser extent. This means managers of Japanese firms who asks their bank manager for a loan can justify the request on the grounds of the profits that will accrue when 'their ship comes in'. Managers in a comparable American firm in a similar situation must be sure that they can see the funnel of the ship in the distance. Hence, US industrial production is much more affected by the short-term interests of shareholders than is Japanese industry. The major goal of Japanese and German bank and enterprise managers is to ensure a firm's long-term competitive position in the market and thus they tend to look favourably on risky investments such as the commercialisation of new technologies. In contrast, the US system favours readily measurable physical (mergers and acquisitions) over intangible assets such as education or R&D. Government policy can shift this short-term perspective towards longer-term economic considerations. However, less than perfect foresight can lead banks into bad loans, which can culminate in financial crisis, as occurred the developing countries during the 1980s or Japan at the end of the 1990s. Japan and the newly developed countries such as Korea had been held up as examples of a successful manufacturing-led development path based on intervention. These Asian countries were delivering 'good news' for a long time. Much of the credit for these achievements went to government planners who 'new what they were doing'. However, when serious regional crises emerged in the late 1990s (essentially because of lightly regulated banking, which was subject to severe moral hazard problems), the truth was revealed: they didn't know. Sceptics argue that Japan and Korea would have had an ever steeper growth curve had it not been for selective intervention. Given macroeconomic stability, equilibrium and a stable exchange rate, high and stable savings and investment rates, an enterprising spirit, a respectable level of education, relatively competitive labour markets and relatively liberal trading system were more than enough to stimulate even faster growth. The contribution of selective intervention was negligible or harmful (Pack, 2000: 51).

Second, in a different case, risk-averse governments may countenance stockpiling in order to cushion the effect of a possible crisis. Private markets may not have the inclination and/or funds to do the same in the long term. A government may estimate the cost of this kind of risk in terms of GDP that would be sacrificed in the case of an unexpected reduction in the availability of certain inputs.

Third, governments may wish to keep some facilities for the home production as a bargaining chip to use with foreign suppliers while negotiating prices of long-term supply contracts. This should deter foreign monopolies from charging monopoly prices.

Fourth, market forces are quite efficient in allocating resources among producers and allocating goods and services among consumers in simple and static settings. Much of the power of markets in these circumstances emerges from the fact that prices convey all the necessary information to participants in the market. This enables them to act independently, without explicit coordination, and still reach a collectively efficient solution. It is possible that markets can, at least in principle, solve simple and static problems in a remarkably efficient way, but it is not entirely surprising to learn that the free market game is less successful in more demanding circumstances with market imperfections. Adjustment problems occur because of the unsatisfactory operation of the market/price game viewed from the long-term vantage point. It is the aim of forward-looking intervention to set the economy on the road towards the desired long-term equilibrium.

Fifth, basic research provides significant positive externalities (spillovers) throughout the economy. These social gains are in most cases difficult for private markets to grasp because the private risks and costs may be very high and the benefits uncertain. In addition, without interventions, such as patents and other intellectual property rights, free markets cannot guarantee sufficient pecuniary returns to the private innovator. The outputs of successful basic research fuel technological progress in the country. In most countries, such research is funded in full or in part by the government either directly (subsidy) or indirectly (tax relief). Governments and private businesses share the risk.

Sixth, industrial policy may ease economic adjustment in a more efficient and equitable way than free market forces. This policy may provide support for R&D, education and training, support for geographical and professional mobility of labour, investment subsidies, protection and other support for the improvement of infrastructure during the early fragile period of a new industry. Free market forces fail to do so. As for adjustment and exit from ailing industries, government policy may offer unemployment benefits, vocational training and early retirement schemes. Industrial policy can, to an extent, both anticipate and shape these changes. It can be involved either directly in picking the winners/losers or indirectly by creating the business environment in which firms can make choices in a potentially successful and desirable way.

Seventh, agriculture is a sector in which every government intervenes. Because of the impact of weather conditions, free market forces cannot achieve the reliability of supply and stability of incomes of the farm population relative to the labour force in the manufacturing sector. In addition, governments seek to secure the domestic supply of farm goods in circumstances of war, as well protecting the landscape and environment.

The eighth reason for the introduction of an industrial policy is that this policy may be able to respond, with various internal and external (retaliatory) measures, to the economic policies of other countries. Left alone, market forces may take advantage of foreign policies in the short term, but if the long-term strategy of foreign competitors is to undermine the importing country's home production by means of predatory pricing in order to create an international monopoly, then the long-term effect may be detrimental for the importing country's welfare. An industrial policy may be a suitable response because it can change the possible free market outcome.

Instruments

Tariffs (trade policy) have historically been the most important instrument of industrial policy. After a number of rounds of multilateral reduction in tariffs under the auspices of GATT/WTO, the use of this instrument has been restricted in scope and reduced in power. However, other methods of intervention have developed. Some of these represent protectionist pressures against adjustment, while others are adjustment oriented. They include:

- subsidies for exports, production, education, R&D and investment;
- NTBs;
- tax, exchange rate and credit policy;
- public purchases;
- price and exchange controls;
- regulation of the market (such as licensing);
- technical and other standards;
- direct production by the state;
- provision of infrastructure;
- competition and concentration policy.

The most benign intervention is the kind that does not harm other businesses and sectors. The most effective instruments of such an industrial policy include macroeconomic stability, education and the provision of infrastructure. Low inflation, a stable exchange rate and slightly positive real rates of interest may be the best tools of such an industrial policy. Savings will increase and entrepreneurs will have the chance to observe and shape their future with a relatively high degree of accuracy. Well-educated managers and a well-trained workforce (investment in human capital as a created factor) provide the economy with the most valuable assets capable of solving problems. Moreover, in many cases, private businesses are not interested in investing in infrastructure (sewage systems, roads, bridges, etc.), so the government needs to step in.

Subsidies may be a distorting instrument of industrial policy. They may diminish incentives for the advance of profitable firms if they are always taxed in order to provide the government with revenue to subsidise inefficient enterprises. A subsidy that stimulates the introduction of new capital may distort a firm's choice of technologies. This is relevant for firms that use capital and labour in different proportions. If a firm has to pay the full cost of capital it might choose another technology. A one-off subsidy to investment may help a firm buy time and adjust to an unexpected change in demand or technology. If the value of subsidies and other favours is smaller than the value added in the given industry, then subsidisation may be justified (but determining this can be quite difficult). If subsidies are provided on a permanent basis for the protection of employment to an industry or firm, there is no incentive for the management to perform as efficiently as in those enterprises or industries where market criteria dominate. A permanently subsidised industry or firm is a very likely candidate for nationalisation.

Sufficient subsidies will always maintain output (in ailing industries) at a level that would be unsustainable in free market conditions. Emerging industries, where investment risk is quite high, have to offer the prospects of relatively higher rewards than elsewhere in the economy in order to attract factors. Gains in productivity in these new businesses may be able to cushion increases in pecuniary rewards to investors without increases in prices. However, faced with the possibility of higher wages in one industry, trade unions may press for increases in wages elsewhere in the economy. Without increases in productivity, the result may be an increase in prices throughout the economy. Nonetheless, the industries that use new technologies and in which productivity is higher than elsewhere in the economy may be one step ahead of other businesses in this race.

The policy of shoring up a 'dying' industry for an excessively long period is like moving forwards but looking backwards. It may be preferable to compensate redundant labour rather than continue to shore up ailing firms. Compensation to redundant labour needs to be provided by the public authorities because the whole society benefits from the process of industrial change and adjustment. Shareholders of dying firms should not be compensated for the depreciation in the value of their shares. They should channel their funds into the growing businesses that need fresh capital for expansion, not to those that are declining and that do not need it (Curzon Price, 1981: 27–9).

In contrast to industries that use ageing technologies, emerging ones require venture capital: they may be quite small, numerous, unstable and have uncertain future. When they are in trouble their voice may not be heard as loudly as that of declining industries. Investment in emerging firms is risky because many of them collapse before they reach maturity.[5] However, these firms are the greatest propelling agents of a modern economy. Although many of them disappear from the market, many of them stay and new ones are created. A high birth rate of new firms is the best indication of the vitality of a system which creates incentives, so that many new enterprises may be started and the risk accepted. Alfred Marshall drew an analogy between the forest (industry, sector or the whole economy) and the trees (individual firms). Trees may grow and decay for individual reasons, but what is important for the economy is that the forest grows.

All protectionist measures offered to an industry should be conditional, otherwise the problems of the industry can be exacerbated. If the protected industry is a declining one, then its adjustment may be postponed or reversed by production or employment subsidies. This increases costs to society in the long term because the desired change (transfer of resources from low-profit to high-profit industries) does not take place. The adjustment policy needs to be of limited duration. It should involve both public funds and private capital, as well as make the cost of action as transparent as possible. In addition, the recipients of assistance should be expected to develop comparative advantages prior to the termination of that help. Market processes should be encouraged and managerial practices improved.

It has been argued, not without dispute, that protectionism did not cost the US economy any more than the trade deficit did. The real harm done by protectionism (reduction in the efficiency of production because of a fragmentation of markets, as well as prevention of specialisation and economies of scale) is more modest than was usually assumed in the case of the US. The major industrial nations suffer more, in economic terms, from the relatively unattractive problems for economic analysis such as 'avoidable traffic congestion and unnecessary waste in defence contracting' than they do from protectionism. To take the most extreme example, the cost to taxpayers of the savings and loan bailout alone will be at least five times as large as the annual cost to US consumers of all US import restrictions' (Krugman, 1990b: 36). The reasons why protectionism features relatively highly on the public agenda can be found in politics and symbolism. Politically, free trade offsets economic nationalism, while symbolically free trade is a cornerstone of liberal democracies. In addition, those involved in protected businesses, such as agriculture and manufacturing industries, that employ ageing technologies tend to vote in large numbers, unlike the rest of the population.

Direct subsidies for R&D or indirect subsidies in the form of public procurement are powerful instruments for the support of industries that introduce new technologies or new goods and services. The volume of demand and its structure provides the most important incentive for production. This is also crucial for the strategic industries, whose activities provide external and non-priced gains through linkages and externalities to the rest of the economy (examples include the machine tool industry, computers, telecommunications and data-processing).[6] If start-up costs create a barrier to entry into a strategic industry, the government may step in and help out. If the governments of other countries are subsidising their strategic industries, the case for intervention by the domestic government can look very persuasive. In the early unstable phase of the introduction of a new production technology, good or service, a secure government demand provides a powerful impetus for the firm to develop the product and open new markets. If this production does not become self-sustaining within a specified period of time, then it may never become profitable and resources that may be allocated for protection may be used elsewhere in the future with a greater efficiency in improving competitiveness.

The costs of subsidies need to be considered before intervention. A subsidy to one firm is a tax on others. If there is the chance of high returns in the future, such a tax might be worth bearing, but the gains are impossible to judge in advance.

Once a government starts handing out subsidies, demands for more go on expanding without end. At that point, political power, rather than 'economic sense', determines who and where gets what. The long isolation of an industry from market forces may remove the incentive to respond swiftly to signals that come from competition in international markets.

When affording protection to an industry, it must be on the condition that the schedule of protection/intervention will be revised downwards over time. Protection that is not temporary and selective may create serious adjustment problems and increase costs in the future. The strategy of selection and the transitory nature of protection may provide a limited adjustment period to an industry by mitigating the full impact of international competition. This programme does not ensure the existence of inefficient industries and firms but rather their adjustment and exit from declining industries. The self-liquidation of protection is perhaps the only way of keeping up the incentive to adjust. If adjustment programmes offer funds to firms, then this must be under the condition that these funds are spent on specified activities. Technical advisory boards that represent a wide community should oversee adjustment programmes (Tyson and Zysman, 1987b: 425).

Public intervention in many countries has primarily, but not exclusively, been directed towards 'problem' industries. These have usually been the coal, steel, textile, footwear and agriculture industries. However, there appears to be growing interest in intervening in emerging industries where technology changes fast. Intervention in this case takes the form of providing or subsidising innovation and R&D, special tax treatment of new technologies (tax holidays and subsidies), training of labour, education of management, government procurement and provision of infrastructure, as well as more general instruments such as planning, policy guidelines and exchange of information.

Many of these instruments may be applied to a single target simultaneously, and may sometimes be in conflict. If the objective is to increase efficiency, then competition and concentration may be conflicting. Many industries may not operate efficiently without a certain degree of concentration dictated by minimum efficient economies of scale. So, this has to be accepted. Small countries usually do not have very restrictive anti-monopoly laws, because efficient production in the home (unprotected) market and possibly even abroad often allows the existence of only one efficient production unit. Countries such as France foster a policy of concentration and efficiency, whereas others such as the US, because of the huge home market, have strong anti-monopoly legislation that favours free competition. Inward-looking industries whose production technologies in the declining phase of their life cycle traditionally lobby in every country for protection, whereas the emerging industries, which are oriented to the widest international market, support free trade.

Small and medium-sized enterprises

It was a strongly held belief in Europe during the 1960s that large American-style companies were the key factor in the economic growth of a country. These enterprises may, among other things, spend substantial funds on R&D and increase the international competitiveness of their output. Hence, mergers and acquisitions were encouraged. That policy left Europe with a number of slumbering industrial giants, ill-equipped to face the challenges of the 1970s and 1980s (Geroski and Jacquemin, 1985: 175). However, experience has shown that those countries that spend most on R&D do not necessarily have the highest rates of growth. It was also realised that SMEs,[7] largely forgotten or pushed to the outskirts of traditional economic analysis, are important players in economic revival and employment. Subsequently, the policy that strongly encouraged mergers and acquisitions was abandoned. It is recognised that, per unit of investment, more jobs are created by SMEs than by large companies. This may be one of the outcomes of the business policy of (large) firms that want to avoid conflicts with organised labour. Product differentiation demands production on a smaller scale and decentralisation of business. This is radically different from the prevailing theoretical expectations during the 1960s.

An expansion of SMEs started after the first oil shock (1973). However, jobs created by SMEs often have the disadvantage of being relatively less secure than those in large firms. Being small, these firms need to be flexible if they want to withstand competition. Flexible SMEs often use hit-and-run tactics in their business, linked with low sunk costs, as they can react faster to new business opportunities than more rigid, large firms. However, SMEs are often less able than large companies to behave 'strategically' and do not have as much lobbying power. Despite this, SMEs are necessary for the balanced growth of an economy, as they provide links among various subsectors. In general, neither large businesses nor SMEs can be efficient in isolation. They both need each other. Big businesses may use specialised SMEs as subcontractors and buffers against fluctuations in demand.

Whereas industrial policy deals with selected industries, policy on SMEs deals with firms of a specific size in all industries. The aim of SME policy is to rectify market imperfections that may work to the disadvantage of smaller firms (uncertain future, high risk, potential isolation, low asset value although not necessarily of 'low quality'). This policy also exploits the positive aspects of relative smallness, such as organisational flexibility, fast and smooth flow of information, product differentiation and custom-made goods and services.

Diversification and reallocation of resources

The promotion of adjustment of some industries does not always go smoothly. Some ailing industries are well-established, relatively large employers of labour with a strong political lobby. This is often the case with the steel industry. However, some steel firms undergo adjustment quite successfully. This was the case with the US Steel Company, which closed thirteen steel-making units and diversified out of steel. This company invested funds in a shopping centre in Pittsburgh, Pennsylvania, and a chemical business in Texas. Steel-making came to account for only 11 per cent of US Steel's operating income (Trebilcock, 1986: 141). Other steel companies prefer a quiet life. They neither innovate nor compete, but they are able to mobilise powerful political forces and government policy instruments (e.g. tariffs, quotas, NTBs, subsidies) in order to resist adjustment (contraction in output and labour redundancies).

The response of a number of US firms to shocks such as an increase in labour costs was to stick to the same technology but to invest abroad where labour costs are lower. In contrast, the response of Japanese firms to the same shock was to change technology and increase productivity. In addition, some Japanese TNCs operating in the US increased the US content of their goods over and above the domestic content of their US counterparts in the same industry. A number of US firms wanted to compete with Japanese TNCs in the home market not necessarily on the basis of productivity, but rather on the grounds of low labour costs. Thus, many US firms started either to source heavily from abroad (developing countries) or to geographically relocate their labour-intensive operations there or both. Japanese TNCs operating in the US increased productivity, so that, for example, by the mid-1980s colour TVs sold in the US by domestically owned firms had less local content than those made by Japanese competitors. In 1987, cars produced in the US by Honda had a local content of over 60 per cent. This was expected to increase to 75 per cent over the following ten years (Graham and Krugman, 1995: 79–80).

The newly industrialised countries have substantially increased their competitiveness in traditional industries such as steel, shipbuilding and textile. Their output position is irreversible in the medium and, perhaps, long term. These industries cannot be recovered in the developed market economies on the grounds of reductions in wages. Such a policy would involve a waste of resources, as trade unions would resist cuts in wages to meet the level of wages prevailing in the newly industrialised countries which have productivity at a level similar to that in developed market economies.

When economic adjustment is spread over a number of years, it may appear that it is easier and less costly per unit of time. Some 'breathing space' for structural change (slowing down the attrition or keeping ailing industries alive) may be achieved, but this argument is not always valid. First, the damage to the rest of the economy is greater the longer a depressed industry is allowed to last and, second, there is no evidence that prolonged adjustment is any easier to bear than quick surgery. Even direct costs may turn out, in practice, to be higher (Curzon Price, 1981: 120).

Picking the winner/loser

The new theory of trade and strategic industrial policy found, in contrast to the neo-classical theory, that some manufacturing and service industries are relatively more important to an economy than others. These are the industries with economies of scale, numerous forward and backward linkages and non-priced spillover effects (externalities) on the rest of the economy. Privileges to these industries *may* create a new irreversible competitive advantage for a country.[8]

It needs to be clear from the outset that the findings of the new theory are not prescriptions for economic policy, but rather an agenda for further research (Krugman, 1993b: 164). A selective industrial policy goes hand in hand with a policy of picking a winner (creating a national champion) or a loser (bailing out). Industries are established or maintained in or removed from certain geographical locations. This process has always been difficult and risky and has demanded considerable and costly information. If this were not so, then you would probably not read this book, but rather look at the stock market report, and invest and increase the value of your assets by several zeros daily. Tomorrow's winner, if wrongly chosen and requiring permanent subsidies, may become the day after tomorrow's loser. When intervening, it is important to have reasonable aims and it is preferable to use policy tools in an indirect way and be ready to withdraw if undesirable events occur in order to prevent even greater damage.

The preference for picking the winner most usually occurs in those countries whose domestic market is small and unable to support the competition of several firms operating at the optimum level of efficiency. In theory, national free market policies can be fostered in large countries, such as the US, which can leave market forces to select the best suppliers. Smaller countries usually have to rely on selective policies, which are potentially riskier. They have to make the best use of the limited amount of available resources. These resources have to be concentrated on selected industries (specialisation). Such an industrial and trade policy may be termed 'cautious activism', which should not be taken to mean protectionism.

Whereas France relies on a relatively centralised model of the economy, Germany has fostered a decentralised model. However, these two countries have achieved a similar level of economic success (de Ghellinck, 1988: 140). When picking the winner, a government chooses between supporting emerging industries and propping up ailing ones (protection of the existing structure which is adjustment-averse). The balance between the two depends upon both the power of the industries involved and the aims of the government.

The policy of singling out certain industries or firms for special treatment inevitably means ignoring the problems of all the others. The 'neglected' businesses may be at a relative disadvantage because they cannot count on direct support from the state if they happen to be in need. In addition, they are taxed in one way or another in order to provide funds for the public support of the 'privileged' businesses. This drains funds for investment in the promising enterprises. Such a policy has a strong impact on the geography of production.

Neglecting emerging and expanding industries with strong positive externalities can reduce the inclination of entrepreneurs to take risks and jeopardise the growth of the economy in the future. If a government cannot formulate the basic structural objectives of national economic policy, then the politically strongest segment of business will seize it.[9] Policy will be formulated in a hurry in response to the political pressures of the moment, with the likely outcome of protecting troubled industries. Independence, resistance to business pressures and clear economic objectives on the part of government remove extemporisations in economic policies. If this were not the case, a country's industrial policy would be an instrument for supporting obsolete industries and a brake on expanding ones (Tyson and Zysman, 1987a:

22). The history of trade and industrial policy (just look at the GATT rounds of negotiations) reveals how hard it is to combat the entrenched interests of producers.

Output grows fastest in emerging industries. These industries do not necessarily create a significant number of direct jobs but, as a result of linkages and other externalities, they have good potential to create indirect jobs. There has, however, been a notable technological improvement in declining industries such as textiles and steel. Thus, the distinction between the two kinds of industries is mostly for analytical purposes, as there are *no industries* with obsolete production technologies, *but* rather *firms* (within those industries) that employ ageing technology. An astute government may note that the industries are no longer sharply divided in 'good' and emerging industries such as electronics and 'bad' and declining ones such as shipbuilding as was the case in 1970s and 1980s. In fact, it has become apparent that there is to a large extent a 'global' structure of manufacturing whatever the industry. In these circumstances, the law of supply and demand will always locate the lowest value-added part of the production chain in the geographical area with the lowest wages. In these circumstances, a smart option for the risk-averse developing country may be to choose first to establish a good 'declining' industry, rather than an uncertain expanding one. Of course, the potential consequence of this type of expectation and choice may be a decline in the standard of living relative to countries that have gone for a different development model and are successful (?!) in its implementation.

Targeting is linked to four basic issues. These are:

- which industries or firms should receive support;
- what kind of support should be provided;
- where they are located;
- how long the assistance should last.

The industries that are singled out for 'special treatment' are usually those that are significant employers and those that have important externalities. In addition, if private markets do not favour risky investments, such as the development of alternative sources of energy, then government may also single out such investments for special treatment.

If domestic regulations regarding safety standards are stricter and more costly to implement than abroad, then, other things being equal, this may place home firms at a disadvantage relative to foreign competitors. Such a case may be used as an argument for demanding some national public 'support' and international involvement in these affairs in order to enforce foreign competitors to adhere to a similar level of environment protection. This issue is important regarding the Eastern enlargement of the EU.

Political reasons such as national defence and pride may influence decisions about support for certain industries. Assistance should cease as soon as the beneficiary becomes profitable; or once it becomes obvious that this will never happen (governments are on the whole known to be unwilling to slash subsidies when there is evidence of failure); or after the expiration of the specified period of assistance.

Japan is an example of a country that has reaped the fruits of conscious targeting of certain manufacturing industries for several decades. As a result it has stayed one step ahead of its competitors with regard to new technologies[10] in the targeted industries. During the 1960s, the target industries were steel and shipbuilding because of their significant externalities. Another target was the toy industry. During the 1970s the targets were machine tools and cars. The target for the 1980s was electronics (photocopiers, computers, audio and video equipment). For the 1990s it was the semiconductors industry. This may be taken as an example of the shaping of comparative advantage in a dynamic context for a specified, relatively limited, period of time. Japanese 'targeting' was first and foremost an information-collecting, interpretation and transmission process which helped the individual firms to make investment decisions. Japan emphasised intervention in technological *areas* that created a large bilateral trade surplus with the US, rather than intervention in *firms*. However, in spite of the success in high-technology industries, average living standards in Japan are below those in the US or EU. Part of the explanation may be found in the relatively high proportion of Japanese national resources that are devoted to stagnant industries compared with in the US.

However, targeting has not always been successful, for a variety of reasons. During the 1960s, the MITI selected steel and shipbuilding as the 'winners'. Intervention (support) was relatively heavy. At that time, Japanese corporations faced an identical business choice and also opted to invest in these industries, although this would have happened even without government intervention. Japan then targeted the production of aluminium and petrochemicals, a choice that was subsequently proven to be mistaken by the first oil shock. In contrast, the MITI was opposed to the promotion of the car industries (nor was electronics on the priority list) during the 1960s as the US and Europe were at that time ahead of Japan in this area. In spite of official opposition to the expansion of the industry, private enterprise continued to invest and was successful without public support (if one leaves aside the relatively closed domestic market). The private policy was right and yielded positive results for some decades to come. If left alone, private businesses may sometimes find superb solutions. Throughout the 1990s, Microsoft was the prime example of such development in the US (which ended up as a global monopoly). However, it is impossible to know in advance which company of today and tomorrow from which industry and in which location will replicate the success of Microsoft.

During the 1990s, Japanese industrial policy was transformed. Increased emphasis was given to deregulation and privatisation in the economy together with safeguarding of the traditional consensus-building spirit. As for the targeting of 'high-growth industries', the evidence that is emerging does not reveal Japanese success in this area. 'Targeting was actually more prevalent in the uncompetitive Japan, while a large proportion of the competitive industries had no government targeting' (Porter, 1996: 88).

Elsewhere in the developed market economies, the policy of targeting has not always been so smooth. After the Second World War, industrial policy relied partly on the unorganised labour that was flowing from agriculture and abroad into the manufacturing industry. This situation has changed. Trade unions organise labour that can influence (i.e. postpone) economic adjustment, even though it may be to the long-term detriment of the economy.

France is a country that is keen to create large and efficient firms that can compete in international markets. It is less concerned with domestic competition. France's Interministerial Committee for the Development of Strategic Industries decides on the key industries, defines the strategy and picks a firm to be national champion to implement that programme. The implementation method takes the form of a contract between the government and the chosen firm. Unfortunately, however, the French government has not always had perfect foresight. Misjudgements were made in very costly projects such as computers and Concorde. Although the Concorde project was a technological success, it was a commercial failure (the project started in 1962 when fuel was cheap).

The French strategy for computers was to try to build large mainframes in order to compete directly with IBM rather than to begin with small computers or peripheral equipment and learn by doing over time. This was too ambitious for the relatively undeveloped French firms to cope with, so the effort failed. The mistake might have been avoided if government industrial policy-makers had consulted more with private experts. Private firms also make mistakes, but they are less likely to ignore market forces and the various choices that they offer (in particular when using their own or shareholders' funds) than government officials who use taxpayers' money and who are often subject to various political pressures and their own re-election goals. This was the main reason why Japanese targeting was more successful than French. The early French mistakes, however, were not in vain. During the Airbus[11] project, the government learned to select the segment of the market for which demand would be high. It also tied customers by early purchasing of aircraft parts in exchange for orders (Carliner, 1988: 164).

Direct targeting of particular industries or firms has not been a striking feature of US industrial policy. This system was established in such a way as to foster, in principle, individual freedom, not to discriminate among firms or industries. The only exceptions are agriculture and sporadic bailouts of firms such as Lockheed (1971) or Chrysler (1979). Government consumption on all levels, however, creates a big overall demand pull to the economy owing to a huge general expenditure and the budget deficit. As a part of public expenditure, defence-related and selective public procurement indirectly influences the development and expansion of high-technology industries with a significant impact on private consumption. For example, NASA demanded computers for spaceships. Those computers had to be small. The industry provided such computers. Once they were commercialised, personal computers flooded the market throughout the world. Hence, the argument that the US government does not intervene in the economy does not hold water. In special situations (e.g. during the Second World War), the US had an explicit industrial policy.[12] In addition, the US has become the major producer of food in the world as a consequence of calculated economic and other policies that embraced various (including credit) subsidies.

Human capital and human resource management are key factors in increasing a country's comparative advantage in a situation of rapidly changing technology (which reduces the need for unskilled labour) and market conditions. Basic choices, such as the education of ethnologists or engineers, singers or mathematicians, lawyers or designers, influence a country's geography of production and competitiveness of its goods and services. Macroeconomic policy may support, in an important way, the creation of comparative advantage, but it is human capital (properly organised, valued and continuously educated) that presents the major lever in the enhancement of a country's competitive advantage.

One has to keep in mind that there is a big redistribution of income: from those less skilled or fortunate towards those with many skills. This takes place among regions within each country, but also on the international scale.[13] 'Old' rules, where real wages go hand in hand with an increase in productivity, no longer apply. High productivity no longer warrants high wages. With high international mobility of goods and capital there is always somebody elsewhere in the world willing to do the same job for less money (Krugman, 1996c).

During the nineteenth and early twentieth centuries, bright British pupils were steered towards the classics in Oxford and Cambridge, while technical subjects were reserved for the less gifted. The situation was the reverse in France, Germany and Japan. After the Second World War, British industry began to recruit widely from the universities. A career in industry, even if a fifth choice after callings at the Foreign Office, BBC, academia or the Church, became socially acceptable for the sons (and increasingly the daughters) of the Establishment (Sharp and Shepherd, 1987: 83–4; Porter, 1990a: 115).

Some may argue that government planners and other public officials in Japan, France and Germany may be more competent and sophisticated than managers in private firms in these countries. The best and most ambitious students aspire to government service. In North America, society has a different attitude. Many people look on government jobs as inferior to those in the private sector because, among other things, they are less well paid. It is not surprising to find that Japan, France and Germany have an industrial policy, while the US and Canada do not, at least no overt industrial policies. Nevertheless, shoddy economic policies in these two countries might be easily amended if civil servants were given a freer hand by the system (Brander, 1987: 40).

4.3 European Union

Rationale

The grounds for the introduction of an industrial policy in the EU can be identified in at least seven related areas:

- If uncoordinated, national policies may introduce a wasteful duplication either of scarce resources for R&D or investment in productive assets of suboptimal capacity. If minimum efficient economies of scale demand access to a market that is wider than the national one, then there is a case for a common EU approach to the issue. Some competition in the diversity of R&D, ideas and production is necessary because it can be a source of creativity. Nonetheless, the authorities need to strike a harmonious balance between competition and coordination, in order to profit from both of them. Hence, a certain degree of coordination of industrial policies at the EU level contributes to the efficiency of the policy.

- A common or a coordinated industrial policy in a large and expanding EU market may wield a deeper (positive or negative) impact on the economy than any isolated national policy can, no matter how big the national market of a member country.

- With a free mobility of factors in the EU, any disequilibria in a national economy may first provoke an immediate and a massive outflow or inflow of capital and, afterwards, of other factors if the disequilibria are not corrected. If a government wants to cool down the economy by increasing the rate of interest, the result may be the opposite from the desired one. High rates of interest will provoke a large inflow of foreign hot capital and the economy may become 'overheated'. EMU eliminated this danger. Therefore, the deeper the integration in the EU, the less effective are national macroeconomic policies that are pursued in isolation. A common or coordinated EU policy in such circumstances is more effective than the sum of national ones.

- Although EU firms are rivals on the EU internal market, they are allies in competition against firms from third countries both in the world and in the internal EU market. If national economic policies used to tackle the same problem are different and have undesirable and unwanted spillover effects on the EU partner countries, then there are grounds for the introduction a common industrial policy of the EU.

- Another argument may be found in the 'unfair' trade and industrial practices of foreign rivals. An EU industrial policy may act as a counter-measure.

- No matter how disputed in theory, concern about employment always carries weight in daily politics.

- Last, but not least, there is a case for externalities that create market failure (the difference between private and social benefits). When there are undesired spillover effects across the frontiers of a single country from, for example, large investments in certain businesses that pollute, then the appropriate response to such events can be found in a common EU policy.

In spite of the arguments in favour of an EU industrial policy, one should not be misled into thinking that this is a substitute for national policies. On the contrary, national and EU policy should be complementary. In fact, EU policy needs to apply only to those areas where it has the potential to be more beneficial than national policies (the principle of subsidiarity). In general, policies at EU level need to be as general as possible, while those with a local dimension need to be custom-made and specific. There has to be coordination between the EU and national/local policies in order to avoid the implementation of conflicting instruments even when there is an agreement about the major goals to be attained.

One of the principal aims of the Treaty of Rome was to increase the competitiveness of domestic firms relative to the US at the time of the creation of the EU (1957). The intention was to locate new and expand existing industries in order to take advantage of the economies of scale that would be provided by an enlarged EU market. It was primarily the expansion of domestic demand that stimulated the development of both the US and, later, Japan. Competitiveness was created in these two countries on the basis of the secure, even protected, large domestic market. In comparison with the US and Japan, no member state of the EU could claim to have a large domestic market. The EU was conceived, among other things, to redress this 'disadvantage'.

Before the establishment of the EU, small European countries' industrial policy was often defensive (e.g. subsidies to protect employment) rather than aggressive (e.g. risky entry into new industries). In the 1960s relatively weak anti-merger laws created the potential for the establishment of large European corporations which could, it was thought at that time, successfully compete with their US and Japanese rivals. However, the problem was not merely in the size of firms in the EU. Fragmented by NTBs, the internal market of the EU had as a consequence economic rigidity that shielded many national firms from both EU-internal competition and the necessary adjustment. The outcome was that in certain manufacturing industries, relative to the US and Japan, the EU came close to being a 'manufacturing museum'.

Protectionism has been the instrument of the EU industrial policy in spite of the costs and postponement of adjustment. Resistance to abandoning obsolete technologies and industries permitted others, most notably Japan, to gain the competitive edge and penetrate the EU market with many high-technology goods. EU manufacturing has valuable attributes in industries where the growth of demand is slow. Competitive advantage is relatively smaller in the expanding manufacturing industries. Without domestic restructuring, and with the exception of German, Dutch and some firms from a few other countries, foreign TNCs that are located in the EU and that operate in the expanding industries may be among the major beneficiaries from the Single Market Programme. If the instruments of protection and cartelisation (e.g. in the coal and steel industry) are not coupled with other tools of industrial policy (e.g. contraction of obsolete industries or assistance for a limited time for the introduction of new technologies), then such a policy will be ineffective from the resource viewpoint. It may be pursued by those who choose to do so and who can afford to be wasteful.

Evolution

The first attempt to introduce a 'real' industrial policy in the EU dates back to 1970. The Commission's *Memorandum on Industrial Policy* (the Colonna Report) aimed to shape the structure of EU industry and set priorities for a common action. As there was no strong legal basis for the introduction of a common industrial policy in the Treaty of Rome, the Report restricted itself to ambitious general statements and five recommendations:

- The Report foresaw the creation of a single EU market (such as the US) based on the abolition of internal barriers to trade.
- It required the harmonisation of legal and fiscal rules that would ease the establishment of enterprises throughout the EU.
- It envisaged the creation of a European Company Statute. Although the EU had existed for more than a decade, firms were very slow to merge businesses across national boundaries. As TNCs were perceived to be important vehicles for improvements in competitiveness and technology relative to foreign rivals, there was a need for the support (intervention) of intra-EU mergers and acquisitions. The absence of EU corporate law presented a serious problem. Large national corporations that tried to merge at the EU level, such as Fiat–Citroën, Agfa–Gevaert, Dunlop–Pirelli or Fokker–VFW, soon gave up. A notable exception is Airbus Industrie (set up in 1970). The pan-EU TNCs that survived to 'adolescence' were those (Philips, Shell, Unilever) that existed long before the establishment of the EU.
- Changing demand conditions create a need for economic adjustment. This adaptation could be made smooth if there was an encouragement of geographical and occupational mobility of labour and upgraded business management.
- The final recommendation was an extension of the EU solidarity regarding foreign competition, R&D and finance.

Consideration of the Report ran into difficulty, as there were two opposing views. On the one hand, Germany did not want any interference in industrial policy at either the national or the EU level. On the other hand, France was in favour of coordinating national economic policies. Other countries sided with one or other of these views.

The next step in the shaping of EU industrial policy was a *Memorandum on the Technological and Industrial Policy Programme* (the Spinelli Report) in 1973. Basically, it was a scaled-down version of the Colonna Report. The new Report argued in favour of the exchange of information, the coordination of national R&D policies, joint R&D projects and the elimination of national technical barriers. The broad strategy did not fully succeed because of different economic philosophies among the member countries. After the oil crisis the member countries pursued nationalistic industrial policies and were not very interested in a joint approach to the issue. In fact, they passed on to the EU the adjustment of the problem industries (steel, shipbuilding, textile and in some cases even cars) via trade, social and regional policies, while keeping the management of expanding industries under national control. During this period there was only some coordination of technical standards and joint actions in R&D.

A profound step towards the elimination of NTBs in internal trade, competition and, hence, industrial policy came with the introduction of the programme *Completing the Internal Market* (the Cockfield Report) of 1985. This supply-side-oriented 'technical' Programme had 282 industry-specific legislative proposals for the elimination of NTBs, as well as a timetable for their implementation by the end of 1992. The adoption of the Cockfield White Paper (1985) and the Single European Act (1987) provided the EU with the means to implement the Single Market Programme. The objective was the achievement of a genuine single internal market through the adoption, implementation and enforcement of 282 measures (directives). This was the outcome of the political determination of the member states to eliminate NTBs on internal trade and change their 'atomised' industrial policies. The EU tried to employ its resources in a more efficient way by a reduction in physical, technical and fiscal barriers to internal trade (elimination of X-inefficiencies).

The classical integration method (elimination of tariffs and quotas) in the EU exhausted its static effects at the end of 1960s. A new approach, the ousting of NTBs, favoured full factor mobility. It was implemented in order to create a genuine frontier-free internal market in the EU. The stress was on a change in the rules, rather than on additional funds. The creation of a homogeneous internal market, such as that in the US, which benefits from enormous economies of scale, was not expected. The Europeans have, on average, far more refined and deeply rooted tastes, hence they value and benefit from variety. They demand and are often ready to pay for superior quality and diversity. The aim of the Single Market Programme was simply to improve competition and market access to diverse national, regional and local markets, as well as to introduce flexible modes of production.

The abolition of customs duties and quotas in the EU benefited only those industries that serve *private consumers*. There is also another market, that for goods and services consumed by *governments*. Industries that employ new technologies failed to serve the entire EU market for these goods and services, as well as to profit from economies of scale because of the existence of NTBs. These national industries compete for public funds and orders. This is why EU firms tended to cooperate more with partners in the US or Japan than among themselves. By entering into a joint venture with a Japanese firm, an EU enterprise made up for its technological gap without forgoing the protectionist shield and/or privileges in the form of public procurement, major export contracts, tax relief and R&D accorded by the state (Defraigne, 1984: 369). Another explanation is that the EU firms were interested in forming partnerships with firms that were market or technology leaders regardless of their nationality, origin or geographical location (Narula, 1999: 718). The outcome of such a policy was that EU standards for high-technology goods were non-existent, and relatively large and protected national corporations, which were not very interested in intra-EU industrial cooperation, were created. These firms were unable to respond swiftly to changes in the international market. An obvious example of this sluggishness was the relatively slow adjustment to the oil shocks.

EU company law was required to help meet the objectives of the Treaty of Rome regarding the harmonious development of economic activities in the Union. Thus, the European Commission proposed the European Company Statute in 1989. The arguments in favour of the Statute include the elimination of the difficulties that come from the current national tax systems for those firms that operate in several EU countries. Business in the entire EU market would be made simpler if the firms were incorporated under a single code of law. The absence of this Statute is estimated to cost business €30bn a year.[14] The case against the Statute is that increased interference by the EU may jeopardise national sovereignty.

The Commission was not without further ideas on industrial policy. A 1990 communication on *Industrial Policy in an Open and Competitive Environment* (the Bangemann Communication) had, basically, the following three proposals. First, industrial policy needed to be adjustment-friendly. This has to take place within the framework of a liberal trade policy. Second, EU industrial policy has to be in accord with other common policies. They need to reinforce each other. Third, difficulties within industries or regions need to be settled by the employment of horizontal measures. The means for the achievement of these ideas should include an improvement in the operation of both the internal market and the international market, as well as the creation of an investment-friendly environment for risk-taking in the EU.

The 1993 Delors White Paper, *Growth, Competitiveness, Employment*, aimed to prepare the EU for the twenty-first century. Its major stated goal was a reduction in unemployment. This was to be achieved, among other means, by an ambitious wave of investment from various sources into the following areas: €400bn over fifteen years into transport and energy in trans-European networks; €150bn until the year 2000 into telecommunications; and €280bn over twelve years into environment-related projects. The Council of Ministers did not support the project and budgetary austerity measures cast it aside.

Following a Council of Ministers Resolution (1992) that called for an overall analysis of the effectiveness of measures taken while creating the Single Market, the European Commission undertook a profound analysis of the entire set of economic policies in the EU. The Monti Report (1996) was followed by thirty-nine volumes of background studies published by Kogan Page in 1997–98 under the title *Single Market Review*. They were split among six headings: manufacturing, services, dismantling of barriers, trade and investment, competition and economies of scale, and aggregate and regional impact of the Single European Market. The full impact of the Single Market Programme could not be fully predicted as the effect of the removal of some NTBs (technical barriers) on the geography of production and welfare would be fully felt only in the longer term. However, the Report gave directions for the preservation of the Single Market and the implementation of EMU from 1999.

The impact of the opening up of the internal EU market as a consequence of the Single Market Programme is most obvious in highly regulated (and hence fragmented) industries such as pharmaceuticals. A major regulatory change in the EU took place with the establishment of the European Agency for the Evaluation of Medicinal Products in 1995. As a result, this traditionally local government-controlled industry changed significantly. The opening up of the EU market altered the business practices of firms in the pharmaceuticals industry in seven ways:

- *Market authorisation*: National regulatory authorities that control the introduction of new products at different rates affect not only the location of production and trade, but also the health and life of patients. To change this, the European Agency for the Evaluation of Medicinal Products became the single decision-making body in the EU in 1995. However, pharmaceutical firms still have the choice of following centralised procedure that leads to a single authorisation for the entire EU (this procedure is mandatory for products derived from biotechnology) or a decentralised procedure based on mutual recognition of national marketing authorisations. It seems obvious that firms will tend to locate in the country with the least regulatory delay and then make use of the principle of mutual recognition to market their products throughout the EU. The result is that pharmaceutical companies are no longer required to follow the sometimes archaic regulations of a single authority but can 'shop around' to find the most flexible one which will give the fastest approval and enable speedy market launch of the products. Biotechnology, an area that arouses tremendous hope for the future expansion of business and at the same time fear of new and unknown, is unified at the EU level. This is gives security to customers in the Single European Market.

- *Dependence on domestic market*: Before 1995, more than 60 per cent of pharmaceuticals produced in France, Germany, Greece, Italy, Portugal and Spain were sold to the domestic market. This was the consequence of preferential government procurement from local firms, insistence on local R&D and local content requirements. Since the opening up of the EU market, firms selling primarily to their national markets have been in jeopardy: in the pharmaceuticals industry it is no good being a large fish in a small pond. Even in the US, large domestic manufacturers have experienced a dramatic fall in their market share, and in the EU 'globalisation' is the only means of survival. This can be achieved by internal growth, alliances and cooperation with other firms or through acquisitions. A lack of preferential treatment (market deepening that came from the Single Market Programme) was a wake-up call to these companies to start sharpening their competitiveness, which had suffered from earlier government protection.

- *Parallel trade*: In 1974, the EU Court of Justice ruled in favour of parallel importation (Centrafarm v. Sterling Drug), i.e. the purchasing of drugs in a low-price market and their repackaging and diversion to other markets. The principle is that medicinal drugs are permitted to move freely from one country to another if the importing country provides a marketing authorisation. As long as drugs are priced differently in different EU countries, this type of trade will continue to exist. This 'temporary situation' will disappear with full market unification. With rising pressure on their health budgets, governments are encouraging these forms of competition and 'price reduction'. At present, prices in southern Europe countries are usually lower, hence most of this trade is going northwards. The introduction of the euro in 1999 marked the beginning of the process of a greater price transparency. Combined with Internet shopping, consumers can find out almost instantly where to buy the cheapest medicines. There is great potential for parallel imports. However, an emerging trend is for TNCs to treat the EU as a unified market and to sell new drugs at the same price throughout the EU.

- *Regulated prices*: The price of drugs varies between EU countries for many reasons: price control schemes, variation in the costs of production, variable exchange rates, differences in reimbursement systems, transfer pricing, patent status, package sizes, rebates and taxes. The difference in price between the cheapest and most expensive country may be as much as tenfold! The Single European Market is bringing a slow convergence in drug prices, but progress is slow and many of the distortions mentioned will continue for some time yet. The introduction of the euro has been the principal factor in bringing price harmonisation throughout the EU. New drugs are registered centrally and are sold at the same price across the Single European Market. Previous obstacles such as exchange rates are disappearing and the EU is treated by firms as one entity. This is the only weapon in the business community's armoury if it wants to have undisturbed presence in all regions.

- *Expenditure for R&D*: Competition will stimulate innovation. R&D for new drugs directed at the regional and global market will increase. R&D in the pharmaceuticals industry has always been mission oriented, regardless of integration.

- *Rationalisation of operation*: Producing a drug involves the manufacture of the active substance and, subsequently, the conversion of this ingredient into different dosage forms. The former has been centralised in the EU, whereas the latter has been decentralised. Many plants are not benefiting from economies of scale as they are operating at between one-third and one-half of their capacity. Overcapacity in the pharmaceutical industry is estimated to be 40 per cent worldwide. Plant closures and alteration in the geography of production are imminent, partly because of new manufacturing methods and partly as a consequence of market opening in the EU, which will bring benefits in the form of economies of scale. At the same time, firms are being attracted to move location within the EU by regional benefits (subsidies) aimed at reducing unemployment in the subsidy-giving region. It is fast becoming irrelevant whether company headquarters or manufacturing capacities are based in Germany, France or Spain, for example. Aventis, the largest European pharmaceutical company, formed by merger of Hoechst and Rhone-Poulenc Rohrer, has its headquarters in Strasbourg and has adopted English as the common language of communication across the company.

- *Mergers and acquisitions*: There is still a great deal of scope for consolidation in the pharmaceutical industry when it is compared with, for example, car manufacturing. Consolidation of the industry is expected to accelerate in the next few years. During the mid-1990s the largest pharmaceutical company in the world commanded less than 5 per cent of the total world market. Expect to witness in the coming years fast growth of companies in this industry as they strive to achieve synergies, to cut cost, to obtain bigger R&D budgets and to reach a bigger 'critical mass'. Examples of this trend so far include the purchase of Syntex by Hoffmann-La Roche and the mergers of Hoechst and Rhone-Polenc Rohrer into Aventis, Ciba Geigy and Sandoz into Novartis, Astra and Zeneca, and Glaxo Wellcome and Smith Kline Beecham. This trend will continue and, in addition to major US mergers, such as that between Pfizer and Warner Lambert, one may expect to see more transatlantic mergers, such as that between Pharmacia and UpJohn. This consolidation is resulting in R&D departments big enough to develop new drugs as well as the ability to produce medicines in the most efficient way unhindered by local differences that were previously limiting factors in the growth of the pharmaceutical industry in the EU.

When a large corporation operating in a declining industry closes down a plant in a city dependent on that industry, the first reaction of the government is often to offer subsidies to large new corporations to settle there. However, industrial rhinoceroses attracted by such subsidies usually remain loyal to the area only as long as the carrot lasts. If it is not certain that the incentives (subsidies) will last until the end of the investment/production programme, firms will not be attracted to the area. Risk-averse enterprises may in this situation request larger incentives and/or invest only in projects with relatively high rates of return.

Locally created jobs can be found in the development of SMEs. Of course, SMEs may not create enough jobs in the short term to make up for the loss of jobs in a geographical area where a large corporation has closed down. However, in the past ten to twenty years, SMEs have accounted for more than half of new jobs in some countries, such as the US. In the EU, SMEs are expected to flourish. In 1999, 18 million SMEs in the EU employed around 70 million people; this is likely to increase considerably in the future.[15] SMEs are often very efficient because, in spite of their size, they can achieve economies of scale by specialising in a very specific market segment and addressing the entire EU rather than a local or national area (assuming demand for their output exists). Large Italian firms such as Fiat, Olivetti and Pirelli dominate the domestic market in their industries, but outside Italy these firms have a (very) modest share of world markets. In contrast, Italian firms in industries dominated by SMEs, such as footwear and clothing, are often world leaders (Porter, 1990a: 445).

A policy of support for SMEs is quite different from one that fosters the development of a few national champions that are easy to control. Until the 1980s, the EU countries generally regarded SMEs as unstable and marginal firms. Although it is true that many SMEs have a much shorter lifespan than large firms (many SMEs disappear from the market before they reach maturity), new ones are continually being created. This is not a worrying sign but rather an indicator that the economic system is healthy and conducive to trying out new business opportunities. Since the mid-1980s, the EU approach towards SMEs has changed. Many industrial policy programmes now support this type of enterprise. SMEs are of vital importance when a market is in the process of opening and deepening, as was the case with the Single Market Programme. Euro-Info Centres act as 'marriage' agencies for SMEs, brokering the establishment of business networks among such firms. This evolutionary and cumulative process needs for its sustenance an educational system that supplies businesses with employees proficient in the skills required. Nonetheless, the EU needs be much more explicit in its industrial policy towards SMEs. Hence, it has been decided that the European Investment Bank (EIB) should in future support SMEs to a much greater degree than in the past.

Spain has traditionally been a relatively closed economy; hence, it is interesting to explore the impact of the Single Market Programme (market opening) on Spanish SMEs. Although the economy was protected, exporting was widespread among Spain's SMEs even before Spain joined the EU in 1986. Jarillo and Martínez (1991) surveyed a sample of SMEs three years after Spain's entry into the EU, by which time the Single Market Programme was in full swing. They found that:

- almost all SMEs were exporters even when the Spanish economy was still relatively isolated from the rest of the world;
- the costs of production were declining as a competitive advantage, whereas design, style and superior technology were assuming increasing importance;
- two-thirds of the SMEs were exporting to the EU even before 1986;
- some SMEs saw the Single Market Programme as a threat (the group of firms for which international activities were secondary to their main business in Spain), while none saw it as a new opportunity as access to the EU market had been almost free since the mid-1970s.

Hence, the Single Market Programme was perceived by Spanish SMEs as a 'bad thing' or as a non-event! In spite of that conclusion, there is a large gap in our knowledge of the relationship between economic integration and the behaviour of SMEs.

The opening and deepening up of the internal EU market prompted by the Single Market Programme brought several advantages to SMEs. They include:

- the rationalisation of distribution networks;
- cheaper and fewer inspections of conformity standards;
- diversification of suppliers;
- more efficient stock controls;
- savings in time and cost of transport.

However, not everything in the garden is rosy. Many SMEs do not fully understand the operation of the Single Market. They may be familiar with the concept, but relatively few understand the conditions under which they can use the 'CE' mark, which shows that the good was produced in the EU and that it meets EU standards. Future EU policy regarding SMEs needs to take account of the following issues:

- easing access of SMEs to financial resources (this was the major weakness of SMEs and is supposed to be mitigated by the new policy orientation of the EIB);

- incentives to individuals to become entrepreneurs;
- a simple and clear regulatory climate in which to start up small business;
- opening up of public contracts to SMEs;
- incentives for advice and technology transfer to SMEs;
- stimulation of innovation in SMEs;
- modification in education and training beyond basic formation in order to assist the unemployed to become entrepreneurs.

Technology policy

Since the 1960s, some of the major factors determining industrial structures in the developed market economies have included changes in technologies, foreign competition, environmental issues, changing employment patterns and an ageing population. With this in mind, the European Commission was initially more concerned with industries in crisis. However, from the 1980s it started to become more involved with the industries and technologies of the future. These are those that have strategic importance for the competitiveness of goods (and services) in the internal as well as external markets. Therefore, during the mid-1980s the EU introduced various technology-push programmes with the aim of creating and sustaining leadership in the market. In design these programmes, the Commission has to balance the interests of the Directorate General for Competition, which advocates *laissez-faire*, and the other Directorates General, which favour an industrial policy (intervention). These programmes have (indirectly) resulted in the technology policy of the EU.

Until the mid-1980s the form and direction of R&D in the EU fell within the remit of national governments (with the notable exception of the Euroatom). The model for the national approach was to some extent Japanese experience of public support to industries from the MITI in the form of exchange of information, cooperation and partial funding of R&D projects. A change came with the Single Market Programme. The legal basis for the EU action in R&D came in 1987 via the Single European Act (Title VI). Although there had been previous initiatives, the member governments decided for the first time to contribute significant funds for R&D to EU programmes. According to the revised Treaty of Rome, the EU will strengthen its scientific and technological bases and encourage competitiveness at international level (Article 163).[16] The Commission and the member states are meant to coordinate policies and programmes carried out at the national level (Article 165).[17] The EU needs to adopt a multiannual framework programme for its R&D projects (Article 166).[18] The EU may cooperate with third countries or international organisations to implement its long-term R&D programme (Article 170).[19]

One goal of the EU is to strengthen links between research institutes and entrepreneurs throughout the EU in order to transform the long-held perception that in Europe science (i.e. R&D) is culture, whereas in the US it is business. However, in the US there is another factor that encourages fast reaction to changing technologies. Vigilant financial markets in the US often look favourable on risky investments by innovative firms. This ethos of support for such innovation, still missing in Europe, forces American firms to adjust rapidly to shifting markets and changing technology. This explains a sizeable part of the difference between the US and EU in terms of commercial exploitation of the results of R&D.

In circumstances in which strong national elements still dominate, the EU should endeavour to coordinate national policies, promote cooperation in R&D and production, and support the flexibility of the industrial structure. Coordination of national policies regarding declining industries should avoid an integration-unfriendly beggar-thy-neighbour mentality. In the light of the (irreversible) changes brought by the Single European Market and the EMU, expanding industries (those in which production technology is changing) should introduce common EU standards that facilitate large-scale production and an increase in competitiveness. The objective is to avoid the creation of incompatible standards, as happened with the PAL and SECAM television systems. If the new, universally accepted standard is not high-definition television (HDTV), and if the EU, Japan and the US adopt three different TV systems (preventing the maximum exploitation of economies of scale), it seems likely from previous experience that the Japanese will excel in the production of TV sets that satisfy all three standards.

The EU's dependence on third-country suppliers of high-technology goods arises for several reasons. On the supply side, the EU investment in R&D is lower than in the US[20] and Japan; the EU also allocates fewer human resources to R&D and there are often delays in the putting into production and marketing the results of R&D. On the demand side, national 'attitudes' (e.g. buy domestic) may limit the potential demand for high-technology products in EU countries, making it difficult for EU manufacturers of high-technology to achieve the necessary economies of scale, European firms are less receptive to new products than their US and Japanese rivals, there is a lack of strong links between producers and consumers, and there is inadequate training in new technologies (Jacquemin and Sapir, 1991: 44–5).[21] Various EU technology programmes are intended to redress this situation.

During the period 1979–85 imports of some products, for example office machines, increased steeply. This trend declined sharply during 1985–87, and there has been no strong inclination since 1988. In electronic goods, transport equipment and industrial and agricultural machinery, the rapid increase in EU imports in the second half of 1970s and first half of 1980s seems to have levelled off. This change, however, dates from 1984, well before the Single Market Programme. This does not permit any strong conclusion concerning the impact of the Single Market Programme on the performance of the EU manufacturing industry (European Commission, 1997a: 32).

Philips and Thomson led the lobby of European companies pressing national governments for the completion of the Single European Market as the principal cure for countering the (past) Japanese ability to be always a few steps ahead in the business game. The Round Table of European Industrialists (rent-seekers) was successful in eliciting support from governments for the Single Market Programme. When the US announced the 'Star Wars' project in 1983, EU industrialists started to worry. First the Japanese took over a large part of the market for consumer electronics, then the Americans seemed to be en *route* to domination of the market for advanced industrial goods. Subsequently, the Round Table, created in 1983, pushed for the creation of a trans-national industrial policy in the form of EU support for high-technology research projects. In spite of budgetary restrictions, the big EU industrialists were successful again (Curzon Price, 1993: 399–400).

Implementation of EU policy in R&D takes the form of four-year Framework Programmes,[22] which were introduced in 1984. The purpose of these medium-term instruments is to integrate and coordinate all assistance/aid for R&D in the EU.[23] These programmes lay down objectives, priorities and the budget for EU-sponsored R&D. By distributing funds to selected research projects, the EU sets guidelines for specific R&D programmes. Based on the findings of the FAST (Forecasting and Assessment in Science and Technology) programme,[24] the EU introduced about twenty publicly supported programmes for industrial cooperation among the EU firms in the R&D stage. Most of the programmes would be beyond the financial capability and will of the participating countries to finance alone. These programmes include the following 'winners':

- A dozen renowned IT firms from Britain, France, Germany, Italy and the Netherlands wanted to pool resources, share risk and attract subsidies from the EU (although this begs the question of why leading-edge companies should need to form cartels and seek such support). Nonetheless, the pressure group they formed (the Round Table) lobbied both national governments and the Commission to adopt the European Programme for Research in Information Technology (ESPRIT) to try to 'correct market failures' in R&D. The European Commission was receptive to the idea and together with the Round Table won approval from the national governments. The EU adopted the Programme, i.e. picked a winner, in 1984. Under the auspices of ESPRIT, the EU funds half of the cost of any project that is in line with the EU terms of reference and that is supported by two or more firms from different EU countries. The other half of the funds has to come from the participating firms and national sources. Eligible projects must be in the field of pre-competitive R&D. So far, the Commission has refused to subsidise joint production in order to avoid criticism from the US about subsidies. Indeed, the Commission has tried to argue that it does not operate a large-scale industrial policy at all, but rather a series of R&D programmes (Curzon Price, 1990: 178).
- Research and Development in Advanced Communication for Europe (RACE) is a spillover programme from ESPRIT. Its aim is to advance the telecommunication network in Europe in the future by the means that include standardisation and coordination of national telecom services.
- Basic Research in Industrial Technologies in Europe (BRITE) aspires to revitalise traditional industries in the EU. This is to be achieved through the introduction of new technologies in these industries although it is not always obvious what is 'strategic' about these industries. Perhaps the concern here is

more about employment than anything else. Public money is spent on projects that financial markets find unattractive.

- The Biotechnology Action Programme (BAP) is small relative to its 'strategic' potential in the future.
- European Collaborative Linkage of Agriculture and Industry through Research (ECLAIR) is like the BAP: relatively small, but with great potential for finding solutions regarding food in the future. It contributes to the establishment and reinforcement of intersectoral links between agriculture and manufacturing.

The European Research Cooperation Agency (EUREKA) was established by seventeen countries (from the EU and the EFTA) at the initiative of the French in 1985. Its formation was a response to the American Strategic Defence Initiative ('Star Wars'). Its objective is the development and *production* of high-technology goods. It is not confined to pre-competitive R&D as the other programmes are. Other countries (such as Turkey) may be included in some of its programmes. EUREKA is, however, *not* an institution of the EU. It has a small secretariat in Brussels and has gained popularity in the business community.

The Fifth Framework Programme (1998–2002) disposes of €14bn. Allocating funds for a period of five years in advance is a much more civilised way of disposing of funds than requiring projects to fight for money every year. The seven 'winning' research areas are (whatever their names mean) quality of life and management of living resources; user-friendly information society; increasing competitiveness; energy and environment; international research; innovation and SMEs; and improvement in human research potential and the socioeconomic knowledge base. These EU-wide programmes should be supported by a number of national plans that spread and reinforce links among the parties involved in R&D and the implementation of the results of those efforts. As a general rule, the admissible aid level in the EU for pre-competitive development projects that are close to the market is 25 per cent of the cost, while for basic industrial research the limit is 50 per cent.

A great deal of public money has been poured into R&D over the past decade in the EU, but the results have been very slow in coming. Of course, the effects of fundamental R&D cannot be predicted with a high degree of accuracy. As public funds are limited, and as the results of R&D are more important than the origin of the work, companies from foreign countries may take part in the R&D projects of the EU on a case-by-case basis, but without any financial help from the Commission. Production everywhere in the world is becoming more and more 'globalised'. Thus, forcing cooperation in R&D only within the EU may squander taxpayers' money. 'Global' production requires an open (global) industrial and trade policy system.

Inter-firm strategic alliances in the development of technology in the EU increased sharply during 1980s. In addition, the Commission became quite heavily involved in projects on a cost-sharing basis. Over 70 per cent of private (largely non-subsidised) strategic technology alliances were formed to exploit joint R&D of new core technologies in informatics, new materials and biotechnology. A major field of cooperation was in information technologies, with over 40 per cent of all strategic technology alliances falling into this area (Hagedoorn and Schakenraad, 1993: 373). A comparison between established 'private' cooperation in R&D and cooperation sponsored by the EU found that they are very similar. In fact, 'subsidised R&D networks simply add to already existing or emerging private networks and merely reproduce the basic structure of European large firm co-operation' (Hagedoorn and Schakenraad, 1993: 387). This being the case, it is difficult to understand why leading and large firms in the EU need subsidies! If the 'official' network largely reproduces the already existing 'private' one, then it is surely largely redundant. The financial resources consumed in promoting cooperation might be better used elsewhere (for instance, on programmes that are not in the field of informatics such as biotechnology or education or infrastructure).

The question of whether replication of R&D networks is the result of a powerful lobby or whether it is necessary to accelerate R&D in the private sector because of significant externalities remains to be answered. Decisions taken at EU level are easy targets for special lobbies as they are too far from the public to monitor. The co-decision procedure between the Council and the Parliament introduced by the Maastricht Treaty was an attempt to overcome this drawback. Although it is a step in the right direction, there is still a danger that EU technology policy may become just a sophisticated new form of protectionism. It is possible that such a waste of scarce public money will be checked in the future by WTO rules on subsidies.

A changed and improved new industrial strategy of the EU and its member states needs to take into account first and foremost the crucial role played by the development of human capital in the long-term competitiveness of the economy. The creation of a prosperous learning society has to give priority to the creation of human capital, especially skills that create, spread, absorb and extend new technology in production, organisation and marketing. In addition, there may be a need for selective intervention in the form of subsidies, promotion of cooperation and information exchange during the pre-commercial phase of R&D projects that may give (oligopolistic) advantages to EU producers relative to foreign rivals. The EU has invested in industries in which is a high risk of failure and where Japan and the US are strong. Part of the reason for the relative failure of electronics in the EU during the 1970s is the fact that domestic firms were sheltered from foreign competition. In contrast, in areas where the EU faced global competition, for example commercial aircraft (Airbus), the EU achieved a considerable degree of success.

If deemed appropriate, selective intervention in new technologies needs to be aimed at those expanding industries in which EU businesses already have or could create internal resources. This means that EU efforts and funds should be focused not on the replication of industries in which the US[25] and Japan[26] are strong (cooperation with them may be a better choice), but primarily where there are grounds for the development of genuine EU technologies and comparative advantages. These may be the development of new production technologies for relatively traditional industries such as food, textiles and furniture. The EU excels also in several high-technology industries such as mobile phones, chemicals and pharmaceuticals, heavy electrical machinery and equipment and super-fast trains.

Not only now, but also in the coming decades, there will be an increased overlap between mechanical, electronic, chemical, medical and biotechnology industries. The EU has a reasonable chance of remaining the leader in some of these fields. This may be aided by the problems in the Japanese economy, which became apparent at the end of 1990s. However, there are many dangers in this area. Although there have been important scientific achievements in genetic engineering [e.g. cloning of animals (sheep) in Britain in 1996–97], these achievements are often associated with serious ethical, moral, social and religious questions. In addition, serious negative side-effects may emerge from biotechnology and genetic engineering, as was the case with 'mad cow disease'[27] in Britain in 1996.

Outlook

The competitiveness of a country's goods and services on the international market in modern times is often much more created than inherited. The leader in some lines of production cannot be sure that this position will endure in the long run. Competition is threatening firms from all sides. Being on the top is no longer a state, but rather a process. Therefore, one can find scope for industrial cooperation and sharing risk in the EU. It could be established both in the pre-commercial and during the commercialisation stages of R&D. In this way, inefficient duplication or multiplication of R&D would be eliminated and resources saved and directed elsewhere. However, the creation of knowledge is not enough to keep a country at the competitive edge. That knowledge needs to be applied in practice with commercial success. Here the US fares much better than the EU. The US system and culture offers wide opportunities to start and restart promising businesses. If sound profit-making ideas fail (for whatever reason) in Boston, there are further chances in Seattle or San Francisco. The Americans treat business failures like battle scars– something to be worn with pride. In Europe, the situation is different. If your business start-up fails, you can forget another one for a while, unless you cross the Atlantic.

The elimination of most NTBs on internal EU trade as a result of the Single Market Programme has had its greatest impact on sensitive businesses, and this will continue to be the case.[28] These businesses are those that were protected by high NTBs and which experienced large price distortions, e.g. the production of goods that are publicly procured either in the high-technology sector (e.g. office machines, telecommunications and medico-surgical equipment) or in traditional manufacturing sectors such as electrical and railway equipment, pharmaceuticals, wine and boilermaking. Businesses protected by relatively modest NTBs will also continue to be affected by market liberalisation and deepening. These include motor vehicles, aerospace equipment, basic chemicals, machine tools for metals and textile and sewing machines.

Some outsiders feared that the Single European Market would lead to the creation of 'Fortress Europe' as a result of a combination of intra-EU liberalisation and an increase in the existing level of external protection. However, the EU has no such plan, nor would it serve its long-term interests. If the word 'fortress' was mentioned, it was only as a potential bargaining chip with major trading partners. It was expected that the Single Market Programme would lead, among other things, to increased competition and efficiency, which would reduce prices in the EU. Therefore, even without any change in the existing level of nominal protection, the real level may rise. Any additional increase would be neither necessary nor desirable. On the contrary, increased efficiency prompted the EU to reduce the level of trade protection in the Uruguay Round deal. Nonetheless, the Single Market Programme has influenced the timing of external FDI in the EU. Many foreign TNCs entered the EU in order to become 'internal' residents of the EU prior to full implementation of the Single Market Programme. They wanted to pre-empt any potential moves towards the creation of an EU fortress from the start of 1993.

Potential changes in the rules of origin and local content may, however, discriminate against 'internal' goods with a relatively high external import content. This may be reinforced by a discriminatory application of testing procedures and standards. A fortress mentality may be introduced in the EU through the social (ist) over-regulation of labour issues. If this is done in the future, it could provoke protectionist winds that would make the security of current jobs more important than the long-term efficiency and adjustment of the economy.

Customs union (phase I in the EU's integration) offered an incentive to economic life, but its effect was spent by the end of 1960s. Something novel and more radical was needed. Phase II is represented by the formation of the genuine single internal market, with unimpeded flow of goods, services and factors, in 1993. This provided the EU with a new momentum. The member countries decided to reintroduce the principle of majority voting (except for fiscal issue, national border controls, working conditions and environmental issues) in order to ease the procedure to implement the Single Market. In 1999, phase III of the integration process, EMU, reinforced earlier achievements in integration and removed all possible internal exchange rate variations for the twelve countries participating in the EMU.

The EU member countries realised that the costs of failing to integrate (i.e. a 'non-Europe') were too high to be ignored. An EU without internal frontiers (at least for residents of the member countries), as envisaged in the White Paper, could increase GNP in the EU by up to 7 per cent and create 5 million new jobs, if accompanied by supporting national policies (Emerson *et al.* 1988: 165). The 'costs' of these real gains are more freedom for business and less regulation. The opponents of the Single Market Programme were not able to create a more attractive and feasible economic strategy and ultimately gave up the attempt to do so. Only inefficient business or those that failed to compete and adjust would lose out in the new situation. As the Single Market Programme was not accompanied by a chain of bankruptcies throughout the EU, this is an indication that the business sector has absorbed the change without any serious and negative shocks. However, the Single Market Programme was merely the first step. One has to keep in mind that the Single Market Programme is merely a medium-term strategy. The Maastricht Treaty rearranged the decision-making process in the EU and set the 'agenda' for the EMU.

Tables 4.1, 4.2 and 4.3 show annual percentage changes in, respectively, growth rate, manufacturing output and capital formation in the EU countries from the mid-1980s to the present. Also shown for comparison are the same indicators for the US and Japan. Although the actual figures differ for each country in the EU, economic cycles show synchronization. The most obvious example is 1993, when most of the EU countries were in recession. That was the first year of the Single European Market in the EU. In addition, industrial production and investments in the EU had been suffering since1991. However, it would be unfair to blame negative macroeconomic trends on the failure of the Single Market Programme. Integration is, after all, no more than a instrument to *support* general national macroeconomic policies. If the policies are right, integration can contribute to their reinforcement. It is still too early to draw any definitive conclusions about the impact of the 'euro', introduced in 1999, on growth. Although the three economic indicators shown in the tables differ between EU countries, the common feature is that they are almost always strongly positive.

Well, 1992 has come and gone, and the single currency, adopted by most of the EU countries, was introduced in 1999, and still the economies of the EU countries have not shown any great expansion despite widespread predictions of the beneficial effects of the Single European Market. There was even a recession in 1992. Has something gone wrong? Perhaps not. Economic integration, including the operation of the Single Market and common currency, is an ongoing process. The Single Market Programme does not have clear deadlines after which one may measure the overall effects with only a small margin of error. Research on the effects of the Single European Market suffers from an identification problem. It is a common shortcoming of all studies that deal with the effects of international economic integration. It is hard to know which changes in the economy and the reaction of enterprises are due to the Programme and which would have happened anyway. For example, external changes include imports of improved foreign technology (software programmes to manage production and inventories) or 'globalisation' of business and competition. It may take another decade or so until all the effects of the Single Market Programme are fully absorbed by the economies of the EU. Perhaps, and again only 'perhaps', the biggest effect on the economies of the EU has already taken place, at the end of the 1980s. Some support for this thesis can be found in the fact that business concentration deals peaked in 1990. It needs to be kept in mind that the Single Market was *a*, rather than *the* reason for change.

In spite of 'grand' expectations regarding employment and growth at the start of the Single Market Programme, as expressed, for example, by Emerson *et al.* (1988), in practice the benefits have been much more modest, although not negligible. It has been estimated that the Programme created between 300,000 and 900,000 jobs, with an extra increase in EU income of 1.1–1.5 per cent over the period 1987–93 (European Commission, 1997b).

Direct intervention in the manufacturing industry by the EU was primarily aimed at declining industries such as steel, shipbuilding and textiles during the 1970s and early 1980s. After 1985, the major emphasis of the policy changed. The EU became much more involved in the expanding high-technology industries

Table 4.1 Real annual growth rate of GDP in EU countries, US and Japan, 1984–2001 (annual percentage change)

Country	1984	85	86	87	88	89	90	91	92	93	94	95	96	97	98	99	2000[a]	2001[a]
Belgium–Luxembourg	2.1	0.8	1.5	2.2	4.9	3.6	3.0	2.0	1.6	-1.5	3.0	2.6	0.9	3.2	2.9	1.8	2.7	2.8
Denmark	4.4	4.3	3.6	0.3	1.2	0.6	1.2	1.4	1.3	0.8	5.8	3.7	2.8	3.1	2.7	1.5	1.9	2.1
Germany[b]	2.8	1.9	2.2	1.4	3.7	3.4	5.7	5.0	2.2	-1.1	2.3	1.7	0.8	1.5	2.2	1.5	2.6	2.7
Greece	2.8	3.1	1.6	-0.7	4.1	3.5	0.0	3.1	0.7	-1.6	2.0	2.1	2.4	3.4	3.7	3.4	3.6	3.9
Spain	1.8	2.3	3.2	5.6	5.2	4.8	3.7	2.7	0.7	-1.2	2.3	2.7	2.3	3.8	4.0	3.6	3.6	3.5
France	1.3	1.9	2.5	2.3	4.5	4.1	2.7	1.0	1.5	-0.9	2.1	1.7	1.1	2.0	3.2	2.5	2.9	3.0
Ireland	4.4	3.1	-0.5	4.6	4.5	6.4	7.6	1.9	3.3	2.6	5.8	9.5	7.7	10.7	8.9	7.8	6.9	5.8
Italy	2.7	2.6	2.9	3.1	4.1	2.9	2.2	1.4	0.8	-0.9	2.2	2.9	0.9	1.5	1.3	1.1	2.2	2.5
Netherlands	3.1	2.7	2.0	0.9	2.6	4.7	4.1	2.3	2.0	0.8	3.2	2.3	3.0	3.8	3.7	3.0	3.2	3.3
Austria	1.4	2.5	1.2	1.7	4.1	3.8	4.6	3.4	1.3	0.5	2.4	1.7	2.0	1.2	2.9	2.1	2.8	2.6
Portugal	-1.9	2.8	4.1	5.3	3.9	5.2	4.4	2.3	2.5	-1.1	2.2	2.9	3.0	4.1	3.5	3.1	3.3	3.3
Finland	3.1	3.3	2.1	4.0	5.4	5.4	0.0	-6.3	-3.3	-1.1	4.0	3.8	4.0	6.3	5.0	3.9	4.0	4.0
Sweden	4.0	2.2	2.2	2.8	2.3	2.4	1.4	-1.1	-1.4	-2.2	4.0	3.7	1.3	1.8	2.6	3.7	3.5	2.8
UK	2.3	3.8	4.1	4.8	4.4	2.1	0.6	-1.5	0.1	2.3	4.4	2.8	2.6	3.5	2.2	1.8	3.8	3.6
US	6.2	3.2	2.9	3.1	3.9	2.5	1.7	-0.2	3.3	2.4	4.1	2.7	3.7	4.5	4.3	3.8	2.8	2.5
Japan	3.9	4.4	2.9	4.2	6.8	4.8	5.1	3.8	1.0	0.3	0.6	1.5	5.0	1.4	-2.8	1.3	1.6	2.1

[a]Estimates and projections.
[b]Including ex-GDR from 1991.

Source: Eurostat (2000).

Table 4.2 Manufacturing output in the EU countries, US and Japan, 1985–99 (annual percentage change)

Country	1985	1986	1987	1988	1989	1990	1991	1992	1993	1994	1995	1996	1997	1998	1999
Austria	4.7	1.2	1.0	4.4	5.8	6.8	1.9	-1.2	-1.5	4.0	4.9	1.0	6.4	8.2	4.7
Belgium	2.5	0.8	2.1	5.8	3.4	1.5	-1.9	-0.4	-5.1	2.1	6.5	0.5	4.7	3.4	0.1
Denmark	4.5	7.3	-3.0	2.2	2.0	3.1	–	3.4	-2.6	10.0	4.6	2.0	5.6	2.2	2.5
Finland	2.9	1.9	5.0	3.2	3.6	-0.6	-8.7	1.3	5.6	11.3	7.2	3.6	10.2	7.0	5.4
France	2.1	0.6	1.2	4.6	3.7	1.5	-1.2	-1.2	-3.9	4.0	2.1	0.2	3.9	4.6	2.2
Germany	4.8	1.8	0.4	3.6	4.9	5.2	2.4	-2.3	-7.6	3.6	1.2	0.6	3.5	4.2	0.8
Greece	3.3	-0.3	-1.2	5.1	1.8	-2.5	-1.0	-1.1	-2.9	1.3	1.8	1.2	1.3	7.1	3.6
Ireland	3.4	2.2	8.9	10.7	11.6	4.7	3.3	9.1	5.6	11.9	18.9	8.0	15.3	15.7	8.6
Italy	0.1	4.1	2.6	6.9	3.9	6.3	-0.4	-1.3	-2.1	6.2	5.0	-1.9	3.8	1.1	–
Luxembourg	-1.1	1.9	-0.6	8.7	7.8	2.6	0.4	-0.8	-4.3	5.9	2.0	0.1	5.8	-0.1	11.4
Netherlands	4.8	0.2	1.1	0.1	5.1	2.4	1.8	-0.2	-1.1	4.9	4.5	2.5	3.1	1.4	0.6
Portugal	-1.3	7.3	4.4	3.8	6.7	9.0	–	-2.3	-5.2	-0.2	11.6	5.3	2.6	5.7	2.8
Spain	1.8	3.3	4.6	3.1	5.1	-0.3	-0.7	-3.0	-4.7	7.6	4.8	-1.3	6.9	5.5	2.6
Sweden	2.9	0.2	2.8	2.9	2.9	0.3	-5.2	-1.7	-0.4	11.5	9.8	1.0	6.5	4.6	2.3
United Kingdom	5.5	1.4	4.1	5.2	2.1	–	-3.3	0.4	2.1	5.2	1.8	1.0	1.0	0.6	0.4
EU(15)	3.1	2.1	2.1	4.5	4.1	3.1	-0.3	-1.3	-3.3	5.1	3.5	0.4	3.9	3.5	1.3
US	1.6	1.2	4.6	4.5	1.8	-0.2	-2.0	3.1	3.4	5.5	4.9	4.4	6.4	4.2	3.6
Japan	3.7	-0.2	3.4	9.4	5.8	4.2	1.9	-5.7	-3.5	1.3	3.3	2.3	3.5	-6.5	0.4

Source: UN/ECE (2000).

Table 4.3 Real gross fixed capital formation in the EU countries, US and Japan, 1985–99 (annual percentage change)

Country	1985	1986	1987	1988	1989	1990	1991	1992	1993	1994	1995	1996	1997	1998	1999
Austria	6.9	2.4	4.4	6.8	6.3	6.6	6.3	0.1	-2.0	8.4	1.2	2.1	0.8	6.8	3.3
Belgium	3.9	3.2	3.3	15.6	12.7	8.5	-4.2	1.7	-3.0	-0.1	5.5	1.1	6.5	3.7	6.0
Denmark	12.6	17.1	-3.8	-6.6	0.2	-0.9	-2.7	-1.0	-1.9	7.4	13.6	4.8	10.4	6.9	1.5
Finland	2.8	1.0	4.9	11.0	13.0	-4.6	-18.6	-16.7	-16.6	-2.7	10.6	8.4	11.9	7.8	4.8
France	3.1	6.0	6.0	9.5	7.3	3.3	-1.5	-1.6	-6.4	1.5	2.0	—	0.5	6.1	7.0
Germany	-0.5	3.3	1.8	4.4	6.3	8.5	6.0	4.5	-4.5	4.0	-0.7	-1.1	0.5	1.4	2.3
Greece	5.2	-6.2	-5.1	8.9	7.1	5.0	4.8	-3.2	-3.5	-2.7	4.2	8.4	13.2	8.0	7.5
Ireland	-7.7	-2.8	-1.1	5.2	10.1	13.4	-7.0	—	-5.1	11.8	14.1	16.3	17.3	15.9	11.8
Italy	0.4	2.3	4.2	6.7	4.2	4.0	1.0	-1.4	-10.9	0.1	6.0	3.6	1.2	4.1	4.4
Luxembourg	-9.5	31.0	17.9	15.0	7.0	2.7	31.9	-9.0	28.4	-14.9	3.5	-3.5	10.5	1.5	7.8
Netherlands	7.0	6.9	0.9	4.5	4.9	1.6	0.2	0.6	-2.8	2.2	4.8	6.3	5.9	5.2	5.8
Portugal	-3.5	10.9	18.0	14.8	4.2	8.2	3.5	4.8	-5.8	3.5	4.7	5.7	11.7	9.7	6.7
Spain	6.1	9.9	14.0	13.9	13.6	6.6	1.6	-4.4	-10.5	2.5	8.2	2.0	5.0	9.2	8.8
Sweden	5.2	0.3	8.2	6.6	11.3	1.3	-8.9	-10.8	-17.2	6.1	9.4	5.0	-2.2	9.4	8.1
United Kingdom	4.0	2.1	8.9	14.8	5.9	-2.3	-8.7	-0.7	0.8	3.6	2.9	4.9	7.5	10.8	5.2
EU(15)	2.5	4.2	5.4	8.7	6.9	4.2	-0.2	-0.3	-5.7	2.6	3.6	2.3	3.4	5.9	5.1
US	6.1	1.9	0.4	2.8	2.9	-0.2	-5.4	5.2	5.7	7.3	5.4	8.4	7.5	10.6	8.2
Japan	5.0	4.8	9.1	11.5	8.2	8.5	3.3	-1.5	-2.0	-0.8	1.7	11.1	-0.8	-7.4	-0.7

Source: UN/ECE (2000).

through its R&D and technology policies. This should not be taken to mean that the EU is no longer concerned with obsolete 'industries', or that it was not interested in the support and development of advanced industries in the past. On the contrary, EU involvement with both types of manufacturing industries existed in the past, and it continues in the present. What changed was only the order of priorities. Nonetheless, high on the agenda for the future are five priorities:

- promotion of investment into intangible assets;
- advancement of industrial cooperation;
- paying special attention to services, SMEs, energy, biotechnology and information technology;
- strengthening of competition;
- modernisation of public intervention.

4.4 Services

Issues

Goods are tangible assets and, as such, are readily defined; the same cannot be said of services. Services have numerous recipients: an individual in the case of a haircut, education, entertainment or transport; a legal entity such as a firm or government in the case of banking or construction; an object such as an aeroplane in the case of guidance, repairs or airport services; or goods in the case of transport and storage. Some services can be provided to more than one recipient. For example, banking, insurance, transport, telecommunication, leasing, data processing and legal advice could be offered to individuals, businesses and governments.

In general, the services sector in the developed market economies contributes more than half to both GNP and employment (around 66 per cent in the EU). And the share of the economy occupied by services has been continuously increasing. This tendency to deindustrialisation has resulted in a shift of emphasis towards the services sector as one of the key solutions to the problems of unemployment and growth. Employment in the manufacturing sector has been declining in the EU since the 1980s, whereas employment in the services sector has been constantly expanding. In 1999, out of 150 million people employed in the EU, 44 million (or 30 per cent) were employed in the manufacturing sector, while 99 million (or 66 per cent) were employed in the services sector. Newly created jobs in the services sector more than compensated for job losses in manufacturing. Production of almost all services takes place in every country. However, the same is not true for the manufacturing of cars, lorries, aircraft or steel. This is the direct consequence of high tradability of goods and restricted tradability of services. Hence, the alleged importance of the creation of new jobs in the services sector.

Notwithstanding its importance and impact on the economy, the services sector has been largely neglected in economic analysis. Classical economists such as Adam

Smith and Karl Marx neglected services as the residual sector of the economy on the grounds that it does not have durable properties and no facility for physical accumulation or trade. The production and consumption of services is simultaneous and requires a degree of mobility of factors. Therefore, the classical economists turned their attention towards the manufacture of physical goods. In addition, rules relating to trade in services were not negotiated for a long time. Trade in services, however, accounted for 20 per cent (or $1.3tn) of total annual world trade in 1998. It comes as no surprise that services were included in the Uruguay Round Accord and the WTO.

The services sector of an economy changes its structure and location over time. The traditional services (such as transport, law, medicine, banking and insurance) are enriched by the new and fast-growing ones (such as telecommunications, information, data processing, engineering and management consultancy).

On the 'technical' side, services differ from other economic activities in at least the following five ways (Buigues and Sapir, 1993: xi):

- The production and consumption of services happen at the same time and at the same location. Therefore, they are regarded as non-tradable as they cannot be stored. Because of a relatively low level of internationalisation, the right of establishment (FDI) is essential for the provision of services abroad. Although services account for around half of the GDP in the EU, their share of total trade is around 20 per cent. This epitomises the non-tradable nature of many services. On the other hand, services account for over half of all FDI in the EU. Internationalisation of services is lowest in distribution, road transport and construction, average in telecommunications, financial and business services; and relatively high in air transport and hotel chains.
- The quality of services cannot easily be ascertained in advance of consumption. Non-price competitive factors such as reputation often play a key role during the decision-making process by consumers. This is important in longer-term relations such as in financial services. Experience plays a part even in one-off relationships in some cases and places.[29]
- Governments in all countries intervene in services more than in other economic activities, because of market failures. These include imperfect competition in a number of services; asymmetric information between providers and consumers (sellers potentially know more about a service, such as an insurance policy, than do buyers); and externalities. Positive externalities are to be found frequently in the services sector, such as in telecommunications or the Internet: in these areas the value for one user increases with the total number of all users. A negative externality may be found, for example, in financial services, where the failure of one bank may cause problems for others (Sapir, 1993: 27). Public intervention influences entry, operation, competition and exit from the sector. Regulation is high and competition low in financial services, air transport and telecommunications. Thus, these industries are served by only a few large companies. Reputation plays a major role in finance and economies of scope are important in air transport, while in tele-

communications there are relatively large sunk costs and economies of scale (in most countries a single public firm used to provide the service). Competition tends to be higher and regulation easier in road transport, business services, construction and hotels.

- Debates about the (in)ability of the government to intervene (in)efficiently to correct market failures, as well as changes in technology, contributed to an ebb in deregulation in the sector first in the US at the end of 1970s, then in Britain during the early 1980s, which subsequently spread to the rest of Europe.
- Services are characterised by a relatively slow growth of labour productivity. Their rate of productivity growth during the period 1970–90 was half of what it was in the manufacturing sector. There are at least two explanations for such development. First, competition in services is obstructed by a high degree of regulation and, second, the substitution of capital for labour is more limited in services than in manufacturing. Technological innovations, however, increased labour productivity in telecommunications and air transport during that period.

Differences between services and other economic activities are not confined to the 'technical' side. There is also a social dimension.

- In the 1990s, half of employees in the service sector were women. This is in sharp contrast with the manufacturing sector, in which women account for only one in five jobs.
- There are many more part-time employees in the services sector than in manufacturing.
- Temporary contracts are increasing in the services sector.
- There is a relatively high level of non-employees.
- Labour unions are not strong in the services sector except in transport and telecommunication services.
- SMEs are the dominant type of business organisation in most service industries.

There are other reasons why the analysis of services is tricky. One is a lack of any profound theory. A wide definition states that 'a service is a change in the condition of a person, or a good belonging to some economic unit, which is brought about as a result of the activity of some other economic unit' (Hill, 1977: 317). Without a proper definition, the measuring unit is lacking. Trade statistics list thousands of items for goods but record only a handful of services (making analysis quite difficult). This reflects the fact that goods have a very high degree of tradability, whereas the tradability of services is low. Hence, the production of services is much more geographically dispersed than is the production of goods. Although many services are not tradable, progress in information and telecom technology has made many services eligible for international trade. Nevertheless, trade in many services is not recorded. For example, the service part of a good, such as repair, may be incorporated in the total price of traded goods.

Apart from transport, financial and telecommunication services, in principle, entry into and exit from a service industry is relatively cheap and easy. However, there are regulatory barriers to such (dis)orderly operation in the service businesses. TNCs release few data on their internal trade in services, whereas other establishments in the sector reluctantly make public this information, as this can endanger their competitive position. In addition, information can be easily, swiftly and cheaply distributed, which jeopardises property rights. Such a lack of hard statistical information makes trade in services difficult to study.

It is easier to sell goods than services in foreign markets. While barriers to trade in goods can be eliminated at the border, problems for the suppliers of services usually start once they pass the frontier control. Provision of services often requires the right of establishment and national treatment of enterprises. Providers of a service frequently need to be physically present in order to provide a service to their customers.

Experts may enter and settle in foreign countries, but their qualifications and licences may not be recognised by the host authorities. Public authorities regulate the supply of services to a much higher degree than they do the production of goods. They often regulate public shareholding, quality and quantity of supply, rates and conditions of operation. Fiscal incentives are often more easily given to firms in the manufacturing industry than to those in the services sector. Because of the wide coverage of regulation of industries in the services sector, an easing or a removal of control of the establishment in services can have a much greater impact on trade and investment than would be the case in the trade and production of goods.

Small and open countries that are net importers of goods may prefer not to rely on their domestic manufacturing industry, as this might not operate on an efficient scale. These countries may choose to develop service industries to create proceeds to pay for imports of goods. Thus, the Netherlands has developed trade and transport, Austria tourism, Norway and Greece shipping, while Switzerland and Luxembourg are highly specialised in financial services.

Services and the jobs that they create may be broadly classified into two groups:

- those that require high skills and pay (such as business, financial, engineering, management, consulting and legal advice);
- those that are geared to consumer and welfare needs.

The suppliers of services in this second group receive poor training, have a high turnover and low pay (such as jobs in shops, hotels and restaurants). Economic development in its post-industrial phase should be aimed at the creation of jobs in the former group, rather than the latter (Tyson, 1987: 79).

European Union

Articles 43–48[30] of the Treaty of Rome grant the right of establishment to EU residents, freedom to supply services throughout the region and freedom of movement for capital. Article 86[31] states that public enterprises and those with special or exclusive rights to provide services of general economic interest 'shall be subject to ... the rules on competition, in so far as the application of such rules does not obstruct the performance, in law or in fact, of the particular tasks assigned to them'. Compared with trade in goods, these rights have not yet materialised in practice on a large scale. The major reason for this is various national restrictions (NTBs). In fact, around half of the 282 measures that came from the Single Market Programme related to services such as finance, transport and telecommunications. It was in the financial services (banking and insurance) that the Single Market Programme advanced most swiftly. This was partly due to the impressive changes in technology (data processing and telecommunications services) and partly a result of international efforts to liberalise trade in services under the auspices of the WTO.

One could ask whether the changes prompted by the Single Market Programme had the same effects on services as they had on manufacturing. A more apposite question is whether the Programme had an impact on the geographical location of services in the EU, as could have happened with manufacturing. In the case of some services that are tradable because of data-processing and telecommunications technology, such as accounting, there was some centralisation and reallocation of business. For most others, significant changes are not expected in the short and medium term. Skilled accountants are able to move around the EU and offer their services, but the Greek islands (tourism) will remain where they are.

The financial services deal with promises to pay. In a world of developed telecom services, these promises can move instantaneously all around the globe. Customs posts do not matter in this business. Nonetheless, restrictive rights of establishment may limit the freedom to supply these services. Traditionally, monetary power has been jealously protected and saved for domestic authorities. This has changed in recent decades. The international mobility of capital can hardly be stopped, therefore countries try to make the best use of it. Not only do financial services generate employment and earnings in their right, but, more importantly, the efficient allocation of resources and the competitiveness of the manufacturing sector depends on wide choice, efficient and low costs of financial services.

The still evolving legislative framework for the single EU market in services is based on the following four principal elements:

- *Freedom of establishment.* Enterprises from other EU countries may not be discriminated against and must receive national treatment in the country of operation. This is important in the services sector because of the need for direct contact between the providers and consumers of services. A single licence is required for the provision of services throughout the EU. This means that a firm that is entitled to provide services in one EU country has the same right in another EU country. The country that issues such a licence is primarily responsible for the control of the licensed firm on behalf of the rest of the EU.
- *Liberalisation of cross-border trade in services.* This element increases the possibility of cross-border provision of services without the actual physical establishment of the business in the host country. A gradual inclusion and a

full permission of cabotage (internal transport service within a country) was one of the key changes. Cabotage in EU air transport was fully liberalised in 1997, while the same happened in road transport in 1998.[32]

- *Harmonisation of the national rules.* This eases the trans-border establishment of business and the provision of services. This is relevant for telecommunications (technical standards) and financial (solvency) services.
- *Common rules of competition.*

As a result of the First Banking Directive (1977), EU-resident banks are free to open branches throughout the Union, but this is subject to host country authorisation. Foreign banks cannot compete successfully with local banks, as the costs of establishment differ widely among countries. In addition, foreign banks may be excluded from certain services (securities) which are reserved for the local residents. The Second Banking Directive (1989) brought a major breakthrough in the EU banking industry as it introduced the single banking licence. From 1993, member countries of the EU accepted the home country control principle, as well as a mutual recognition of each others' licensing rules for the banks.

Full harmonisation of the banking laws in the EU countries is, however, neither easy nor necessary. Banking laws among the states in the US differ, but this has never been a major handicap to the economic performance of the country. As financial services become globalised, the challenge to the EU and its member countries is to adjust to this change and remain competitive, become mature or lose out to other competitors. If third-country banks wish to benefit from the Single European Market, the Second Banking Directive asks for reciprocal treatment. However, it subsequently became evident that this would be an unrealistic provision in relation to US banks. These banks are not allowed to enter into certain financial operations (such as securities) across the boundaries of federal states. It would be unreasonable to give EU banks operating in the US more favourable treatment than domestic US banks and/or to expect the US to change the domestic rules because of a different regulation in the EU. In the end, the reciprocity provision did not apply to subsidiaries of US banks that were established in the EU prior to 1 January 1993.

The insurance business is very special and complex indeed. There are few homogeneous products and there is usually a long-term relation between the parties. If a consumer purchases a bottle of Scotch whisky, he still has the pleasure of consuming this drink even if the producer goes out of business. The same is not true for an insurance policy. Control of the insurance business is exercised by regulating entry into the business. Insurers in the EU are granted the general right to establish (locate operations in another partner country), but they are often permitted to solicit business only through local agencies. This is particularly true for compulsory insurance.[33] The rationale for such restrictions can be found in the protection of consumers' interests because of the asymmetric information between the seller and the buyer (the seller may know much more about the policy than the buyer),[34] but it can be employed for the protection of local businesses too. Where a sound case for the protection of local consumers ends and where a barrier to trade in the insurance business and protection of the local industry begins is difficult to determine. Buyers of an insurance policy may appreciate the benefits of relatively tougher regulation but may not wish to accept the higher costs involved.[35]

Progress in the EU was faster in the non-life than in the life insurance business. The directive (1988) on the freedom to supply non-life insurance distinguished between two kinds of risks. Mass risks (commercial risks) and large risks (transport, marine, aviation) are covered by the home country regulation of the insurer, whereas personal insurance is covered by national regulations in the country where the policy-holder resides. Integration in the insurance business in the EU has not advanced as much as in the field of banking. EU insurance companies are allowed to compete only under the host country rules, which significantly reduces the opportunity for real competition. In fact, the insurance industry is hardly affected by the 'globalisation' of business. Highly protected national insurance markets would require a great deal of harmonisation before real competition could take place and before a 'single EU insurance passport' could be introduced. The process may take longer than in banking because distortions in the insurance business are much more complex and because the interpretation of the Cassis de Dijon case has not yet been applied to insurance services.

As part of the implementation of the Single Market Programme, personal insurance policies started to be sold and advertised freely in the EU in 1994. This is not to say that insurers and consumers had reason to rejoice. One reason for this is that national tax treatment still favours local companies. These firms have a wide network of tied agents that may not be easily and swiftly replicated by foreign competitors. Another reason is national restraints on the sale of certain types of policies. For example, Italy banned the sale of kidnap insurance because of the concern that it would encourage abductions.

Uncoordinated national laws can no longer provide the basis for future developments of financial services in the EU. This is increasingly important in the light of increasing globalisation and a loss of an EU-specific dimension in business, especially in banking. If the EU wants to preserve or even increase the existing amount of business and employment that goes with it, it is crucial that it fosters the development of an open and efficient market for financial services. Consumers will gain a wider choice, better quality and cheaper financial services, which is essential for the competitiveness of the manufacturing industry and the smooth operation of the whole economy.

The Debauve case (1980) dealt with advertising. It showed how complicated may be cases in the services sector. Belgium prohibited advertising on TV. Nonetheless, cable TV programmes that originated in other countries without such restrictions and which were marketed in Belgium contained advertising messages. The issue was whether the government of Belgium had the right to ban advertising on channels received in the country but which originate in other countries. The EU Court of Justice concluded that, in the absence of the EU action, each member state would regulate and even prohibit advertising on TV on its territory on the grounds of general interest. The question here is what was the 'general interest' in this case? A typical argument for regulation would be the protection of consumers (viewers). An increase in the choice of channels would not be against the interests of the viewers regardless of whether or not foreign programmes contain advert breaks. Therefore, the argument that an improvement in the welfare of those in Belgium who wished to watch foreign channels was increased by the ban cannot hold water (Hindley, 1991: 279). If Belgian viewers watch foreign programmes (with or without advertising), they will watch fewer domestic channels. Hence, support for the public financing of domestic TV will decrease. An additional reason for the Belgian policy was the protection of the advertising revenue of the local newspapers.

Both large-scale and flexible modes of production require efficient and reliable transport services. The sophistication of consumer demand and a reduction in own-account transportation have increased demand for transport services. Just-in-time delivery systems (frequent, punctual and reliable shipments) are favoured by sophisticated logistics as they reduce storage costs but they rely on competitive transport services. The majority of firms in the haulage industry are small or medium-sized. Around 95 per cent of the companies have fewer than six vehicles. This reflects the fact that road haulage markets are mainly local (Carlén, 1994: 89). Two-thirds of all goods transported by road in the EU travel less than 50 km, a further 20 per cent travel between 50 and 150 km, leaving only 14 per cent travelling distances of over 150 km (European Commission, 1992: 11). This finding suggests the existence of a geographical clustering of manufacturers in the vicinity of consumers in the EU. While in most of the EU countries road transport is geared towards the domestic service (most obvious in Greece, Spain and Portugal), the Netherlands and Belgium direct around a half of their road transport services to other countries (primarily Germany) because of their important ports (Rotterdam and Antwerp respectively).

In the past, the operation of commercial transport vehicles and the supply of transport services was highly restricted throughout the EU. Free competition did not exist. This is understandable as all countries apply qualitative controls (safety standards), but also operate quantitative controls. Cabotage was generally prohibited, while bilateral permits negotiated between member states regulated haulage between them.

The EU was relatively successful in introducing special transport permits valid for a limited time throughout the EU. However, the number of these permits was relatively small in relation to demand. The shortage of international haulage licences that are acceptable for business throughout the EU has created a black market for them. The price of an annual permit for a lorry to carry goods around the EU could be as high as a fifth of a lorry's operating costs. International road transport in the EU was fully liberalised from 1993. Liberalisation of rules regarding EU road haulage, including cabotage (from 1998), increased the potentials for efficiency of transport and reduced the costs of this service to the manufacturing sector, trade and distribution.[36] Initially, there was a quota of around 30,000 authorisations (valid for two months) for cabotage in the EU. This number was progressively increased until 1998, after which EU hauliers were free to pick up or deliver their cargo anywhere in the EU without any restrictions. Nonetheless, cabotage represents a negligible part of the EU transport market (less than 1 per cent). The Single Administrative Document for carrying goods among the member countries of the EU is a significant step in the direction of improving the transport service.

The EU skies were opened to all EU-domiciled air transport companies in 1997. These companies are allowed to operate domestic air service (cabotage) in the EU country of their choice. In addition, they can offer air transport services between EU countries. However, anyone who expects seismic changes in this market will be disappointed. Few companies are likely to start a domestic air service in other countries. Barriers to 'real' competition in this industry involve various national bilateral deals holding sway over long-haul flights to non-European destinations. Alitalia cannot operate flights between Paris and New York because the Franco-American deal does not allow for such a possibility. These bilateral deals are the result of arrangements between governments, not airlines. Hence, the solution needs to be found in administration. Nonetheless, there are slow moves towards reshaping the EU air travel market.

One of the fastest growing industries in the services sector is telecommunications. This is due to the profound technological changes that have taken place since the 1960s, which include communication via satellite, microwaves and digital technology. New goods and services, such as fax machines, electronic mail and mobile phones, also appeared. At total of €450bn has been invested in the EU information industry. The natural monopoly argument for the provision of long-distance as well as local services has vanished. EU policy in the telecommunication field was slow and late to appear. During the mid-1980s, the EU was concentrating its efforts on R&D and common standardisation. Subsequently, the aim of having an open network was translated into a directive in 1990. In addition, public contracts that exceed €0.6m in the industry must be transparent and officially published. Directive 96/19/EC introduced full competition in the telecommunications market in 1998, although Greece, Portugal and Spain were allowed a few years' grace. This means that EU consumers have the right to have a phone connected, access to new services, have services of a specified quality and benefit from new methods of solving problems between the consumer and the provider of the service. The obvious benefit was an increase in the number of telecommunication services (often free access to the Internet, huge growth in mobile telecommunications) and a sharp decline in the price of these services.

Business services have high rates of growth too. They include accountancy, auditing, legal, R&D, information, data processing, computing and various engineering and management consultancy services. Different technical standards, licensing of professionals and government procurement of services represent barriers to the free supply of services throughout the EU. A liberal treatment of these services may reduce their costs and increase the efficiency of business. In a world undergoing continuous changes in technology, markets, laws and so on, consultants who manage to stay at least one step ahead of their clients will survive.

Outlook

The policy of the EU towards services should be founded on three major freedoms: the freedom to establish business (geographical liberty), the freedom to offer services and the freedom to transfer capital. Deregulation in the services sector increased competition, which reduced costs for consumers, increased opportunities and improved the competitive position of the entire economy. Apart from deregulation, the promotion of the development of the EU-wide service industries needs to be encouraged. Initial steps towards this objective include recognition of qualifications, single banking and insurance licences, removal of restrictions on transport and the opening up of government procurement over a certain (small) threshold to all EU suppliers.

Although the general interests of a member country do not always conform with the overall interest of the EU, the EU Court has often been reluctant to question national stances. This has limited the effectiveness of Articles 49–55[37] as well as Article 86[38] of the Treaty of Rome. While the Cassis de Dijon case was applied to internal trade in goods, the application of the same principle to services is waiting for 'better times'. The relatively 'soft' stance of the EU regarding restrictive agreements and abuse of dominant position in services cannot easily be explained only by the properties of services; one also needs to add the influence of entrenched businesses, lobbies and the public protection of specific interests. Nonetheless, it is slowly being realised that regulation which limits competition prevents, rather than stimulates, efficiency in services such as telecommunication, transport and finance.

As the provision of most services has a local character (because many of them are non-tradable), there will be no big change in the geographical location of their production. Local incumbents have established and operate strong retail networks, and their own reputation (accounting may be an exception) may act as an additional barrier to entry. Because of this aspect of services, national regulation may remain dominant in many industries within the services sector in the future. The structure of ownership, however, may change as local firms enter into the network of large TNCs in the industry. However, one should not exaggerate the potential expansion of TNCs in the services sector as most mergers and acquisitions in the sector have a strong national dimension. An international, i.e. EU, dimension in the services sector is growing in the insurance industry. Allianz, the biggest insurer in the EU, earned 48 per cent of its premium income outside Germany in 1990, compared with only 18 per cent in 1985 (Sapir, 1993: 37).

The impact of the Single European Market on the changing geography of production is much more obvious in the manufacturing sector than in services. This is the consequence of a much higher degree of tradability of goods than is the case with services. The impact on services may not be immediately obvious. It will take a long time to materialise in reality. The Single Market brought certain benefits to the consumers of services. The most obvious are in telecommunications. However, large-scale benefits may be absent because of important barriers that include the reputation of the already established service firms, past experience, excess capacity and cultural differences. It may be wrong to expect that the genuine internal market will cause an equalisation of prices of services throughout the EU. Prices will only tend to converge because of increased competition. Nonetheless, some price differentials will persist because of differences in productivity and taxation as well as the needs and preferences of the local markets.

Some trends are, however, obvious. There is a general movement for the share of services in the economy to expand, while that of the manufacturing industry shrinks. In addition, the services sector of the economy is more dispersed (because of limited tradability) than the manufacturing sector. As personal income increases, there is a disproportional increase in demand for services. At the same time, many manufacturing industries are farming out various services (from cleaning to accounting and design) and relying on external specialist firms to provide them. Finally, as manufacturing in the EU undergoes some degree of geographical reallocation, this will have an impact on the location of services, which may follow their clients in the manufacturing sector.

4.5 Conclusion

Consideration of the various problems that arose during the creation and implementation of an industrial policy in the manufacturing and services sectors of a country has given an insight into the magnitude of the problems in this field which face schemes that integrate countries. There is at least one forceful argument that favours the introduction of an industrial policy. The neo-conservative school argues that a free market system is the best existing method for solving economic problems. However, this cannot be accepted without reservations. Neither the economic performance of the US prior to the New Deal nor contemporary economic performance in the most successful industrialised countries such as Germany, Japan or Sweden supports this view. Strategic government intervention and comprehensive social welfare programmes, rather than free markets, have been the engines of economic success throughout the advanced industrial world (Tyson and Zysman, 1987b: 426). In fact, free markets were often no more than 'fine-tuning' policy choices of the government.

A country with a flexible policy towards manufacturing industry in response to market signals (such as Japan during the 1960s and 1970s) or one that shapes the market (France during the 1950s and 1960s) is better able to adapt to changes than a country that largely resists such changes (such as in Britain in the case of coal and steel production during the 1970s). Industrial policy that ignores market signals and that supports industries with obsolete technologies introduces confusion over future developments and increases the cost of inevitable change. These costs may be much higher in the future than they were in the past because of social rigidities and rapid changes in technology. The success of an industrial policy may be tested by its effectiveness in shifting resources from industries that use ailing technologies, not by how effective it is in preventing this adjustment. However, the problem is that even the most sophisticated national or international institutions do not know exactly what will happen in the future (recall the debt crises in the 1980s and another case about the impact of Microsoft on the economy).

A policy of picking a winner (a strategic industry with important externalities) *ex ante* may propel the economy of a country in the future. This may have a favourable outcome for the country or the EU if the choice is correct, if this policy is coordinated with the suppliers of inputs and if it is limited to a defined period of time in which the national champion is expected to become self-reliant. The other interventionist approach of rescue (*ex post*) may simply postpone the attrition of the assisted industry and increase the overall costs of change to the society.

The shifts out of industries that use obsolete production technologies into modern ones seems easy in theory but can be quite difficult, costly and slow in practice. This is, of course, a matter of political choice. The inability to do something is different from an unwillingness to do it. The EU opted for the creation of the Single European Market as the environment that favours change. Nonetheless, its direct industrial policy is in many respects a set of R&D policies coupled with public procurement. Other dimensions of industrial policy are implemented within the domain of competition, trade, regional, education and monetary (stability) policies. It is to be hoped that the 'social dimension' in the future of the EU will remain only as a set of non-obligatory standards that will not mislead the EU into the complacency that would kill the urge for continuous change for the better.

The shaping of an industrial policy in every country requires detailed data about the available factors, competition, externalities, changes in the production and management technology, policies of the major trading partners, as well as about the tax, legal and political environment. Even then, industrial policy prescriptions should be taken with a pinch of salt. At the time when Britain was industrialising it was the textile industry that was the leader in technology. The capital required to start up a textile firm was much smaller than that required to build a steel mill, which was the leading manufacturing industry when Germany started to industrialise. The problems of development had to be solved by government incentives (intervention) and bank loans. Modern industries require not only capital investment (in many cases this entails reliance on banks) but also, and more importantly, investment in highly qualified personnel. Education policy is always shaped to a large extent by government.

There are justifiable reasons for pessimism about the ability to create and implement an effective industrial policy in a decentralised country or a group of integrated countries. Many agents and issues need to be taken into account during the decision-making process about uncertain events. Remember the story about debt crises and the success of Microsoft from Chapter 2. Numerous agencies have an impact on industrial policy, including ministries of trade, finance, social affairs, education, regional development, energy, technology, defence and foreign affairs. Most of these departments exist at the federal, regional and local levels. There are also labour unions, banks, industrial associations and non-governmental organisations. They all have diverse and often conflicting goals. The complexity of coordination, communication and harmonisation of all these players increases exponentially with their number. In spite of all those organisational difficulties, the rewards are worthwhile.[39] However, while numerous agents may, of course, be a source of creativity, in practice they often turn out to be a source of disagreement over the distribution of instruments of industrial policy. The interaction of all these players has an amalgamating effect on the national industrial policy. To reconcile all these diverse demands is a great political challenge.

Luckily, the evidence in the cases of Japan (1960–90) and Germany may serve as examples to other countries in the shaping of national industrial policies. The crucial property of a promising industrial policy is that if it cannot be organised centrally then it ought to coordinate measures taken at lower levels. Without a consensus about the basic objectives of industrial policy among the major players and their commitment to these goals, such a policy will not come about. Exchange of views, mutual understanding, trust, support and, finally, an agreement about the goals and means of industrial policy between governments at all levels, business community and labour is an essential element of its effectiveness.

While the EU creates conditions for competition, its member countries implement their own national industrial policies. The divergence in industrial policy philosophies among the member countries and a lack of funds has prevented the EU from playing a more influential role. The variety of uncoordinated national policies has introduced confusion and uncertainty regarding the future actions of the EU. Until the member countries take advantage of a vast Single European Market, they may not profit from the potentials for an increase in the competitive edge in a number of industries primarily *vis-à-vis* the US, but also Japan and some newly industrialised countries. If it attempts to be durable and successful, an EU industrial policy will require the agreement of the member states about their objectives and policy means. A new philosophy by the European Commission regarding industrial policy is based on the idea that this policy needs to offer primarily a stable macroeconomic environment. The EMU epitomises this policy stance. It is expected that enterprises can be left alone within such ambience to do their best to remain competitive.

The 'golden rules' for a respectable industrial policy include the following:

- The policy should not harm other parts of the economy.
- The policy needs to be continuous and stable.
- The policy instruments should reinforce each other.
- Inflation needs to be low, rates of interest positive and exchange rates stable. In such an environment incentives exist for savings and investment.
- Public borrowing needs to be small in order to give the private sector better opportunities for obtaining investment funds.
- If necessary, intervention needs to be general and offer support to industries, rather than individual firms within them.
- There always needs to be an element of choice among various courses of action, as well as the flexibility to respond to crises and opportunities.
- If certain support (such as subsidies, tariffs or quotas) is offered, it should have a timetable, be transparent and be of limited duration, after which it has to be withdrawn.
- There needs to be a reference to investment in human capital. Well-trained labour and an educated management are the most valuable created assets

that an economy can have. The policy needs to create a 'learning society' that supports and rewards the acquisition of new skills and promotes the flexibility needed for adapting to constant changes in the economy and technology.[40]

- Measures to ease the adjustment frictions are often a necessary element in an industrial policy. Emphasis needs to be on all industries (including traditional ones) that use modern technologies.
- A relatively easy international transfer of production from one location to another within a liberal trading system has to be kept in mind. National location-specific advantages for the production of specific goods and services need to be cultivated.
- The policy should not neglect the creation of SMEs, which form valuable links throughout the economy, not only with large firms, but also with producers and consumers.
- There needs to be a consensus among the major players (employers, employees and the government) in the economy about the global economic goals and means for their achievement. These players should also be committed to the achievement of the agreed goals. This implies that the long-term vision of the goals needs to be realistic.
- Public support to R&D and innovation should increase the exchange of information among the interested parties.
- As private capital is generally uninterested in investment in infrastructure, the government needs to step into this field on its own and to stimulate public–private partnership.

Although industrial policy is wider than trade or competition policy, the boundaries between them are blurred. Whether an industrial policy increases national GDP compared with what would happen without it can be debated for a long time without a solution to satisfy everyone. A promising industrial policy should neither shield expanding industries from competition for an excessively long period of time nor prevent the attrition of declining industries forever. It ought to facilitate the movements of factors from industries that employ obsolete technologies to industries that use modern technologies.

Industrial policy has to be well coordinated at all levels of government with other economic policies that affect the manufacturing and services sectors. Without successful communication, harmonisation and coordination, intervention in industry will be similar to the work of a brain-damaged octopus. This holds both for single countries and for integration schemes that integrate countries. Nonetheless, traditional behaviour is sometimes hard to change in reality, even though the need for change is recognised. The EU has chosen the Single Market and the EMU as paths to create conditions for change according to market criteria of efficiency. It is up to the economic agents to take advantages of these opportunities.

Certain results from such a choice began to emerge. The industrial structure of the EU countries became more specialised from the early 1980s than was the case before. This confirms the theoretical expectations of both the standard, neo-classical and new theory of economic integration. A new pattern of industrial production is emerging in the EU. The major features of this process of divergence in the economic structure of the EU countries include the following (Midelfart-Knarvik *et al.*, 2000: 46–7):

- The process is slow and does not provoke great adjustment costs.
- There was a certain convergence among the geography of production in the EU countries towards the EU average during the 1970s, whereas since the early 1980s countries have tended to diverge from the EU average. This is a general sign of increased national specialisation in the EU. The most remarkable national change in the geography of production was the spread of relatively high-technology and high-skill industries to the peripheral countries of Ireland and Finland.
- Not all industries follow the same path as a reaction to economic integration. Some of them concentrate, while others spread (contrary to the expectations of the neo-classical theory). Several forces, therefore, propel such changes in the structure of production. Strong functional intra-industry linkages (high share of intermediate goods from the same industry and/or the need for a large pool of highly skilled labour and researchers) stimulate agglomeration. Weak functional linkages acts as an incentive to the spread of production.
- While 'economic integration' has made the US geography of industrial production more similar (less specialised) since 1940s, integration in the EU had as its consequence growing disparity (increasing specialisation) in manufacturing production. This slow process in both regions shows no signs of abating. The driving force for this is still not known.
- The slow change in the geography of production has not provoked major adjustment costs in the EU. If this continues, and if it is associated with production linkages and comparative advantages, there will be long-term benefits for everyone.
- Availability of highly skilled and educated workers and engineers is becoming an increasingly important determinant of industrial location.
- Agglomeration tendencies towards the central locations became more pronounced for industries that use many intermediate inputs.
- High returns to scale are weakening as centripetal (agglomeration) forces.

Notes

1 Lipsey (1993: 12), first used the term 'massaged-market economies'.
2 Strategic is not taken here to have any military sense, but rather refers to businesses that have important forward and backward links with other industries, as well as strong and positive externalities (spillovers) on the rest of the economy.
3 There is a growing awareness that *most* external economies apply at a regional or metropolitan level, rather than at an international one. Therefore, the fears that external economies would be geographically dissipated abroad is mostly wrong (Krugman, 1993b: 161, 167).

4   Akio Morita, the chairman of Sony Corporation, argued that 'an economy can be only as strong as its manufacturing base. An economy that does not manufacture well cannot continue to invest adequately in itself. An economy whose only growth is in the service sector is built on sand. Certainly, the service sector is an important and growing economic force. But it cannot thrive on its own, serving hamburgers to itself and shifting money from one side to another. An advanced service economy can thrive only on the strength of an advanced manufacturing economy underlying it ... The notion of a postindustrial economy that is based principally on services is a dubious one' (Morita, 1992: 79).

5   Entrepreneurs (sometimes seen as 'maniacs with a vision') often have genuine ideas, but many of them do not have the necessary knowledge about how to run a business.

6   New technologies are less and less sector or industry specific. The same holds for modern firms. Many of them cannot be easily classified in the group of enterprises that belongs to only one industry or sector.

7   A common definition of an SME uses the number of employees as the determining factor. Small enterprises are taken to be those with up to twenty-five employees, while medium-sized ones have up to 250 workers.

8   A few examples are given in Chapter 2.

9   Groups that lobby in Brussels include 400 trade associations, around 300 large firms, 150 non-profit pressure groups, 120 regional and local governments and 180 specialist law firms (*The Economist*, 15 April 1995: 26). Together, they have around 10,000 lobbyists, and their number is steadily rising since the start of the Single Market Programme because of its implication for business (*The European Voice*, 17 February 2000: 8). A very high concentration of lobby services in Washington, DC, made, in some cases, a collection of some (private) interests stronger than those of the government.

10   A lack of natural resources made Japan invest in the development of human and technological capital.

11   Airbus was established in 1970. It is a publicly sponsored consortium of British (British Aerospace, 20 per cent), French (Aérospatiale, 37.9 per cent), German (Deutsche Airbus, 37.9 per cent) and Spanish (CASA, 4.2 per cent) enterprises. It was established without the involvement of the EU and under the French law as a *Groupement d'Intérêt Economique*. As such, it makes no profits or losses in its own right. This means that the accounts of the group are available only to the four shareholders. Unlike Boeing's accounts, which are accessible to the public, Airbus's accounts are concealed from the public and the profit disguised in the accounts of its shareholders. It is, therefore, difficult to assess the commercial success of the best-known consortium in Europe. Why then does Boeing not pressure the US administration to do something about this? As around half of the value built into Airbuses is of US origin, the producers of these components have a strong lobbying power in Washington, DC, and could counter that of Boeing.

Airbus received in subsidies for new models of aircraft in the period 1970–94 between $10 and $20bn, depending on whether the source of the data is Europe or America (*The Economist*, 8 July 1995: 14). If these subsidies have been granted for such a long time and in such a large volume, one wonders if the artificial comparative advantage has really been successful!

Airbus is expected to become a limited company in 2001. Only a fully integrated company can know what its costs are and introduce policies that will drive costs down in order to keep the company competitive. Such a corporate strategy is enhanced because of Boeing's (in 1997 it sold seven out of ten commercial aircraft with more than 100 seats) takeover of McDonnell-Douglas.

12   The policy goal was to acquire the production of war materials. There was little concern about antitrust laws, international competitiveness or competing national objectives (Badaracco and Yoffie, 1983: 99). Governments have always affected industrial

development through trade policy, public procurement, taxes and subsidies, as well as provision of public goods.

13 One has, however, to remember extreme cases which are not very numerous, but exist everywhere. The most highly paid people are not always highly educated. Many pop singers or sportspeople have a poor education. However, one cluster of educated people that is being paid most are managers and lawyers (in the countries where law means something).

14 *Single Market News*, February 1996: 13.

15 *The Week in Europe*, 1 July 1999.

16 Old Article 130f.

17 Old Article 130h.

18 Old Article 130i.

19 Old Article 130m.

20 In the period 1987–93, the total public funds for R&D in the US were €168bn, while in Europe 'only' €66bn was allocated for that purpose (Jacquemin, 1996: 176). Europe invests 2 per cent of GNP in R&D, while the same investment in the US is 3 per cent. Japan invests even more in R&D (Micossi, 1996: 160).

21 In the US, small, high-technology firms sell as much as half of their output to the federal government and benefit from R&D support. In contrast, public procurement in Europe is effected through a small number of large national suppliers. This suggests that fostering of a free entry and mobility within flexible industries may be a superior policy choice than supporting a few giants that react to changes with some delay (Geroski and Jacquemin, 1985: 177).

22 Nobody in the European Commission uses the term 'five-year plan'. That would remind many on the five-year plans in the former centrally planned economies of Eastern Europe.

23 The First Framework Programme (1984–87) disposed of a budget of €3.7bn, the Second Framework Programme (1987–91) had a budget of €6.5bn, while the Third Framework Programme (1991–94) was allocated €8.8bn.

24 FAST is a shared-cost programme involving a number of research and forecasting centres in the EU. It is an instrument for studying future developments, as well as the impact and social uses of science and technology.

25 Software, aerospace, telecommunications, advance materials, semiconductors, biotechnology and defence technology.

26 Electronics and cars.

27 Even a layperson would say 'Cows were created as herbivorous animals. Don't make them eat meat products!'.

28 They include businesses in both manufacturing and services sectors. The impact on services is discussed below.

29 Do you remember your first (or for that matter even your second or third) taxi ride from the airport in a south European country as a foreigner? If you have not yet experienced this pleasure, be assured it is one you will remember.

30 Old Articles 52–68.

31 Old Article 90.

32 Cabotage operations in road transport grew considerably in the period 1990–98. Most cabotage (68 per cent in 1997) was carried out in Germany. Nonetheless, this represented only 1 per cent the German national transport market (European Commission, COM[2000] 105, 28.2.2000: 9). Cabotage in air transport is also rather small: not more than 4–5 per cent of the total internal EU air transport market.

33 The number of car accidents per motor car or per inhabitant may be higher in one country than another. Hence, because of higher risk, differences in insurance premiums among countries will remain in spite of increased competition.

34 'As patriotism is the last refuge of scoundrels (according to Dr Johnson), the welfare of widows, orphans, and the incompetent is the last refuge of supporters of regulation.

Individuals free to make their own decisions will indeed make mistakes. Even if potential buyers are clearly informed of the regulatory regime, some will not understand its significance. Even if large amounts of information are available on that significance, some will not bother to obtain it ... Protection of the foolish against error provides a rationale for almost infinite extension' (Hindley, 1991: 272–3).

35 Everyone may appreciate the benefits of a car such as a BMW or a Mercedes. It is quite another thing, however, whether consumers are willing to pay or have the means to pay for such a motor car. A small Fiat may be the ultimate limit for many of them.

36 The US offered a convincing example of deregulation of the inter-state transport services in 1980.

37 Old Articles 59–66.

38 Old Article 90.

39 Without the highest degree of coordination one would not be able to fly to the Moon and return safely to the Earth.

40 Education may be a subsidised input for which the business sector has not paid the full price. Nonetheless, countervailing duties cannot be introduced by foreign partners as education often takes a long time and cannot be easily and directly valued as is the case with other subsidies, such as those for exports.

5 Geography of foreign direct investment

5.1 Introduction

The geography of production is shaped not only by national firms and governments, but also by foreign-owned (controlled) firms and organisations that impose international rules. Some preferential trading or integration agreements such as common markets permit the free movement of factors among member countries on the condition that factors originating in partner countries are not subjected to discrimination. The promotion of geographical and sectoral factor mobility results in more efficient allocation of resources from the group's standpoint. These improvements in the locational advantages of the group for business are due to the free internal factor flow from low- to high-productivity locations and businesses within the common market. In this situation, factors respond to signals that include demand, higher productivity and higher returns within a common market.

This chapter is devoted to the mobility of capital. It considers the relation between factor mobility and trade, including globalisation; major aspects of TNCs; intervention and the nature and significance of the impact of integration on TNCs and vice versa; and FDI flows in the EU.

5.2 Factor mobility and trade

Let us start by assuming a model that consists of two countries A and B, two final goods X and Y and two factors of production K and L. Suppose further that factor mobility is perfect within each country but prohibited between countries. If there are no barriers to trade and no distortions, if technology is the same and freely accessible to both countries, if production functions are completely homogeneous, if both goods are produced in both countries and isoquants intersect only once (there is no factor intensity reversal), then free trade in goods will equalise relative prices in goods. This will equalise both relative factor prices and their returns in each country. This stringent situation is illustrated in Figure 5.1.

In Figure 5.1, X_a represents the unit isocost line (the combination of factors which keeps output constant) for good X in country A (production of which is relatively labour 'intensive'), while X_b describes the same cost line for good X in country B, where its production is relatively capital 'intensive'. Equilibrium occurs

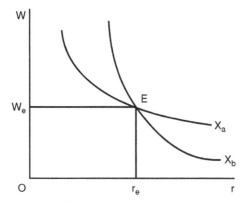

Figure 5.1 Equalisation of factor prices.

at point E, where factor prices are equalised through trade at levels Or$_e$ for capital and OW$_e$ for labour. In this model trade is a substitute for factor mobility.

The exclusion of balance of payments adjustments from comparative statistics implies that the adjustment process between the two distant points in time has worked well and that the balance is in equilibrium. However, in reality, such a process may last for up to a generation. Thus, a static model, which usually neglects the adjustment process, can hardly be justified. Capital accumulation, economies of scale and economic growth produce different results in the long term from the straightforward static model.

Free international trade in goods and factor movements are prevented by the existence of various barriers. In this framework, according to one view, commodity movements are still a substitute for factor movements. An increase in trade restrictions stimulates factor movements while an increase in barriers to international factor mobility enhances trade in goods (Mundell, 1957: 321).

So far it has been assumed that technology is the same in both countries. This is, however, not always the case. Differences in technologies among countries enhances, rather than reduces, the opportunities for international capital mobility. Some developing countries export raw materials in return for FDI, which enables them to produce and later export manufactured goods (Purvis, 1972: 991). When technologies differ, factor mobility may increase the volume of trade, rather than reduce it. Factor mobility and commodity movements may act in this case as complements.

If factor mobility leads to a reduction in the volume of trade in goods, then factor movements and trade in goods are substitutes. This is the case when there are differences in the prices of goods between countries. If labour moves from country A, where good X is dearer, to country B, where this good is cheaper, this decreases the demand for and price of good X in country A and increases demand and price in country B until the two prices are equalised. If relative differences in factor endowments are not the only basis for trade, international mobility of factors and trade may stimulate each other and become supplements (Markusen and Melvin, 1984).

Theoretical explanations of the relation between trade and FDI require further study. If FDI is a response to trade barriers, then FDI acts in a trade-replacing way. If, however, FDI is an efficiency-seeking investment (developing natural resources), then it operates in a trade-promoting way. In any case, there is some evidence that FDI has increased trade in the EU (van Aarle, 1996: 137). An extensive survey of the impact of the Single Market Programme on FDI in the EU found strong evidence that FDI and trade are complementary (European Commission, 1998: 1).

The basis for trade can be something other than a simple difference in factor endowments (factor proportions). Alternative bases for trade include:

- returns to scale;
- imperfect competition;
- difference in market structure;
- difference in production and factor taxes;
- differences in efficiency in production and technology (production functions);
- differences in tastes;
- differences in growth rates.

In this case, free geographical mobility of factors results in countries becoming relatively well endowed with the factors used 'intensively' in the production of export goods (Markusen, 1983: 355). International mobility of factors and trade are often taken to be complements, rather than substitutes. A high mobility and concentration of factors (designers in northern Italy, chemical engineers in Basle, financial experts in London and New York or computer scientists in California or Boston) will create an additional comparative advantage, which will, in turn, enhance trade. 'Globalisation' of international business and the integrated international operations of TNCs contribute to this situation. This is most obvious in the EU, where an expansion of intra-group FDI and TNC operation has accompanied a high level of intra-group trade.

The factor price equalisation theorem anticipates that free trade will have as its consequence parity of wage levels among countries. This need not always be the case. Migration is a necessary condition for the equalisation of wages if the majority of labour in both high-wage countries and low-wage countries is employed in the production of non-tradable goods. In this case free trade is not a sufficient condition for the equalisation of wages between the countries involved.

Substitutability between trade in goods and mobility of factors (the Hecksher–Ohlin model) may be the exception, rather than the rule. If countries are quite different in relative factor endowments and with weak economies of scale, then individuals who draw their income from factors that are relatively scarce end up worse off as a result of trade. If countries are similar and trade is mostly motivated by economies of scale (intra-industry trade), then one might expect to find that even scarce factors gain (Krugman, 1990b: 80).

5.3 Mobility of capital

General considerations

The theory of preferential trade explores the effect of integration on the location of production, structure of trade and welfare. Little attention has been devoted to the geographical origin of ownership of firms. This gap is bridged by the theory of FDI, which studies locational advantages for investment in different countries, competitive advantages of firms that originate in different countries, as well as the interaction between firms, local natural and government resources and capabilities in the context of spatial distribution of economic activities and economic integration.

Entrepreneurs view a country's preferential trading and integration arrangements as a long-term economic indicator, unlike changes in prices, which may reflect only a temporary situation on the market. Entrepreneurs may form expectations with a higher degree of certainty. Hence, TNCs may locate a part of their production in such an expanding area and increase FDI by the creation of 'tariff factories'.

The creation of tariff factories within an integrated area is a strategy that TNCs pursue not to take advantage of their efficiency or to employ a foreign resource (resource efficiency), but rather to benefit from (or avoid) the shield provided by the common external tariff and NTBs. This could be one of the reasons why Japanese TNCs were eager to establish a presence in the EU prior to 1993 and the full implementation of the Single Market Programme to become EU residents and thus circumvent the threat of a 'Fortress Europe'. In addition to such an *investment creation effect* (a strategic response of foreign firms to potential trade diversion), new prospects for improved business without tariffs and quotas on trade within the (protected) region may prompt local firms to rearrange production facilities within the group. This may produce the *investment diversion effect*. This strategic response of firms to trade creation may have as its effect an increase in FDI in some countries in the group and a decrease in FDI in others.

Foreign direct investment reflects the goal of an entrepreneur from country A to acquire a lasting interest (including management) in an asset in country B. In principle, FDI asks for freedom of establishment and, if possible, national treatment in foreign markets. This distinct type of international capital flow has a strong risk-taking and, often, industry-specific dimension. In addition, it is coupled with a transfer of technological know-how as well as management and marketing skills.

Capital moves among countries in the form of portfolio and direct investment. Portfolio investment is most often simply a short-term movement of claims that is speculative in nature. The main objectives include an increase in the value of assets and relative safety. This type of capital mobility may be prompted by differences in interest rates. The recipient country will probably not wish to use these funds for investment in fixed assets that must be repaid in the long term, so these movements of capital may be seen by the recipient country as hot, unstable and 'bad'. Volatility of portfolio investment complicates their analysis. The large number of portfolio investments, made in many cases by brokers, obscures who is doing what and why.

Foreign direct investment is often the result of decisions by TNCs. Therefore, FDI may be a part of a proxy for the investment and location activities of TNCs (keeping in mind that TNCs may control operations abroad simply by issuing licences).

Globalisation

Liberalisation in the national and international economy is a policy choice of *governments*, primarily in the developed world. It is linked with privatisation and downsizing of the activities of the public sector and the expansion of the activities of the private sector. *Globalisation* of the economy and production is a fact. It is the outcome of the behaviour of *firms* (TNCs), their organisation, changing technology in production and distribution, control and finance, as well as economies of scale. In part, it is also the consequence of a change in the behaviour of consumers (declining loyalty to national producers and some national products)[1] and liberalisation of national and international economies for trade, production and finance.

As a process primarily driven by the actions of the TNCs (power is shifted from states to firms),[2] globalisation lacks two important components: transparency and accountability.[3] This process deals with the change in the geography of (integrated international) production and consumption as it reduces the importance of proximity to inputs or markets. It widens boundaries and deepens space for the geographical location of production and consumption because of the declining costs of getting goods and services to the market. A rapid expansion of FDI is the key component of this process. Capital market liberalisation and increased capital mobility have radically reduced the influence of governments in the monetary sphere. However, governments have gained increased control in other areas. For example, computers and information technology have greatly simplified data collection and processing, and consequently enabled increased control over firms and citizens, which is relevant for tax and other purposes. However, the failure to launch a new round of trade negotiations in Seattle in 1999 may slow down the process of globalisation.

The rapid international expansion of TNCs has made them the most visible features of globalisation. As foreign, often large, organisations which sometimes make visible and highly publicised mistakes, TNCs are easy targets for non-governmental organisations (NGOs), which can run successful campaigns to disgrace a mighty TNC. NGOs increased public awareness and pushed through agreements on the control of 'greenhouse gases' at the 'Earth Summit' in Rio de Janeiro in 1992. They also helped in torpedoing the Multilateral Agreement on Investment in 1998 and made a big fuss in Seattle, which contributed to the failure to start a new WTO round of trade negotiations.

Apart from a partial integration of international production, globalisation brings risks and disruptions. Volatile capital flows, speculative attacks on currencies, financial crises and unpredictable reallocation of jobs are obvious examples of increased economic and social vulnerability of many countries. To wrap up the issue, Henry Kissinger labelled globalisation as 'another name for the dominant role of the United States'.[4]

The fashionable term 'globalisation' is not clearly defined. Hence, this fuzzy and powerful metaphor is overused and often abused and it is misleading. Basically, it refers to the choices and strategies, as well as the shape, extent, direction and significance, of the activities of TNCs. Globalisation is also linked with and invigorated by new technologies in communications and information processing. Another incentive to the process of globalisation can be found in changes in economic strategy in many countries as outward-looking economic models replace inward-looking and TNC-hostile economic approaches. The diminished importance of national borders has led some observers to argue that there is little scope for meaningful national policies.

The Internet symbolises borderlessness brought about by globalisation. Physical presence in a specific location is not necessary. In cyberspace, users are 'everywhere and nowhere' at once. However, one does not need to give an absolute value to globalisation. In spite of this process, localisation and clusters (as already seen) still matter. Firms that went furthest in 'globalisation' report that face-to-face contact is essential for the smooth organisation of business within the firm and marketing outside it.

The imposition of 'global' standards may be justified in the case of relatively new goods and services such as photocopiers, fax machines, computers, mobile phones and electronic commerce; if this were not so, international communication could be difficult and costly. However, imposing such standards on traditional goods (e.g. food), except for health reasons, is less readily justified. If preferences for different types of a food are strongly region specific (for example, in Italy the thickness of pizza crust differs between regions) why should one favour or impose global (e.g. Pizza Hut type) standards? Yet another cost of globalisation is exemplified by the financial crises experienced by Mexico, Thailand, Indonesia, South Korea and Russia in the second half of 1990s. Without exposure to global capital markets, the crises would not have developed as they did. The critics of this view argue that these countries would not have developed so quickly before the crises without such exposure.

On the one hand, there is a search by efficiency-seeking enterprises, particularly some TNCs, for seamless and wide international markets regarding trade and investment. The *globalisation* of economic activity is making national frontiers less divisive than was the case a few decades ago.[5] Such worldwide economic integration and integrated international production of goods and services, whereby competitors are in each others' backyards, are made possible by the expansion of information and telecommunication technologies.[6] However, the process is sometimes reversed, i.e. *regionalism* (in the developing world), by relatively inefficient firms and governments that are driven by short-term election interests, especially where the conditions required for a successful integration process, such as prevail in Western Europe, are largely absent.

Regional integration (a second-best solution) may be a promising form of supranational governance in areas where there is a strong case for coordination and harmonisation of national policies. Integration may resolve conflicts through positive cooperation but, if pushed to the limit, it may undermine multilateral (first-best) trade and investment systems and fragment the world economy into conflicting regional blocs. Regionalism and globalisation/multilateralism do not necessarily need to conflict. If the regional blocs adopt fairly liberal external trade and investment policies, and if they cooperate, the general outcome may be an overall welfare improvement. The pace of international trade liberalisation since the 1960s, as well as the extension of the GATT into new areas such as services and agriculture, might have been much slower in the absence of the challenge posed by progress in EU integration. The debate should not be between regionalism and multilateralism, but rather between liberalism and interventionism (Blackhurst and Henderson, 1993: 412).

It is often forgotten that the spirit of 'globalisation' does not bring anything essentially new. The aim is for more freedom for trade in goods and services and a greater liberty for capital mobility (FDI). The economic role of national frontiers declines as national economies merge in a single 'global' unit. To put it bluntly, the objective is to return to the essentials of the system that was prevailing before 1914. In this situation, re-globalisation may be a more appropriate term.

An enlarged market is an important gain for efficiency-seeking firms in a small country. Without integration, foreign countries can simply threaten a small country that they will introduce protectionist measures or sanctions against it (witness the frequent US threats to the Latin American and many other countries). Such a warning can seriously undermine the quality of all economic decisions in the small country. Integration enhances and ensures market access to the partner countries, as well as increasing the potential for the long-term competitiveness of a small country's economy. A common market eliminates or harmonises national incentives to foreign TNCs to locate in the partner countries (which were previously subject to the countervailing duties). It also mitigates non-economic considerations, such as political pressures on third countries' investors to locate in a particular country.

Foreign investors will locate their activities in the country that offers the lowest costs of operation (production and marketing). Nonetheless, FDI is made simpler by regionalisation of the world economy and international economic integration. However, integration/regionalisation is only a supporting tool for the tendencies that bring globalisation of international business. Modern competitive firms are usually TNCs which are globalising their business in the search for seamless and widest markets. Thus, an increasing share of domestic output even in the developed countries is under the control of foreign TNCs. The same holds for an increasing share of foreign output of domestic TNCs. Strong FDI relations may exist even though the countries or groups of countries are not formally integrated. Consider the example of two-way FDI flows between the US and the EU (see Tables 5.5 and 5.7).

In the case of developing countries, it is important to be aware that they sometimes use tariff proceeds for investment purposes. In this case, a customs union may bring to an end an important part of domestic investments by reducing tariff revenue. In a situation with many market imperfections, the opportunities for gains and losses are numerous. Hence, long-term gains in growth that originate in international economic integration may offset this loss of tariff revenue. However, the question asked by the public choice theory is: are we sure that the government of the day in a developing country cares or can afford to care about long-term gains?

Linkages of transnational corporations

Targeting some key productive activities that have significant linkages with the rest of the economy requires some form of government intervention. Japan's decision to target steel, shipbuilding and toys in the 1950s and 1960s was highly profitable. This choice turned out to be questionable in the 1970s, so Japan turned to cars and machine tools. The Japanese have chosen electronics as their target industry in the 1980s and 1990s (Tyson, 1987: 70). This target may, in turn, become obsolete in the near future as software overtakes hardware in importance, and in this sector the US leads. However, in the past the selected industries have had important spillover effects throughout the economy. Telecommunications affect the dissemination of information, computers have an impact on data processing, while transportation equipment affect the size of the market. As a result of these linkages, private returns from these industries are smaller than social returns. The targeting and location, in a common market or any other type of integration, of key industries that may have significant linkages with other industries or partner countries may have important and long-term beneficial spillover effects on the group. Various linkages between the operation of TNCs and the growth process are presented in Figure 5.2.

Investment activity is one of the most sensitive indicators of a country's economic climate. What exactly it indicates, however, is not always clear. Increases in investment may indicate the emergence of new business opportunities, interest in the future, reactions to international competition and response to increasing cost pressures. In any case, sluggish investment activity, as during the 1970s, is an indication of rough economic times (Schatz and Wolter, 1987: 29).

When a firm wants to locate and produce abroad it does not necessarily need to export capital. A firm may rent capital abroad instead of purchasing or building a production unit. Instead of using its own funds, a firm may borrow in its home, host country's or a third country's financial market. In the case of fixed exchange rates, countries may enter into an 'interest rate war' in order to attract capital into their economies. Integrated capital markets with harmonised rates of interest and mobility of capital may prevent this outcome. While labour markets are most often regional (in Europe), capital markets were national and are becoming international.

Neither firms nor governments depend on savings in their home markets. Interest rates and demand for funds in one country are affected by money (short-term) and capital (long-term) markets in other countries because of the links among financial markets. Small countries are interest rate takers, so that even the

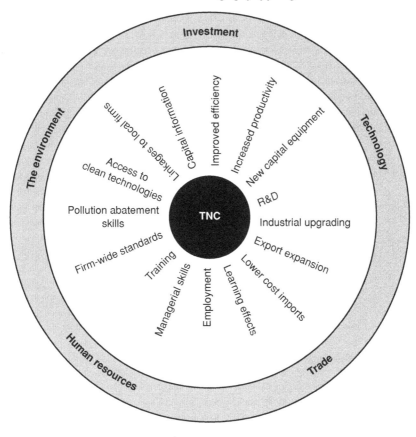

Figure 5.2 Transnational corporations and the growth process.

Source: World Investment Report: Transnational Corporations as Engines of Growth. New York: United Nations, 1992.

national housing (non-traded good) market feels the impact from foreign markets by means of changes in interest rates. Free mobility of capital prevents the independent conduct of monetary policy. If a country lowers interest rates in relation to third countries, then capital will flow abroad. This also destabilises the exchange rate if all else is equal. In addition, if a country increases interest rates in relation to foreign countries, if other things are constant, capital will flow into the country. The supply of money increases, hence inflation is the consequence.

Financial markets may sometimes favour large companies and countries and discriminate against small companies and countries. Large companies and countries provide greater security that the funds will be returned and interest paid. A large stock of assets provides this confidence. These markets may discriminate against risky investments such as seabed research, new sources of energy and the like. By integrating capital markets, small countries may mitigate the effect of their relative disadvantage.

The electronics industry in Taiwan has benefited from a geographical variety of foreign investors (mainly from the US and Japan). These TNCs provided education for managers and training for workers, improved efficiency and quality of production and created stable markets and production and marketing links with local suppliers. These initiatives provided a solid foundation for the creation of an indigenous electronic industry in Taiwan. The industry evolved with global standards. Mexico's misfortune in the electronics industry was that it received FDI only from declining US parts makers and assemblers. This was coupled with a lack of integration with the domestic Mexican electronics industry. Crediting the Taiwanese government for the success of this industry and blaming the Mexican government for its failure would be too simplistic (Lowe and Kenney, 1999: 1439). Sceptics argue that Japan and Korea would have experienced superior growth trajectories had it not been for selective intervention. Given macroeconomic stability, equilibrium and a stable exchange rate, high and stable savings and investment rates, an enterprising spirit, a respectable level of education, relatively competitive labour markets and a relatively liberal trading system were more than enough to stimulate even faster growth. The contribution of selective intervention was negligible or harmful (Pack, 2000: 51).

Trans-border business activities

There are four main types of trans-border business activities that are conducted by TNCs: market seeking, resource based, rationalised and strategic asset seeking (Dunning, 1999: 3–4). *Market seeking* (demand-oriented) investments search for new markets, but they replace trade. They are influenced by the relative size and growth of the foreign market in which the investment is made, the relative costs of supplying that market through imports or local production, as well as the relative advantage of engaging in direct local production or licensing.

Resource seeking (supply-oriented) FDI is motivated by the availability and cost of both natural resources and labour in the target location. As the products of such investments are often exported abroad, the economic climate in foreign markets, changes in technology, transport costs and barriers to trade influence the attractiveness of such investment to TNCs.

Rationalised investments seek efficiency. Like resource-based investments, they are complementary to trade. Their attractiveness is found in cost considerations. They are influenced by the ease with which intermediate or final products (linked to economies of scale and specialisation) can be traded on the international market. A case in question is the US loss of competitiveness as a site for labour-'intensive' production. The domestic US enterprises from this area of manufacturing locate abroad (Mexico and Asia).

Strategic asset-seeking FDI is aimed at protecting and augmenting the existing ownership-specific advantages by the investing firm. Alternatively, such FDI may be aimed at reducing the advantages of competitors.

5.4 Transnational corporations

Introduction

Any firm that owns, has a lasting interest in or controls[7] assets in more than one country may be called a TNC. It is a wider concept than FDI since it includes non-equity business participation in another country. FDI is often the result of decisions by TNCs. Therefore, FDI may be a relatively good proxy for the investment activities of TNCs. A note of caution has to be added, however. TNCs may control trans-border business operations by non-equity involvement such as licensing. In the case of licensing, a TNC must be assured that the goods or services provided conform with the original quality standards.

The total world outward *stock* (the production potential) in 1999 was estimated to be $4.7tn. The stock of FDI in a national economy indicates what proportion of the home economy is owned/controlled by foreign firms. Worldwide *inflows* of FDI in 1999 were $865bn. Inflows of FDI reflect the ability of a country to attract FDI (national location-specific advantages). *Outflows* of FDI mirror the willingness and capacity of a country's firms to enter and stay in trans-border business activities. The distribution of the stock of FDI is asymmetrical. In 1999, 68 per cent of FDI stock was located in developed countries (UNCTAD, 2000). This is confirmation that FDI activity is strongest among comparable, mainly highly developed, countries.

The sectoral distribution of FDI reveals that the industries that are absorbing the largest slices of FDI are those dominated by high technology and highly qualified personnel. They also have higher than average expenditure on R&D relative to sales. The reasons for such a distribution may be found in the excessive transaction costs of arm's-length contacts through the market, so internalisation of these links within a firm seems to be a better business choice. In addition, they include those that benefit from strong economies of scale in the production of (sophisticated) intermediary goods; their output of final products is highly differentiated; and their production is sensitive to information.

Determinants

Large companies are in most cases TNCs. They are not directly or completely accountable to any government but rather have their own ethos. Chauvinism (regarding the location of business, personnel matters are a different thing) is alien to international firms, for their business decisions are not likely to be based on either ideological or nationalistic grounds (Rubin, 1970: 183). The most crucial determinants of FDI are the relative difference in returns and profit maximisation in the long run, market presence, availability of resources, expectations of growth in demand and political stability. They may be more important than a country's participation in a regional economic bloc.

Transnational corporations behave like other firms: they primarily look for opportunities to make a profit. The size and rate of growth of a local market, including privileged access to international markets (instead of mere differences in the cost of labour) are the most prominent motivators for their trans-border business operations. This is because of the impact of market size on the minimum efficient scale for production. In addition, where market liberalisation is a widely accepted policy choice, created assets (technology and ability to create it, business culture, capability to organise and control production and marketing, communications infrastructure, marketing networks) are increasingly important determinants for FDI. This is why roughly 70 per cent of the activities of TNCs are geographically located in developed market economies (measured by the stock of FDI). In spite of talk about 'globalisation,' a significant part of the output of most companies is still sold on the local market. In this situation, the developing countries and those whose economy are in transition face very tough competition in attracting TNCs.

Other motivators for FDI include the availability of resources (although this depends on the attitude of target countries towards TNCs), local suppliers (just-in-time delivery), efficiency in production, diversification, available technology and exchange of threat (what Du Pont does in Europe, BASF will try to do in the US). Neo-classical theory cannot predict with absolute certainty the geographical location of activities resulting from capital mobility within a common market. TNCs that use complex technologies do not worry about tariffs and quotas. They are concerned, rather, with domestic regulations such as environmental standards.[8] A degree of government intervention may influence the geographical location of TNCs with important implications for the future distribution of output and trade.

Some goods and services must be adapted in order to meet local needs (e.g. food). This may be done more cheaply by locating at least a part of the production process near the place of consumption. Other reasons for FDI instead of, or together with, exporting include taking advantage of a range of host country's incentives such as financial incentives (subsidies, reduced taxes), tariff protection, exemption from import duties, public purchases and granting monopoly rights. Other motives include market pre-emption, increase in market power, as well as empire-building ambitions of firms.

The literature that is based on surveys and case studies suggests that government strategies such as tax incentives and industrial policies have little, if any, effect on the location of industry. All studies are aware of the difficulties in ascertaining the impact of public policy measures on the location of production. Public policies have mixed effects on the location of firms. On the one hand, higher taxes increase the operating costs of firms. On the other hand, higher taxes in some areas may go to pay for better public services, such as education or infrastructure, that support the operation of firms (Smith and Florida, 1994: 31).

In a survey of thirty TNCs covering seventy-four investment projects in cars, computers, food processing and petrochemicals, many TNCs revealed that government incentives were not an issue and, where they existed, simply made an already attractive country for the location of business operations even more attractive. Investment decisions were made on the grounds of economic and long-term strategic conditions regarding inputs, costs and markets. Overall, incentives are not an important factor in the set of elements that determine inward FDI.

Once the decision is made to invest in the target country (or region), the incentives may have an impact on the exact choice of location within the target country (UNCTAD, 1998: 103–4).

As for the geographical origin of the TNCs, most of them originate in countries with decentralised political systems such as the US, Britain and the Netherlands. These countries have the longest history of transnationalisation of national economic activity. In these countries, the TNCs and the state foster relations of complementarity. In centralised states, the administration does not want to share power with any enterprise; however, this has changed in past decades.

If producers and government in a big country A make a credible threat to close its market to exporters from a small country B, then one of the options for country B is to establish 'fifth column' production in country A. This would preserve country B's market share in country A's market. If overheads are covered in country B's home market, then its firm in country A may sell on a marginal cost basis. Many European and Japanese TNCs have concentrated on breaking into the US market and become 'US nationals' in order to avoid unilateral US economic sanctions and changes in the American trade regime. Making profit from such an investment has played a secondary role, at least in the short term. A similar observation in the EU was the flurry of non-EU TNCs that settled in the EU prior to the full implementation of the Single Market Programme at the end of 1992.

The success of Japanese firms in reducing the labour content of the final output is one of the factors contributing to the expansion of their FDI into relatively high labour cost areas such as North America or the EU. High labour productivity can make up for higher wages. This is why the most significant part of all activities by TNCs takes place in a select group of developed countries. Relatively low nominal wages do not necessarily equal low labour costs. In addition, low or declining wages may mean a (local) shrinking market. If this were the case, and if TNCs are interested in the local market, this may act as a deterrent to FDI. Despite the advantage of cheaper labour in Italy, Greece and Portugal, relative to the central and northern EU countries in the 1960s, labour outflow, rather than capital inflow was the equilibrating force at that time.

Foreign direct investment is a tool used by enterprises that want to exploit long-term profit-making opportunities abroad. Before embarking upon FDI, an enterprise compares alternative geographical locations at home and at various places abroad. If investing abroad seems to be the more promising option, then the enterprise has to make sure that it possesses or can obtain certain mobile income-generating firm-specific advantages in production or transactions that could enable it to operate profitably in the foreign environment (Dunning, 1988a: 42). These advantages include exclusive or privileged access to specific assets and better organising capabilities for both production and transactions.

Local firms have several advantages over foreign ones. For example:

- They have a better knowledge of local consumer and supplier markets.
- They do not have the costs of operating at a distance.
- They often receive favours from the government.

- They do not operate in a different, often hostile, language, tax, legal, exchange rate, social and political environment.
- Last but not least, TNCs may sometimes have some disadvantages in the eyes of certain local politicians in target countries. Basically, they are foreign and, often, relatively large.

A difficulty for TNCs may be that they have to attract key managers and technicians from the headquarters to a foreign subsidiary. This may require both higher wages for such personnel and higher allowances for their families. TNCs that extract and export natural resources are forever at risk of becoming a target for nationalisation. If a TNC wants to operate in such a geographical and social environment, it must have or control a special and mobile advantage over its domestic competitors, such as superior technology and management, a well-known brand name or, especially important for services, access to markets and quality control. For these reasons, it is no surprise that TNCs are often more profitable and successful than local competitors in the same industry.

While firm-specific income-generating and mobile advantages are a necessary condition for FDI, they are not a sufficient condition. If trade were free, firms could simply use their advantages by exporting instead of producing abroad. Various market imperfections limit the size of the market for free trade and, hence, justify FDI. These include tariff and NTBs, differences in factor prices, sunk costs and aftersales service. Therefore, an enterprise with a specific and mobile income-generating advantage considers a number of different possibilities and restraints at various foreign locations before settling abroad.

Transfer pricing

Foreign ownership and control of domestic output potentials is often seen by the man in the street as a burden on the domestic economy that is brought by TNCs. A more serious argument against the operation of TNCs is that they behave in the market of the host country in an anti-competitive way through various business practices such as predatory pricing, monopolisation or transfer pricing.

One argument against TNCs used by host countries is their internal (transfer) pricing system.[9] TNCs internalise intermediate product and service[10] markets. Prices in trade among different sister enterprises are arrived at by non-market means.[11] For example, if transfer of technology is measured by international payments of royalties and fees, then around 80 per cent of payments are undertaken on an intra-firm basis (UNCTAD, 1997: 20). By doing so, TNCs may shift profits out of countries with relatively high taxes to those with the lowest corporate taxes (tax avoidance)[12] or they may oust competition by cross-subsidising product lines. In order to shift profits, vertical TNCs may overprice imports of inputs and underprice exports. This pricing system may distort the efficient geographical location of production (resource-wise) and flows of trade.

One way to control operations of the TNCs in the host country could be to request that the internal pricing system treats the parent and its subsidiary as if they were two separate companies. The enforcement and control of this request may be seriously endangered if there are no substitutes for these internally traded goods and various (headquarters) services. Another solution may be to harmonise fiscal systems in countries where TNCs operate. Nonetheless, a note of caution needs to be added. Transfer pricing is probably used much more commonly than TNCs are willing to admit, but much less frequently than is supposed by outsiders (Plasschaert, 1994: 13). In any case, transfer pricing is not widespread in small and decentralised TNCs or in TNCs that operate in competitive markets.

Internalisation of intermediate goods or services markets within TNCs is not always done with the primary goal of avoiding taxes on corporate profits. Another possible reason is to maintain high quality in the supply of goods and services, as local or external suppliers may not necessarily be able to maintain the high standards requested by the TNC. Nonetheless, fiddling with transfer pricing is more widespread in the developing countries than in the developed world. The balance of payments position of developing countries often drives them to control flows of foreign exchange. Strict controls may induce TNCs to manipulate transfer pricing in order to protect and/or increase profits. The developing countries are not well equipped either to detect or to control manipulation of the internal prices of TNCs.

Research and development

A potential case in the host country against TNCs is that TNCs rely heavily on the R&D of their parent companies and that their head offices charge for their services in a way that might not be controlled by the host country. This can make both subsidiaries and host countries too dependent on foreign R&D and technology. Is this really the case? Some empirical research in Canada found that the subsidiaries of TNCs undertook more R&D than domestic Canadian firms (Rugman, 1985: 486). In another example, European manufacturers of lifts undertake their R&D of lifts for tall buildings in their US subsidiaries because there are so many skyscrapers there.

While there is historical evidence that most R&D takes place in the headquarters of TNCs, this is no longer necessarily on a large scale. There are many instances of foreign subsidiaries having developed technologies that have benefited the parent firm. For example, IBM's (US) breakthroughs in superconductor technology took place in Switzerland; Hoffmann–La Roche (Switzerland) developed important new pharmaceuticals such as Librium and Valium in New Jersey (US); Toshiba made advances in audio technology in its British laboratory; and Matsushita's R&D facilities for air-conditioners are in Malaysia. However, for a solid conclusion, more evidence at a much more disaggregated level is needed. Affiliates of foreign TNCs in the US look a lot like the domestic firms. There are no particular signs of headquarters effects (Graham and Krugman, 1995: 73–4, 119).[13]

The geographical spread of R&D centres is driven by several factors, including:

• the need to adapt output to the requests of the local market;

- subsidies or pressure from the host government to establish local R&D facilities;
- the available sophisticated and experienced local R&D staff;
- the possibility of establishing a 'listening and learning post' in the host country.

However, an international spread of locations for R&D does not mean, as seen in Chapter 3, that the innovation process has become a 'global' trend.

A small country often does not have the necessary resources for large-scale basic research in relation to a big country. By importing technology a small country may have access to the results of a much larger volume of R&D wherever it is carried out. It can be both complementary and supplementary to R&D already undertaken in the domestic economy. Relying on the domestic operation of foreign-owned TNCs may be a superior economic policy choice for a risk-averse (poor and small) country than being dependent on foreign supplies of the same good produced elsewhere.

Inter-firm strategic alliances in the development of technology in the EU increased sharply during the 1980s. In addition, the European Commission became heavily involved in projects on a cost-sharing basis. Over 70 per cent of private (largely non-subsidised) strategic technology alliances were related to joint R&D of new core technologies in the fields of informatics, new materials and biotechnology. A major field of cooperation was in information technologies, as over 40 per cent of all strategic technology alliances were in this field (Hagedoorn and Schakenraad, 1993: 373).

A comparison between established 'private' cooperation in R&D and cooperation sponsored by the EU found that the two forms are very similar in the case of leading enterprises. In fact, 'subsidised R&D networks add to already existing or emerging private networks and merely reproduce the basic structure of European large firm co-operation' (Hagedoorn and Schakenraad, 1993: 387). This being the case, it is difficult to understand why leading and large firms in the EU need subsidies! If the 'official' (EU-sponsored) geographical network largely reproduces the already existing 'private' one, then it may be redundant. Financial resources could have been used elsewhere (for instance, to fund programmes that are not in the field of informatics, such as biotechnology or education or infrastructure). Is such replication of R&D networks the outcome of the lobbying power of powerful firms or is it necessary to accelerate R&D in the private sector because of significant externalities?[14] Perhaps such waste of scarce public money will be checked in the future by WTO rules on subsidisation.

There is a tendency to reduce the risks and costs of R&D within TNCs. Over 70 per cent of international strategic technology alliances between companies from the EU and NAFTA are focused on R&D (Hagedoorn, 1998: 184). This may be an important incentive for mergers and acquisitions in the pharmaceuticals industry (the major reason is still the very fragmented nature of the pharmaceuticals industry compared with car manufacturing). High risk and uncertainty as well as excessive R&D costs drive firms to centralise these functions (usually in their country of origin). Another reason is the exploitation of host countries' incentives to R&D (subsidies, tax brakes, secure contracts). In this case, the basic research remains in the headquarters, while subsidiaries undertake applied development according to local demand, regulations and incentives. It is often forgotten that many firms that create knowledge are neither TNCs nor large (e.g. in the areas of computer hardware and software). The only condition for their creation in some locations is that they operate in a competitive environment, which is often lacking in small countries.

Host countries and transnational corporations

The greatest power of TNCs stems from their high international mobility to enter and exit from an industry. TNCs can act as geographical capital arbitrageurs. They may borrow in countries where the rate of interest is lowest and invest in countries where they expect the highest returns. TNCs may spread overheads and risk among their subsidiaries. These enterprises also extend control over international markets. If a subsidiary is producing final goods, then other parts of a TNC may increase export components to this subsidiary.

Many TNCs create sophisticated and complicated technologies. They avoid the transfer of this technology through the market in order to prevent competitors from copying it. The longer the technology gap with imitators, the longer the TNC can behave like a monopolist. Thus, a TNC usually transfers technology only among its subsidiaries.

Relations between TNCs and host countries may sometimes be quite tense. Mining is an industry that requires a huge amount of investment before commercial exploitation. Different countries often compete and offer incentives for FDI and effectively engage in 'locations tournament' (David, 1984). At this stage a TNC has the strongest bargaining position. When TNCs locate their operations in host countries they may react to changes in, for example, the host country's tax system or interest rates quite differently from domestic firms, which may not be able to withdraw from the home market. Thus, TNCs may become a threat to the host country's national economic policies. To counter this danger, the common market member countries should coordinate and harmonise their policies regarding competition, capital mobility and TNCs.

If TNCs produce final goods in host countries and if they import raw materials and components from countries which are outside the common market instead of purchasing them from the local suppliers, then they may jeopardise the process of integration within a common market. The external dependence of the area may increase instead of reducing. Where the member countries of a common market or other type of international economic integration compete among themselves for FDI in the absence of an agreed industrial policy, it is unreasonable to expect the operation of the TNCs to result in an optimal allocation of resources (Robson, 1983: 32). This has happened in the Caribbean region.

A large amount of investment may, however, keep a TNC as a hostage of the host country. These sunk costs with limited or no 'salvage value' may represent a barrier to exit from the host country. In this case, the host country government can show the TNC who is boss. The host governments may renegotiate the deals with the TNCs. This kind of danger may induce the TNCs to borrow predominantly on the host country financial market and transfer from elsewhere only the technical and managerial expertise. A possible closure of a subsidiary in the host country would cost some local jobs in both the subsidiary and supplying firms. The affected local workers and their families may lobby in favour of the interests of the TNC. Those corporations may find allies among industries in the host country. As long as TNCs purchase from them, both subsidiaries and local firms may work together in lobbying the government for protection, subsidies, tax breaks and procurement agreements.

A serious threat to the market structure of a host country may be introduced by a TNC. It may monopolise the whole domestic market and by predatory pricing prevent the entry to the industry of potential host country firms. It may introduce technologies that use relatively more of the resources in short supply (capital) and relatively less of the component that is abundant (labour) in the host country. TNCs may offer relatively higher wages to qualified domestic labour in order to attract it. This labour may flow from the host country's firms into TNCs. However, this may be due, in part, to the fact that the home firms do not value sufficiently a resource that is in short supply. Vacancies in the domestic firms may be filled by less well-trained labour, which may have an adverse effect on the growth of production in the host country. Although technologies used by the TNCs in the host countries may not be the most up to date, they can be superior to those which are currently in use in developing countries (environmentally sound technologies are an obvious example).

TNCs may have an adverse impact on the allocation of resources in the host country if their operation account for a significant proportion of production, employment, purchases and sales. Thus, the operation of TNCs may have a greater influence in certain segments of industry in developing countries than in developed countries. This state of affairs asks for a coordinated approach towards TNCs by the regional groups in the developing world, as was the case with the controversial Decision 24 (1970) in the Andean Pact.[15] It also requires the establishment and enforcement of a common industrial policy. This can be supported by the regional development banks and/or by joint planning. Openness to and participation in an integrated network of international production of TNCs will contribute to the growth potential of the developing countries.

This analysis suggests that the TNCs do not pay much attention to the overall needs of the host countries. This is true. However, it is not a duty of TNCs to meet the social needs, including the infrastructure needs, of the host country. Nobody forces host countries to accept TNCs. The fulfilment of these social demands is the role of the host country's government. In the presence of unemployed resources, inflation, foreign and budgetary debt, famine and underdevelopment, any hard currency investment is welcome. Any attempt by the host government to restrict the entry and operation of TNCs may dry up this thin trickle of capital inflow. Host countries sometimes behave (or used to) as if they want FDI but not the foreign investor. Unfortunately, the developing countries are those that most need these investments.

In order to increase local embeddedness, some TNCs involve themselves in local communities through sponsorship of local sporting and cultural events, even education and training. Whether this is a calculated public relations ploy (as in the case of some Japanese and German TNCs that operate in Britain) to avoid criticism or a real and deep commitment towards the local communities remains unanswered (Dicken *et al.*, 1995: 41).

Economic adjustment in the developing world may be facilitated by the presence of TNCs. These corporations have the know-how, ability to raise funds and the widespread marketing channels that help export growth.

The local content[16] requirements for locating FDI in a particular country may be criticised on the grounds that they distort investors' input choices, stimulate suboptimal input mixes and potentially increase prices. In a survey of 682 projects, it was found that, in 83 per cent of cases in which there was a requirement to accomplish the objectives of trade-related investment measures (TRIMs) such as local sourcing and exporting, the firms planned to do so anyway (UNCTC, 1991a: 4). That is to say, TRIMs were redundant.

Mineral resources, including oil, are in many developing countries the property of the state. It is the government that negotiates terms of entry with TNCs. In manufacturing, the role of the government is somewhat less pronounced. In this case, the government usually sets general terms of entry, performance and exit from an industry. While the developing countries, as a rule, regulate the conditions for entry of TNCs with greater scrutiny, industrialised countries control their exit and the possible consequences of loss of jobs and the environment.

It is popularly argued that TNCs invest most often in fast-growing manufacturing industries such as electronics and pharmaceutical industries. These industries thus 'fall into foreign hands'. Foreigners may thus have undue influence in the host country and interfere with sovereignty. An example was when the US introduced a ban on the export of technology for the gas pipeline from the then USSR to Western Europe in the early 1980s. Many subsidiaries of US TNCs in Western Europe were affected by this decision. It is much harder for a host country to influence the parent country of a TNC through a subsidiary.

In spite of allegedly lower environmental standards in the developing countries, a large-scale transfer of polluting business activities to these countries has not taken place. This is the consequence of the constant focus of TNCs on the developed countries and the adherence of TNCs to the application of environmental standards (often the same as their home country) that are superior to those prevailing in the host developing country.

As noted earlier, modern technologies complicate the employment impact of FDI. Modern technologies substitute capital for labour. A 'greenfield' business start-up increases employment in the host country if it does not put domestic competitors out of business. A takeover of an existing firm does not necessarily increase employment and may reduce it if the merged firm rationalises the existing activity (Buckley and Artisien, 1987: 212). A foreign-located subsidiary may begin as a unit for marketing of the final good. If it develops further, it may become a product specialist, which may increase employment (direct and indirect) of a particular type of labour. However, one has to remember that employment is determined by demand for final goods and services.

Transnational corporations treat their business in different countries as a single market operation. Therefore, their financial service is always centralised as it may best meet the needs of the firm as a whole.[17] It represents the backbone of overall efficiency. This is most pronounced in the case where ownership-specific advantages of a TNC are generating high returns. Other operations such as employment, wage and labour relations are always decentralised within TNCs. Labour markets are local and often highly regulated, so decentralisation of these issues is the optimal policy for TNCs. Multiplant coordination of a growing part of business activities is one of the greatest advantages of TNCs. For example, Nike (an American 'producer' of sports goods) keeps its R&D in Oregon but subcontracts the actual manufacturing of those goods in some forty geographical locations, principally in Asia. If wages increase in one country, Nike simply moves production into another.

Takeovers (mergers and acquisitions) provide means for the 'external' growth of TNCs. They are attractive to TNCs that have wide international marketing networks and are tempting to sellers who are interested in penetrating the widest possible market. This is enhanced if the acquired (or merged) enterprise is not linked to any industrial group, which helps to avoid conflicting interests. This is the reason why the Anglo-Saxon enterprises dominate cross-border mergers and acquisitions in Europe. TNCs may also grow 'internally' through subsidiaries. Mergers and acquisitions are, however, virtually unknown in Japan.

National and international regulation

The basis of the Organisation for Economic Cooperation and Development (OECD) Declaration on International Investment and Multinational Enterprises (1976) is the principle of national treatment of foreign companies. This principle means that, provided national security is not jeopardised, TNCs have the same rights and obligations as domestic companies in similar situations. It does not put all foreign suppliers on an equal footing in the importing country market (which is what the most favoured nation clause does), rather it refers to the treatment of foreign suppliers in comparison with domestic ones.

Resource-rich and prosperous countries such as Canada may exercise the greatest leverage on TNCs.[18] The experience of this country is one of the most interesting examples of control of TNCs. It is relevant, as a significant part of the economic integration between Canada and the US has an FDI dimension.

Both Canada and the US are signatories to the OECD Declaration. In 1973, a few years before this Declaration was delivered, Canada established the Foreign Investment Review Agency (FIRA) to survey inward FDI. This move was a reaction to a relatively large share of foreign ownership of Canadian industry. One may argue that much of the foreign ownership of the host country industry may be attributed to the level of the host country's tariffs, taxes, subsidies and other incentives. TNCs overcome tariff obstacles by locating 'tariff factories' in the host country. The intention of the FIRA was not to stop FDI in Canada, but rather to allow FDI only if it resulted in beneficial effects to Canada. The criterion upon which the FIRA evaluated both the takeovers of existing Canadian firms and the establishment of new businesses included expanded exports, use of Canadian resources, increase in investment, employment and productivity, as well as compatibility with the national industrial and other economic policies.

The FIRA's rejection rate of 20 per cent was an important barrier for certain investors and was high compared with rates of some 1 per cent in other countries that used a similar screening process (Lipsey, 1985: 101). This caused many firms to withdraw their applications in order to avoid uncertain and costly application procedures, while other firms that might have been potential investors have not even applied. At the beginning of the 1980s, the rejection rate of the FIRA was reduced. The Conservative government transformed the FIRA from a nationalistic authority aimed at increasing Canadian ownership in domestic industry into an organisation for the attraction of FDI and in 1984 renamed it Investment Canada. The fear of too much foreign capital had given way to a fear of too little (Lipsey and Smith, 1986: 53).

Access to growing national and international markets and a stable macroeconomic environment are major incentives for locating of FDI in some geographical areas. However, a stable, predictable and transparent legal situation also encourages FDI as it lowers risk and potentially increases profits. There exist global rules that regulate international trade in goods (WTO), but such rules do not exist regarding FDI. A complex set of bilateral[19] and some regional treaties regulate FDI. The coverage of these rules is not full. In addition, many governments offer incentives to attract FDI. Diversity in treatment of FDI in bilateral deals and the possibility of a sudden reversal in the liberalisation trend in the times of crisis (Asia 1997–98) create a need for a multilateral treaty.

The OECD drafted a Multilateral Agreement on Investment (MAI) with the aim of providing a sound legal environment, including open markets, based on the principle of non-discrimination between domestic and foreign investors. In addition, there would be instruments for dispute settlement among all involved parties (various combinations of public and private players) and enforcement of decisions.

In spite of grand expectations, the MAI project got into serious trouble and was put aside in 1998. The critics argued that the exclusive OECD 'club' of twenty-nine countries did not take into account the needs of the developing countries. Another criticism was that the MAI gave excessive power to TNCs regarding protection of the investment, transfer of funds, right of establishment and most favoured nation treatment.

The legal system that regulates FDI in most OECD countries is well developed. Hence, the MAI was of little real significance for these developed countries, even though most of the FDI activity in the world is within the OECD group. The drafters' intention was to lure the emerging players in the FDI flows to join the agreement. However, few developing countries were ready to sign a deal that they had no part in shaping (exchanging concessions such as domestic opening markers for FDI in return for the opening of OECD markets for agricultural goods). Some critics saw the MAI as a tool of neo-colonialism. However, the work on the MAI was not in vain. It raised an important issue. Better luck with it in the future perhaps may be had by the WTO, which has a wider membership (135 countries), dispute settlement instruments and experience in handling difficult negotiations.

Benefits

Estimates of the potential gains to be had from economic integration and operations of TNCs are generally based on the classical assumption that the set of traded goods is both complete and *fixed*. In such a case, the gains from trade and FDI appear to be quite small. Prices in the economy could be changed by government (tariff) intervention, so the quantity of produced and traded goods would change but the list of the manufactured and traded goods would remain the same.

Suppose now that the list of goods is *expandable*. The neo-Schumpeterian economic model assumes that there are no limits for the introduction of new goods and services in an economy. Let us assume, in addition, that the introduction of a new commodity requires a large amount of fixed costs.[20] This is especially true in the case of the developing countries. Perfect competition and free trade exclude (major) fixed costs from consideration. Once the fixed costs are included in the picture, their presence is often used as a justification for the introduction of government intervention. When important fixed costs enter the model, a substantial volume of the good needs to be sold in order to make a profit. In such a case, a tariff on the good in question may reduce demand. If this reduction in (international) demand is important, then the commodity may never appear on the market. Losses from such a development or gains in the reverse case may not be easily estimated, at least, not for the time being. In any case, if the new goods are left out of consideration, then this kind of analysis can bring substantial underestimates of the welfare cost of trade restrictions (Romer, 1994). These new goods and services are usually brought (to the developing countries) by TNCs.

Integrated countries may obtain certain benefits from the trans-border business activity of firms. These gains, specific to the operation of TNCs within the area, include not only *tangible* resources (transfer of capital on more favourable terms than could be obtained on capital markets, tax receipts, economies of scale, sourcing of inputs from local suppliers and employment) that it provides at lower cost than through the market, but also various *intangible* assets. These intangible assets include new technologies in production, management and control that make the existing resources more productive; positive externalities in production through linkages;[21] international marketing networks that can overcome barriers for exports into foreign markets; new ideas; clustering of related firms; training of labour; and competition. The pecuniary element of these spillovers is quite difficult to measure and could easily escape the attention of a non-economist. Monopolisation, restrictive business practices, increased sourcing from the parent country with a negative impact on the balance of trade, transfer pricing, transfer of profits abroad[22] and geographical polarisation of economic activity may be found on the other side of the benefits coin. All of them affect the geographical allocation of resources in a way that is not always favourable to either the integrated country or the whole group.

Despite a relative academic hostility, public sensitivity, polemics against foreigners that export home resources and some official anxiety about the operation of TNCs, the situation has changed since the 1980s. All countries in the world welcome TNCs. There is a tendency towards a convergence in the national rules regulating FDI. Apart from some screening, these countries provide TNCs with various incentives which include the provision of infrastructure, subsidised loans, tax exemptions, export incentives, opportunities for complete ownership and exemptions from duties. However, these countries have to bear in mind that they compete with other possible locations (and countries), hence there is a tendency towards a liberal and converging national systems towards TNCs. The growing and wide markets in the US and EU are still the most preferred locations for TNCs. If other regions want to attract TNCs, then, ideally, they should have some 'unique selling point' that TNCs cannot find in Europe or North America.

Apart from these drawbacks, host countries experience significant gains and thus invite the location and operation of the TNCs. These corporations may bring in technology that is superior to existing domestic technology. This has the effect, in the host country, of increasing output capacity, jobs and tax proceeds, as well as resulting in savings in unemployment benefits and perhaps also creating exports. TNCs enter into growth industries and provide technological expertise that would otherwise be missing. Some TNCs produce brand-name drinks or cigarettes. These are goods whose consumption is burdened by excise duties. Governments may need or want these proceeds and become an ally of the TNCs. If there are barriers to entry, such as huge initial capital investment in an industry, then TNCs may provide this advantage. When the host country's policy is to promote exports or substitute imports, then TNCs may fill part of this role.

One major incentive to persuade TNCs to locate their operations in a country or an integrated region is to offer them a stable macroeconomic environment and a growing market. International economic integration provides this opportunity. Other carrots include tax holidays,[23] subsidies, tariff protection and secure public purchases. In the medium and longer term, the best policy is to influence the supply of educated local labour (a created factor) as an additional incentive to TNCs to select the country for the location of their operations. Sticks include performance criteria, exports, employment, withholding taxes, as well as repatriation and re-investment rules.

Potential benefits from the location of TNCs in a national economy may not be measured directly and in the short term. Nonetheless, many of them can be listed. They include:

- access to wide international manufacturing and marketing networks;
- linkage of the economies of different countries;
- introduction of new resources and capabilities in the national economy;
- an improvement in the quality of the existing resources and capabilities;
- increased capital formation and growth (creation of wealth);

- access to new technology, R&D, innovations, standards and know-how in production, management, marketing networks and pollution control;
- economies of scale and more efficient use of resources and capabilities;
- improved efficiency in production and increased competitiveness;
- improved quality of output;
- product differentiation;
- externalities (including sourcing from the local firms);
- employment of local resources;
- benefits of learning.

5.5 Intervention

If market imperfections permit rents (above average profits), then the governments of the integrated countries may wish to intervene. The larger market of an integrated area may be better able to absorb the cost of intervention owing to the spread of such costs than would be in the case of individual countries acting alone. For instance, a simplified (prisoner's dilemma) example is presented in Table 5.1.

Suppose that there are just two firms capable of producing aircraft: British Aerospace in Britain and Aérospatiale in France. Assume also that, because of sunk costs, R&D and economies of scale, only one firm can produce aircraft efficiently (profit-wise) within the EU and that public authorities prefer to purchase domestically made goods. The numbers in Table 5.1 then show the profit of the two firms. If there is no intervention by the government, the firm that moves first captures the market and makes a profit. If both produce, both lose; if neither produces, there is neither gain nor loss. The example is important as, if only one country has the ability to produce aircraft, the government of the other may then try to persuade a foreign TNC to locate its production within the confines of its borders, thus putting the potential competitor from the partner country out of business. This possibility for a geographical location of production is a strong case for a joint treatment of TNCs by the integration groups.

Now suppose that there is no domestic producer of aircraft in Britain and that the domestic government decides that it may be sensible to have aircraft production located at home and to move first to strategically and irreversibly pre-empt any other player.[24] The reasons may include employment, export and prestige, but also, and more importantly, various externalities, including obtaining the leading edge in one of the high-technology industries and also national pride. Some early movers sustain their position for decades. For example, Procter & Gamble, Unilever

Table 5.1 Profit in the aircraft industry, without intervention

| France | Britain | |
	Production	No production
Production	−3; −3	10; 0
No production	0; 10	0; 0

and Colgate have been international leaders in washing powder production since the 1930s. With this in mind, the government decides to invite Boeing to come and locate its production in Britain. As bait, it offers various subsidies and protection to capture the aircraft market in the integration arrangement with France. The major reason for the subsidy is not simply to increase export sales, but rather to improve the terms of trade and secure rents for the home firm, a cluster of related domestic enterprises and, finally, for the country itself. Of course, such a policy may have a significant balance of payments effect in the medium and long term. Hence, the structure of markets and the operations of TNCs matter for the geography of production.

Engineering comparative advantages of countries and firms are becoming more important in modern footloose industries and are eroding, to an extent, inherited comparative advantages. For example, trade within the EU is to a large extent of an intra-industry character. It is much more driven by economies of scale than by the 'classic' comparative advantages of those countries. If pushed to the limit, a national reaction to a monopoly in a foreign country is the creation of a national monopoly. That is fighting fire with fire (Curzon Price, 1993: 394)!

What is important here is that the neo-classical model deals with the given and perfect resources and capabilities, whereas the new theory studies market imperfections, multiple equilibria and government intervention in a dynamic set-up that suppresses market constraints and pushes economic frontiers outwards. It considers economies of scale, externalities, differentiated products, changing technology and FDI. These are all features of modern manufacturing. The new theory questions the proposition that free markets may successfully take advantage of the potential benefits in the new situation. Such an approach is different from the neo-classical one, in which TNCs were, by definition, excluded from consideration. The assumption in free markets is that there is no grounds for trans-border business activities as the geographical and sectoral allocation of resources is perfect (first-best solution). The new theory explains why countries can trade not only when their resource endowments and production capabilities are *different*, as in the neo-classical situation, but also when their resource endowment and production capabilities are *identical*. The case in question is the intra-industry trade (i.e. intra-EU trade in cars).

One thing, however, ought to be clear from the outset. The new theory does not replace the neo-classical one. The new theory considers only market imperfections that can be mitigated by intervention, which may introduce an adjustment instrument into an already highly imperfect situation. Table 5.2 shows what would happen to the profits of the two aircraft producers if the British government subsidised its (foreign owned/controlled) firm with monetary units that equal 5. If the firm located in Britain decides to produce, it will always have an advantage over its non-subsidised French rival.

When market imperfections exist, the British government can influence the geography of production (allocation of resources and specialisation). Nonetheless, if the choice of national champions is to be a good one, the government should be competent and well informed, otherwise the result may be costly commercial

Table 5.2 Profit in the aircraft industry, with intervention

France	Britain	
	Production	*No production*
Production	−3; 2	10; 0
No production	0; 15	0; 0

failures, such as the Franco-British Concorde project or computers in France. Many governments in East Asia have intervened successfully in their economies. However, governments in many East European and developing countries have intervened much more, and yet have singularly failed to achieve the economic successes seen in East Asia. In any case, intervention is facilitated when the number of potentially competing firms is small and production output is standardised.

In order to intervene/subsidise in an intelligent way, governments need a great deal of information that is quite costly to obtain: information not only about technology and demand, but also about the strategies of other governments and TNCs. If they chose wisely, strategic policy can be a superb device. In practice, a subsidy in one country may provoke retaliation in another in the form of a subsidy or a counterbalancing duty. The retaliation and counter-retaliation cycle makes everyone worse off. Integration may offer some advantages to developing countries in such a situation. It may inspire these countries to negotiate the distribution of strategic industries within the area or attract TNCs in order to maximise positive externalities and reduce unnecessary subsidies. The basic argument for the government's involvement may be that without intervention in the area, and owing to imperfections, there may be *underinvestment* in strategic industry. If, however, intervention is not well managed, *overinvestment* may be the consequence.

The simple model of strategic investment, industrial and trade policy is based on the expectation that the subsidised home production of a tradable good or service shifts monopoly profits (rents) to the home country and to the firms owned/controlled by it. These profits should be over and above the cost of the subsidy. If the domestic firms are affiliates of foreign TNCs, then the effect on the home country's welfare may be uncertain. No matter what the circumstances are, the expectation that profit shifting may enhance the home country's welfare holds *only* when foreign countries do not retaliate against domestic subsidies. A cycle of retaliation and counter-retaliation would make everyone worse off. In addition, when there is a liberal treatment of FDI, bilateral trade deficits may point to misleading signals. For example, if Japan (or any other country) invests in China in order to take advantage of relatively low labour costs and export output to the US, the bilateral deficit in trade between the US and Japan may shrink, but the overall US trade deficit may increase because of extra US imports from China.

Governments need to keep in mind that general favours (subsidies) handed out to domestic firms may trickle out to foreign beneficiaries located within the confines of the jurisdiction of the government. A more effective policy may be to use subsidies to develop and upgrade the skills of domestic human capital as footloose capital is increasingly attracted by, among other factors, created factors such as the local availability of skilled, highly trained and experienced labour.

In advanced countries such as the US, the constituent parts may compete with each other by offering substantial grants (and grant equivalents) in order to attract world-scale manufacturing projects. The size of these grants is increasing all the time. In 1984, Michigan offered state and local incentives worth $120m (equivalent to $14,000 per job) to attract Mazda; in 1986, Indiana offered $110m ($51,000 per job) to Subaru–Isuzu; in 1989, Kentucky offered $325m ($108,000 per job) to Toyota (UNCTC, 1991b: 73–4); in 1983, Alabama gave $252m ($168,000 per job) to Mercedes–Benz; and North Carolina handed out $130m ($108,000 per job) to BMW. In spite of strict rules of competition, countries in the EU are sometimes allowed to dispense 'incentives' to TNCs to settle within their confines. Britain gave $89m ($29,675 per job) to Samsung in 1994, while France granted $111m ($56,923 per job) to Mercedes–Benz and Swatch in 1995 (UNCTAD, 1995: 18). These kind of subsidies and participation in 'location tournaments' are well beyond the financial capabilities of developing countries.

The self-reinforcing aspect of FDI begins to operate only after a certain level of development. The developing countries 'which are already doing well in these categories do not need location tournaments. The others are not likely to profit from them' (Wheeler and Mody, 1992: 72). The ability of the developing world to attract FDI depends on many factors that these countries cannot control. They need to try to stabilise their macroeconomic and political situation, improve the quality and quantity of human capital and infrastructure, liberalise trade and investment policies, actively promote their advantages to the business community and study potentials for integration or preferential trade with other (neighbouring) countries. Such a policy approach would stimulate domestic private investment and growth. It could be argued that they might wish to pursue such policies even if they had little effect on FDI.

In an examination of annual FDI flows (1960–90) towards the major integration groups in the developing world, Jovanović (1995) found no difference in FDI flows before and after the creation of the integration group. The national economic (and political) situation played a much more important role in FDI than did participation in the integration deal. This conclusion was later reconfirmed by Blomström and Kokko (1997: 39). In considering the situation in Ireland, it was found that 'recent FDI growth has taken place at a time when the relative value of Ireland's incentives has been eroded. This erosion stems both from domestic reductions in incentives and from the increasing use of regional incentives elsewhere in the EU. This may suggest that incentives are necessary but not sufficient to attract internationally mobile investment?' (Braunerhjelm *et al.*, 2000: 85).

5.6 Transnational corporations and international economic integration

Many business activities entail high costs and uncertainties and face rapid changes in technology and demand, so the operation of such activities in relatively small markets may not be commercially viable from an efficiency point of view. Worldwide free trade may not be achieved in the short or medium term (if ever), so, as the first-best neo-classical solution suggests, international economic integration or preferential trade may be an attractive second-best policy option. Such integration, although to an extent an inward-looking strategy, widens/pools the markets of the participating countries. Larger and growing markets provide greater confidence than relatively smaller ones to both domestic and foreign investors.

Domestic markets in most countries are so small that even a high degree of protection of growth-propelling manufacturing industries and services aimed at supplying the local market may not be viable in terms of efficient employment of resources. By supplying a larger market provided by the integration arrangement, participating countries may increase production, capacity utilisation, employment and investment; reduce vulnerability to external shocks; capture economies of scale; improve bargaining positions in international markets; and increase average standards of living. Those results should be viewed in comparison with the situation in which all countries act alone under heavy domestic protection.

The production and distribution of goods and services in an integrated area is not the sole prerogative of domestic firms, but can also be carried out by TNCs and their affiliates. This consideration adds an extra element to the theoretical analysis that brings it closer to the real world, but it also introduces some analytical drawbacks to the pure and simple theoretical models. In an early work, Mundell (1957) argued that, within the Hecksher-Ohlin theoretical model, trade in goods and trade in factors may substitute for each other. Markusen (1983) has shown that the operations of TNCs (flow of factors) are complementary to international trade, rather than substitutes, and that Mundell's proposition may describe only a special case.

Foreign direct investment is the result of market imperfections, as in a free trade situation the geographical and sector-wise allocation of resources is perfect and there are no grounds for FDI. Nonetheless, TNCs are a source of powerful enterprise-created links that may integrate national economies. Countries should aim to set realistic objectives in relation to integration or preferential trade: to determine how TNCs fit into the picture, to structure their entry, operation and exit and to negotiate deals. In addition, if the integrated countries master the production of goods and services to such an extent that it increases their international competitiveness, firms within the area may expand abroad and themselves become TNCs. They may increase the employment of home resources and enter new markets beyond the confines of the market of the integrated area.

Suppose that a monopolist TNC exports a good to a group of integrated countries protected by a common binding quota. If the TNC decides also to locate within the integrated area, it may choose to produce there any quantity of the good it wishes. In such a case, the integration scheme (as a whole, but not necessarily every part of it) may benefit significantly as there is additional employment of domestic factors and domestic consumers also gain because the price of the good may fall. In another case, if local firms are competing with a TNC in the home market, the location of the TNC within the integrated area may benefit both consumers (price falls) and resource utilisation as domestic firms must become more competitive if they want to remain in business. If such a process works well, then there is no justification for restrictions on the operation of foreign TNCs in an integrated area (be it in the developed or developing world).

An arrangement that integrates countries may improve the terms of trade of the group with the rest of the world. If the price of a good or service that is imported to the group falls after integration, then such an arrangement increases the rents of the scheme to the detriment of those previously made by foreign firms. Suppose that country A and country B integrate. If a TNC outside the integration scheme that produces good X is located in country B prior to integration and continues to operate there after the regional arrangement is formed, then the price of good X may fall as a result of either competition in the integrated market or the increased efficiency that comes from economies of scale. If country A starts importing good X from country B, then country A experiences other benefits in addition to the stimulation of trade. The rents of the TNC dwindle, whereas the surplus of country A's consumers rises. In this case country A experiences the so-called *foreign profit diversion effect*. If another TNC in country A were to produce good Y, which is then exported to the partner country B after integration, country A experiences the opposite effect of *foreign profit creation effect* (Tironi, 1982: 155–6).

Foreign profit creation/diversion effects are of vital importance to integration schemes whose economic structures are dominated or influenced by TNCs. This may be the case in countries that are involved in the 'globalisation' of international business, as well as in many developing countries. If such countries integrate, then TNCs are mostly interested in favourable foreign profit creation effects. Consider two countries contemplating integration, each of which has in its market a TNC that manufactures the same undifferentiated good. If the leverage of the two TNCs on decision-making is significant in the two countries, then the TNCs may collude and undermine the integration efforts.

Governments usually respect the opinions of the business community, especially if the business has a significant effect on the welfare of the country. Hence, in some cases, TNCs may even play one government against another and continue with an inefficient (from a resource allocation point of view) but, for them, profitable production.[25] This is one reason why the integration arrangements of developing countries may include provisions that refer to TNCs. Nonetheless, the policy of an integrated area towards TNCs depends on the basic objectives of the group. If the basic objective of the group is an increase in *employment*, then ownership of the firms is irrelevant. FDI is, after all, an investment. If the goal of the group is to *shift rents* towards the integrated countries, then it matters who is the owner of the manufacturing and services production and marketing units.[26] In reality, however, governments are not indifferent to who owns 'national' assets.

If the integrated market of the (developing) countries is still small enough for the establishment of a cluster of related suppliers, then the major beneficiaries may be TNCs that assemble goods and/or perform only limited (usually final) manufacturing operations. Such a tendency may be enhanced when the integrated countries have relaxed rules of origin for goods that qualify for liberal treatment in internal trade. Although the internal trade of the group increases, so does the extra-group import content of the traded goods. Broad regional deepening of production linkages does not take place. Estimates of the potential increase in trade should refer to the dual pattern of trade (imports of components from abroad and export of finalised goods within the group) and discount the gross increase in internal trade of the region. Instead of the expected relative reduction in the dependency on external markets, integration on such terms may have the completely opposite effect.

The governments of potential host countries may compete with each other in offering subsidies to TNCs to entice them to invest and locate in their country. In this game, the principal winners may be the TNCs themselves as their bargaining power is enhanced. One outcome may be that TNCs locate in more than one country, supply the local protected market and engage in parallel production on a scale that is suboptimal from a resource allocation point of view, while these countries lose interest in the integration process. Such a strategy requires a common competition policy, a joint industrialisation programme and coordinated treatment of TNCs by countries in the group, otherwise the linkages with the suppliers from the local economy and integration partner country may be superficial. Integration may lead to a production structure that is dominated by firms alien to the integrated group and in which potentially positive absorption and spread of changes in the market (created by the involvement of TNCs) by the local enterprises fails to take place.

Transnational corporations have an interest in promoting integration among developing countries with small markets, but only in countries where they have not been involved before integration. In medium and large developing countries, the position of TNCs may be quite different and they may in fact attempt to prevent integration among countries of this size. The primary concern of TNCs may not be efficiency in production, but rather the likely reactions of other TNCs as well as the avoidance of conflicts (UNCTAD, 1983: 12).

5.7 European Union

Issues

Free capital mobility largely results in the loss of national monetary independence. For example, all else being equal, an increase in a member country's interest rate relative to those in the outside world, intended to slow down the economy and curb inflation, would have the result of increasing the domestic money supply. Many TNCs would invest funds in that country in order to profit from higher rates of interest. The reverse situation, of a country lowering its interest rates with the intention of stimulating economic activity by cheap loans, would lead to a decrease in available funds as TNCs would transfer financial resources to countries with higher rates of interest (Panić, 1991: 212). It is unlikely that national firms would be able to influence exchange rate policy to the same degree as TNCs.

However, this does not mean that TNCs render government policies irrelevant. The governments of large countries still have significant autonomy to pursue policies in the national interest for two reasons. First, they have more self-sufficient economies that small countries and, second, the size of their market is such that TNCs do not want to be excluded from it. Hence, TNCs will be careful not to irritate the host government (Panić, 1998: 273–4).

The establishment of the European Economic Community, as phase 1 in the integration process, stimulated TNCs from the US to invest and later expand activities in this region during the 1960s and 1970s. The implementation of the Single Market Programme (phase 2 in the integration process) and the completion of the internal market was expected to increase investment of Japanese TNCs in the EU. However, the realisation of this expectation also depended, in part, on the evolution of the tariffs and NTBs in the EU. The establishment of EMU as phase 3 in the EU integration process may reinforce the attractiveness of the EU as a location for FDI. This was supported by a relative decline in the value of the euro relative to the dollar in the first year of its operation.

While phase 1 in the integration process eliminated (among other things) tariffs on internal trade, the objective of phase 2 was to eliminate NTBs on internal trade, which was expected to increase efficiency of production (rationalised investments), reduce transaction costs, increase competition and demand and harmonise standards. This required some adjustments of internal production in the EU. The rationale for the existence of 'tariff factories' was removed. Thus, investment in production that avoided internal EU barriers was significantly reduced or even eliminated. In any case, phase 2 was expected to increase the operation and investment of TNCs originating in the EU, as well as cooperative agreements and strategic alliances between them. An additional effect would be investment creation. In the longer term, it was thought that European TNCs could become like those in the US and take full advantage of economies of scale. Europeans generally have more sophisticated tastes than US consumers, and demand differentiated goods. Hence, large-scale production of homogenised goods, as occurs in the US, has never been expected in the EU. The objective of phase 3 in the EU integration process is to 'level the monetary playing field' in the EU and to remove all exchange rate risks that jeopardise competition, trade and investment.

Foreign TNCs initially feared that the EU would create a 'Fortress Europe' whose aim would be to protect the home market through the Single Market Programme. Some of them rushed to establish themselves in the EU before the potential 'discrimination' took place. Target enterprises in the EU became overvalued to the extent that other locations, most notably in the US, began to appear more attractive. Despite this, the EU continued to be an interesting location for FDI, as foreign TNCs were also hoping to enter into strategic alliances with EU firms.

Horizontally integrated TNCs such as 3M responded to the Single European Market with specialisation of production in their plants. 'Post-it' notes are made in 3M's British plant, while Scotch tape is produced in Germany. Previously, 3M produced a wide range of goods in each country to serve predominantly the local market. Vertically integrated TNCs such as Ford responded to the new opportunities by vertical specialisation. Differentials and gear boxes are produced in France, while engines are made in Spain. In addition, there emerged a special kind of relation among the competing firms. Removal of NTBs on internal trade and liberalisation of public procurement 'forced' inter-firm specialisation in similar goods. For example, ICI (Britain) specialised in marine, decorative and industrial paints, whereas BASF (Germany) specialised in automobile paints (Dunning, 1994a: 296–7).

Evolution

Unlike the Exxon–Florio amendment (1988) in the US, which gives the US President the right to block mergers, acquisitions or takeovers of domestic firms by foreign TNCs when such action is likely to jeopardise national security, the EU does not have a common policy regarding FDI. Only Article 43[27] of the Treaty of Rome gives the right of establishment to businesses throughout the EU for the nationals of any member state. The EU 'has one of the most liberal regimes for incoming FDI' (UNCTAD, 1996: 117). The obstacles mainly include personnel restrictions, local content requirements and government procurement. Japan also has few formal barriers to inward FDI. Nonetheless, the real obstacles to FDI in Japan are not found in the legal sphere. They exist as a cost of 'doing business in Japan', such as close and strong informal links among businesses, tight labour markets, language barriers and difficulties in obtaining the necessary data.

The impact of the creation of the EU on the attraction of FDI from the US was at the centre of early studies of the relationship between integration (or, as it was then called, 'tariff discrimination' introduced by the EU and EFTA) and FDI. The expectation was that the geographical location of FDI would be influenced by integration, and in particular that the establishment of the EU would lure TNCs there. Scaperlanda (1967: 26), in examining the American FDI trend in Europe between 1951 and 1964, found that the formation of the EU(6) did not attract a large share of American FDI. FDI from the US to the EU(6) since 1958 has amounted to $3.5bn, compared with $4bn to non-EU European countries over the same period. Factors such as familiarity with the country in which the investment was to be located, differences in the application of technology and the financial liquidity to fund foreign investment had a greater effect on the distribution of FDI than the creation of the EU(6). In addition, the American TNCs were more interested in the French market than in the EU(6).

Instead of calculating the FDI trend for the whole period 1951–64, merging 'before' and 'after' EU effects (as did Scaperlanda) and masking investment shifts rather than revealing them, Wallis (1968) divided the period of analysis into two subperiods. The share of the American FDI in the EU(6) moved along a continuous and increasing path in the period 1951–64 with a kink in 1958. Before 1958, the EU(6) share increased by 0.7 per cent a year, whereas after 1958 the average annual increase was 2.7 per cent. An increase in the US FDI in Europe was also observed in the following way: 'Fifteen years from now it is quite possible that the world's third largest industrial power, just after the United States and Russia, will not be Europe, but *American industry in Europe*. Already, in the ninth year of the Common Market, this European market is basically American in organisation' (Servan-Schreiber, 1969: 3).

D'Arge (1969; 1971a,b) attempted to determine the impact of European integration on American FDI in the EU and EFTA. The effect of the formation of a trading block on the location of FDI may follow three patterns:

- a one-off (intercept) shift in trend;
- a gradual increase in trend (slope shift);
- a combination of the other two.

The data showed that, in the case of the EFTA, there was a positive intercept shift (a one-off effect), while in the period following the creation of the EU(6) there was a combination of shifts in both slope and intercept.

Scaperlanda and Reiling (1971) found that European integration had no significant effect on US FDI flows in this region: FDI flows to the EU(6) and EFTA were similar after 1959, although it had been expected that the EU would attract more FDI than the EFTA. However, it is important to remember that at that time the major beneficiary of US FDI was the UK, which was a member of the EFTA but not the EU(6). Thus, early studies of the impact of integration on FDI do not give a clear picture of the effect of integration on FDI.

Clarification of the situation came later with evidence that, in the case of American FDI in the EU(6), size and growth of market played an important role (Goldberg, 1972: 692; Scaperlanda and Balough, 1983: 389). However, Culem (1988) argued that FDI is not in direct competition with domestic investments. A foreign country may be desirable in its own right, either because it has a specific factor (not available at home) that is necessary for the production process, or because an external outpost may be better placed to monitor developments in foreign markets or because the foreign government has exerted political pressure to locate there. Culem found that 'the size of the European market does not appear to exert any attraction on U.S. direct investments' (p. 900).

Econometric modelling of FDI is a formidable task. The results of models depend greatly on the assumptions made, so the conclusions can only be tentative. Nonetheless, there is general support for the hypothesis that tariff discrimination, regionalism and integration influence FDI. However, this cannot be translated into a statement that an *x* per cent change in tariffs will induce a *y* per cent change in FDI. Therefore, strong policy recommendations on the basis of such models are reckless (Lunn, 1980: 99).

Recent studies report that the net effect of integration has been to increase both internal EU and non-EU investment in the EU. The elimination of import duties on internal EU trade encouraged non-EU investors to locate in the EU (Dunning and Robson, 1987: 113), while the elimination of NTBs (Single Market Programme) and widening of the internal market prompted both EU and third-country TNCs to invest.[28] An increase in the FDI activity following the establishment of the Single Market Programme has been confirmed not only by Eurostat statistics, but also by studies including those by Aristotelous and Fountas (1996: 579), Dunning (1997: 13), Jovanović (1997: 324–9; 1998a: 158–64), European Commission (1998) and Clegg and Scott-Green (1999: 612).

The Single Market Programme prompted TNCs to rationalise their operations in the EU. Hence, the absence of any reference to TNCs in the official reports generated by the Single European Act, such as Emerson *et al.* (1988) and Cecchini (1988), comes as a surprise. The assumption in those reports seems to be that international specialisation and trade is carried out by firms whose operational facilities are confined to a single country. The growth and predominance of TNCs in most areas of economic activity make this kind of analysis inappropriate (Panić, 1991: 204).

Britain has always been a relatively attractive location for TNCs, although its economic performance relative to other EU major economies has often been poor. What is the reason for this interest? Regional incentives are no more generous there than in the rest of the EU.[29] One reason for its appeal that is often cited is the commonality of the English language, although large TNCs are able to afford to ease the language barrier. Another reason that is sometimes put forward is that a presence in Britain can serve as a springboard to the rest of the EU, but this could equally apply to other member countries. However, where Britain does score well is in its labour force, which can be highly competent and experienced but relatively low paid (compared with other major EU countries), and in its industrial and education infrastructure and social and political stability.

Japanese TNCs have not been reluctant to invest in Britain. However, they prefer to build new factories in rural areas rather than to take over existing plants. They also prefer takeovers to joint ventures. Where Japanese TNCs have a clear comparative advantage they prefer 'greenfield' entry (the preferred way to locate). One advantage of this is that previous managerial habits and labour relations are not inherited. In addition, such sites are often in depressed areas which attract subsidies. Greenfield locations enable Japanese TNCs to introduce their own technology, work practices and management style, with high productivity (Ford and Strange, 1999: 124). In Britain, Japanese TNCs were not always attracted to existing clusters, but created new ones. In industries where their comparative advantage is weaker, Japanese TNCs are more likely to form alliances and joint ventures.

In the US, Japanese investors tend to prefer locations (states) where labour unionisation is low. This has less to do with saving on labour costs and more to do with the Japanese organisation of production. Japanese manufacturing plants often require fewer job categories than is the case in their American counterparts. Labour unions are perceived as impediments to flexible production practices. In some cases, Japanese TNCs prefer to locate in rural areas as they mistrust urban workers because they perceive them as having developed 'bad work habits' and because they have greater mobility (Woodward, 1992: 696–9). In addition, Japanese TNCs in the car industry offer relatively high wages in order to ensure the development of higher levels of human capital and workforce stability. This is in sharp contrast to the hypothesis in the earlier literature that that TNCs predominantly seek locations for their investment in the areas where they can profit from low wage costs (Smith and Florida, 1994: 29–30; 39).

Yamawaki (1993: 19–20) argued that the decision about the location of production depends not only on factor costs, but also on comparative advantage in technology in the target country. A Japanese TNC from a particular industry invests in the country that already has a comparative advantage in the same industry over its counterparts in the EU partner countries.

Geographical choice of location of Japanese TNCs has the following policy implications for the countries that consider the location of these TNCs as an astute policy choice (Ford and Strange, 1999: 133–4):

- Japanese TNCs are attracted to areas with a cluster of manufacturing industries in which they operate and where there exists a high density of previous Japanese FDI.
- A highly educated and innovative workforce attracts Japanese TNCs, with consequent policy implications for education and R&D.
- Labour market flexibility and low level of labour unionisation are preferred by the Japanese TNCs. This may be a stimulus to labour market reform.
- Relatively low wages are also an attractive factor for Japanese TNCs.

Flow of foreign direct investment

Table 5.3 summarises internal EU FDI outflows per investor country during the period 1984–98. The start of the Single Market Programme in 1985 marked the beginning of a sharp increase in annual FDI flows. These outflows increased almost sixfold in the period 1985–89. Firms wanted to consolidate their competitive position before full implementation of the Programme. Over the period 1989–94, annual FDI outflows were relatively stable at (well) over €30bn. Then came a period of acceleration in FDI activity. Internal FDI outflows in the EU(15) almost tripled in the period 1994–98. This was for the most part due to the 'global' trend in mergers and acquisitions. The largest investors were Britain, Germany, the Netherlands, France and Belgium/Luxembourg.[30]

The destination of internal EU FDI flows is given in Table 5.4. These flows were geographically concentrated in Britain, the Netherlands, Belgium/Luxembourg, Germany, France and Spain (in that order).[31] Apart from Spain, these countries were at the same time major internal investors in the EU. Internal flows of FDI in the EU, therefore, suggest a trend towards agglomeration.

The discrepancies between the reported data in Tables 5.3 and 5.4 arise for various reasons, including differences in the definition of FDI, data collection systems, recording of short-term loans, borrowing on the local market, exchange rates and date of recording as well as the treatment of reinvested earnings and authorised and actual investment. These are the main reasons for the discrepancies in the data for intra-EU FDI in 1998, which was €25.5bn or 23 per cent of average intra-EU flows.

Table 5.3 Intra-EU(15) FDI (equity and other) flows, 1984–98 (€m) (FDI investor EU country)

Destination	1984	1985	1986	1987	1988	1989	1990	1991	1992	1993	1994	1995	1996	1997	1998	Total
Belgium–Luxembourg	878	368	379	1,460	2,163	1,970	2,481	3,958	5,147	3,849	5,098	3,663	3,311	7,597	8,524	50,846
Denmark	110	105	186	177	290	542	438	949	828	398	1,156	836	1,630	1,240	436	9,321
Germany[a]	657	1,234	2,033	1,534	2,119	4,771	8,089	8,681	8,070	9,528	6,328	10,172	8,301	11,174	16,962	99,653
Greece	9	6	2	1	4	-2	14	-4	10	-7	-81	22	46	339	527	886
Spain	16	32	67	167	235	604	551	469	293	362	81	219	919	1,928	1,542	7,485
France	713	627	933	3,211	5,031	9,232	8,479	7,143	7,616	3,652	3,774	3,017	5,736	5,408	8,492	73,064
Ireland	26	37	55	65	258	448	548	561	347	357	1,203	1,764	1,531	3,896	3,457	14,553
Italy	491	218	583	661	1,162	924	1,687	1,501	3,294	1,674	1,672	2,012	2,967	2,664	4,727	26,237
Netherlands	318	539	2,784	1,453	6,757	5,518	7,083	6,141	1,611	3,185	10,458	7,802	8,061	8,456	12,928	83,094
Austria									400	465	643	736	340	504	535	3,623
Portugal	5	14	2	4	26	41	63	227	368	223	118	173	211	261	500	2,236
Finland									827	1,236	480	555	935	1,427	13,060	18,520
Sweden									151	910	-77	2,153	388	2,321	11,173	17,019
UK	1,108	2,425	2,503	3,421	6,151	8,522	3,953	2,791	3,755	8,777	5,248	9,900	10,103	14,496	19,376	102,529
EU(12)	4,366	5,694	9,579	12,371	24,414	33,234	33,592	32,332	31,356	31,778	35,055	39,675	42,846	57,473	77,470	
EU(15)									32,734	34,389	36,101	43,119	44,509	61,725	102,238	

[a]Including ex-GDR from 1991.

Source: Eurostat (2000).

Table 5.4 Intra-EU(15) FDI (equity and other) flows, 1984–98 (€m) (FDI recipient EU country)

Destination	1984	1985	1986	1987	1988	1989	1990	1991	1992	1993	1994	1995	1996	1997	1998	Total
Belgium–Luxembourg	1,063	499	957	1,179	3,806	5,363	7,996	4,390	7,633	5,522	5,209	5,864	6,966	11,769	19,351	87,567
Denmark	8	6	72	177	136	499	155	252	712	512	1,291	1,788	−563	412	3,197	8,654
Germany[a]	632	617	589	438	1,372	4,907	7,576	7,433	7,123	3,949	8,441	5,876	5,132	8,525	11,483	74,093
Greece	15	114	136	102	86	242	229	330	387	233	308	398	436	729	957	4,702
Spain	573	597	1,170	1,523	1,892	3,397	4,880	5,338	5,020	4,199	4,728	2,540	2,695	3,385	6,190	48,127
France	1,215	1,236	1,434	1,346	4,426	3,949	4,262	3,597	6,812	3,903	5,627	5,445	8,382	6,595	13,898	72,127
Ireland	141	279	61	160	300	1,087	2,233	4,105	1,713	1,849	850	1,934	1,677	1,395	−1,124	16,660
Italy	970	488	1,105	769	1,276	2,341	2,196	1,740	3,190	2,985	2,251	4,128	5,656	4,878	8,251	42,224
Netherlands	2,803	698	2,799	1,291	3,789	4,555	5,102	2,588	7,673	5,289	7,941	12,467	10,245	12,512	15,193	94,945
Austria									325	914	−137	1,826	3,637	1,484	1,890	9,939
Portugal	82	186	114	190	314	734	888	974	1,226	660	715	449	1,186	1,329	1,577	10,624
Finland									270	526	555	599	491	673	9,420	12,534
Sweden									1,223	1,840	5,663	1,125	2,976	3,128	16,521	32,476
UK	1,886	1,629	2,847	5,243	2,595	7,703	10,054	7,426	5,957	7,692	6,763	9,179	13,752	15,179	19,848	117,753
EU(12)	4,059	6,204	11,319	12,316	20,219	35,736	44,998	37,477	47,461	36,924	44,239	50,014	55,450	66,600	99,607	
EU(15)									49,279	40,204	50,320	53,564	62,554	71,885	127,438	

[a]Including ex-GDR from 1991.

Source: Eurostat (2000).

Before phase 2 of the integration process, endogenous EU firms generally had a primarily national orientation, whereas foreign-owned TNCs (mainly American) had a pan-European business perspective. The removal of NTBs that came with the Single Market Programme was aimed at addressing this disequilibrium in European business operations. It had an obvious and positive impact on internal FDI flows from 1985. EU internal FDI flows became more important than outflows from the EU to third countries in the period 1990–96. Another interesting observation is that the southern countries such as Greece and Portugal (but also Denmark) were initially left out of the internal EU flows of FDI, but began slowly to catch up in the course of the 1990s.

The EU countries were investing not only within their group, but also outside of it. Data on external EU FDI outflows are given in Table 5.5. The US and EFTA countries have always been both major locations (targets) for FDI from the EU and, at the same time, major sources of FDI coming into the EU. It is interesting to note that favourable trade and cooperation together with prospects for the full entry of the EU were incentives for an ever-increasing flow of FDI from the EU to the candidate countries. Hence, the possibility of EU accession contributed to the changing geography of production in the region. A similar development occurred in the case of Mexico and the US (NAFTA). The principal investor outside the EU was Britain, followed by Germany (Table 5.6). Another two important investor countries were France and the Netherlands.

A comparison of Table 5.3 and Table 5.5 shows that intra-EU FDI flows became very important from 1989 and from 1990 were more important for the EU than external flows. From 1990 until 1994 investors invested more within the EU than outside it. Previously, regional integration was only one factor that influenced FDI flows from the EU countries within and out of the EU. While the liberalisation of internal EU trade had a strong impact on trade integration, study of FDI flows shows that before 1989 and after 1995 integration was stronger on the global plane than on the EU one.

Thomsen and Nicolaides (1991: 103) argued that the Single Market Programme had its greatest influence not on the *quantity* of FDI in that period in the EU, but rather on its *timing*. Such an argument should be viewed with caution. The Single Market Programme has the potential to affect (enhance) the long-term growth prospects of the EU. In addition, the Programme changed the EU business regime and created advantages additional to the already existing EU specific locational advantages. Hence, the long-term level of inward FDI in the EU is higher than it would have been otherwise (European Commission, 1998: 96).

The EU was, together with the US, the major target for the location of FDI from third countries. The principal foreign (third-country) investor was the US (Table 5.7), followed at a large distance by the EFTA. Japan also invested in the EU, but its investment was only a quarter of that invested by the EFTA (originally seven countries, reducing to four following the departure of the UK, Denmark and Ireland to join the EU). Yamada and Yamada (1996) reported that the principal goal of Japanese investors in the EU was to avoid emerging protectionism. The

Table 5.5 Extra-EU(15) outward flows of FDI (equity and other), 1984–98 (€m) (EU FDI abroad)

Destination	1984	1985	1986	1987	1988	1989	1990	1991	1992	1993	1994	1995	1996	1997	1998	Total
EFTA(7)[a]	952	722	163	1,789	2,593	1,992	3,226	2,471	1,539	1,758						13,908
EFTA(4)[b]											4,279	1,797	4,368	8,421	22,323	44,485
Candidate countries[c]											2,824	5,489	5,482	6,975	9,416	30,186
United States	11,537	10,061	17,772	23,885	22,120	24,053	7,155	9,232	6,941	13,789	7,426	24,534	17,272	36,936	112,319	345,032
Japan	294	34	104	12	247	682	911	341	445	−1,229	272	854	2,159	525	1,048	6,699
Others	4,624	4,288	3,893	4,984	6,720	6,555	9,235	14,688	8,903	9,839	9,328	12,906	18,131	37,238	45,392	196,724
Extra EU(12)	17,407	15,105	21,932	30,670	31,680	33,282	20,527	26,732								
Extra EU(15)									17,828	24,157	24,129	45,580	47,412	90,095	190,498	

[a]European Free Trade Association until 1994 (AT, CH, FI, IS, LI, NO, SE).
[b]European Free Trade Association (CH, IS, LI, NO).
[c]Candidate countries (BG, CY, CZ, EE, HU, LV, LT, PL, RO, SK, SI).

Source: Eurostat (2000).

Table 5.6 Outward FDI flows (equity and other) by EU member countries outside EU(15) 1984–98 (€m) (who invests outside the EU)

Origin	1984	1985	1986	1987	1988	1989	1990	1991	1992	1993	1994	1995	1996	1997	1998	Total
Belgium–Luxembourg	60	52	605	545	1,839	1,145	1,175	370	698	1,333	151	2,379	3,994	890	6,035	21,271
Denmark	222	147	390	219	297	397	415	835	269	779	1,123	1,345	371	1,240	120	8,169
Germany[a]	2,978	4,020	5,364	5,266	5,961	4,515	5,369	4,884	4,425	3,830	5,929	10,924	18,469	22,241	51,713	155,888
Greece																0
Spain			241	227	552	415	733	1,116	727	820	2,864	2,330	2,762	7,210	11,612	31,609
France	1,747	2,379	3,531	3,483	3,958	6,205	6,864	7,801	2,628	4,381	8,976	5,379	11,263	14,159	18,585	101,339
Ireland																0
Italy	1,512	598	865	495	1,144	242	1,031	4,362	1,910	1,442	1,101	783	932	3,704	5,605	25,726
Netherlands	1,011	2,373	1,029	3,607	2,612	5,182	4,497	3,179		2,978	3,035	4,827	10,892	10,541	18,563	74,326
Austria												543	858	617	813	2,831
Portugal	11	17	5	6	2	15	26	60	67	6	76	115	422	742	1,446	3,016
Finland	385	259	464	331	1,065	1,705	1,412	675	290	177	251	369	699	1,182	1,253	10,517
Sweden	1,183	1,183	2,206	1,346	1,298	2,505	1,422	984	729	127	685	3,392	396	5,264	5,264	26,801
UK	9,627	5,105	9,799	16,728	14,710	14,819	392	3,130	504	4,704	2,634	11,604	3,281	20,484	67,594	185,115
EU(12)	17,407	15,105	21,932	30,670	31,680	33,282	20,527	26,732	17,828	24,157	24,129					
EU(15)		15,105										45,580	47,412	90,095	190,498	

[a] Including ex-GDR from 1991.

Source: Eurostat (2000).

Table 5.7 EU(15) inward FDI (equity and other) flow from third countries, 1984–98 (€m) (FDI receipts from abroad)

Origin	1984	1985	1986	1987	1988	1989	1990	1991	1992	1993	1994	1995	1996	1997	1998	Total
EFTA(7)[a]	1,663	1,838	3,258	3,833	8,509	8,351	11,284	6,883								45,619
EFTA(4)[b]									3,303	2,016	5,630	7,064	6,298	3,441	14,922	42,674
Candidate countries[c]											524	226	118	145	356	1,369
United States	2,951	1,788	2,660	2,337	2,551	9,846	9,178	5,411		11,296	10,347	24,293	19,989	20,782	61,715	185,144
Japan	390	719	465	1,572	2,584	4,354	5,406	1,682	1,859	1,600	1,454	1,535	468	2,562	2,532	29,182
Others	1,148	1,366	736	5,249	4,497	5,392	6,885	6,957	17,598	6,592	3,859	4,102	4,955	11,258	9,755	90,349
Extra EU(12)	6,152	5,711	7,119	12,991	18,141	27,943	32,753	20,933								
Extra EU(15)									22,760	21,504	21,814	37,220	31,828	38,188	892,80	

[a] European Free Trade Association until 1994 (AT, CH, FI, IS LI, NO, SE).
[b] European Free Trade Association (CH, IS LI, NO).
[c] Candidate countries (BG, CY CZ, EE, HU, LV, LT PL, RO, SK, SI).

Source: Eurostat (2000).

Table 5.8 Inward FDI flows (equity and other) from extra-EU(15), 1984–98 (€m) (who receives FDI from abroad)

Destination	1984	1985	1986	1987	1988	1989	1990	1991	1992	1993	1994	1995	1996	1997	1998	Total
Belgium–Luxembourg	64	507	151	693	1,282	1,868	1,355	1,774	1,998	2,899	1,658	2,229	1,792	1,239	4,550	24,059
Denmark	32	159	156	151	422	640	567	637	243	582	1,076	609	397	610	4,387	10,668
Germany[a]	115	295	246	215	–383	1,670	2,187	440	658	2,087	2,444	5,503	3,562	3,018	2,636	24,693
Greece																0
Spain			1,076	1,338	1,799	2,127	2,956	2,139	2,065	1,186	2,379	1,036	1,745	918	1,098	21,862
France	1,387	1,677	1,386	2,056	1,813	2,100	3,365	4,287	4,096	2,647	4,495	7,013	4,984	5,702	4,621	51,629
Ireland																0
Italy	927	30	–456	1,745	33,063	291	3,020	1,288	940	673	416	1,112	515	1,039	208	14,811
Netherlands	139	507	938	664	947	2,704	3,013	2,807		272	2,331	3,658	6,646	1,298	17,518	43,342
Austria												171	112	323	279	885
Portugal	135	122	47	97	211	365	586	520	317	227	376	117	–58	568	543	4,173
Finland	64	50	307	52	106	190	604	–164	221	181	244	152	–265	144	141	2,027
Sweden		188	683	249	622	927	603	552	397	1,002	1,716	8,351	1,314	2,876	1,622	21,102
UK	1,996	623	3,366	5,619	8,748	15,690	14,661	5,612	8,756	7,904	2,398	8,592	9,415	17,981	47,950	159,311
EU(12)	6,152	5,711	7,119	12,991	18,141	27,943	32,753	20,933								
EU(15)									22,760	21,504	21,814	37,220	31,828	38,188	89,280	

[a]Including ex-GDR from 1991.

Source: Eurostat (2000).

EU candidate countries invested modestly in the EU, predominantly in trade-related services.

The geographical distribution of incoming FDI in the EU in the period 1984–98 is given in Table 5.8. The major location in the EU for external investors was Britain, followed by France, the Netherlands, Germany and Belgium/Luxembourg (in descending order). Again, there was a clustering of FDI in the 'core' EU countries. In addition to these countries, external investors were also interested in Sweden and Spain.

Spain can provide a useful example for other EU-rim countries. With its improved infrastructure, unimpeded access to the EU market and relatively abundant well-qualified and cheap (according to EU standards) labour force, it provides an attractive springboard for external TNCs that are interested in operating in a pan-EU market. The noted enthusiasm of external investors in Spain points to a relative spread of external FDI in the EU.

Foreign direct investment flows are a strongly cyclical phenomenon. After a slowdown at the start of the 1990s, FDI flows recovered in Europe as it came out of a recession. Japan's importance as a foreign direct investor country has declined since its economic 'bubble' burst at the end of 1990s. In the 1990s, the persistent growth of the US economy dominated the world FDI stage. The booming economy maintained and strengthened strong incentives to invest in the US. Annual FDI inflows in the US were \$84bn (1996), \$105bn (1997), \$186bn (1998) and \$275bn (1999) (UNCTAD, 2000: 283).

Large global interpenetration of FDI reduces the chance that regional arrangements may turn into closed blocs. A 'hostage population' of TNCs may reduce the fear of retaliatory measures. Extensive FDI links between the US and the EU helped reduce any potential conflict between the two partners regarding market access. The same is not yet true of Japan. There is a hope that Japan will mature as a foreign investor in future and that potential conflict with that country will be defused.

A drive towards a reciprocal treatment of FDI with Japan (or any other country) may not be highly productive. It is generally accepted that TNCs bring benefits that more than compensate for the possible costs. The EU is, after all, the major source of FDI, so the demand for a reciprocal treatment may be counterproductive. The principle of reciprocity in FDI often means the aligning of regulations upwards (reciprocal treatment in trade is often different as it levels down trade provisions).

Table 5.9 shows the annual rates of growth of GDP (expansion of markets) in the EU member countries, US and Japan in the period 1984–2001. It has already been said that there was a degree of concentration of FDI in the 'core' EU countries. This was in spite the fact that these countries did not (always) have the highest rates of growth. Ireland and Portugal (even Greece towards the end of 1990s) had higher rates of growth than the UK. However, in spite of this and increasing integration, the size of an individual country market may still be a very important determinant for the location of FDI. The highest growth countries are not always the principal locations for FDI.

The distribution of *incoming* FDI from third countries among sectors and

Table 5.9 Real annual growth rates of GDP in EU countries, US and Japan, 1984–2001 (per cent)

Country	1984	85	86	87	88	89	90	91	92	93	94	95	96	97	98	99ᵃ	00ᵃ	01ᵃ
Belgium–Luxembourg	2.1	0.8	1.5	2.2	4.9	3.6	3.0	2.0	1.6	-1.5	3.0	2.6	0.9	3.2	2.9.	1.8	2.7	2.8
Denmark	4.4	4.3	3.6	0.3	1.2	0.6	1.2	1.4	1.3	0.8	5.8	3.7	2.8	3.1	2.7	1.5	1.9	2.1
Germanyᵇ	2.8	1.9	2.2	1.4	3.7	3.4	5.7	5.0	2.2	-1.1	2.3	1.7	0.8	1.5	2.2	1.5	2.6	2.7
Greece	2.8	3.1	1.6	-0.7	4.1	3.5	0.0	3.1	0.7	-1.6	2.0	2.1	2.4	3.4	3.7	3.4	3.8	3.9
Spain	1.8	2.3	3.2	5.6	5.2	4.8	3.7	2.7	0.7	-1.2	2.3	2.7	2.3	3.8	4.0	3.6	3.6	3.5
France	1.3	1.9	2.5	2.3	4.5	4.1	2.7	1.0	1.5	-0.9	2.1	1.7	1.1	2.0	3.2	2.5	2.9	3.0
Ireland	4.4	3.1	-0.5	4.6	4.5	6.4	7.6	1.9	3.3	2.6	5.8	9.5	7.7	10.7	8.9	7.8	6.9	5.8
Italy	2.7	2.6	2.9	3.1	4.1	2.9	2.2	1.4	0.8	-0.9	2.2	2.9	0.9	1.5	1.3	1.1	2.2	2.5
Netherlands	3.1	2.7	2.0	0.9	2.6	4.7	4.1	2.3	2.0	0.8	3.2	2.3	3.0	3.8	3.7	3.0	3.2	3.3
Austria	1.4	2.5	1.2	1.7	4.1	3.8	4.6	3.4	1.3	0.5	2.4	1.7	2.0	1.2	2.9	2.1	2.8	2.6
Portugal	-1.9	2.8	4.1	5.3	3.9	5.2	4.4	2.3	2.5	-1.1	2.2	2.9	3.0	4.1	3.5	3.1	3.3	3.3
Finland	3.1	3.3	2.1	4.0	5.4	5.4	0.0	-6.3	-3.3	-1.1	4.0	3.8	4.0	6.3	5.0	3.9	4.0	4.0
Sweden	4.0	2.2	2.2	2.8	2.3	2.4	1.4	-1.1	-1.4	-2.2	4.0	3.7	1.3	1.8	2.6	3.7	3.5	2.8
UK	2.3	3.8	4.1	4.8	4.4	2.1	0.6	-1.5	0.1	2.3	4.4	2.8	2.6	3.5	2.2	1.8	3.6	3.6
United States	6.2	3.2	2.9	3.1	3.9	2.5	1.7	-0.2	3.3	2.4	4.1	2.7	3.7	4.5	4.3	3.8	2.8	2.5
Japan	3.9	4.4	2.9	4.2	6.8	4.8	5.1	3.8	1.0	0.3	0.6	1.5	5.0	1.4	-2.8	1.3	1.6	2.1

ᵃEstimates and projections.
ᵇIncludes ex-GDR from 1991.

Source: Eurostat (2000).

Table 5.10 Sectoral distribution of FDI inflow (equity and other) into EU(12) from outside EU(12), 1984–91 (€m)

	Destination	1984	1985	1986	1987	1988	1989	1990	1991	Total
btp	Building and construction	76	235	-2	-376	17	92	-188	-215	-361
e00	Energy	236	1,031	787	-172	-2,087	901	5,786	-742	5,740
i01	Agriculture and food	294	732	4	1,297	3,495	-739	-1,396	274	3,961
i02	Metallics	105	57	-276	109	86	174	316	-594	-23
i03	Machinery	-267	718	-183	-444	443	386	716	308	1,677
i04	Transport equipment	-25	-594	1,796	419	-1,189	3,431	1,623	3,856	9,317
i05	Electrical and electronics	1,412	474	-458	536	1,991	2,115	889	-711	6,248
i06	Chemical industries	781	-428	-50	1,649	1,233	988	-2,515	1,780	3,438
i07	Other industries	-156	-45	371	1,573	1,562	3,754	2,785	2,595	12,439
i08	Industries not allocated	0	1	-1	0	-2	-1	0	-379	-382
i09	Total industries	2,144	915	1,203	5,139	7,619	10,108	2,419	7,129	366,676
ind	Not allocated	79	538	133	61	222	258	1,568	455	3,314
s01	Finance and banking	2,419	-129	3,160	5,162	6,562	5,928	11,320	5,908	40,330
s02	Insurance	-136	210	-214	233	704	2,116	-517	-537	1,859
s03	Trade, hotel and catering	455	1,781	715	301	1,140	4,012	7,047	4,653	20,104
s04	Transport, storage and communication	51	289	155	49	379	986	352	490	2,751
s05	Real estate	781	948	1,006	1,129	2,018	2,782	2,987	1,903	13,554
s06	Other services	46	-108	175	1,463	1,566	760	2,087	1,539	7,528
s07	Services not allocated	0	0	0	0	0	0	-108	347	239
s08	Total services	3,616	2,991	4,997	8,337	12,369	16,584	23,168	14,305	86,367
tot	Total	6,152	5,711	7,119	12,991	18,141	27,943	32,753	20,933	131,743

Source: Eurostat (2000).

Table 5.11 Sectoral distribution of FDI inflow (equity and other) in EU(15) from outside EU(15), 1992–98 (€m)

	Destination	1992	1993	1994	1995	1996	1997	1998	Total
595	Agriculture and fishing	105	−49	71	19	−282	179	4	47
1495	Mining and quarrying	752	655	1,873	1,216	−537	−210	−712	3,037
1100	Extraction of petroleum and gas								0
3995	Manufacturing	8,333	7,855	5,331	15,170	6,526	10,314	27,926	81,455
1605	Food products			790	912	−664	−310	1,828	2,556
1805	Textiles and wearing apparel								0
2205	Wood, publishing and printing								0
2295	Total textiles and wood activities			826	2,413	795	1,090	1,825	6,949
2300	Refined petroleum products and other treatments								0
2400	Manufacture of chemicals and chemical products								0
2500	Rubber and plastic products								0
2595	Total petroleum, chemical, rubber and plastic products			1,364	8,473	3,522	3,718	5,742	22,819
2805	Metal products								0
2900	Mechanical products								0
2995	Total metal and mechanical products			487	617	−161	1,439	2,882	5,264
3000	Office machinery and computers								0
3200	Radio, television, communication equipment								0
3295	Total office machinery, computers, RTV, communication equipment			435	1,927	1,094	1,571	12,732	17,759
3400	Motor vehicles								0
3500	Other transport equipment								0
3595	Total vehicles and other transport equipment	404	144	165	−57	1,731	1,704	991	4,534
4195	Electricity, gas and water	−25	417	−35	2,661	1,321	3,420	9,154	17,069
4500	Construction			79	−215	2,322	821	63	3,462
5295	Trade and repairs	2,760	2,763	2,757	2,242	5,091	3,325	3,141	22,079
5500	Hotels and restaurants	284	202	64	127	457	811	1,680	3,625
6495	Transport, storage and communication	604	606	311	36	538	2,488	6,464	11,047
6000	Land transport					11	337	56	404
6110	Sea and coastal water transport					95	557	267	919

Code	Activity								
6200	Air transport					290	154	155	599
6295	Total land, sea and air transport				51	392	1,047	475	1,965
6420	Telecommunications				126	−39	618	4,410	5,115
6895	Financial intermediation	5,614	5,633	4,708	5,596	8,836	5,020	24,191	59,598
6510	Monetary intermediation				1,432	1,176	3,743	3,392	9,743
6520	Other financial intermediation				5,161	5,710	−168	18,670	29,373
6524	Financial holding companies								0
6730	Insurance and activities auxiliary to insurance				−994	1,894	1,325	1,758	3,983
6795	Total other financial intermediation and insurance				4,166	7,603	1,155	20,431	33,355
7395	Real estate and business activities	2,807	3,306	5,227	9,879	6,327	10,176	15,873	53,595
7000	Real estate				1,622	846	154	770	3,392
7200	Computer activities				419	162	303	1,112	1,996
7300	Research and development				327	532	31	430	1,320
7400	Other business activities				7,451	4,482	8,994	13,213	34,140
7410	Business and management consultancy								0
7415	Management activities of holding companies								0
7440	Advertising								0
7495	Total computer, research, other business activities				8,197	5,173	9,327	14,754	37,451
9995	Other services	302	61	464	336	1,034	1,385	1,710	5,292
9996	Not allocated	1,013	−87	770	152	170	401	−218	2,201
9997	Subtotal	22,760	21,504	21,618	37,220	31,804	38,128	89,276	262,310
9998	Private purchases and sales of real estate								0
9999	Total	22,760	21,504	21,814	37,220	31,828	38,188	89,280	262,594

Source: Eurostat (2000).

industries in the EU in the period 1984–98 is presented in Tables 5.10 and 5.11. EU services received by far the largest share of FDI. Financial intermediation, real estate and trade, repairs, hotel and catering were the principal target industries for FDI in EU. The petroleum, chemical, rubber and plastic industries, electrical and electronics and transport equipment were the major targets for FDI within the manufacturing sector.

These data permit only cautious conclusions about the impact of the Single European Market and EMU on the geographical concentration of FDI in the EU. In the car-making industry, Britain lost its previous attractiveness for FDI, but Spain increased its attractiveness. In the electrical equipment manufacturing sector, Germany became the preferred location for FDI, in particular for the higher value-added operations. However, it is still a moot analytical point whether inward FDI brings to the EU high-value-added employment and technology or low-level, tariff-jumping assembly work (European Commission, 1998: 141).

Data for the sectoral distribution of *outgoing* FDI to third countries in the period 1984–98 are presented in Tables 5.12 and 5.13. EU investors were primarily interested in the extraction of petroleum and gas. They also had a huge interest in financial intermediation, real estate, insurance, computers, research and other business activities. Within the manufacturing sector, the principal targets were the petroleum, chemical, rubber and plastic industries, as well as office machinery and communication equipment.

The sectoral distribution of internal EU(15) FDI flows in the period 1992–98 is given in Table 5.14. Financial services, real estate and trade-related services absorbed the largest share of intra-EU FDI. Extraction of petroleum and gas, petroleum processing, chemicals, plastic and rubber were the major targets for FDI on the non-services side of the economy.

5.8 Conclusion

A popular perception, based on shoddy economics, is that the export of goods is beneficial for a country and, therefore, needs to be supported, whereas (some) imports are perceived to be dangerous as they might jeopardise the national output and employment potential.[32] FDI is, however, treated in a different way. Outflows are being deterred as there is a fear that exporting capital means exporting exports and exporting jobs, while inflows are welcomed!

Capital mobility has its costs and benefits. If these effects are desirable, they should be stimulated, otherwise they should be taxed and/or regulated and controlled. Simultaneous inflow and outflow of FDI in integrated countries is possible and quite likely. This was confirmed in the case of the EU. However, FDI flows and the consequent geography of production may be significant and dominant even without formal integration. Just look at trans-Atlantic FDI flows. TNCs primarily follow the opportunities for making profits in large and growing markets in the long term. Therefore, regional economic integration is *a*, rather than *the* cause of FDI.

The relative loss of the international competitive position of the EU in relation

Table 5.12 Sectoral distribution of FDI outflow (equity and other) from EU(12) outside EU(12), 1984–91 (€m)

	Destination	1984	1985	1986	1987	1988	1989	1990	1991	Total
btp	Building and construction	278	127	432	674	365	954	461	972	4,263
e00	Energy	8,555	1,689	1,537	5,256	4,961	7,516	-1,763	4,196	31,947
i01	Agriculture and food	532	-402	841	2,295	4,183	6,409	-179	1,166	14,845
i02	Metallics	318	-3	309	522	880	1,835	1,048	735	5,644
i03	Machinery	613	591	278	848	1,194	586	1,000	836	5,946
i04	Transport equipment	947	327	342	424	487	372	913	3,121	6,933
i05	Electrical and electronics	637	293	1,513	2,762	3,430	1,573	1,364	1,756	13,328
i06	Chemical industries	-70	4,757	5,061	3,110	3,477	2,095	5,216	939	24,585
i07	Other industries	-114	-119	2,017	1,885	4,293	-118	427	2,204	10,475
i08	Industries not allocated	0	0	3	4	1	1	1	-549	-539
i09	Total industries	2,863	5,444	10,364	11,850	17,945	12,753	9,792	10,209	81,220
ind	Not allocated	39	28	428	103	213	183	1,694	755	3,443
s01	Finance and banking	3,052	3,037	2,707	1,922	1,648	2,790	5,523	7,934	28,613
s02	Insurance	722	1,513	1,643	1,209	1,579	1,991	1,846	-111	10,392
s03	Trade, hotel and catering	1,234	2,146	1,716	4,599	168	913	1,710	-139	12,347
s04	Transport, storage and communication	87	121	366	192	717	2,543	-123	1,635	5,538
s05	Real estate	433	666	93	337	206	819	1,263	958	4,775
s06	Other services	143	332	2,646	4,529	3,881	2,820	185	660	15,196
s07	Services not allocated	0	0	0	0	0	0	-61	-338	-399
s08	Total services	5,671	7,815	9,171	12,788	8,199	11,876	10,343	10,599	76,462
tot	Total	17,407	15,105	21,932	30,670	31,680	33,282	20,527	26,732	197,335

Source: Eurostat (2000).

Table 5.13 Sectoral distribution of FDI outflow (equity and other) of EU(15) outside EU(15), 1992–98 (€m)

	Destination	1992	1993	1994	1995	1996	1997	1998	Total
595	Agriculture and fishing	37	12	138	18	−1,640	194	287	−954
1495	Mining and quarrying	−248	455	1,906	610	1,071	7,508	62,874	74,176
1100	Extraction of petroleum and gas								0
3995	Manufacturing	7,475	7,444	16,825	19,841	17,754	30,948	55,832	156,119
1605	Food products			1,572	2,073	1,279	2,969	1,263	9,156
1805	Textiles and wearing apparel								0
2205	Wood, publishing and printing								0
2295	Total textiles and wood activities			2,434	1,938	1,495	1,911	4,188	11,966
2300	Refined petroleum products and other treatments								0
2400	Manufacture of chemicals and chemicals products								0
2500	Rubber and plastic products								0
2595	Total petroleum, chemical, rubber, plastic products			6,884	7,112	7,871	9,558	3,741	35,166
2805	Metal products								0
2900	Mechanical products								0
2995	Total metal and mechanical products			1,752	2,678	1,747	4,551	2,349	13,077
3000	Office machinery and computers								0
3200	Radio, television, communication equipment								0
3295	Total office machinery, computers, RTV, communication equipment			2,435	386	641	749	3,204	7,415
3400	Motor vehicles								0
3500	Other transport equipment								0
3595	Total vehicles and other transport equipment	−185	155	−1	1,817	291	5,801	38,532	46,440
4195	Electricity, gas and water			455	1,030	808	2,965	2,211	7,439
4500	Construction	128	554	557	352	1,098	739	131	3,559
5295	Trade and repairs	1,114	2,022	−1,688	1,468	7,089	5,883	11,029	26,917
5500	Hotels and restaurants	438	263	412	−234	−180	−840	−1,810	−1,951
6495	Transport, storage and communication	761	−430	−139	2,935	2,755	6,289	7,096	19,267
6000	Land transport					82	6	103	191
6110	Sea and coastal water transport					575	−16	−70	489
6200	Air transport					−314	−126	−262	−702

Code	Description								
6295	Total land, sea and air transport				812	339	−136	−229	786
6420	Telecommunications	5,706	7,063	3,136	1,836	2,054	4,902	5,126	13,918
6895	Financial intermediation				10,181	9,958	23,284	42,783	102,111
6510	Monetary intermediation				2,749	1,956	5,392	9,234	19,331
6520	Other financial intermediation				6,380	5,268	7,319	28,007	46,974
6524	Financial holding companies				0	0	0	0	0
6730	Insurance and activities auxiliary to insurance				1,145	2,475	10,171	−8,558	5,233
6795	Total other financial intermediation and insurance				7,525	7,740	17,488	19,451	52,204
7395	Real estate and business activities	827	4,262	2,859	7,645	8,257	11,574	10,035	45,459
7000	Real estate				264	791	−483	−1,287	−715
7200	Computer activities				236	102	865	2,809	4,012
7300	Research and development				269	283	57	10	619
7400	Other business activities				7,695	6,066	11,017	7,380	31,258
7410	Business and management consultancy								0
7415	Management activities of holding companies								0
7440	Advertising								0
7495	Total computer, research, other business activities				7,301	6,448	11,937	10,198	35,884
9995	Other services	682	248	−400	801	−148	987	433	2,603
9996	Not allocated	1,082	2,182	567	932	528	537	−531	5,297
9997	Subtotal	17,789	24,157	24,619	45,580	47,353	90,069	190,364	439,931
9998	Private purchases and sales of real estate								0
9999	Total	17,828	24,157	24,129	45,580	47,412	90,095	190,498	439,699

Source: Eurostat (2000).

Table 5.14 Sectoral distribution of FDI flow (equity and other) from EU(15) to EU(15), 1992–98 (€m)

	Destination	1992	1993	1994	1995	1996	1997	1998	Total
595	Agriculture and fishing	49	33	−24	−2	−873	−78	93	−802
1495	Mining and quarrying	743	615	231	1,001	669	1,534	−4,468	325
1100	Extraction of petroleum and gas								0
3995	Manufacturing	16,680	11,270	19,695	10,382	20,006	22,088	43,457	143,578
1605	Food products			3,642	166	1,502	2,405	−1,390	6,325
1805	Textiles and wearing apparel								0
2205	Wood, publishing and printing								0
2295	Total textiles and wood activities			2,558	2,404	2,503	2,940	6,627	17,032
2300	Refined petroleum products and other treatments								0
2400	Manufacture of chemicals and chemicals products								0
2500	Rubber and plastic products								0
2595	Total petroleum, chemical, rubber, plastic products			5,419	1,077	6,804	7,501	10,421	31,222
2805	Metal products								0
2900	Mechanical products								0
2995	Total metal and mechanical products			2,500	1,197	3,077	6,915	5,720	19,409
3000	Office machinery and computers								0
3200	Radio, television, communication equipment								0
3295	Total office machinery, computers, RTV, communication equipment			865	75	2,825	−38	6,324	10,051
3400	Motor vehicles								0
3500	Other transport equipment								0
3595	Total vehicles and other transport equipment			2,936	2,094	2,505	−477	3,568	10,626
4195	Electricity, gas and water	172	523	670	493	555	1,999	2,623	7,035
4500	Construction	318	82	573	940	535	946	485	3,879
5295	Trade and repairs	3,885	3,077	3,783	4,527	7,444	9,570	13,254	45,540
5500	Hotels and restaurants	1,108	70	552	1,658	2,048	209	68	5,713
6495	Transport, storage and communication	657	567	1,234	1,500	3,126	2,787	1,337	11,208
6000	Land transport					−56	−714	−1,531	−2,301
6110	Sea and costal water transport					238	986	960	2,174
6200	Air transport					789	−50	358	1,097

6295	Total land sea and air transport				-252	969	221	-226	712
6420	Telecommunications				1,693	2,067	2,327	1,604	7,691
6895	Financial intermediation	18,647	18,136	12,145	19,796	15,198	12,121	38,891	134,934
6510	Monetary intermediation				5,106	4,053	3,146	20,717	33,022
6520	Other financial intermediation				9,029	9,544	9,400	9,863	37,836
6524	Financial holding companies								0
6730	Insurance and activities auxiliary to insurance				5,542	1,335	-122	18,532	25,287
6795	Total other financial intermediation and insurance				14,571	10,879	9,281	28,396	63,127
7395	Real estate and business activities	5,020	4,620	9,694	10,612	9,039	16,576	24,628	80,189
7000	Real estate				817	254	893	2,294	4,258
7200	Computer activities				564	197	786	200	1,747
7300	Research and development				577	12	108	139	836
7400	Other business activities				8,446	7,864	14,840	20,817	51,967
7410	Business and management consultancy								0
7415	Management activities of holding companies								0
7440	Advertising								0
7495	Total computer, research, other business activities				9,586	8,068	15,735	21,159	54,548
9995	Other services	723	468	581	1,178	1,398	3,564	5,201	13,113
9996	Not allocated	1,256	671	1,183	1,477	3,201	246	1,506	9,540
9997	Subtotal	49,279	40,204	50,320	53,564	62,346	71,564	127,076	454,353
9998	Private purchases and sales of real estate								0
9999	Total	49,279	40,204	50,320	53,564	62,554	71,885	127,438	455,244

Source: Eurostat (2000).

to the US, Japan and the newly industrialised countries (in several lines of production) in the 1970s and 1980s has increased both interest in and the need for strengthening the competitiveness of TNCs from the EU. These TNCs are the key actors in improving the international competitiveness of the EU. Ambitious and well-funded public research programmes in the EU may assist the EU first to catch up and later to improve its position *vis-à-vis* its major international competitors if astutely linked with the production resources and potentials, as well as demand.

US investors in the EU were market seeking in the 1950s and 1960s. The same was true of Japanese FDI in the 1970s and 1980s. As EU consumers were not able to purchase what they wanted because of NTBs, Japanese TNCs invested in the EU in order to satisfy an existing and growing local demand. TNCs from both source countries have always looked at the EU market as a single unit. Their advantages over local EU enterprises included, in some cases, not only a superior capability to innovate products and technologies and manage multiplant production and supply, but also a willingness, experience and ability to serve consumers from a local base, rather than through exports, which was the favourite method of operation of many national firms in the EU.

There is, however, at least one difference between Japanese and American FDI in the EU. Nearly half of Japanese FDI was concentrated in banking and insurance in the early 1990s. At the same time, more than a half of American FDI was in the manufacturing industry, while around a third was in financial services. Therefore, Japanese FDI has relatively less impact, at present, on EU manufacturing industry than the American TNCs (Buigues and Jacquemin, 1992: 22; European Commission, 1998: 3). This focus by Japanese investors may come as a surprise as Japan has the advantage in electronics and cars. A concentration of Japanese FDI in financial services (relying on human, rather than physical, capital) both in the EU and the US is, however, a partial reflection of Japanese balance of payments surpluses and the appreciation of the yen. However, from 1994, the interest of the Japanese TNCs shifted predominantly towards the Pacific Rim countries.

In order to avoid weakening the competitive position of EU firms in global markets, the EU may follow two courses, although employing a mix of the two has its attractions. First, the EU may increase protection of domestic firms against foreign TNCs through measures such as rules of origin, local content requirements and other TRIMs. Second, the EU may open its domestic market and encourage foreign, in particular high-technology, TNCs to locate their manufacturing operations in the EU. As widely argued, EU firms in many manufacturing industries are less efficient than their counterparts in the US and Japan. If the EU were to adopt a liberal economic policy and EU firms were to adjust and withstand competition from foreign TNCs, then they may, in relative terms, gain more from market liberalisation than their foreign competitors.

The incomplete internal market in the EU was the major cause of a suboptimal production structure in the region. All economic agents, including TNCs, behave as welfare-maximising units in the long term, subject to the prevailing conditions. These private agents should not be criticised for actions that may be in conflict with public objectives. The completion of the Single Market Programme in the EU, which included the removal of NTBs, assisted in a rationalisation of production and enhanced the location-specific advantages of the EU. The introduction of the single currency in 1999 removed internal EU exchange rate risks and solidified earlier achievements in integration. This will continue to increase both the size and the growth of the EU market, which could, in turn, further increase investment expenditure in the region in the longer term.

An extensive survey of the impact of the Single Market Programme on FDI in the EU found strong evidence that FDI and trade are complementary (European Commission, 1998: 1). Concerns that the Single Market Programme would lead to a concentration of general economic activity into the 'core' EU countries were not justified. There has been only a limited spread of economic activity to the 'peripheral' EU countries that enjoy certain cost advantages (European Commission, 1998: 145).

As one of the major players in the international capital mobility scene, the EU would like to see multilateral rules for FDI.

- Foreigners would have the right to invest and operate competitively in all sectors of the economy; only a few exceptions to the general rule should be allowed.
- There should be no discrimination of foreign investors based on their origin. A 'stand still' commitment would prevent the introduction of new restrictions.
- There should be a 'roll-back' principle to gradually eliminate national (or group) measures that run counter to the liberalisation of FDI rules.

However, as seen above, the MAI will have to wait for some time in the future.

Notes

1 One should not accord an absolute value to the decline of consumer loyalty to local brands. Regional rather than 'global' strategies in some food and health-care products may offer a superior business outcome. Some 'global success' was achieved, however, by Coca-Cola, which succeeded in replacing a part of the consumption of milk and natural fruit juices with an artificial and sweet liquid that has at best a questionable impact on health.
2 Now governments court firms (TNCs) to try to persuade them to locate within the confines of their control. Critics say that the protection of the vulnerable in society or the safeguarding of the environment is weakened, even that it is left at the mercy of big businesses. This may be the case in some lines of production.
3 The same holds for the increase in the influence of special influence groups such as non-governmental organisations (NGOs). Do these unelected groups of people with sometimes questionable accountability represent a risky shift of power towards special vested interests? Or do they represent a move towards the new 'civil society' (does anyone know the definition of this type of society)?
4 H. Kissinger, 'Globalisation: America's role for the millennium', *The Irish Independent*, 13 October 1999.
5 Increased international mobility of factors, increased international intra-firm transactions, expanding international cooperative arrangements between firms,

increasing importance of knowledge, as well as a reduction in transport and communication costs, support the process of 'globalisation' and are constituent parts of it. In these circumstances, individual actions of national governments may not increase global welfare (pollution is an example). In these circumstances, some supranational rules may be necessary in order to deliver more beneficial outcomes.

6   Trade is relatively more concentrated within regions than FDI. This suggests that trade plays a more prominent role in intra-regional integration arrangements, while FDI has a greater influence on global integration (UNCTAD, 1993: 7).

7   Control may not be easy to define in all circumstances. A 51 per cent ownership of a firm is a clear sign of full control. However, in some cases 20 or even 10 per cent ownership is sufficient for the control of a firm if other shareholders are widely dispersed.

8   According to research carried out by the location division of Ernst & Young, firms now appear to accept higher costs of production in return for high environmental standards. 'Regions that sell themselves on the basis of relaxed environmental legislation may soon find their approach counterproductive' (*Business Europe*, 12 March 1997).

9   Intra-company pricing refers to transactions among related units of the same firm. Not every manipulation of transfer prices increases the overall profits of the entire company, as these extra revenues stem from sales to outside customers (Plasschaert, 1994: 1).

10   Trade in services is expanding. Monitoring internal prices for services is a much more complex task than inspecting the same prices for goods by the employment of free market criteria.

11   Firms are reluctant to comment and release data on their internal prices. Hence, there is a black hole in this area of research.

12   Tax avoidance, unlike tax evasion, does not involve breaking any laws but rather making the best use of positive regulations. In practice, the difference between the two is often ambiguous.

13   TNCs that come from the US and operate in the EU reported an annual R&D of almost $2,500 per employee in 1989. In contrast, Euro-affiliates of Japanese TNCs reported R&D per employee of around $725 in the same year (Gittelman *et al.*, 1992: 18). The reasons for the difference include a relatively strong headquarters effect, as Japanese FDI in Europe is a fairly novel phenomenon compared with FDI from the US. American TNCs have been present in Europe on a larger scale since the 1950s. In addition, Japanese TNCs may be more involved in the EU in relatively mature manufacturing industries and services where R&D expenditure is not as high as in other activities.

14   Decisions taken at the EU level are easy targets for special lobbies as they are far from the public gaze. The co-decision procedure between the Council and the Parliament introduced by the Maastricht Treaty tried to ameliorate this shortcoming. This is a step forward compared with the past, but there is still a danger that EU technology policy may become a sophisticated new form of protectionism.

15   One of the most widely cited attempts to introduce a common policy towards TNCs in the groups that integrate developing countries was *Decision 24*. This was the first attempt by an integration group of developing countries to develop and implement a policy towards TNCs. It should be mentioned at the outset that the aim of Decision 24 was not to obstruct FDI inflows into the region. On the contrary, the member countries wanted to encourage such inflows, but in a structured way that would benefit members and increase economic efficiency within the region. In addition, they wanted to increase the bargaining power of home firms in relation to foreign TNCs in order to promote equitable distribution of gains from FDI.

The thrust of the complicated and controversial Decision 24 was the regulation of FDI and transfer of technology. It permitted the establishment of national screening and registering bureaus; outlawed new FDI in utilities and services; prohibited an annual reinvestment of corporate profit of more than 5 per cent without approval; allowed the annual transfer of profits of up to 14 per cent; and compelled TNCs to disclose all data that relate to the transferred technology, including data on the pricing of inputs. In addition, the expectation from the divestment stipulation (the most polemic feature) imposed on TNCs was a gradual reduction in foreign ownership of local assets, national capital accumulation and a basis for the development of local technology (Mytelka, 1979: 190).

Foreign investors loudly criticised Decision 24 as an unfriendly measure, but in practice they took a more pragmatic and longer-term approach. In spite of stringent conditions for FDI, the flows to the region did not decrease; on the contrary, in some cases they even increased. In order to enhance the inflow of FDI in the region the group replaced Decision 24 and introduced a more liberal *Decision 220* in 1987. This move introduced a set of common rules for FDI but gave independence to the member states in the implementation of the policy. Decision 220 was replaced in 1991 by *Decision 291*, which offered national treatment of FDI. The intention of the group was to remove obstacles to FDI and promote a free inflow of capital to the region.

16 Local content usually means 'national content' (value added within a country) or value added within the group such as the EU or NAFTA.

17 For example, Pirelli (Italy) coordinates and guarantees its global financial duties from a Swiss affiliate which is in charge of finance for the whole corporation. The US affiliate of Siemens (Germany) transmitted daily financial data to headquarters, which is in charge of global financial management (UNCTAD, 1993: 124).

18 Investment in natural resources has three distinct features. First, the geographical location of non-renewable resources is not mutable; second, investments require huge amounts of capital which is linked with significant economies of scale; and, third, processing of minerals is linked with a considerable consumption of energy.

19 It is estimated that there are around 1,600 bilateral investment treaties (*The Economist*, 14 March 1998: 85).

20 The introduction of a new good depends not only on the fixed costs and expected benefits, but also on substitution and complementarity with the goods that already exist on the market. Of course, there must be or needs to be created real demand for the new good or service.

21 Linkages with the local suppliers (local embeddedness) depend on the choice of the TNC and the existence of the suitable local firms with which a TNC can do business.

22 Transfer of profits out of the country takes place when TNCs do not find the country in question a promising geographical location for the reinvestment of earnings. Such a transfer may send a warning signal to the local government that something is wrong in the economy and that something needs to be done about it.

23 Recent research shows that FDI in the manufacturing industry from the US became increasingly sensitive to tax rates in the period 1984–92 (Altshuler *et al.*, 1998: 2).

24 According to an influential view, no matter what a government does to influence competitiveness and increase exports in the short term would still cause the adjustment of the exchange rate and factor prices in the long term (Johnson and Krauss, 1973: 240). The new theory disputed such an approach and argued that, in the presence of increasing returns to scale, externalities and the economies of learning, the policy of the government does matter. Such a policy may, if handled properly, bring irreversible advantages for the country in question.

25 In the situation where TNCs do not dominate in the economy of a country or an integrated group of countries, then, of course, their impact may be marginal. The situation, however, in virtually all present-day regional groupings of developing countries is that TNCs play a dominant role (Robson, 1987: 209).

26 Educated management and a trained labour force (domestic human capital) is what matters for the country, rather than ownership of the business (Reich, 1990). Tyson (1991) disagreed with such a view and argued that ownership still mattered. This view is, however, opposed to the traditional US stance that favours free trade and free flow of capital.

27 The 'old' Article 52 of the original Treaty of Rome.

28 Yannopoulos (1990) surveyed the diversity of views expressed in the debate on the effect of European integration on FDI.

29 Government incentives influenced TNCs such as Ford to make new investments in the north-west of the country and Wales. Honda, Nissan and Toyota benefited from public grants as they settled in regions with unemployment problems. However, those allowances were equally available in Britain to other firms from the EU or third countries, whether they were from car production or other industries.

30 One has to be careful when interpreting the data for a country such as Luxembourg (or Switzerland). Such countries often act only as intermediaries for the inflow and outflow of funds.

31 There was an increased flow of FDI in the EU-rim countries in 1991–92.

32 Through trade a country acquires useful things from abroad. Therefore imports is a gain, rather than a cost. To pay for imports, the country has to 'send' its useful goods and services abroad. In these terms exports is a cost, rather than a gain!

6 Regional policy in the European Union

6.1 Introduction

Various theoretical and policy-oriented aspects that affect regional policy, such as the choice of geographical location of domestic and foreign-owned firms, competition and industrial policies, have been encountered in the preceding chapters. The purpose of this chapter is to present the regional policy of the EU in the following way. Section 6.2 spells out basic theoretical issues linked with regional policy. Sections 6.3 and 6.4 consider, respectively, objectives and instruments of a regional policy. Various aspects of regional policy in the EU are the subject matter of section 6.5. It is concluded that the EU should pay attention to regional and cohesion matters for three reasons. First, in an EMU, balance of payments disequilibria are replaced by regional disparities. Second, Eastern enlargement would deepen the regional problem. Third, there is a constant need for the coordination on all levels of government of various policies that have a regional impact.

Regional policy, as a part of the EU Cohesion[1] Policy, affects the daily life of almost half of the 377 million people who live in the EU. Such a policy involves various subsidies and development projects, including infrastructure, training and support to SMEs, in order to ease and remedy regional disparities. The objective is to strengthen the output potential of the disadvantaged locations and regions, as well as to reinforce the unity (with diversity) of the EU.

In 2000, annual expenditure from structural funds[2] was €9.6bn, or 35 per cent of the overall EU budget (this is next to the EU expenditure on agriculture). As a result, European integration has a direct and significant impact on a substantial number of EU citizens and businesses. This EU policy will gain in importance in the future at least because of two crucial developments:

- EMU: Member countries can no longer deal with national economic problems by the use of policy instruments such as interest rate, inflation, excessive deficit-financed expenditure or changes in exchange rate. Potential national balance of payments disequilibria became regional disequilibria in an EMU. Hence, one of the policy instruments to deal with such problems is regional policy.

- *Eastern enlargement*: The EU is in negotiations with ten Central and East European countries with economies in transition, as well as Cyprus and Malta, while Turkey may also join the group in the future. Eastern enlargement would introduce significant regional disparities into the EU. Thus, the EU will be assisting the candidate countries for some time to come to ensure that they are well prepared for full entry into the EU.

6.2 Issues

Recall that a region may be more easily discerned than defined. The definition of a region depends on the problem that one encounters. A region is a geographical phenomenon with distinct borders with others, but it also has political, governmental and administrative features and is an ethnic and social concept with human and cultural characteristics. A region is also an economic concept defined by its endowment factors, their combinations and mobility. Therefore, a region can be defined in theory as a geographical area that consists of adjoining particles with similar unit incomes and more interdependence of incomes than between regions (Bird, 1972: 272). A region of a country or an economic union may be thought of as an open economy.

There are many *causes* of regional disequilibria. They include (Vanhove and Klaasen, 1987: 2–7):

- market rigidities (such as relatively low mobility of factors);
- geographical factors;
- differences in the availability of resources;
- education of management and training of labour;
- regional economic structure (in some regions industries with ageing technologies, in others industries with modern technologies);
- institutional factors such as the centralisation of public institutions (Paris is an obvious example);
- national wage setting in spite of differences in productivity and labour market conditions across different regions.

Regional disparities adopt numerous *forms*. They include not only differences in income levels per capita, rates of growth or rates of unemployment, economies of scale, externalities, output and consumption structures, productivity, access to public services, but also the age structure, population density and the pattern of migration.

Regional policy is basically aimed at influencing economic adjustment in the four (theoretical) types of regions.

- Regions in which agriculture accounts for a relatively high share of production and employment. These are usually underdeveloped rural areas with relatively low levels of income, high levels of unemployment and poorly developed infrastructure.

- Regions whose former prosperity was founded on industries that are now in decline, such as coal, steel, shipbuilding or textiles. These are the regions that failed to keep pace with changes in technology and were unable to withstand external competition (in some cases because of earlier excessive protection). In the case of recession, labour in these regions is the first to be made redundant.
- Regions with a high concentration of manufacturing and resulting congestion and pollution problems. In these areas, of course, there are benefits to be had from the joint use of goods and services available in these areas. Regional policy may, however, try to reduce the existing congestion (concentration) and pollution and/or prevent their further increase.
- Frontier regions, which are far from the strongest areas (poles of growth) of a country's or union's economic activity.

Jobs can be located in regions where there are people with suitable qualifications, training and experience. Therefore, regions with unskilled labour cannot be expected to attract any significant number of industries that use modern technologies and require trained labour and educated management. The location of business near large and/or growing markets saves transport costs. If returns to scale were constant, as the neo-classical theory assumes, this could tend to equalise factor owners' rewards in different regions. With economies of scale and other market imperfections (the situation with multiple equilibria), these tendencies may, but will not necessarily, increase rather than decrease regional disequilibria.

Convergence in the level of development among different regions is not a self-sustaining process. It is easier during an economic recovery than during recessions. Lagging regions/countries have usually a higher proportion of both 'sensitive industries' and public enterprises than prosperous ones. Therefore, they may be hit harder by a recession and budgetary restrictions (no subsidies and public purchases) than other regions.

In the 1960s, the regional problem was usually tackled with supply-side subsidies for the provision of infrastructure and the reallocation of various (public) manufacturing and service industries. Foreign competition, in particular from the newly industrialised countries, placed in jeopardy a number of industries that failed to adjust. As there had been little luck with earlier approaches to the regional problem, and coupled with austerity programmes in public finances, there was a major change in national regional policies during the 1980s. Outright subsidies were reduced or slashed and the policy was supplemented by a system intended to make the lagging regions more self-reliant (support to indigenous development). This included the development of human resources, the attraction of private investors (in particular foreign ones) and the provision of technical services.

There is a great deal of uncertainty regarding the impact of international economic integration on regional matters. One thing, however, needs to be mentioned here. Having a 'peripheral' location is not an irreversible economic disadvantage. Its impact can be mitigated and even reversed, as has been successfully shown by countries such as Ireland and Finland (or Australia and

Japan). What matters most for the competitiveness of a country's goods and services on the international market is the efficient creation, employment and reward to the most precious economic factor: human capital.

Regional policy was neglected in the EU before its first enlargement in 1973. This was followed by a period of interest in an active regional policy. However, enthusiasm for this policy waned in the 1990s as there were few obvious positive results from intervention. Public intervention in regional issues is still a highly controversial issue. Is there or is there not a self-equilibrating process among the regions in the long term? Is intervention (regional policy) necessary or not? Hence, can regional policy work at all?

National governments introduced regional policies in order to promote growth in poor regions. The policy was based on the assumption that market failures exist. The instruments of the policy included investment aid, direct investment by the state, wage subsidies, tax allowances, licensing and the provision of infrastructure and services. However, since the 1990s, the emphasis of regional policy has moved away from the attraction of extraregional investment and general subsidies, primarily towards the development of endogenous regional growth and human resources. The national regional policy was transformed in most EU countries into an enterprise and entrepreneurship development policy.

The situation regarding regional policy at the EU level has been ambivalent. On the one hand, cohesion is becoming a *leitmotif* of European integration, hence EU involvement in this issue. On the other hand, market liberalisation and an active regional policy (intervention) do not go hand in hand! As an automatic market-led adjustment mechanism operates too slowly to be politically acceptable, EU structural funds for regional development and social issues emphasise supply-side intervention. They provide assistance to infrastructure and training.

6.3 Objectives and justification

Regional policy is intervention by the state in order to influence the 'orderly' distribution of economic activity and to reduce social and economic differences among regions. It was usually a reactive (*ex post*) policy that primarily tried to reduce the existing regional disparities, rather than a policy that primarily prevented the creation of new regional disequilibria.

Trade liberalisation and/or economic integration can easily provoke a country's economic adjustment (geographical, sectoral and professional reallocation of resources). Enhanced competition may force certain regions to embark upon a painful, but potentially rewarding, alteration in the structure of the geography of production (transfer of resources from unprofitable into profitable economic activities). The politicians in the affected regions often blame integration or trade liberalisation for adjustment 'pains'. However, this objection may not always be justified. The most basic reason for a painful adjustment process is often earlier protection. A policy of long and excessive sheltering of the domestic economy reduces the reaction time of local enterprises to international structural pressures and opportunities and, hence, increases the cost of adjustment in the future.

Adjustment costs and 'pains' are always present, but the potential benefits from such a change may more than compensate for the effort.

Relatively low wages may attract investment into a region; however, there may be at the same time some agglomeration and concentration tendencies in other regions. If wages are set at a national level, this may act as a structural barrier that works against the lagging regions. In this case, the lack of flexibility in the level of wages among regions despite relative differences in productivity and in the labour market conditions means that the less developed areas are unable to respond to this situation by reduced wage costs. One cannot know in advance where the balance will tilt. Some developed regions may become more developed, while some less developed regions/countries may become poorer (if nothing is done to alleviate the situation), but other less developed regions may move to the group of advanced ones.

The objectives of a regional policy are various, but their common denominator is that they aim to employ the regions' unemployed or underemployed resources and potentials, to locate new ones, to attract missing factors, as well as to increase output and incomes. In congested or polluted areas, this policy restricts the expansion of firms and stimulates exit from the region. In the developing countries, the primary concern is economic development. This is most often coupled with regional imbalances, but their solution is not as high on the agenda as increases in economic potentials and capabilities. In areas of economic integration, the problem of regional (in)equalities is of great concern. Countries are reluctant to lag behind their partners for any length of time. This is of great concern in an EMU, where there are no balance of payments disequilibria but rather regional disparities. Depressed regions/countries can no longer resort to devaluation as there is a single currency, while advanced regions/countries will not always be willing to finance regional disequilibria without proof that there is structural adjustment and improvement taking place in the regions assisted. With this in mind, a regional policy can be justified on nine counts.

The first justification for a regional policy (intervention that is supposed to assist in the process of economic adjustment), in contrast to free market adjustment, can be found in the structural deficiencies of regions. These include market rigidities, conditions of access to the market and the structure of output. When such imperfections exist, a free market system is 'unable' to achieve a satisfactory equilibrium from the social standpoint in the short and medium term, so there may be a need for intervention in order to enhance the creation and use of the regional income-generating potentials and capabilities.

Regional imports consists of goods and services. In France, for example, most of the country's regions purchase financial, insurance, legal and other services from Paris. This is not easily quantified. A reduction in a region's exports, for instance, may be obvious from the outset. Regional solutions to these disequilibria are inhibited by rules of competition and by the existence of a single currency. Hence, the second 'justification' for regional intervention in an economic union.

The third reason for intervention may be found in the employment of factors. The neo-classical theory of international trade usually assumes free and full international mobility of factors, which ensures full employment. However, even Adam Smith noted that a man is the most difficult 'commodity' to transport. During recession, the employment situation is tough everywhere, therefore the potential advantages of some regions that are abundant in labour are removed. Reduced mobility of labour prevents the equalisation of discrepancies in economic unions. Hence, growth in one region may create conditions for even higher growth in the same region and increase inequalities among regions (polarisation effect). This may, however, act as a 'locomotive' for development in other regions as there may be increased markets for food, economies of scale and innovation in other regions (spread effect). In order to adopt the idea that there are benefits from the spread effect, one must assume that there is a complementarity between the regions in question.

In a situation closer to reality and which includes economies of scale, large sunk costs, externalities and other market failures, adjustment does not happen according to a relatively smooth neo-classical expectation. The regional absorption capacity of new technologies requires industrial and general culture that incorporates continuous learning, adaptation, spread and development of human capital, as well as flexibility. Therefore, the introduction of new technologies is often uncertain and quite risky. That is why certain technologies diffuse quite slowly among the regions. The reallocation of resources induced by the spread effect works at a (much) slower pace than may be politically acceptable, hence the need for intervention.

The fourth rationale could be found in the 'need' for compensation. Two forces created by economic integration affect regional development. The first one, specialisation, leads the backward regions to specialise in labour-intensive production according to their comparative advantage. The second force includes economies of scale and externalities. This can lead to a divergence in regional incomes. As integration extends the size of the market, firms take advantage of economies of scale and externalities. The Single Market Programme provided incentives for the concentration of industries with strong internal links. In the case of other regions, the Programme reduced trade costs, hence there are potentials for a spread of other industries that may benefit the EU periphery, where labour costs are lower. However, if this does not happen, or takes place at a very slow pace, there is a possibility that some regions may actually be damaged by integration if there are no instruments for compensation. Hence, another justification for a regional policy.

Subsidies may be one of the tools of a regional policy. However, the distribution of subsidies is always subject to political pressures. The final disbursement of subsidies often reflects more the balance of political powers than the comparative (dis)advantage of a region. At the end of the process, regional policies implemented in such a way may do more harm than good if they diminish local incentives for adjustment and flexibility or, at best, they may have a dubious effect. Nonetheless, public policies in the backward regions, such as support for education, infrastructure and selected public goods as well as aid to the creation of SMEs in the form of loan guarantees for the start-up of a business, have the potential to assist regional development.

The fifth reason for intervention may be found in the improved allocation of resources. Free markets usually direct capital towards already developed regions in the short and medium term. Private investors tend to maximise the speed of the safe return of their invested funds and to minimise investment in infrastructure. Thus, it is understandable why they direct their funds towards already advanced regions. These tendencies of agglomeration (adjoint locations of linked productions), where the developed tend to become more developed while the underdeveloped remain at best where they are, have significant private benefits but also social costs and benefits. A society may reap the benefits of large-scale efficient production. However, if private entrepreneurs are not impeded in their decision-making by government policy, the geographical location of their business may introduce significant social costs such as pollution, congestion and traffic jams in some regions and unemployment and increased social assistance in others.

The sixth reason for intervention may be found in the improvement of stabilisation (macroeconomic) policy. Regional differences in rates of unemployment may reduce the opportunities to control inflation and introduce a stabilisation policy. The reduction of inflation in some regions may increase unemployment in others. This may not always be the desired outcome. Diversified regions with a variety of employment opportunities will be able to adjust in a less painful way than specialised regions with entrenched market rigidities.

The seventh justification for the introduction of a regional policy is that it may reduce public expenditure in the assisted region in the long run. Public support to firms to locate in certain regions may propel economic activity towards these regions. Unemployment may drop, reducing welfare payments and in the long term increasing tax receipts that may be spent on something else. In addition, 'employment' in public administration used to provide a shelter for the unemployed. Such artificial employment may be reduced or even eliminated once the private sector (with superior wages and career prospects) starts thriving in the assisted region.

The eighth rationale for intervention points out that regional policy is targeted at regions with some disadvantage (underdevelopment, unemployment, obsolete technologies and output structure, congestion or pollution). The benefits of a regional policy are not confined to the assisted area. Other regions, through externalities, enjoy part of the benefit. The beneficial effects of a regional policy extend beyond the assisted area itself. This is why the Germans and Swedes have an interest in helping out the Greek or Portuguese, even though they might have achieved their greatest gains from integration and the Single European Market (restructuring, economies of scale) around 1990. In general, integration may be reinforced, unwanted migration of labour may be prevented, factors may be employed in a superior way and there are important non-economic gains.

Finally, apart from the above arguments for regional policy, which mostly deal with 'economic' efficiency, there are political grounds which are at least as important as the economic ones. Solidarity, tolerance and perception of a common future are the core of any social community. The mitigation of economic disparities among the constituent regions may be the necessary reason for the unity of a state or an economic union. This is relevant as the costs and benefits of international economic integration tend to be unequally spread among the participating countries in a situation with market imperfections and multiple equilibria. Arguments of equality require the solution and/or mitigation of intolerable or growing differences in the distribution of wealth among the population which lives in different regions. The national political system does not always take fully into account the needs of backward regions. For example, the national system of setting wages may significantly reduce the wage cost advantages of many regions, whereas welfare expenditure can contribute to a greater regional equilibrium. Complete equalisation in the standards of living in different regions is neither possible nor desirable because it may reduce incentives for change and improvement. What is needed in regional matters is a continuous adjustment of regional development within commonly agreed guidelines, as well as the protection of the standard of living accepted as desirable by the group.

Regional intervention may be quite costly. In addition, there may be an inefficient replication of effort at various levels of government. Therefore, one may use the coordination argument in favour of a EU regional policy. The EU is best placed to coordinate various national and regional actions, to improve their efficiency and to collect and transfer resources from the prosperous to the backward regions of the EU.

The goals of regional policy, such as balanced growth, equal shares of social and cultural progress of the society, solidarity, regional distinctiveness and stability, are vague and may not be accurately measured. Specific objectives such as job creation, reduction in unemployment, improved housing and development of infrastructure introduce fewer problems in quantification. Care has to be given to select policy tools in order to ensure that the regional policy does not evolve into protection of the present economic structure; rather it needs to assist in continuous structural adjustment of the regions.

6.4 Instruments

Instruments of regional policy are often directed towards entrepreneurs and factor owners. They can be employed either directly (e.g. support of existing technologies or shifting towards new technologies or business activities) or indirectly (e.g. improvement in infrastructure). Their joint effects may alter and increase employment, investment and output in the assisted regions, at least in the short term.

The dilemma of the state may be whether to stimulate regional development through private investment, to invest directly in production and infrastructure for which there is no interest in the private sector and/or to stimulate public–private partnership. The available policy tools include those that provide incentives and disincentives to firms to move and to locate in or out of specific geographical regions. Major instruments include:

- subsidies – regional allocation of capital, investment, infrastructure, output, social security and income/wage;
- vocational training;
- public procurement and provision of goods, services and infrastructure;
- reduction in interest rates;
- tax concessions;
- decentralisation of government offices, education and health services;
- reductions in energy and public transportation costs;
- free locations;
- licences for the location of business;
- trade protection.

As seen from this short list, the choice of policy tools is rather limited. The secret of success in this situation is not the wide range of instruments, but rather their astute combination and application.

If offered, cash grants may be preferred to reduced tax liabilities as regional policy instruments. Grants apply horizontally and directly to all firms, whereas reduced tax liabilities help only those that are profitable. Trade restrictions are not the wisest instruments of a regional policy. The costs fall on the whole economic union, but they bring benefits to one or only a few regions.

Disincentives for regional expansion in congested areas are a relatively novel feature. In Britain, for example, they appeared in the form of industrial development certificates that had to be obtained prior to expansion or location in non-assisted regions. However, after the second oil shock, as unemployment increased, these certificates were abandoned as an instrument of regional policy. In France, for instance, there were certain constraints on the expansion of manufacturing and service industries in the Paris region. They included a special tax on office floor construction and authorisations for large-scale investments.

The policy of moving workers to jobs views the regional problem as being exclusively one of unemployment. It neglects the fact that other problems in a region may be worsened further by this 'forced' mobility of labour. The productive sector of the population moves out of the region while the consuming sector remains in it. The local tax base may not be able to provide sufficient funds to cover the costs of local health care, schools and other social services. The overall situation may be worsened by the multiplier effect. In advanced regions that receive the migrants, new disequilibria may be created. The additional population increases congestion and rents for a certain type of housing, which may reduce the quality of life there. Education and training are often emphasised as key elements in the solution to the unemployment problem. Although they are necessary, they are not sufficient conditions to fight unemployment. Creating new jobs also requires investment and increased flexibility in the labour markets.

Unemployment rates may be one of the most telling indicators of regional variations. If labour mobility is relatively low, then the movement of jobs to workers may diminish regional disparities in unemployment. An argument against this is that it may increase costs, as alternative locations may not be optimal for the efficient conduct of business. However, as more industries become footloose, these costs to firms may diminish. Improvements in infrastructure, including the training of labour and the education of management together with the spread of timely information, help the location of footloose industries which are at the beginning of their product cycle in the assisted regions.

6.5 European Union

Introduction

International economic integration brings multiple equilibria and may, in some cases, aggravate the situation of already backward and peripheral regions in comparison with previous circumstances. This is recognised in part by the existence of national and EU regional policies. Nonetheless, having a peripheral location does not mean that a country is destined to have a poor economic performance. The accumulation and efficient employment of human (and physical) capital is the most important factor in a country's economic performance. Although countries such as Finland, Sweden, New Zealand, Australia and even Japan and South Korea have relatively unfavourable geographical locations regarding major transport routes, the irreversibility of their 'peripheral' geographical position is mitigated and more than compensated for by the accumulation and efficient employment of their national human and physical capital. The expansion of infrastructure and further development of human and physical capital alleviated Spain's location at the fringe of the EU. It is expected that the EU candidate countries from Central and Eastern Europe with economies in transition will do likewise in the future.

The regional policy of an economic union can be justified at least on the grounds of solidarity, unity, harmonisation of national regional policies and the (re)distribution of wealth within the group. Policy coordination at the central level is defended on the grounds that it prevents clashes of different national regional policies with common objectives. The policy needs to ensure, at the very least, that the existing regional problems are not made worse by economic integration, otherwise the less developed regions/countries will have no incentives to participate in the project.

Evolution

The evolution of the regional policy of the EU can be divided into four broad phases. Regional issues did not feature highly on the agenda among the original six member countries. During the late 1950s and 1960s, only Italy gave weight to the regional problem because of its southern part (Mezzogiorno). This is why regional policy in the EU was practically non-existent until 1973. Following the entry of Britain, Denmark and Ireland in that year, the situation changed. The second phase in the development of the regional policy began after the first enlargement of the EU. Britain was particularly interested in the inclusion of regional issues in the EU. The first tool to implement the policy was the European Regional Development Fund (ERDF). The entry of Greece in 1981, and Spain and Portugal in 1986, increased the desire and need for an EU regional policy. This policy mainly gives benefits to the EU-rim countries (Britain, Greece, Ireland, Italy, Portugal and Spain), just as the Common Agricultural Policy favours the 'northern' countries.[3] The third phase started with the reform of policy and the ERDF in 1988. The fourth phase is linked with two events: the creation of EMU in 1999 and the forthcoming Eastern enlargement of the EU.

Following the first enlargement of the EU, the new regional conditions of the EU were officially analysed for the first time in the *Report on the Regional Problems of the Enlarged Community* (the Thomson Report) of 1973. The Report identified two types of regions in the EU that have problems. First are the farming regions that are located in the periphery of the EU. The Italian Mezzogiorno and Ireland fit into this group. In both regions there is a relatively high long-term structural unemployment and dependence on farming. The second type of problem regions are those that have a high proportion of regional output and employment in industries with obsolete technologies and those with declining demand. These problem regions have a slow rate of shifting resources out of such industries and technologies, as well as a relatively high level of long-term structural unemployment. Some regions in Britain fall into this group. A renegotiation of the British entry and concerns by Italy and Ireland led to the creation of the ERDF in 1975 under Article 308[4] of the Treaty of Rome. However, the ERDF only provides resources for regional development that are *additional* to those available from national funds.

Regional discrepancies

Differences in economic development among regions exist in every country, but at the EU level they seem much larger. Less developed regions in one country may have different characteristics from less developed regions in others, including large variations in income. In addition, congestion in southern Italy is greater than that in the south-west of France. Table 6.1 presents GDP per capita in the EU(15) and thirteen candidate countries at market prices in 1998 in order of decreasing level. This comparison of the relative difference in GDP per capita among regions and countries at current prices may well overestimate the real difference between advanced and backward regions or countries. The difference within the EU between Luxembourg, the richest country according to this indicator, and Portugal, apparently the least developed, is 4:1. For comparison, on this criterion the difference between Luxembourg and Bulgaria would be 28:1, while the EU(15) average GDP per capita in 1998 was fifteen times higher than in Bulgaria.

A useful device for overcoming part of the problem associated with the inter-country comparison of GDP at market prices can be found in the use of current purchasing power standard (PPS). This statistical indicator is based on the relative prices of a basket of representative and comparable goods and services. The PPS

Table 6.1   GDP per capita at current prices (€) and population in the EU and candidate
countries, 1998

Country	GDP per capita	Population in million
Luxembourg	38,185	0.4
Denmark	29,265	5.3
Sweden	23,933	8.8
Germany	23,428	82.0
Austria	23,328	8.1
Netherlands	22,272	15.7
Finland	22,277	5.1
Belgium	21,930	10.2
France	21,478	60.4
United Kingdom	21,145	59.2
Ireland	20,473	3.7
Italy	18,472	57.6
Spain	13,213	39.4
Greece	10,330	10.5
Portugal	9,795	10.0
EU(15)	20,179	376.5
Cyprus	12,183	0.7
Slovenia	8,796	1.9
Malta	8,298	0.4
Czech Republic	4,869	10.3
Hungary	4,133	10.1
Poland	3,627	38.7
Slovakia	3,365	5.4
Estonia	3,196	1.4
Turkey	2,770	63.4
Lithuania	2,586	3.7
Latvia	2,334	2.4
Romania	1,639	22.5
Bulgaria	1,327	8.3

Source: Eurostat (2000).

represents more adequately the real level of the local purchasing power, and it
often gives significantly different results from the ones given in current euros, in
particular during times with volatility in exchange rates. The PPS is not affected
(in the short term) by fluctuations in the exchange market. This problem has
disappeared in the case of the countries that take part in the EMU. Significant
differences between data given in current euros and those in the PPS are assigned
to differences in price levels in the member countries. If prices in an individual
member country are higher than the EU average, then the GDP per capita is
higher in current euros than according to the PPS. The reverse is true for the
countries whose GDP per capita in current euros is below the EU average. In
these countries, the PPS gives a higher value than the GDP in current prices.

Table 6.2 provides data in descending order on the differences in GDP per
capita in the EU(15) and thirteen candidate countries in 1998 in order of decreasing

Table 6.2   GDP per capita at purchasing power standard in
the EU and candidate countries, 1998 (€)

Country	GDP per capita, PPS
Luxembourg	35,497
Denmark	23,995
Netherlands	22,759
Belgium	22,507
Austria	22,437
Germany	21,801
Ireland	21,672
United Kingdom	20,611
Finland	20,526
Sweden	20,524
Italy	20,388
France	19,960
Spain	16,293
Portugal	14,989
Greece	13,333
EU(15)	20,180
Cyprus	15,947
Malta	–
Slovenia	13,721
Czech Republic	12,166
Hungary	9,664
Slovakia	9,263
Estonia	7,349
Poland	7,249
Turkey	6,381
Lithuania	6,175
Romania	5,942
Latvia	5,497
Bulgaria	4,624

Source: Eurostat (2000).

level. This kind of presentation changes, to an extent, the picture of the relative wealth of countries in comparison with Table 6.1. According to this indicator, the difference in average real income between the richest country, Luxembourg, and the poorest, Greece, was only 2.7:1. These measures are an indicator of differences in the level of economic development, whereas disparities in unemployment rates may be an indicator of a relatively poor capacity to adjust to various economic shocks. Differences between the two measures also have implications for the regional problem as they show that local output is below its potential. The ratio between average EU(15) GDP and that in Bulgaria as measured by the PPS is 4.4:1, which is much less dramatic than the difference expressed in current prices. However, the combined GDP of the thirteen candidate countries at current prices in 1998 was *only* 6.9 per cent of the total GDP of the EU(15), whereas according to the PPS the same ratio was *only* 16 per cent.[5]

There are regional differences within countries too.[6] These discrepancies may be capable of dividing the EU. The objective of the EU is to mitigate existing and prevent the creation of new regional imbalances. Data for 1998 in the PPS reveal that the most developed regions of the EU, those with per capita GDP of 150 per cent or more of the EU average (100), were Inner London (229), Hamburg (198), Luxembourg (172), Brussels (170), Darmstadt (167), Vienna (166), Oberbayern (165) and Paris (156). The most backward regions (excluding the French overseas departments) were the Greek region of Iperios (43), Açores (50), Voreio Aigaio (51), Extramadura (54), Madeira (55), Dytiki Ellada (57), Peloponnese (57) and Andalucia (58).[7]

In a comparison of worker productivity and per capita income, Paci (1997) found that European workers are becoming more similar as differences in their productivity are diminishing. However, European citizens are becoming less equal as disparities in per capita income are not diminishing. Therefore, the EU and national governments have much work to do in order to assist the poorer regions to increase the standards of living of their population (Paci, 1997: 630).

Action

Regional policies that are carried out at a local level by the member states and their regional authorities can have an advantage over EU regional policy because the local authorities may be better informed about local needs and problems. On the other hand, the EU is better placed to coordinate regional as well as other national policies. In addition, the EU may contribute its own resources and introduce common priorities and standards, and it may take into account regional interests when it reaches certain policy decisions. The EU has to ensure through the use of the rules of competition that the member governments do not distort competition by a 'subsidy war'. Normally, the EU puts a ceiling on the permitted subsidy per establishment and/or a job created in various regions.

The ERDF was established in 1975. Its expenditure was allocated to the member states in fixed quotas as compensation to the countries that contributed more than average to the EU budget. Those national quotas were set according to the following four criteria:

- the national average GDP per capita had to be below the EU average;
- the assisted region had to have an above-average dependence on farming or a declining industry;
- there had to be structural unemployment in and/or emigration from the region;
- EU policies (such as free internal trade) had to have had a detrimental impact on the region.

Put in simple terms, to obtain EU funds, the governments of the member states had to submit regional projects to the EU to meet the allocated financial quota and to commit certain funds themselves to these projects. The EU had no leverage on the selection process – it simply reacted to national initiatives. There was also a minuscule non-quota section of the ERDF, which absorbed only 5 per cent of the resources. The EU was able to use these funds freely. This situation came in for much criticism and the ERDF was reformed in 1985.

The reformed ERDF divided its funds among the EU member states by indicative ranges instead of fixed quotas as was the case previously. A government is guaranteed to receive the minimum of the range over a period of three years only if it has submitted a sufficient number of suitable projects. The projects submitted are evaluated according to criteria that are consistent with the EU priorities and objectives. The intention is to stimulate a greater number of applications in order to increase competition among various proposals. ERDF support may be up to 55 per cent of public expenditure on regional projects; in addition, it is allowed to co-finance programmes and it may prop up the development of indigenous potential in regions. The ERDF also attempts to mobilise local resources because it is increasingly difficult to attract private investment from wealthy to poor regions. Additional attention is devoted to the coordination of both member countries' regional policies and EU policies that have an impact on regions (agriculture, trade, environment, for example).

A further modification of EU regional policy followed the Single European Act (1987) and the entry of Spain and Portugal, which deepened the EU regional problem. The Act introduced a new Title into the Treaty of Rome on Economic and Social Cohesion. Article 158[8] requests the promotion of a harmonious development in the EU and 'reducing disparities between the level of development of the various regions'. Article 159[9] requires the coordination of economic policies among the member countries and authorises the EU to support those actions and other objectives through structural funds. Apart from these grant-awarding funds, loan-awarding institutions such as the European Investment Bank (EIB) and the European Coal and Steel Community are also involved in regional projects.

Special regional problems emerged in the EU in 1986 after the entry of Spain and Portugal. Therefore, during the preparations for enlargement, the EU introduced the Integrated Mediterranean Programme in 1985. The goal of this coordinated Programme was to help the Mediterranean regions of the EU (Greece and the southern regions of Italy and France, with a combined population of around 50 million) to adjust to competition from the two new member countries. The Programme disposed of €4.1bn in grants and €2.5bn in loans over a period of seven years. It integrated all available sources of finance on the levels of the EU, national, regional and local authorities. In addition, it coordinated other policies of the EU. The Programme was aimed not only at adjustment of agricultural production (olive oil, wine, fruit, vegetables), but also at the adjustment of existing and the creation of new SMEs. Alternative employment for jobs lost in agriculture was to be found in services (tourism) and SMEs. Apart from the border regions of Finland, the largely 'unnoticed' entry of three developed countries (Austria, Finland and Sweden) in 1995 has not introduced new regional distortions in the EU.

The modification of regional policy and the ERDF took place in 1988 following the southern enlargement of the EU. It had one basic objective: to improve the coordination of various structural funds in order to support the Single Market Programme. The 1988 reform introduced the following six basic *principles*:

- Member countries are to submit plans according to priority objectives.
- There needs to be a partnership between the administration at the local, regional and national level.
- EU measures play only an additional role.
- There needs to be compatibility with other EU policies such as competition and environment.
- Different EU policies need to be coordinated.
- Resources need to be concentrated on the least developed regions.

At the same time, six priority *objectives* of the regional policy included:

- promotion of the development of the backward regions (Objective 1);
- economic adjustment and conversion of the production structure in the regions that were affected by a large-scale industrial decline (Objective 2);
- a fight against structural unemployment (Objective 3);
- the promotion of youth employment (Objective 4);
- structural adjustment in agriculture, in particular in the regions affected by the reform of the Common Agricultural Policy and fisheries (Objective 5a);
- promotion of development in rural areas (Objective 5b).

Another decision in the reform package was to more than double the resources of structural funds from €6.3bn in 1987 to €14.1bn in 1993.[10] Nonetheless, these funds had to be only additional regional expenditure to that undertaken by national governments. The objective was to make the structural policy a tool with a real impact, to move from an informal project to multiannual programme financing, to increase the predictability of the policy (as the funds were allocated for a period of five years) and to increase partnership with authorities that are involved in regional policy at all levels of government. In practice, all these tasks turned out to be quite bureaucratic; the methodology for the designation of regions that had to receive assistance permitted a high degree of political influence, so the coverage of the assisted areas was wider than originally planned, and support was less concentrated (Bachtler and Mitchie, 1993: 722–3).

The provisions that regulate the operation of the structural funds were revised in 1993. The main thrust of the 1988 reform was, nonetheless, preserved. Alterations included only a simplification of the decision-making procedure and its greater transparency; the planning period over which the structural funds operate was extended to six years (1993–99); the resources for the period 1994–99 totalled €144.5bn; and there was the inclusion of a few new regions that are eligible for the assistance.

As always when there is a disbursement of funds, the European Commission has to be careful. It has to find a balance between, on the one hand, its aim of having effective policies that do not introduce distortions that may be damaging for the EU in the long term and subsidy-seeking regions and firms on the other. To be eligible for EU assistance, a disadvantaged region has to have per capita GDP of 75 per cent or less of the EU average. In reality, the application of this official ceiling is quite 'flexible' as aid has also been given to regions with average income that is 80 per cent of the EU average. As a result, half of the population of one of the richest and most developed regions in the world became eligible for assistance because of the relative drawbacks of the region in which they live.

The regional policy of the EU is simply a supranational policy that is additional to, rather than a partial replacement of, various national regional policies. Its first shortcoming is that the ERDF is modest in relation to regional needs. It should not be forgotten, however, that the regional policy of the EU, and particularly its Cohesion Policy, is relatively new although it is improving over time. In 2000, structural funds accounted for 35 per cent of the entire EU budget. The attempt to reduce disparities between rich and poor countries in the EU is great in circumstances of relatively slow growth and cuts in expenditure. National governments also act as a brake on the development of regional policy, as they prevent, in some cases, greater involvement of the EU in their own regional affairs. A greater degree of coordination of national economic policies may avoid dissipation of scarce EU funds, which may result in help to the rich in the relatively less developed regions to the detriment of the poor in the developed ones.

It could appear that there is a tendency to redirect structural spending from rural to urban areas. Regional problems are starting to concentrate in the urban areas of the problem regions. The principal beneficiaries of economic integration in the EU are urban areas in the central regions. This process has also created disadvantages in urban areas and in *other* regions of the EU. This is because the EU is a heavily urbanised group of countries.

The impact of the Single European Market on regional disequilibria in the EU is ambiguous. There is an identification problem. First and foremost, one needs to answer difficult questions: what are the short- and long-term effects of the Programme on the regions and, what is the impact of the changes on the regional disequilibria that would have happened on their own? If the longer-term effects of the Single Market Programme include the liberalisation of EU trade, then output may continue to be concentrated in the already advanced regions in order to benefit from positive externalities (this implies a fall in output and wages in the less advanced regions). However, internal trade liberalisation may reallocate some EU production activities towards the periphery in order to take advantage of lower wages and other production costs there. As the outcome is uncertain in a situation with market imperfections and multiple equilibria, the effects of the Programme on the regions will continue to be debated for quite some time in the future.

Traditional forms of national regional policy started to change and to decline in importance from the early 1990s in most of the EU member countries.[11] Denmark, for example, abolished all regional development grants and loans in 1991. The Dutch have restricted their regional assistance to a relatively small part of the country in the north. Owing to budgetary constraints, France had to scale down its regional aid. Germany has severely curtailed regional policy in the western part of the country, while placing priorities in the new eastern *Länder*. Even the less developed countries such as Greece or Ireland have had to be careful with their regional expenditure because of the restrictions that originated in recession. The new spirit of national regional policies in the EU countries includes (Bachtler and Michie, 1993: 721–2):

- reduction of the importance of regional policy in the northern countries;
- transfer of responsibilities to regional and local levels;
- automatic aid replaced by discretionary assistance;
- increased involvement of the European Commission in regional matters, in particular through the rules on competition.

Contemporary regional policy also includes the local development of producer services. This feature was gradually incorporated into regional policy only in the second half of the 1980s. Nonetheless, the creation of jobs in new manufacturing businesses, their extension in existing ones or relocation of businesses still account for the major part of regional intervention. The Commission may authorise investment aid of up to 75 per cent net grant equivalent in the least developed regions. The same limit is 30 per cent in other areas where aid is allowed. The upper limit for aid in the least favoured areas is intended to increase the competitiveness of these regions in attracting private investment. In practice, the country that has such regions within its confines may face severe budgetary problems and lack the necessary funds to finance projects in these areas. Hence, the impact of this concession is significantly eroded. In any case, a relatively high proportion of the allowed aid of up to 75 per cent may seriously question the degree of commercial risk borne by the private firm (Yuill *et al.*, 1994: 100).

EU regional policy is governed by six key principles (Armstrong, 1996: 194–6):

- coordination of various EU policies and funds;
- partnership with member state governments, regional and local authorities, private businesses and banks;
- multiannual and multiproject programming;
- subsidiarity: policy should be carried out at the lowest possible level of government;
- concentration of assistance on the priority objectives;
- additionality: the EU regional policy should be additional to, rather than a replacement for, national or regional or private expenditure.

The objective of *Agenda 2000* (European Commission, 1997b) was to offer an overall medium-term plan (2000–06) for the future of the EU. It wanted to prepare the EU for the new millennium when the EU expects to enlarge eastwards. As far as regional policy is concerned, for reasons of efficiency and visibility *Agenda 2000* merged earlier objectives for the structural funds into two regional objectives and one pan-EU objective (European Commission, 1997c: 22–5):

- Objective 1: Backward regions with per capita GDP of 75 per cent of the EU average or below. This covers around 20 per cent of the EU population.

- Objective 2: Rural and urban reconversion regions. Economic and social restructuring in areas undergoing economic change in manufacturing and services, declining rural areas, urban areas in difficulty and crisis-hit areas depending on fisheries. This covers around 18 per cent of the EU population.
- Objective 3: Development of human resources in regions not covered by Objective 1 or 2. This supports training, education and employment.

Structural funds will dispose of €218bn over the period 2000–06. *Agenda 2000* also reduced the percentage of the EU(15) disadvantaged population covered by Objectives 1 and 2 from 51 per cent (in one of the richest areas in the world) to 35–40 per cent. This is much more in line with the intention to concentrate EU resources on those areas that really need them. In addition, candidate countries were allocated as a pre-accession aid €45bn for the period 2000–06. However, the level of annual assistance to a candidate country cannot exceed 4 per cent of that country's national GDP. This shifting of funds eastwards has aroused some hostility towards such developments as the beneficiary regions and countries (Spain, France) in the EU feel that they are losing out to the East.

It is apparent that the EC is exerting increasing influence in EU regional matters, mainly through competition rules and funds with an impact on regional markets. National governments also conduct regional policies; however, they are becoming increasingly selective and are making sure that the policy provides value for money. In addition, outright general assistance to the regions is being replaced by transparent grants for capital investment.[12]

There is concern among member countries that the EC relies heavily on quantitative indicators in the designation of areas for assistance and that it does not take sufficient cognisance of the specific circumstances of each area. For example, unemployment data in rural areas may hide the 'real' regional problem as there may be a high level of emigration from those areas. Unemployment rates that are below the national average do not reflect a buoyant local economy, but rather a lack of local job opportunities. The quantitative approach by the Commission may be justified on the grounds that it must be impartial. The Commission can be questioned in its work by the European Parliament or by the Court of Justice, so it must be able to justify its actions. Although quantitative criteria play an important role in the first phase of the consideration of the problem by the Commission, the second phase of analysis provides for a greater flexibility and consideration of other, more qualitative elements (Yuill *et al.*, 1994: 98–100).

Mezzogiorno[13]

Since the early 1950s, Italy has implemented a range of inconsistent regional policies that have failed to enable Mezzogiorno to catch up on the rest of the Italian economy to any great extent.[14] Public intervention started after the Second World War with the development of a regional infrastructure. Poor transport links may have 'protected' local industries in the backward regions of southern Italy. The building of the Autostrada del Sole led to a chain of bankruptcies in the local food, textiles and clothing businesses because of a fall in trade costs with the rest of the country. The Mezzogiorno started to 'import' cheaper goods from elsewhere in Italy, hence the previously protected local businesses suffered.

Towards the end of the 1950s, the major infrastructure was built, but it was not sufficient to attract firms to invest south. At that time regional policy started to offer hefty financial and fiscal incentives to businesses that wanted to locate their activities in the Mezzogiorno. In the late 1960s public enterprises increased their role in the production geography of the south. At the same time wage, subsidies were employed as means of industrial policy. In 1968, a national wage agreement laid down a common wage throughout the country. This introduced a major rigidity in the economy of the Mezzogiorno. Private firms abstained from hiring because of wage costs that were not linked to productivity. The south lost wage flexibility to respond to shocks, while public enterprises were overmanned. This type of economy was vulnerable to shocks, as was exemplified in the early 1970s after the increase in the price of oil (Braunerhjelm *et al.*, 2000: 72).

The policy reaction to such geography of production was support to SMEs. However, this policy change came too late to be effective. The gap between the north and the south began to grow again from the mid-1970s. During the 1980s, Italian regional policy was restricted to income support (public employment and pensions). Growing taxes and continuous transfers to the Mezzogiorno were frustrating the north of the country. In addition, the European Commission requested the removal of wage subsidies to firms in the south as they were distorting competition.

Dissatisfaction with previous regional policies carried out since the 1950s, pressure from the northern regions and involvement of the European Commission in regional and competition affairs contributed to the introduction of Law 488 in December 1992. This law effectively abolished special intervention (*intervento straordinario*) for the Mezzogiorno and extended the coverage of the policy (grant-based support) to the centre-north of Italy. This means that regional policy in Italy is no longer tantamount to a policy directed at the southern part of the country. The abolition of this special treatment for the Mezzogiorno may be considered as one of the most significant developments in regional policies during the past four decades.

One of the policy tools that was used to support industrialisation in the region was law provisions that requested public corporations to direct the majority of their investments towards the south. These firms were regarded in the receiving area more as providers of jobs (hence, as supporters of the local demand) than as contributors to the growth of the national economy. As such, a relatively low efficiency of investment in the Mezzogiorno comes as no surprise at all. Because of these 'results' there was growing pressure for a reconsideration of the public policy towards the south, as well as open opposition to the policy from the northern regions of the country.

During the first half of the 1950s GDP per capita income in the south of Italy was around 55 per cent of that in the north and centre of the country. In the second half of the 1980s the equivalent figure was 57 per cent. In spite of this, the

Mezzogiorno cannot be described as a 'poor' region, particularly in terms of consumption. Large transfers of resources from outside the region support the artificially high levels of consumption. Therefore, the Mezzogiorno may be described as a structurally dependent economy (*European Economy*, 1993: 21–2).

The source of the regional problem of the Mezzogiorno lies not necessarily in a lack of funds or infrastructure, but rather in the non-material sphere. One of the major obstacles can be found in the absence of an 'entrepreneurial culture'. In addition, a survey of TNCs that already operate in or have considered investment in the Mezzogiorno revealed that the major obstacles to foreign investors include the existence of criminal organisations and political factors. A lack of infrastructure featured highly only for those TNCs that have not yet established their branches there. Factors that contributed to the attractiveness of the Mezzogiorno included the availability of relatively low-cost labour (both quantity and quality), the availability of land, as well as various public incentives to locate business operations there.[15]

6.6 Conclusion

A country or economic union in which there are differences in the levels of development and/or living standards among constituent regions that do not have at least a tendency towards equalisation cannot be regarded as having a well-integrated economy. Therefore, all countries and economic unions have a certain commitment to reduce regional disequilibria for a few economic and, more importantly, a variety of non-economic reasons. The objectives of EU regional policy are to diminish existing and prevent new regional disparities.

If a regional policy is to be effective, then the authorities at all levels of the government have to coordinate their activities in order to influence decisions about the allocation of resources (location of economic activity). In spite of these coercive powers, the regional policies of countries have had relatively limited positive achievements. It should therefore come as no surprise that the achievements of the regional policy of the EU, which often relies more on rules of competition, persuasion and on certain funds than on coercion, are scant indeed.

Regional policy has been based on a number of compromises, to the detriment of the purity of principles. Previous attempts to shape regional policy relied mainly on the alleviation of transport and communication costs through the expansion of infrastructure, as well as the mitigation of agglomeration disequilibria. More recently, attention has shifted towards a greater self-reliance for those regions that are lagging in development, as well as the enhancement of enterprise competitiveness in these regions.

Enterprise policy and the policy of macroeconomic stability are gradually being used instead of regional policy to tackle the regional (spatial) problems of a country. The new regional (development) policy includes the following features:

- reduction in the usual financial regional support;
- emphasis on SMEs, business 'incubators' and start-ups of new firms;

- backing of the producers' services;
- aid to increase flexibility to face and adapt to challenges;
- assistance to innovation;
- coordination with other policies.

The critics of this policy stance believe that the two policies lack the firmness needed to have a direct influence on a given spatial problem.

Raw materials are traded without major restrictions, while manufacturing industry and services are protected. On these grounds, resource-exporting regions (countries) may be supporters of free trade in a country or an economic union, because they would be able to obtain manufactured goods at more favourable terms of trade.

The question, however, arises as to whether regional policy increases or decreases market imperfections. In the second-best world, all answers are possible but not always desirable. If the costs of such a policy are less than the benefits it brings, then the policy is justified. The rationale for a regional policy that basically redistributes income (equity) must be found in solidarity among regions that constitute countries and/or the EU, as well as the fact that the area of benefit is larger than the assisted region.

Demand, technology and supplies of factors often change. Regions that fail to adjust continuously to the new challenges and opportunities remain depressed. One of the broad objectives of regional policy is to help the redistribution of economic activity among different regions. Its impact cannot be measured easily as it is not a simple task to construct a counterfactual world that would specify what would have happened without this policy. The difference between the actual and counterfactual situation may be attributed to regional policy.

Cohesion will remain one of the major issues in the EU. Hence, there are at least three major arguments in favour of the EU regional policy:

- In the absence of policy instruments such as tariffs, NTBs, devaluation or changes in rates of interest, regions that are not able to adjust as fast as the rest of the EU face increases in unemployment and decreases in living standards. In this situation, there is some case for the demand for short-term fiscal transfers at the EU level to ease the adjustment process. The possibility of such transfers in unforeseen cases ought to be permanent in an EMU. Otherwise, when in need, the regions that are in trouble may not be sure that other partner countries will provide resources on a case-by-case basis. EMU may not be able to operate efficiently without an effective regional policy. Structural funds are expected to involve a third of the EU budget in the period 2000–06.
- Coordination of national regional policies at the EU level can avoid self-defeating divergent regional programmes that are taken in isolation.
- Footloose industries, multiple equilibria, economies of scale and externalities do not guarantee that integration will bring an equitable dispersion of economic activities. Some direction for economic adjustment and allocation of resources

in the form of regional policy may be necessary. Expanding structural funds are employed in the EU in order to preserve unity with diversity in the group. This has to be reinforced in the light of the forthcoming Eastern enlargement, which will bring new and serious regional disequilibria in the EU.

In contrast to the decentralisation and trimming down of national regional policies, EU regional policy has continued to widen its coverage and scope. It is, however, hard to determine the point at which regional policy distorts competition beyond the interest of the EU. Hence, uncertainty over regional policy will continue in the future. There are many arbitrary elements in the policy, as well as special cases. EU regional policy has revealed its limitations. It is still Byzantine in its complexity. If this is already true of the integration of the member countries that established the EMU, the situation will be worse if Central and East European transition countries join the EU in the future. A solution to the regional development problem, as well as to achieving some balance among various regions, is an urgent, difficult, but highly rewarding challenge for the EU. Instability in regional policy at national and EU levels seems likely to continue. It is possible that the trend to decentralise the creation and implementation of national regional policy will continue in the future. There is, however, a danger in the expansion of regional incentives that compete with each other.

Regional policy is another facet of social policy. Hence, the EU faces difficult political choices regarding regional policy. Challenges in this area include the Eastern enlargement, monetary union, continuous unemployment, structural change and international competition. Obstacles to a stronger influence in this policy area come from EMU restrictions in the monetary and fiscal fields, lack of a federal EU system of transfer of funds, slower growth and little internal migration of labour. However, one has always to keep in mind that the amount of funds at the disposal of a particular economic policy intervention is not always what matters most. What matters is the amount of funds that is necessary to change a particular type of behaviour. The amount of funds and their astute combination and use to change certain types of behaviour will continue to be a matter for a debate long into the future.

Notes

1 Economic and social cohesion is defined as 'overall harmonious development' [Article 158 (old Article 130a) of the Rome Treaty]. As cohesion is defined in such a vague way, it can mean different things to various persons. Does it mean equalisation of income; or equalisation of opportunities; or providing an incentive to stay in the EU?

2 Guidance Section of the Agricultural Fund, European Regional Development Fund, European Social Fund, Cohesion Fund and Financial Instrument for Fisheries Guidance.

3 Federal countries such as the US, Canada, Australia or Switzerland have different regional policies from that of the EU.

4 Old Article 235.

5 Silke Stapel (2000), 'The GDP of the candidate countries', *Statistics in Focus*, Theme 2 – XX/2000, Eurostat: 3.

6 In Finland, for instance, the southern region of Uusimaa (including Helsinki) is the most prosperous. GDP per capita there is 131 per cent of the EU average. The rest of the country has a GDP that is around 90 per cent of the EU average.

7 Axel Behrens (2000), 'Per capita GDP below 75% of the EU average in 50 of the 211 EU regions', *Statistics in Focus*, Theme 1 – 1/2000, Eurostat: 2.

8 Old Article 130a.

9 Old Article 130b.

10 The European Coal and Steel Community has exerted its own influence on regions that are involved in the coal, iron and steel industries. Loans were given for the retraining and redeployment of workers, as well as for a modernisation of the industry. The EIB has been giving loans for projects in the less developed regions of the EU.

11 Britain changed its regional policy in 1980. The most important features of this alteration were the following three elements. First, the regional disequilibria started to be seen as a *regional*, rather than a *national* issue, one that had to be resolved by indigenous development, rather than by a transfer of resources and business activity from elsewhere. Second, direct subsidies for employment were replaced by a system of regional aid programmes based on employment creation through improved competitiveness. Third, the policy became increasingly reliant on employment cost-effectiveness (Wren, 1990: 62).

12 Regional support started to include producer services and incentives for the introduction of innovations such as licences or patents.

13 The Mezzogiorno is the area south of Lazio.

14 Regional policy in Ireland, another formerly backward EU country, was consistent for over four decades. The policy emphasised the role of markets, selected electronics and pharmaceuticals for special treatment, invested in infrastructure (tele-communications) and more than anything else invested in education (creation of human capital).

15 *Business Europe*, 31 May 1991: 3.

7   Conclusion

The traditional (static) model of preferential trading areas considered the effect of a reduction in tariffs on welfare. It concluded that the elimination or lowering of tariffs increased competition which, in turn, could lead to an improvement in welfare. The new theory focuses on the dynamic effects of integration. In the case of perfect competition, a narrow range of outcomes is clear. However, in the situation of imperfect competition and multiple equilibria, many outcomes can take place. With economies of scale and imperfect competition, there are no unconditional expectations that all countries will gain from integration, even less that they will gain equally. In the absence of adjustment policies, such as industrial, regional and social policies, integration may impose costs on some countries, rather than give them benefits. Therefore, cooperation among countries regarding the distribution of gains and losses is a necessary condition for successful integration. In any case, integration alters the geography of production in participating countries, which must modify, and even abandon, the established domestic monopolies and autarkic traditions.

When there exist economies of scale, changes in technology, sunk costs, imperfect competition and FDI, it is select intervention in the form of economic policy (for example, development of human resources through education; investment/production subsidies; protection for a limited period of time) which may successfully correct those market imperfections. The theory of strategic trade and industrial policy which takes into account market imperfections supplements the smooth and straightforward conclusions of the neo-classical theory. Under certain assumptions, free trade may be an attractive economic policy. In more realistic conditions, however, 'astute' intervention, of which integration is a part, may fare even better. However, this is not a definite outcome, as the 'lone-wolf' development strategies of Sweden (until it joined the EU in 1995), Switzerland, Taiwan, South Korea, Singapore and Hong Kong have shown. However, the economic performance of these countries may be the exception, rather than a general rule.

An analytical difficulty stems from the fact that the theory of integration includes simultaneously both free trade within the group and protection against third parties in the form of the common external tariff (and NTBs). Economic integration reduces trade costs among some countries, so it may seem beneficial in relation to a situation where each country applies its own system of tariffs. Tariffs are removed on the internal trade, but a common external tariff is erected. One distortion is replaced by another, so, as far as the final effect on welfare is concerned, all outcomes are possible. If free trade is the first-best policy, then integration is the second-best situation. Hence, a universal prescription for the success of an integration arrangement may not be found.

International economic integration takes place for a variety of powerful political and influential economic reasons. They include the following:

- Integration supports security and assists in avoiding wars. This was the major reason why economic integration between France and Germany started in the early 1950s.
- In the world of rapid change in technology and conditions in the market, a country cannot be certain that its current comparative advantages will be secured in the future. So, a country may wish to secure markets for the widest variety of its goods and services to protect against abrupt changes in the trade policy of its partners. Hence, integration can be seen as an 'insurance policy' against sudden and unilateral economic actions by partners.
- Trade barriers can be adapted according to the preferences of the involved countries.
- Integration fosters between partners a degree of mutual understanding and trust that is often lacking on the global scale. A relatively small number of participants may create cosy relations and make monitoring of the deal easier and friendly, while positive cooperation within the group may facilitate the exchange of favours and enable agreement to be achieved and (perhaps) disputes settled in a faster and more efficient way than is the case in multilateral institutions.
- Integration agreements can be employed as a bargaining tool with external partners.
- Gains to exporters from preferential trading agreements and terms of trade effects from integration are not available to countries through simple unilateral trade liberalisation policies.
- Integration can strengthen national reform. International commitments can be used as a scapegoat for unpopular domestic economic policies. International action limits, to some extent, the possibility for unnecessary public intervention in the economy because it extends the scope of economic policy across several countries.
- There is increased efficiency of the use of resources due to increased competition, specialisation and returns to scale. This both stimulates innovation and increases average standards of living.
- The potential for monetary stability is created. Secure markets and stable currencies enable investors to make decisions with a high degree of certitude.
- There is likely to be a reduction in the cost of a national import substitution policy.

- Relatively larger markets have a potentially greater capacity for coping with various distortions than smaller markets, because larger markets may more easily offset the impact of both favourable and unfavourable effects. Vulnerability to external shocks can be reduced.
- In 'normal' circumstances countries grow richer together, not at each others' expense, hence the need for cooperation (if not integration) on a larger international scale.

In general, geographical space is becoming less important as a barrier to the specific location of business. However, a higher international mobility of capital has made the selection of the location of business wider. Integration arrangements enlarge markets and create the potential for increased growth. This is often considered an incentive for FDI.

While these real gains arouse substantial interest in integration, countries are also aware that there are costs of adjustment (alteration in the geography of production) that limit enthusiasm for integration. However, integration is not a cure for all economic ills. It is only a tool to support national economic policy. Integration creates opportunities for increased competition on an enlarged market, but its success also depends on an astute national macroeconomic policy and similar policies in education (investment in human capital that is supposed to solve problems), R&D and investment in capital goods, as well as the willingness of firms to take advantage of the newly created environment.

A regional trading bloc may be seen as a compromise between two groups of protagonists promoting seemingly irreconcilable principles of economic policy: free traders and protectionists. Having made the compromise in a regional group, the former are happy about the abolition of barriers on intra-bloc trade, while the latter are pleased by the continuation of barriers against extra-bloc imports. Does it make any sense to ask who has made the greater concession in reaching the compromise? The question makes sense indeed, and the answer depends on the height of the trade barriers abolished and that of the barriers retained (Machlup, 1979: 102).

It is hard to forecast with a high degree of accuracy when and how the effects of integration will turn out. In the short term, just after the lifting of barriers to trade, production, GNP and commerce may increase while some prices may fall. In addition, some increase in unemployment may occur in the short term because of intensified competition and the unfinished adjustment process. In the medium and long term, structural adjustment takes place and economies of scale occur, while retraining and mobility of labour reduces unemployment because new jobs are being created. Market rigidities are eased as agents change their behaviour as a result of increased opportunities for business and competition. It is in this context that the dynamic effects of integration materialise.

A relatively large and partly integrated market is not a guarantee in itself that international economic integration will bring the desired economic outcomes. The evidence for this can be found in the cases of Russia and India, as well as China (perhaps until the 1990s). Contrasting evidence is supplied by the impressive experience of individualistic development of the small countries mentioned. A country's prosperity does not depend on its size and natural resources; more important are human resources, as well as the political and regulatory framework. Nonetheless, relatively larger markets may have the potential for a greater capacity in coping with distortions than smaller markets, because they may more easily offset the impact of both favourable and unfavourable effects. This supports the case for integration. Although all countries are not under the same kind of pressure to adjust, a joint country action may offer attractive economies of scale compared with the situation when each country acts alone.

One of the difficulties of international economic integration is that its long-term gains accrue to everybody, but in relatively small instalments. The costs of integration may be more easily identified. They affect some visible and vociferous segments of business and labour, but their effects may have only a relatively short-term impact on the national economy. The coordination of economic policies which may be brought by regional integration has the potential to exercise its full beneficial effects only in the long term. These joint economic policies should not be abandoned even if they do not bring the desired results in the short term. Enhanced competition and economies of scale exert a downward pressure on costs and prices. This enables an increase in non-inflationary growth. Nonetheless, it is unclear how this would happen in practice. It may occur through increased output with unchanged inflation or less price inflation or, most likely, a mixture of both. One real problem is that non-economists may not easily comprehend the gains from international economic integration.

A move from a fragmented to an integrated market can create some of the most striking results of economic integration. However, integration does not affect all industries in an equal way. The industries most affected are those that produce traded goods and services with increasing returns to scale. Links between integration, trade, FDI and geography of production are complex and vary with the types of integration as various types permit different freedoms to factor mobility and introduction of joint economic policies.

According to the classical trade theory, a reduction in trade costs is expected to bring benefits via an increase in a country's specialisation. The neo-classical theory predicts that national specialisation would mirror differences in comparative advantage. Countries trade in order to take advantage of their differences. The 'new economic geography and spatial economics' and the 'new trade' theories argue that countries specialise in production and trade according to the potential for greater economies of scale even if they are the same size and have identical endowment of factors.

An additional point of interest for the 'new school' is the impact of economies of scale on geographical agglomeration of production. The specialisation process (reallocation of resources) is, however, not without adjustment costs. These costs are lower in the case of intra-industry trade than when the adjustment has an inter-industry dimension. This aspect needs to be taken into consideration when ascertaining the net effect. The two 'new economic theories' study production linkages. These theories confirm that, depending on the strength of the functional production linkages, regional, national or international geography of production may change in response to the alteration in trade costs. This change in the costs of trade may originate in changes in marketing, transport and communication technology, as well as in bilateral, regional or international reductions in trade barriers.

Economic integration and its deepening may affect the EU geography of production. This depends on the intra-industry production links, barriers to the reallocation of resources, factor mobility and public policy. There are four principal influences:

- Trade costs are higher in the EU than in the US because of differences in culture, languages and preferences that segment markets. Nothing will change as integration is not sufficiently strong to alter these entrenched differences (Krugman and Venables 1996: 966).
- Economic activity may spread in such a way that each region becomes specialised in a particular activity. This type of concentration does not mean income polarisation as is exemplified in North America. The US economy is less geographically polarised than the EU.
- Integration may alter the EU geography of production but not sufficiently to threaten the existing geography of production. On the one hand, there may be reinforcement of the existing 'multicentric' geography of production. A long-term polarisation may split a country or an economic grouping into advanced regions with high incomes and low unemployment and depressed regions with low income and high unemployment. On the other hand, with dependence on the might of functional intra-industry production links and the reduction in trade costs, there may be a spread of production throughout the EU (Krugman and Venables 1996: 966–7).
- Economic activity may agglomerate in core regions, leaving others (e.g. some mountainous or peripheral regions) without production potentials and without residents. However, free competition within the group is not likely to destroy all business in participating countries. Two instruments will prevent such a disastrous scenario. First, a period of adjustment to new circumstances will enable firms to reallocate resources gradually. A country with serious adjustment problems may seek free access to the markets of partner countries some time before it offers the same concession to these partners. The exchange rate is the second safety valve that will prevent such a catastrophe. The experience of the EU, EFTA and NAFTA has shown that economic adjustment to integration can take place smoothly. Trade, production, economic growth and employment tend to increase in the long term. Structural problems that did occur were most likely caused by increases in prices for oil, competition from the newly industrialising countries and a poor national macroeconomic policy, and not by integration.

Industrial clusters create economies that are external to individual firms but internal to a network of firms in a cluster. This brings gains as firms improve links with other suppliers. Consequently, adjustment and relocation improve comparative advantages. There are sound reasons to welcome and support such changes. Public policies had nothing to do in the creation of clusters. Sometimes they worked against them. The case in question is when the authorities want to spread industrial activities, rather than to concentrate them in a specific area. Mistaken public (regional) policies not only choke the growth of clusters that would benefit the entire region and country, but can also increase polarisation that they are intended to prevent and reverse. The case of Mezzogiorno in Italy is a striking example of this.

Specialisation increased in Denmark, Germany, Greece, Italy and the Netherlands in the period 1968–90. A significant increase was recorded in Belgium, Britain, France, Portugal and Spain from 1980 to 1990. Data indicate that there was either a fall in specialisation or no noteworthy change in Britain, Portugal and Spain between 1968 and 1990. The likely explanation is that, prior to EU entry, these countries had relatively high trade barriers that protected production for which there was no national comparative advantage. Entry into the EU eliminated administrative trade barriers and reduced trade costs. All countries, however, increased specialisation in the period 1980–90. 'So with integration, specialisation may initially fall during structural adjustment and then increase. This would explain why Spain, Portugal, and the UK, which were all late joiners to the EU, show a fall in specialisation when comparing 1968–1990, and an upward trend starting in the late 1970s and early 1980s' (Amiti, 1999: 579).

Each country's geography of production within the EU has become different from the rest of the Union. While this reallocation of resources has obvious benefits that come from specialisation, it also creates problems for specialised countries, which may react in a different way to asymmetric shocks and require diverse policy instruments to counter them. Therefore, in the light of the EMU and Eastern enlargement, there is a strong need for the creation of EU policy tools to counter such obstacles in handling the smooth operation of the Single European Market. Without clear and strong policy instruments (predominantly linked with fiscal and competition policy tools in the short term) the smooth operation of the Single European Market and the EMU may be in jeopardy. The EU still lacks the federal financial power to provide equalisation grants to needy or poor states/regions and manage interpersonal transfers of social security, health and unemployment benefits or pensions.

Regions that are not able to adjust to the changed situation as fast as the rest of the EU face increases in unemployment and decreases in living standards. This is the consequence of absence of policy instruments such as tariffs, NTBs, devaluation or changes in rates of interest at the national level. In this situation, there is some justification for short-term fiscal transfers at the EU level to ease the adjustment process. The possibility for such transfers in unforeseen cases should be permanent in the EMU. Otherwise, the regions in trouble will be left alone to face their problems, which may provoke disintegration tendencies. An effective regional policy is necessary if the EMU is to operate efficiently.

As for the industrial structure of the EU, the conclusion is that the EU countries became more specialised from the early 1980s than was the case before. This confirms the theoretical expectations of standard, neo-classical and the new theory of economic integration. A new pattern of industrial production is emerging in the EU (Midelfart-Knarvik *et al.*, 2000:46–7). The major features of the geography of industrial production in the EU countries are as follows:

- The process is slow and does not provoke great adjustment costs. The Single Market Programme had no clear effect of on the reallocation of manufacturing production and specialisation.
- There was some convergence in the geography of production in the EU countries towards the EU average during the 1970s, whereas from the early 1980s countries diverged from the EU average. This is a general sign of increased national specialisation in the EU. The most remarkable national change in the geography of production was the spreading of relatively high-technology and high-skill industries to Ireland and Finland.
- The availability of highly skilled and educated workers is becoming an increasingly important determinant of industrial location. National economic policies concerning investment, industrial change, R&D, mobility of people and knowledge, investment in human capital (education) that develops and extends skills, experience and organisational competencies of this most important factor are crucial for the efficiency side of the economy; and regional and social matters also play a role.
- Not all industries follow the same path as a reaction to economic integration. Some of them concentrate, while others spread (contrary to the expectations of the neo-classical theory that all industries will be affected in the same way). Several forces, therefore, propel such changes in the structure of production. Strong functional intra-industry linkages (high share of intermediate goods from the same industry and/or the need for a large pool of highly skilled labour and researchers) stimulate agglomeration. Where these functional linkages are weak, this acts as an incentive to spread production.
- While 'economic integration' has made the US geography of industrial production more similar (less specialised) since the 1940s, integration in the EU has resulted in a growing disparity (increasing specialisation) in manufacturing production. This slow process shows no signs of abating in either region. The forces that drive this process are still unknown.
- Agglomeration tendencies towards the central locations became more pronounced for industries that use many intermediate inputs.
- High returns to scale are becoming less important as centripetal (agglomeration) forces.

An extensive survey of the impact of the Single Market Programme on FDI in the EU found strong evidence that FDI and trade are complementary (European Commission, 1998: 1). Concerns that the Single Market Programme would lead to a concentration of general economic activity in the 'core' EU countries were not borne out. There has been only a limited spread of economic activity to the 'peripheral' EU countries that enjoy certain cost advantages (European Commission, 1998: 145).

If a country or an economic union has different levels of development and/or living standards among the constituent regions and there is no tendency towards equalisation, such a country/economic union does not have a well-integrated economy. Thus, all countries and economic unions have a commitment to influence the spatial distribution of production and disequilibria in it for various economic and, more importantly, non-economic reasons. It follows that the aim of EU regional policy is to diminish existing and prevent new regional disparities. If a regional policy is to be effective, then the government must coordinate its activities in order to influence decisions regarding the allocation of resources. In spite of these coercive powers, the regional policies of countries have had relatively limited achievements. Regional policy has been based on a number of compromises, with the result that the purity of principles has suffered. Therefore, it should come as no surprise that the achievements of the regional policy of the EU are few because of the organisation's heavy reliance on persuasion and certain funds in the field of regional policy, rather than on coercion (apart from the competition policy).

Europe can be divided into six groups of countries that move at different speeds. Each of them has a different impact on the change in the continental geography of production. The first and fastest group includes the twelve EU countries that are participating in the EMU. The second set of four EU countries includes those (Britain, Denmark and Sweden) that do not (yet) participate in the EMU. The third group consists of the EU countries that are members of the Schengen agreement. A fourth group contains ten candidate countries from Central and Eastern Europe with economies in transition, as well as Cyprus and Malta, all of which are individually negotiating full entry into the EU. Within this group one may single out Bulgaria and Romania as the 'slowest' countries. The fifth group comprises only Turkey. It has only the title of a candidate country. In the sixth unit are other European countries, mainly in the Balkans and east of Poland and Romania.[1]

The analysis of spatial economics and economic integration relies on the study of particular cases. Nonetheless, many useful things can be learned from exceptional cases. The examination of the issue is still highly suggestive (in particular how a historical accident may shape production geography in the future) rather than convincing and conclusive. A coherent theory of the subject is not yet in sight. However, there are various approaches that contribute to the raising of new questions and understanding of the issue. This leaves the topic open to further theoretical and empirical analysis.

The objective of this book has been to promote and to contribute to the debate and policy on spatial economics and economic integration. Natural factor endowment (geography of resources) may have determined production geography in the past but need not do the same in the future. Education, progress in human capital development, market structure and economies of scale will play a vital role in shaping the geography of production in the future. In this model, relatively small beginnings can have large and irreversible consequences for the geography of production in a country or in an integrated group. New thoughts about the subject can be set off by small events such as reading this book.

Note

1 In addition, the EU is becoming a more and more complicated place. The Union finds ways to interfere directly not only in the composition of governments of member states, but also in the leadership of individual national parties. Many people question the wisdom of surrendering additional sovereign rights to a supranational administration. In this situation enthusiasm for integration is vanishing.

8 Research agenda

The objective of this list is to suggest certain research topics in the area of spatial economics and economic integration.

- A lesson for the EU is that the Single Market Programme (integration deepening) provided some opportunities for concentration of production in select hotspots, as well as for rationalisation of business operations. Amiti (1998; 1999) found some evidence that this took place in some manufacturing industries, including industrial chemicals, petroleum, textiles, plastics, iron and steel, machinery and transport equipment. These are all industries that are subject to economies of scale and which have a high proportion of intermediate inputs in final production. Hence, this provides some support for the arguments of the new theory of spatial economics. In the period 1976–89 geographical concentration increased in thirty out of sixty-five recorded industries, concentration fell in twelve industries (the biggest fall was in the manufacturing of concrete for construction), while there was no significant change in geographical concentration in other industries (Amiti, 1999: 580). On the other hand, a study by the European Commission observed that an 'examination of data offers mixed evidence for the contention that the single market is leading to a geographical concentration' (European Commission, 1998: 67) and that there is 'little evidence of concentration occurring in the EC' (European Commission, 1998: 69). Hence, this topic demands further research.
- There was (and perhaps still is) confusion about whether external trade policy including integration affects the aggregate level of employment. Trade only increases competition, improves allocation of resources and dwindles the clout of several privileged, monopolistic and entrenched interests. Therefore, trade widens opportunities for the vast majority of players and can assist them to join the group of prosperous countries. It alters the geography of production and the structure of employment within different economic sectors. Trade influences the overall standard of living and the kind of jobs available, rather than making them available.
- The future of the inflow of foreign labour in the EU is highly uncertain. On the one hand, an ageing population in the EU will demand extra expenditure

by the state. On the other hand, an inflow of foreign labour to rectify demographic trends in the EU may ease the pressure from labour shortages in the EU. But an inflow from where? – an 'orderly' inflow from the countries in transition or a 'disorderly' inflow from the Islamic and unstable countries which are undergoing a demographic 'explosion', such as the south Mediterranean countries? Background research on how to cope with such developments is lacking.

- The social issue of an ageing population and its needs as well as the trend for retired people to move to southern EU countries has an impact on the geography of production of services in the EU. Another issue that needs more research is the effect of the entry of women in the specific part-time labour market.
- Innovation is one of the major dimensions of competition. Creation of knowledge and technology and their spread and extension (upgrading technological capabilities) gain in importance. Should research capabilities and finance be clustered in an integrated area, reducing risk and benefiting from economies of scale? Alternatively, should one decentralise these efforts to introduce competition, to avoid routine and to benefit from multiplicity of ideas? Should one be active and subsidise training and innovation or be passive and let market forces do the upgrading of production potential and capabilities? What is the impact of national research institutes? Should they be centralised at the EU level? What are the instruments and incentives to create and sustain a permanent 'learning culture' and inspire human capital accumulation?
- Whereas economic integration from the 1940s made the US geography of industrial production more similar (less specialised), integration in the EU has had as its consequence growing disparity (increasing specialisation) in manufacturing production. This slow process shows no signs of abating in either region. The forces driving this process are still not known.
- What is the impact of deurbanisation on the geography of production? Migration out of metropolitan areas such as Rome has been shown to have an impact on urban development and employment.
- North–south and east–west integration change the geography of production. A possible research issue is the theoretical consideration of economic integration between countries with different levels of development, e.g. integration between the EU and the transition economies. What are the chances of integration between the EU and Mediterranean countries? Is integration, such as a free trade area, between the US, Canada and Mexico without special treatment for the weaker country a good thing?
- Will there be a greater spread (deconcentration) of EU industry towards the 'periphery' and Central and East European countries as a consequence of integration?
- One of the most difficult obstacles facing the Central and East European countries before they can join the EU is the environmental dimension of the *acquis communautaire*. How do EU and other international quality and environmental standards affect the geography of production?

- What is the effect of slower growth on the 'spread' effects that benefit peripheral regions?
- Relations between regionalism and multilateral solutions to the trade and investment problems offer another challenging research topic. Is there any way to prevent the creation and evolution of regional blocs that inhibit global liberalisation? What is the consequence of each policy choice on the geography of production? This is particularly important in agriculture and services.
- The relation between economic integration and NTBs has received relatively little research attention so far.
- Another global item for research is the impact of integration on various industries. Integration has had the strongest impact on the higher value-added industries that produce tradable goods with significant economies of scale. This, however, has to be studied in greater detail, in particular its relevance for developing countries.
- One should not forget the development of the theory of public choice. What do the voters want regarding economic integration and what are they ready, able and willing to pay in terms of taxes, prices and security of employment? Does that public choice change over time? How can integration arrangements be adjusted to accommodate these changes? Do governments care more about re-election than about the long-term future of their country?
- There are also unresolved issues regarding fiscal federalism in integration groups with members at different level of development. How will the EMU operate without the ability to temporarily run up large budget deficit and without (semi)automatic federal transfers to disadvantaged regions or countries when hit by asymmetrical shocks?
- There is a large shady area in our knowledge regarding the need for an industrial and technology policy (intervention) for an increase in competitiveness of an integrated group. Is simple economic integration and liberalisation in an enlarged market sufficient for an increase in competitiveness? What are the corporate strategies regarding economic integration? How will they change over time? Is business consolidation (mergers and acquisitions) a necessary consequence of an enlarging and integrating market? Is it going to be reversed in the future? What is the impact of integration on concentration ratios?
- What is the relation between international economic integration and SMEs?
- What is the effect of economic integration and trade liberalisation on the existing clusters of industries? Does integration stimulate the creation and expansion of new clusters? Do TNCs provoke clustering?
- Is there a need for the harmonisation of regulation in an integrating group of countries, or can/should one leave competition within national regulations about, for example, labour or environment issues?
- As regional policies had very limited results in the past, one wonders whether it is necessary to have such a policy at the level of an integration scheme. If not, how can EMU take place among countries that are at different levels of economic development? Can one leave the solution of the 'regional problem'

exclusively to market forces? How will this cope with the regional problem of the EU once the transition countries start entering the EU?

- As for the services sector, the question is whether a liberal regulatory framework within a group of countries is sufficient to bring about the integration of and competition in this sector? If not, what else is necessary? Why?
- High and ever-increasing environmental standards will continue to introduce NTBs to trade. What is the best way to cope with this problem – through mutual recognition of national standards in the EU or should the highest standards be imposed throughout the group? If the highest standards are to be imposed in the EU, then some countries may face financial difficulties in implementing them. Who should pay for this: national taxpayers, the taxpayers of the standard-imposing country and/or the EU?
- Last, but not least, there is the question of regional integration and multilateral rules for trade and investment. Almost all countries in the world are and will be involved in some type of integration arrangement. International economic integration is here to stay. The issue is the strengthening of the complementarity between regional economic integration and the WTO, and preventing regional groups turning into blocs that inhibit global liberalisation. Researchers and practitioners will have to find the ways and means to make sure that integration and the multilateral process continue to reinforce each other in the decades to come.

In any event, there are so many dilemmas regarding the relation between geography of production and international economic integration that anyone embarking upon studying these issues should not worry that the circle is closed and that their research efforts will be in vain.

Bibliography

Adams, G. (1983). 'Criteria for US industrial policy strategies', in *Industrial Policies for Growth and Competitiveness* (eds G. Adams and L. Klein). Lexington, MA: Lexington Books, pp. 393–418.

Adams, G. and L. Klein (1983). 'Economic evolution of industrial policies for growth and competitivenss: overview', in *Industrial Policies for Growth and Competitiveness* (eds G. Adams and L. Klein). Lexington, MA: Lexington Books, pp. 3–11.

Allen, C., M. Gasiorek and A. Smith (1998). 'The competition effects of the Single Market in Europe', *Economic Policy*, 441–486.

Altshuler, R., H. Grubert and T. Newlon (1998). 'Has U.S. investment abroad become more sensitive to tax rates?', NBER Working Paper No. 6383.

Amin, A. (1993). 'The globalization of the economy: an erosion of regional netwirks?', in *The Embedded Firm* (ed. G. Grabher). London: Routledge, pp. 278–295.

Amin, A. and A. Malmberg (1992). 'Competing structural and institutional influences on the geography of production in Europe', *Environment and Planning*, 401–416.

Amiti, M. (1998). 'New trade theories and industrial location in the EU: a survey of evidence', *Oxford Economc Papers*, 45–53.

Amiti, M. (1999). 'Specialization patterns in Europe', *Weltwirtscahftliches Archiv*, 573–593.

Ando, K. (1998). 'The Single European Market and the location strategy of foreign car multinationals', *Discussion Paper* No. 249, University of Reading, Department of Economics.

Aristotelous, K. and S. Fountas (1996). 'An empirical analysis of inward foreign direct investment flows in the ECU with emphasis on the market enlargement hypothesis', *Journal of Common Market Studies*, 571–583.

Armington, P. (1969). 'A theory of demand for products distinguished by place of production', *IMF Staff Papers*, 159–178.

Armstrong, H. (1995). 'Convergence among regions of the European Union, 1950–1990', *Papers in Regional Science*, 143–152.

Armstrong, H. (1996). 'European Union Regional Policy: sleepwalking to a crisis', *International Regional Science Review*, 193–209.

Armstrong, H. and R. de Kervenoael (1997). 'Regional economic change in the European Union', in *The Coherence of EU Regional Policy* (eds J. Bachtler and I. Turok). London: Jessica Kingsley, pp. 29–47.

Armstrong, H. and R. Vickerman (eds)(1995). *Convergence and Divergence among European Regions*. London: Pion.

Arthur, B. (1989). 'Competing technologies, increasing returns, and lock-in by historical events', *Economic Journal*, 116–131.

Arthur, B. (1990a). 'Positive feedbacks in the economy', *Scientific American* (February), 92–99.

Arthur, B. (1990b). 'Silicon Valley locational clusters: when do increasing returns imply monopoly', *Mathematical Social Sciences*, 235–251.

Arthur, B. (1994a). 'Industrial location patterns and the importance of history', in *Increasing Returns and Path Dependence in the Economy* (ed. B. Arthur). Michigan: University of Michigan Press, pp. 49–67.

Arthur, B. (1994b). 'Urban systems and historical path dependence', in *Increasing Returns and Path Dependence in the Economy* (ed. B. Arthur). Michigan: University of Michigan Press, pp. 99–110.

Audretsch, D. (1989). *The Market and the State*. New York: New York University Press.

Audretsch, D. (1993). 'Industrial policy and international competitiveness', in *Industrial Policy in the European Community* (ed. P. Nicolaides). Dordrecht: Martinus Nijhoff, pp. 67–105.

Audretsch, D. (1998). 'Agglomeration and the location of innovative activity', *Oxford Review of Economic Policy*, 18–29.

Audretsch, D. and M. Feldman (1995). 'Innovative clusters and the industry life cycle', *CEPR Discussion Paper* No. 1161.

Audretsch, D. and M. Feldman (1996). 'R&D spillovers and the geography of innovation and production', *American Economic Review*, 630–640.

Auyang, S. (1998). *Foundations of Complex-system Theories in Economics, Evolutionary Biology and Statistical Physics*. Cambridge: Cambridge University Press.

Azhar, A., R. Elliott and C. Milner (1998). 'Static and dynamic measurement of intra-industry trade and adjustment: a geometric reappraisal', *Weltwirschaftliches Archiv*, 404–422.

Bachtler, J. (1995). 'Policy agenda for the decade', in *An Enlarged Europe: Regions in Competition?* (eds S. Hardy, M. Hart, L. Albrechts and A. Katos). London: Jessica Kingsley, pp. 313–324.

Bachtler, J. and R. Michie (1993). 'The restructuring of regional policy in the European Community', *Regional Studies*, 719–725.

Bachtler, J. and R. Michie (1995). 'A new era in EU regional policy evaluation? The apprisal of the structural funds', *Regional Studies*, 745–751.

Bachtler, J., and I. Turok (1997). *The Coherence of EU Regional Policy*. London: Jessica Kingsley.

Badaracco, J. and D. Yoffie (1983). 'Industrial policy: it can't happen here', *Harvard Business Review* (November-December), 97–105.

Bak, P. and K. Chen (1991). 'Self-organized criticality', *Scientific American* (January), 26–33.

Balassa, B. (1977). 'Effects of commercial policy on international trade, the location of production and factor movements', in *The International Allocation of Economic Activity* (eds B. Ohlin, P. Hesselborn and P. Wijkman). London: Macmillan, pp. 230–258.

Balassa, B., and L. Bauwens (1988). 'The determinants of intra-European trade in manufactured goods', *European Economic Review*, 1421–1437.

Baldwin, R. (1989). 'The growth effects of 1992', *Economic Policy*, 248–270.

Baldwin, R. (1997). 'Review of theoretical developments on regional integration', in *Regional Integration and Trade Liberalization in SubSaharan Africa* (ed. A. Oyejide, I. Elbadawi and P. Collier). Houndmills: Macmillan, pp. 24–88.

Baptista, R. and P. Swann (1998). 'Do firms in clusters innovate more?', *Research Policy*, 525–540.

Barro, R. and X. Sala-i-Martin, (1991). 'Convergence across states and regions', *Brookings Papers on Economic Activity*, 107–182.

Basevi, G. (1970). 'Domestic demand and ability to export', *Journal of Political Economy*, 330–337.

Bayliss, B. and A. El-Agraa (1990). 'Competition and industrial policies with emphasis on competition policy', in *Economies of the European Community* (ed. A. El-Agraa). New York: St. Martin's Press, pp. 137–155.

Beckmann, M. (1999). *Lectures on Location Theory*. Berlin: Springer.

Beckmann, M. and J. Thisse (1986). 'The location of production activities', in *Handbook of Regional and Urban Economics* (ed. P. Nijkamp). Amsterdam: Elsevier, pp. 21–95.

Begg, I. and D. Mayes (1993). 'Cohesion in the European Community', *Regional Science and Urban Economics*, 427–448.

Begg, I. and D. Mayes (1994). 'Peripherality and Northern Ireland', *National Institute Economic Review*, 90–100.

Belderbos, R. (1997). 'Antidumping and tariff jumping: Japanese firms' DFI in the European Union and the United States', *Weltwirschaftliches Archiv*, 419–457.

Bernhofen, D. (1999). 'Intra-industry trade and strategic interaction: theory and evidence', *Journal of International Economics*, 225–244.

Bhagwati, J. (1989). 'United States trade policy at the crossroads', *World Economy*, 439–480.

Bhagwati, J., D. Greenaway and A. Panagariya (1998). 'Trading preferentially: theory and policy', *Economic Journal*, 1128–1148.

Bhagwati, J. and E. Tironi (1980). 'Tariff change, foreign capital and immiserization', *Journal of Development Economics*, 71–83.

Bird, R. (1972). 'The need for regional policy in common market', in *International Economic Integration* (ed. P. Robson). Harmondsworth: Penguin books, pp. 257–277.

Bird, R. (1975). 'International aspects of integration', *National Tax Journal*, 302–314.

Blackhurst, R, and D. Henderson (1993). 'Regional integration arrangements, world integration and GATT', in *Regional Integration and the Global Trading System* (eds K. Anderson and R. Blackhurst). New York: Harvester Wheatsheaf, pp. 408–435.

Blais, A. (1986). 'Industrial policy in advanced capitalist democracies', in *Industrial Policy* (ed. A. Blais). Toronto: University of Toronto Press, pp. 1–53.

Blomström, M. and A. Kokko (1997). 'Regional integration and foreign direct investment', *Policy Research Working Paper* No. 1750, Washington, DC: World Bank.

Boschma, R. (1997). 'New industries and windows of locational opportunity', *Erkunde*, 12–22.

Boschma, R. and J. Lambooy (1999a). 'Evolutionary economics and economic geography', *Journal of Evolutionary Economics*, 411–429.

Boschma, R. and J. Lambooy (1999b). 'The prospects of an adjustment policy based on collective learning in old industrial regions', *GeoJournal*, 391–399.

Borrus, M. and J. Zysman (1997). 'Wintelism and the changing terms of global competition: prototype of the future?', *BRIE Working Paper* No. 96B, Berkeley: University of California.

Brada, J. and J. Méndez (1985). 'Economic integration among developed, developing and centrally planned economies: a comparative analysis', *Review of Economics and Statistics*, 549–556.

Brainard, W. and J. Tobin (1992). 'On the internationalization of portfolios', *Oxford Economic Papers*, 533–565.

Brander, J. (1987). 'Shaping comparative advantage: trade policy, industrial policy, and economic performance', in *Shaping Comparative Advantage* (eds R.G. Lipsey and W. Dobson). Toronto: C.D. Howe Institute, pp. 1–55.

Brander, J. (1995). 'Strategic trade policy', in *Handbook of International Economics* (eds G. Grossman and K. Rogoff). Amsterdam: Elsevier, pp. 1395–1455.

Brander, J. and B. Spencer (1985). 'Export subsidies and international market share rivalry', *Journal of International Economics*, 83–100.

Braunerhjelm, P. and K. Ekholm (eds) (1998). *The Geography of Multinational Firms*. Boston: Kluwer.

Braunerhjelm, P., R. Faini, V. Norman, F. Ruane and P. Seabright (2000). *Integration and the Regions of Europe: How the Right Policies Can Prevent Polarization*. London: CEPR.

Brecher, R. and J. Bhagwati (1981). 'Foreign ownership and the theory of trade and welfare', *Journal of Political Economy*, 497–511.

Brülhart, M. (1998a). 'Trading places: industrial specialization in the European Union', *Journal of Common Market Studies*, 319–346.

Brülhart, M. (1998b). 'Economic geography, industry location and trade: the evidence', *World Economy*, 775–801.

Brülhart, M. and R. Elliott (1998). 'Adjustment to the European single market: inferences from intra-industry trade patterns', *Journal of Economic Studies*, 225–247.

Brülhart, M. and R. Elliott (1999). 'A survey of intra-industry trade in the European Union', in *Intra-Industry Trade and Adjustment: The European Experience* (eds M. Brülhart and R. Hine). Houndmills: Macmillan, pp. 98–117.

Brülhart, M. and R. Hine (eds) (1999). *Intra-Industry Trade and Adjustment: The European Experience*. Houndmills: Macmillan.

Brülhart, M. and J. Torstensson (1996). 'Regional integration, scale economies and industry location in the European Union', *CEPR Discussion Paper* No. 1435.

Buckley, P. and P. Artisien (1987). 'Policy issues of intra-EC direct investment', *Journal of Common Market Studies*, 207–230.

Buckley, P. and M. Casson (1998). 'Models of the multinational enterprise', *Journal of International Business Studies*, 21–44.

Buigues, P. and A. Jacquemin (1992). 'Foreign direct investment and exports in the Common Market', paper presented at the Japanese Direct Investment in a Unifying Europe, conference held in INSEAD, Fontainebleau, 26–27 June 1992, mimeo.

Buigues, P. and A. Sapir (1993). 'Market services and European integration: issues and challanges', *European Economy Social Europe*, No. 3, ix–xx.

Buigues, P. and J. Sheehy (1995). 'The impact of the Internal Market Programme on European integration', in *35 Years of Free Trade in Europe: Messages for the Future* (ed. E. Ems). Geneva: European Free Trade Association, pp. 38–63.

Bumbacher, U. (1995). 'The Swiss watch industry', in *Studies in Swiss Competitive Advantage* (eds M. Enright and R. Weder). Bern: Peter Lang, pp. 113–151.

Canova, F. and A. Marcet (1995). 'The poor stay poor: non-convergence across countries and regions', *CEPR Discussion Paper* No. 1265.

Cantwell, J., S. Iammarino and C. Noonan (2000). 'Sticky places in slippery space – the location of innovation by MNCs in the European regions', *Discussion Paper* No. 281, University of Reading, Department of Economics.

Capello, R. (1999). 'Spatial transfer of knowledge in high technology milieux: learning versus collective learning processes', *Regional Studies*, 353–365.

Carlén, B. (1994). 'Road transport', *EFTA Occasional Paper* No. 49, pp. 81–111.

Carliner, G. (1988). 'Industrial policies for emerging industries', in *Strategic Trade Policy and the New International Economics* (ed. P. Krugman). Cambridge, MA: The MIT Press, pp. 147–168.

Casella, A. (1996). 'Large countries, small countries and the enlargement of trade blocs', *European Economic Review*, 389–415.

Castells, M. and P. Hall (1994). *Technopols of the World*. London: Routledge.

Caves, R. (1996). *Multinational Enterprise and Economic Analysis*. Cambridge: Cambridge University Press.

Cecchini, P. (1988). *The European Challenge 1992*. Aldershot: Wildwood House.

CEPR (1994). *The Location of Economic Activity: New Theories and Evidence*. London: CEPR.

Chandler, A., P. Hagström and Ö. Sölvell (eds) (1998). *The Dynamic Firm*. Oxford: Oxford University Press.

Chang, H. (1994). *The Political Economy of Industrial Policy*. London: Macmillan.

Chatterji, M. and R. Kuenne (eds) (1990). *New Frontiers in Regional Science*. Houndmills: Macmillan.

Chaudhry, P., P. Dacin and P. Peter (1994). 'The pharmaceutical industry and European Community integration', *European Management Journal*, 442–453.

Christaller, W. (1933). *Die Zentralen Orte in Süddeutschland*, Jena: Gustav Fischer. [Translated from German by C. Baskin *Central Places in Southern Germany* (1966), Englewood Cliffs: Prentice-Hall].

Cini, M. and L. McGowan (1998). *Competition Policy in the European Union*. Houndmills: Macmillan.

Clegg, J. and S. Scott-Green (1999). 'The determinants of new FDI capital flows into EC: a statistical comparison of the USA and Japan', *Journal of Common Market Studies*, 597–616.

Cossentino, F., F. Pyke and W. Sengenberger (eds) (1996). *Local and Regional Response to Global Pressure: The Case of Italy and Industrial Districts*. Geneva: ILO.

Cowan, R. and W. Cowan (1998). 'On clustering in the location of R&D: statics and dynamics', *Economics of Innovation and New Technology*, 201–229.

Culem, C. (1988). 'The location determinants of direct investments among industrialized countries', *European Economic Review*, 885–904.

Curzon Price, V. (1981). *Industrial Policies in the European Community*. London: Macmillan.

Curzon Price, V. (1987). *Free Trade Areas, the European Experience*. Toronto: C.D. Howe Institute.

Curzon Price, V. (1990). 'Competition and industrial policies with emphasis on industrial policy', in *Economics of the European Community* (ed. A. El-Agraa). New York: St. Martin's Press, pp. 156–186.

Curzon Price, V. (1991). 'The threat of "Fortress Europe" from the development of social and industrial policies at a European level', *Aussenwirtschaft*, 119–138.

Curzon Price, V. (1993). 'EEC's strategic trade-cum-industrial policy: a public choice analysis', in *National Constitutions and International Economic Law* (eds M. Hilf and E. Petersmann). Deventer: Kluwer, pp. 391–405.

Curzon Price, V. (1996). 'Residual obstacles to trade in the Single European Market', *Euryopa*, Institut européen de l'Universite de Genève.

Curzon Price, V. (1997). 'The European Free Trade Association', in *Economic Integration Worldwide* (ed. A. El-Agraa). London: Macmillan, pp. 175–202.

d'Arge, R. (1969). 'Note on customs unions and direct foreign investment', *Economic Journal*, 324–333.

d'Arge, R. (1971a). 'Customs unions and direct foreign investment', *Economic Journal*, 352–355.

d'Arge, R. (1971b). 'A Reply', *Economic Journal*, 357–359.

Darwent, D. (1969). 'Growth poles and growth centers in regional planning – a review', *Environment and Planning*, 5–32.

David, P. (1984). 'High technology centers and the economics of locational tournaments', Stanford University, mimeo.

David, P. and J. Rosenbloom (1990). 'Marshallian factor market externalities and the dynamics of industrial localization', *Journal of Urban Economics*, 349–370.

de Bernardy, M. (1999). 'Reactive and proactive local territory: co-operation and community in Grenoble', *Regional Studies*, 343–352.

Defraigne, P. (1984). 'Towards concerted industrial policies in the EC', in *European Industry: Public Policy and Corporate Strategy* (ed. A. Jacquemin). Oxford: Clarendon Press, pp. 368–377.

de Ghellinck, E. (1988). 'European industrial policy against the background of the Single European Act', in *Main Economic Policy Areas of the EEC – Towards 1992* (ed. P. Coffey). Dordrecht: Kluwer, pp. 133–156.

de la Fuente, A. and X. Vives (1995). 'Infrastructure and education as instruments of regional policy in the European Community', *Economic Policy*, 13–51.

de la Mothe, J. and G. Paquet (eds) (1996). *Evolutionary Economics and the New International Political Economy*. London: Pinter.

Dertouzos, M., R. Lester and R. Solow (1990). *Made in America*. New York: HarperPerennial.

Dicken, P., M. Forsgren and A. Malmberg (1995). 'The local embeddedness of transnational corporations' in *Globalization, Institutions and Regional Development in Europe* (eds A. Amin and N. Thrift). Oxford: Oxford University Press, pp. 23–45.

Donges, J. (1980). 'Industrial policies in West Germany's not so market-oriented economy', *World Economy*, 185–204.

Dosi, G. (1988). 'Sources, procedures and microeconomic effects of innovation', *Journal of Economic Literature*, 1120–1171.

Dosi, G. (1997). 'Opportunities, incentives and collective patterns of technological change', *Economic Journal*, 1530–1547.

Dosi, G., K. Pavitt and L. Soete (1990). *The Economics of Technical Change and International Trade*. New York: Harvester Wheatsheaf.

Drabek, Z. and D. Greenaway (1984). 'Economic integration and intra-indusrtry trade: the EEC and CMEA compared', *Kyklos*, 444–469.

Dunning, J. (1988). *Explaining International Production*. London: Unwin Hyman.

Dunning, J. (ed.) (1993). *The Theory of Transnational Corporations*. London: Routledge.

Dunning, J. (1994a). 'MNE activity: comparing the NAFTA and the European Community', in *Multinationals in North America* (ed. L. Eden). Calgary: University of Calgary Press, pp. 277–308.

Dunning, J. (1994b). 'Globalization: the challenge for national economic regimes', *Discussion Paper* No. 186, Department of Economics, University of Reading.

Dunning, J. (1995). 'Think again professor Krugman: competitiveness does matter', *International Executive*, 313–324.

Dunning, J. (1997). 'The European Internal Market Programme and inbound foreign direct investment', *Journal of Common Market Studies* (Part I), 1–30, (Part II), 189–223.

Dunning, J. (1998a). 'Location and the multinational enterprise: a neglected factor?', *Journal of International Business Studies*, 45–66.

Dunning, J. (1998b), 'Globalization, technological change and the spatial organization of economic activity', in *The Dynamic Firm* (A. Chandler *et al.*, eds). Oxford: Oxford University Press, pp. 289–314.

Dunning, J. (1998c). 'Regions, globalization and the knowledge economy: the issues stated', Rutgers University, mimeo.

Dunning, J. (1999). 'The eclectic paradigm as an envelope for economic and business theories of MNE activity', *Discussion Paper* No. 263, Department of Economics, University of Reading.

Dunning, J. and P. Robson (1987). 'Multinational Corporate Integration and Regional Economic Integration', *Journal of Common Market Studies*, 103–124.

Eaton, C. and R. Lipsey (1975). 'The principle of minimum differentiation reconsidered: some new developments in the theory of spatial competition', *Review of Economic Studies*, 27–49.

Eaton, C. and R. Lipsey (1976). 'The non-uniqueness of equilibrium in the Löschian location model', *American Economic Review*, 77–93.

Eaton, C. and R. Lipsey (1979). 'Comparison shopping and the clustering of homogeneous firms', *Journal of Regional Science*, 421–435.

Eaton, C. and R. Lipsey (1982). 'An economic theory of central places', *Economic Journal*, 56–72.

Eaton, C. and R. Lipsey (1997). *On the Foundations of Monopolistic Competition and Economic Geography*. Cheltenham: Edward Elgar.

Eaton, J., E. Gutierrez and S. Kortum (1998). 'European technology policy', *Economic Policy*, 405–438.

El-Agraa, A. (1997). 'UK competitiveness policy vs. Japanese industrial policy', *Ecnomic Journal*, 1504–1517.

Ellison, G. and E. Glaeser (1997). 'Geographic concentration in U.S. manufacturing industries: a dartboard approach', *Journal of Political Economy*, 889–927.

Ellison, G. and E. Glaeser (1999). 'The geographic concentration of industry: does natural advantage explain agglomeration?', *American Economic Review* (Papers and Proceedings), 311–316.

Emerson, M., M. Aujean, M. Catinat: Goybet and A. Jacquemin (1988). 'The Economics of 1992', *European Economy*, March.

Enright, M. (1998). 'Regional clusters and firm strategy', in *The Dynamic Firm* (A. Chandler et al., eds). Oxford: Oxford University Press, pp. 315–342.

Enright, M. and R. Weder (eds) (1995). *Studies in Swiss Competitive Advantage*. Bern: Peter Lang.

European Commission (1992). *The Future Development of the Transport Policy*. Brussels: European Commission.

European Commission (1997a). *Regional Growth and Convergence*. London: Kogan Page.

European Commission (1997b). *The Impact and Effectiveness of the Single Market*. Luxembourg: EU.

European Commission (1997c). *Agenda 2000 for a Stronger and Wider Union*. Luxembourg: European Communities.

European Commission (1998). *Foreign Direct Investment*. London: Kogan Page.

European Communities (1991). *XXth Report on Competition Policy*. Brussels: European Communities.

European Economy, (1990). *One Market? One Money*. No. 44.

European Economy, (1993). *The Economic and Financial Situation in Italy*, No. 1.

European Economy, (1994). *Competition and Integration; Community Merger Control Policy*. No. 57.

European Economy, (1996). *Economic Evaluation of the Internal Market*. No. 4.

Feldman, M. (1994). *The Geography of Innovation*. Dordrecht: Kluwer.

Findlay, R. (1995). 'The philosophy of locational competition', in *Locational Competition in the World Economy*, (ed. H. Siebert). Tübingen: J.C.B. Mohr, pp. 3–16.

Finger, M. (1975). 'A new view of the product cycle theory', *Weltwirschaftliches Archiv*, 79–99.

Fontagné, L., M. Freudenberg and N. Péridy (1998). 'Intra-industry trade and the single market: quality matters', *CEPR Discussion Paper* No. 1959.

Ford, S. and R. Strange (1999). 'Where do Japanese manufacturing firms invest within Europe and why?', *Transnational Corporations*, 117–142.

Frankel, J. (1997). *Regional Trading Blocs*. Washington DC: Institute for International Economics.

Freeman, C. (1994). 'The economics of technical change', *Cambridge Journal of Economics*, 463–514.

Friedman, J., D. Gerlowski and J. Silberman (1992). 'What attracts foreign multinational corporations? Evidence from branch plant locations in the United States', *Journal of Regional Science*, 403–418.

Fujita, M. and R. Ishii (1998). 'Global location behavior and organizational dynamics of Japanese electronics firms and their impact on regional economies', in *The Dynamic Firm* (A. Chandler *et al.*, eds). Oxford: Oxford University Press, pp. 343–383.

Fujita, M., P. Krugman and A. Venables (1999). *The Spatial Economy*. Cambridge: MIT Press.

Fujita, M. and T. Mori (1996). 'The role of ports in the making of major cities: self-agglomeration and hub-effect', *Journal of Development Economics*, 93–120.

Fujita, M. and J. Thisse (1996). 'Economics of agglomeration', *Journal of the Japanese and International Economies*, 339–378.

Fukao, K. and R. Benabou (1993). 'History versus expectations: a comment', *Quarterly Journal of Economics*, 535–542.

Gallup, J., J. Sachs and A. Mellinger (1999). 'Geography and economic development', in *Annual World Bank Conference on Development Economics 1998* (eds B. Pleskovic and J. Stiglitz). Washington: World Bank, pp. 127–178.

Garofoli, G. (1991a). 'Industrial districts: structure and transformation', in *Endogenous Development and Southern Europe* (ed. G. Garofoli). Aldershot: Avebury, pp. 49–60.

Garofoli, G. (1991b). 'Endogenous development and southern Europe: an introduction', in *Endogenous Development and Southern Europe* (ed. G. Garofoli). Aldershot: Avebury, pp. 1–13.

Geroski, P. (1987). 'Brander's 'shaping comparative advantage': some comments', in *Shaping Comparative Advantage* (eds R.G. Lipsey and W. Dobson). Totonto: C.D. Howe Institute, pp. 57–64.

Geroski, P. (1988). 'Competition and innovation', in Commission of the European Communities, *Studies on the Economics of Integration*. Brussels: European Community, pp. 339–388.

Geroski, P. (1989). 'European industrial policy and industrial policy in Europe', *Oxford Review of Economic Policy*, 20–36.

Geroski, P. and A. Jacquemin (1985). 'Industrial change, barriers to mobility, and European industrial policy', *Economic Policy*, 170–218.

Gittelman, M., E. Graham and H. Fukukawa (1992). 'Affiliates of Japanese firms in the European Community: performance and structure', paper presented at the Japanese Direct Investment in a Unifying Europe, conference held in INSEAD, Fontainebleau, 26–27 June 1992, mimeo.

Gleiser, H., A. Jacquemin and J. Petit (1980). 'Exports in an Imperfect Competition Framework: An Analysis of 1,446 Exporters', *Quarterly Journal of Economics*, 507–524.

Goldberg, M. (1972). 'The determinants of U.S. direct investment in the E.E.C.: comment', *American Economic Review*, 692–699.

Goodman, E. and J. Bamford (eds) (1989). *Small Firms and Industrial Districts in Italy*. London: Routledge.

Gordon, I. and P. McCann (2000). 'Industrial clusters: complexes, agglomeration and/or social networks?', *Urban Studies*, 513–532.

Görg, H. and F. Ruane (1999). 'US investment in EU member countries: the internal market and sectoral specialization', *Journal of Common Market Studies*, 333–348.

Grabher, C. (1993). 'The weakness of strong ties: the lock-in of regional development in the Ruhr area', in *The Embedded Firm* (ed. G. Grabher). London: Routledge, pp. 255–277.

Graham, E. (1978). 'Transatlantic investment by multinational firms: a rivalistic phenomenon?', *Journal of Post Keynesian Economics*, 82–99.

Graham, E. (1996). 'Foreign direct investment in the new multilateral trade agenda', Occasional Paper WTO Series, No. 4, Graduate Institute of International Studies, Geneva.

Graham, E. (1998). 'Market structure and the multinational enterprise: a game-theoretic approach', *Journal of International Business Studies*, 67–83.

Graham, E. and P. Krugman (1995). *Foreign Direct Investment in the United States*. Washington: Institute for International Economics.

Greenaway, D. and R. Hine (1991). 'Intra-industry specialization, trade expansion and adjustment in the European Economic Space', *Journal of Common Market Studies*, 603–622.

Greenaway, D. and C. Milner (1987). 'Intra-industry trade: current perspectives and unresolved issues', *Weltwirschaftliches Archiv*, 39–57.

Greenaway, D. and J. Torstensson (1997). 'Back to the future: taking stock on intra-industry trade', *Weltwirschaftliches Archiv*, 248–269.

Greenaway, D. and J. Torstensson (2000). 'Economic geography, comparative advantage and trade within industries: evidence from the OECD', *Journal of Economic Integration*, 260–280.

Greenhut, M. (1956). *Plant Location in Theory and Practice*. Chapel Hill: The University of North Carolina Press.

Grubel, H. and P. Lloyd (1975). *Intra Industry Trade*. London: Macmillan.

Gual, J. (1995). 'The three common policies: an economic analysis', in *European Policies on Competition, Trade and Industry* (eds P. Buigues, A. Jacquemin and A. Sapir). Aldershot: Edward Elgar, pp. 3–48.

Haberler, G. (1977). 'Survey of circumstances affecting the location of production and international trade as analysed in theoretical literature', in *The International Allocation of Economic Activity* (eds B. Ohlin, P. Hesselborn and P. Wijkman). London: Macmillan, pp. 1–24.

Hagedoorn, J. (1998). 'Atlantic strategic technology alliances', in *The Struggle for World Markets* (ed. G. Boyd). Cheltenham: Edward Elgar, pp. 177–191.

Hagedoorn, J., and J. Schakenraad (1993). 'A comparison of private and subsidized R&D partnerships in the European information technology industry', *Journal of Common Market Studies*, 373–390.

Hague, D. (1960). 'Report on the proceedings: summary record of the debate', in *Economic Consequences of the Size of Nations* (ed. E. Robinson). London: Macmillan, pp. 333–438.

Hanson, G. (1998). 'North American economic integration and industry location', *Oxford Review of Economic Policy*, 30–44.

Harrison, R. and M. Hart (eds) (1993). *Spatial Policy in a Divided Nation*. London: Jessica Kingsley.

Hartley, K., A. Cox and D. Mayes (1997). 'The impact of rules' in *The Evolution of the Single European Market* (ed. D. Mayes). Cheltenham: Edward Elgar, pp. 87–113.

Hay, D. and G. Liu (1997). 'The efficiency of firms: What difference does competition make?', *Economic Journal*, 597–617.

Hayek, F. (1978). *New Studies in Philosophy, Politics, Economics and History of Ideas*. London: Routledge.

Helliwell, J. (2000). *Gloalization: Myths, Facts and Consequences*. Toronto: C. D. Howe Institute.

Henderson, J. (1974). 'The sizes and types of cities', *American Economic Review*, 640–656.

Hepworth, M. (1986). 'The geography of technological change in the information economy', *Regional Studies*, 407–424.

Herin, J. (1986). 'Rules of origin and differences between tariff levels in EFTA and in the EC', Occasional Paper No. 16, EFTA, Geneva.

Herzog, H. and A. Schlottmann (eds) (1991). *Industry Location and Public Policy*. Knoxville: The University of Tennessee Press.

Hill, T. (1977). 'On Goods and services', *Review of Income and Wealth*, 315–338.

Hillman, D. and D. Gibbs (1998). *Century Makers*. London: Weidenfeld & Nicolson.

Hindley, B. (1991). 'Creating an integrated market for financial serices', in *European Economic Integration* (eds G. Faulhaber and G. Tamburini). Boston: Kluwer, pp. 263–288.

Holmes, P. and A. Smith (1995). 'Automobile industry', in *European Policies on Competition, Trade and Industry* (eds P. Buigues, A. Jacquemin and A. Sapir). Aldershot: Edward Elgar, pp. 125–159.

Holmes, T. (1998). 'The effects of state policies on the location of manufacturing: Evidence from state borders', *Journal of Political Economy*, 667–705.

Hotelling, H. (1929). 'Stability in competition', *Economic Journal*, 41–57.

Humphrey, J. and H. Schmitz (1996). 'The triple C approach to local industrial policy', *World Development*, 1859–1877.

Hymer, S. (1976). *The International Operations of National Firms: A Study of Direct Foreign Investment*. Boston: MIT Press.

Isard, W. (1954). 'Location theory and trade theory: short run analysis', *Quarterly Journal of Economics*, 305–320.

Isard, W. (1956). *Location and Space-Economy*. Cambridge: Technology Press of MIT.

Isard, W. (1977). 'Location theory, agglomeration and the pattern of world trade', in *The International Allocation of Economic Activity* (eds B. Ohlin, P. Hesselborn and P. Wijkman). London: Macmillan, pp. 159–177.

Isard, W. and M. Peck (1954). 'Location theory and international and interregional trade theory', *Quarterly Journal of Economics*, 97–114.

Jacquemin, A. (1984). *European Industry: Public Policy and Corporate Strategy*. Oxford: Clarendon Press.

Jacquemin, A. (1990a). 'Mergers and European policy', in *Merger and Competition Policy inthe European Community* (ed. P. Admiraal). Oxford: Basil Blackwell, pp. 1–38.

Jacquemin, A. (1990b). 'Horizontal concentration and European merger policy', *European Economic Review*, 539–550.

Jacquemin, A. (1996). 'Les enjeux de la competitivite europeenne et la politique industrielle communautaire en matiere d'innovation', *Revue du Marché commun et de l'Union europeenne*, March, 175–181.

Jacquemin, A., P. Lloyd, P. Tharakan and J. Waelbroeck (1998). 'Competition policy in an international setting: the way ahead', *World Economy*, 1179–1183.

Jacquemin, A. and L. Pench (1997). *Europe Competing in the Global Economy*. Cheltenham: Edward Elgar.

Jacquemin, A. and A. Sapir (1991). 'The internal and external opening-up of the Single Community Market: efficiency gains, adjustment costs and new Community instruments', *International Spectator*, 29–48.

Jacquemin, A. and A. Sapir (1996). 'Is a European hard core credible? A statistical analysis', *Kyklos*, 105–117.

Jacquemin, A. and D. Wright (1993). 'Corporate strategies and European challenges post-1992', *Journal of Common Market Studies*, 525–537.

Jaffe, A., M. Trajtenberg and R. Henderson (1993). 'Geographic location of knowledge as evidenced by patent citations', *Quarterly Journal of Economics*, 577–598.

Jarillo, J., and J. Martinez (1991). 'The international expansion of Spanish firms: towards an integrative framework for international strategy', in *Corporate and Industry Strategies for Europe* (eds L. Mattsson and B. Stymne). Amsterdam: Elsevier, pp. 283–302.

Jianping, D. (1999). 'Agglomeration effects in manufacturing location – are there any country's preferences?, *Economia Internazionale*, 59–78.

Johnson, C. (1984). 'The idea of industrial policy' in *The Industrial Policy Debate* (ed. C. Johnson). San Francisco: Institute for Contemporary Studies.

Johnson, H. (1977). 'Technology, technical progress and the international allocation of economic activity', in *The International Allocation of Economic Activity* (eds B. Ohlin, P. Hesselborn and P. Wijkman). London: Macmillan, pp. 314–327.

Johnson, H. and M. Krauss (1973). 'Border taxes, border tax adjustment, comparative advantage and the balance of payments', in *Economics of Integration* (ed. M. Krauss). London: George Allen & Unwin, pp. 239–253.

Jovanović, B. (1982). 'Selection and the evolution of industry', *Econometrica*, 649–670.

Jovanović, M. (1995). 'Economic integration among developing countries and foreign direct investment', *Economia Internazionale*, 209–243.

Jovanović, M. (1997). *European Economic Integration*. London: Routledge.

Jovanović, M. (1998a). *International Economic Integration*. London: Routledge.

Jovanović, M. (ed.) (1998b). *International Economic Integration: Critical Perspectives on the World Economy – Theory and Measurement* (Volume I). London: Routledge.

Jovanović, M. (ed.) (1998c). *International Economic Integration: Critical Perspectives on the World Economy – Monetary, Fiscal and Factor Mobility Issues* (Volume II). London: Routledge.

Jovanović, M. (ed.) (1998d). *International Economic Integration: Critical Perspectives on the World Economy – General Issues* (Volume III). London: Routledge.

Jovanović, M. (ed.) (1998e). *International Economic Integration: Critical Perspectives on the World Economy – Integration Schemes* (Volume IV). London: Routledge.

Jovanović, M. (2001). 'Why and how firms cluster', *Brown Economic Review*, forthcoming.

Keeble, D. and F. Wilkinson (1999). 'Collective learning and knowledge development in the evolution of regional clusters of high technology SMEs in Europe', *Regional Studies*, 295–303.

Keeble, D., C. Lawson, B. Moore and F. Wilkinson (1999). 'Collective learning process, networking and 'institutional thickness' in the Cambridge region', *Regional Studies*, 319–332.

Kim, S. (1995). 'Expansion of markets and the geographic distribution of economic activities: the trends in U.S. regional manufacturing structure, 1860–1987', *Quarterly Journal of Economics*, 881–908.

Kimura, Y. (1996). 'Japanese direct investment in the peripheral regions of Europe: an overview', in *Japan and the European Periphery* (ed. J. Darby). Houndmills: Macmillan, pp. 13–36.

Kleinknecht, A. and J. ter Wengel (1998). 'The myth of economic globalisation', *Cambridge Journal of Economics*, 637–647.

Knickerboker, F. (1973). *Oligopolistic Reaction and Multinational Enterprise*. Boston: Harvard University.

Komiya, R. (1988). 'Introduction', in *Industrial Policy of Japan* (eds R. Komiya, M. Okuono and K. Susumura). Tokyo: Academic Press, pp. 1–22.

Kravis, I. and R. Lipsey (1982). 'The location of overseas production and production for export by U.S. multinational firms', *Journal of International Economics*, 201–223.

Krätke, S. (1999). 'Regional integration or fragmentation? The German–Polish border region in a new Europe', *Regional Studies*, 631–641.

Krueger, A. (1995). 'Free trade agreements versus customs unions', NBER Working Paper No. 5084.

Krugman, P. (1980). 'Scale economies, product differentiation, and the pattern of trade', *American Economic Review*, 950–959.

Krugman, P. (1987). 'The narrow moving band, the Dutch disease, and the competitive consequences of Mrs. Thatcher', *Journal of Development Economics*, 41–55.

Krugman, P. (1990a). *Rethinking International Trade*. Cambridge MA: The MIT Press.

Krugman, P. (1990b). 'Protectionism: try it, you'll like it', *International Economy* (June/July), 35–39.

Krugman, P. (1991). 'History versus expectations', *Quarterly Journal of Economics*, 651–667.

Krugman, P. (1992). *Geography and Trade*. Cambridge MA: The MIT Press.

Krugman, P. (1993a). 'On the number and location of cities', *European Economic Review*, 293–298.

Krugman, P. (1993b). 'The current case for industrial policy', in *Protectionism and World Welfare* (ed. D. Salvatore). Cambridge: Cambridge University Press, 160–179.

Krugman, P. (1993c). 'First nature, second nature, and metropolitan location', *Journal of Regional Science*, 129–144.

Krugman, P. (1995). 'A reply to professor Dunning', *International Executive*, 325–327.

Krugman, P. (1996a). 'What economists can learn from evolutionary theorists', A talk given to the European Association for Evolutionary Political Economy, November (http://web.mit.edu/krugman/www/).

Krugman, P. (1996b). *Pop Internationalism*. Cambridge, MA: The MIT Press.

Krugman, P. (1996c). 'The Adam Smith Address: What Difference does Globalization Make', *Business Economics*, 7–10.

Krugman, P. (1996d). 'Urban concentration: the role of increasing returns and transport costs', *International Regional Science Review*, 5–30.

Krugman, P. (1997). 'What should trade negotiators negotiate about', *Journal of Economic Literature*, 113–120.

Krugman, P. (1998a). 'What's new about the new economic geography', *Oxford Review of Economic Policy*, 7–17.

Krugman, P. (1998b). *The Accidental Theorist*. New York: Norton.

Krugman, P. (1999). 'The role of geography in development', in *Annual World Bank Conference on Development Economics 1998* (eds B. Pleskovic and J. Stiglitz). Washington: World Bank, pp. 89–107.

Krugman, P. (2000). 'Can America stay on top?', *Journal of Economic Perspectives*, 169–175.

Krugman, P. and A. Venables (1990). 'Integration and the competitiveness of peripheral industry', in *Unity with Diversity in the European Economy: the Community's Southern Frontier* (eds C. Bliss and J. Braga de Macedo). Cambridge: Cambridge University Press, pp. 56–75.

Krugman, P. and A. Venables (1995). 'Globalization and the inequality of nations', *Quarterly Journal of Economics*, 857–880.

Krugman, P. and A. Venables (1996). 'Integration, specialization, and adjustment', *European Economic Review*, 959–967.

Kuhn, T. (1972). *The Structure of Scientific Revolutions*. Chicago: Chicago University Press.

Lall, S. (1994). 'The east Asian miracle: does the bell toll for industrial strategy?', *World Development*, 645–654.

Lambooy, J. (1997). 'Knowledge production, organisation and agglomeration economies', *GeoJournal*, 293–300.

Lancaster, K. (1980). 'Intra-industry trade under perfect monopolistic competition', *Journal of International Economics*, 151–175.

Lawson, C. and E. Lorenz (1999). 'Collective learning, tacit knowledge and regional innovative capacity', *Regional Studies*, 307–317.

Leamer, E. (1984). *Sources of International Comparative Advantage*. Cambridge, MA: The MIT Press.

Leamer, E. and J. Levinsohn (1995). 'International trade theory: the evidence', in *Handbook of International Economics* (eds G. Grossman and K. Rogoff). Amsterdam: Elsevier, pp. 1339–1394.

Levin, R., A. Klevorick, R. Nelson and S. Winter (1987). 'Appropriating the returns from industrial research and development', *Brookings Papers on Economic Activity*, 783–820.

Linder, S. (1961). *An Essay on Trade and Transformation*. Uppsala: Almquist & Wiksells.

Lindholm Dahlstrand, Å. (1999). 'Technology-based SMEs in the Göteborg region: their origin and interaction with universities and large firms', *Regional Studies*, 379–389.

Lipsey, R. E. (1999). 'The role of foreign direct investment in international capital flows', NBER Working Paper No. 7094.

Lipsey, R.G. (1985). 'Canada and the United States: the economic dimension', in *Canada and the United States: Enduring Friendship, Persistent Stress* (eds C. Doran and J. Stigler). New York: Prenctice Hall, pp. 69–108.

Lipsey, R.G. (1987a). 'Models matter when discussing competitiveness: a technical note', in *Shaping Comparative Advantage* (eds R.G. Lipsey and W. Dobson). Toronto: C.D. Howe Institute, pp. 155–166.

Lipsey, R.G. (1987b). 'Report on the workshop', in *Shaping Comparative Advantage* (eds R.G. Lipsey and W. Dobson). Toronto: C.D. Howe Institute, pp. 109–153.

Lipsey, R.G. (1992a). 'Global change and economic policy', in *The Culture and the Power of Knowledge* (eds N. Stehr and R. Ericson). New York: De Gryter, pp. 279–299.

Lipsey, R.G. (1992b). *An Introduction to Positive Economics*. London: Weidenfeld and Nicolson.

Lipsey, R.G. (1993). 'Globalisation, technological change and economic growth', Annual Sir Charles Carter Lecture, mimeo.

Lipsey, R.G. (1994). 'Markets, technological change and economic growth', Canadian Institute for Advanced Research, Vancouver, mimeo.

Lipsey, R.G. (1997). 'Globalization and national government policies: an economist's view', in *Governments, Globalization and International Business* (ed. J. Dunning). Oxford: Oxford University Press, pp. 73–113.

Lipsey, R.G. and M. Smith (1986). *Taking the Initiative: Canada's Trade Options in a Turbulent World*. Toronto: C.D. Howe Institute.

Lipsey, R. G. and R. York, (1988). *Evaluating the Free Trade Deal: A Guided Tour through the Canada-US Agreement*. Toronto: C.D. Howe Institute.

Lloyd, P. (1998). 'Globalisation and competition policies', *Weltwirschaftliches Archiv*, 161–185.

Loertscher, R. and F. Wolter, (1980). 'Determinants of intra-industry trade: among countries and across industries', *Weltwirschaftliches Archiv*, 280–293.

Longhi, C. (1999). 'Networks, collective learning and technology development in innovative high technology regions: the case of Sophia-Antipolis', *Regional Studies*, 333–342.

López-Bazo, E., E. Vayá, A. Mora and J. Surinah (1999). 'Regional economic dynamics and convergence in the European Union', *Annals of Regional Science*, 343–370.

Lösch, A. (1938). 'The nature of economic regions', *Southern Economic Journal*, 71–78.

Lösch, A. (1940). *Die Räumliche Ordnung der Wirtschaft*, Jena: Gustav Fischer [Translated from German by W. Woglom and W. Stolper, *The Economics of Location* (1973), New Haven: Yale University Press].

Lowe, N. and M. Kenney (1999). 'Foreign investment and the global geography of production: why the Mexican consumer electronics industry failed', *World Development*, 1427–1443.

Lucas, R. (1988). 'On the mechanics of economic development', *Journal of Monetary Economics*, 3–42.

Lunn, J. (1980). 'Determinants of US direct investment in the EEC', *European Economic Review*, 93–101.

McCann, F. (1995). 'Rethinking the economics of location and agglomeration', *Urban Studies*, 563–577.

McFetridge, D. (1985). 'The economics of industrial policy', in *Canadian Industrial Policy in Action* (ed. D. McFetridge). Toronto: University of Toronto Press, pp. 1–49.

Machlup, F. (1979). *A History of Thought on Economic Integration*. London: Macmillan.

Malmberg, A. (1996). 'Industrial geography: agglomeration and local milieu', *Progress in Human Geography*, 392–403.

Malmberg, A., Ö. Sölvell and I. Zander (1996). 'Spatial clustering, local accumulation of knowledge and firm competitiveness', *Geografiska Annaler*, 85–97.

Marcus, M. (1965). 'Agglomeration economies: a suggested approach', *Land Economics*, 279–284.

Markusen, A. (1996a). 'Sticky places in slippery space: a typology of industrial districts', *Economic Geography*, 293–313.

Markusen, A. (1996b). 'Interaction between regional and industrial policies: evidence from four countries', *International Regional Science Review*, 49–77.

Markusen, A. (1999). 'Fuzzy concepts, scanty evidence, policy stance: the case for rigour and policy relevance in critical regional studies', *Regional Studies*, 869–884.

Markusen, J. (1983). 'Factor movements and commodity trade as complements', *Journal of International Economics*, 341–356.

Markusen, J. and A. Venables (1998). 'Multinational firms and the new trade theory', *Journal of International Economics*, 183–203.

Markusen, J. and J. Melvin, (1984). *The Theory of International Trade and Its Canadian Applications*. Toronto: Butterworths.

Marshall, A. (1890). *Principles of Economics*. London: Macmillan.

Mayes, D. (ed.) (1997). *The Evolution of the Single European Market*. Cheltenham: Edward Elgar.

Meiklejon, R. (1999). 'An international competition policy: do we need it? Is it feasible?', *World Economy*, 1233–1249.

Messerlin, P. (1996). 'Competition policy and antidumping reform: an exercise in transition', in *The World Trading System: Challenges Ahead* (ed. J. Schott). Washington DC: Institute for International Economics, pp. 219–246.

Micossi, S. (1996). 'Nouvelles orientations de la politique industrielle dans l'Union europeene', *Revue du Marche commun et de l'Union europeenne*, 158–164.

Midelfart-Knarvik, K., H. Overman, S. Redding and A. Venables (2000). 'The location of European industry', *Economic Papers*, No. 142, European Commission.

Miller, S. and O. Jensen (1978). 'Location and the theory of production', *Regional Science and Urban Economics*, 117–128.

Morita, A. (1992). 'Partnering for competitiveness: the role of Japanese business', *Harvard Business Review*, May–June, 76–83.

Moses, L. (1958). 'Location and the theory of production', *Quarterly Journal of Economics*, 259–272.

Mulligan, G. (1984). 'Agglomeration and central place theory: a review of the literature'. *International Regional Science Review*, 1–42.

Mundell, R. (1957). 'International trade and factor mobility', *American Economic Review*, 321–335.

Mytelka, L. (1979). *Regional Development in a Global Economy*. New Haven: Yale University Press.

Nadvi, K. (1998). 'International competitiveness and small firm clusters – evidence from Pakistan', *Small Enterprise Development*, 12–24.

Narula, R. (1999). 'Explaining the growth of strategic R&D alliances by European firms', *Journal of Common Market Studies*, 711–723.

Nelson, R. (1999). 'The sources of industrial leadership: a perspective on industrial policy', *De Economist*, 1–18.

Neven, D. (1990). 'EEC integration towards 1992: some distributional aspects', *Economic Policy*, 14–46.

Neven, D., R. Nuttall and P. Seabright (1998). 'Enforcement of the European merger regulation', in *Applied Industrial Economics* (ed. L. Philips). Cambridge: Cambridge University Press, pp. 413–435.

Norman, V. (1990). 'Discussion of D. Neven's Paper', *Economic Policy*, pp. 49–52.

Norman, V. (1995). 'The theory of market integration: a retrospective view', in *35 Years of Free Trade in Europe: Messages for the Future* (ed. E. Ems). Geneva: European Free Trade Association, pp. 19–37.

Oakley, R. and S. Cooper (1989). 'High technology industry, agglomeration and the potential for peripherally sited firms', *Regional Studies*, 347–360.

Ohlin, B. (1933). *Interregional and International Trade*. Cambridge: Harvard University Press.

Ottaviano, G. (1999). 'Integration, geography and burden of history', *Regional Science and Urban Economics*, 245–256.

Ottaviano, G. and D. Puga (1998). 'Agglomeration in the global economy: a survey of the "new economic geography" ', *World Economy*, 707–731.

Ottaviano, G. and J. Thisse (1999). 'Integration, agglomeration and the political economics of factor mobility', *CEPR Discussion Paper* No. 2185.

Oughton, C. (1997). 'Competitiveness policy in the 1990s', *Economic Journal*, 1486–1503.

Paci, R. (1997). 'More similar and less equal: economic growth in the European regions', *Weltwirschaftliches Archiv*, 609–634.

Paci, R. and S. Usai (1999). 'The role of specialisation and diversity externalities in the agglomeration of innovative activities', University of Cagliari and University of Sassari, mimeo.

Pack, H. (2000). 'Industrial policy: growth elixir or poison?', *World Bank Research Observer*, 47–67.

Paelinck, J. and M. Polèse (1999). 'Modelling the regional impact of continental economic integration: lessons from the European Union for NAFTA', *Regional Studies*, 727–738.

Palmeter, D. (1993). 'Rules of origin in customs unions and free trade areas', in *Regional Integration and the Global Trading System* (eds K. Anderson and R. Blackhurst). New York: Harvester Wheatsheaf, 326–343.

Panić, M. (1991). 'The impact of multinationals on national economic policies', in *Multinationals and Europe 1992* (eds B. Bürgenmeier and J. Mucchelli). London: Routledge, pp. 204–222.

Panić, M. (1998). 'Transnational corporations and the nation state', in *Transnational Corporations and the Global Economy* (eds R. Kozul-Wright and R. Rowthorn). Houndmills: Macmillan, pp. 244–276.

Papageorgiou, G. (1979). 'Agglomeration', *Regional Science and Urban Economics*, 41–59.

Parr, J. and A. Reynolds-Feighan (2000). 'Location theory: analysis and applications', *Urban Studies*, 439–442.

Paul, C. and S. Siegel (1999). 'Scale economies and industry agglomeration externalities: a dynamic cost function approach', *American Economic Review*, 272–290.

Peck, M. (1989). 'Industrial organization and the gains from Europe 1992', *Brookings Papers on Economic Activity*, 277–299.

Penrose, E. (1952). 'Biological analogies in the theory of the firm', *American Economic Review*, 804–819.

Peroux, F. (1955). 'Note sur la notion de, "pôle de croissance" ', *Économie Appliqué*, 307–320.

Perroux, F. (1950). 'Economic space: theory and applications', *Quarterly Journal of Economics*, 89–104.

Perroux, F. (1961). *L'Économie du XXe Siècle*. Paris: Presses Universitaires de France.

Petit, P. and L. Soete (1999). 'Globalization in search of a future', *International Social Science Journal*, 165–181.

Pinch, S. and N. Henry (1999). 'Paul Krugman's geographical economics, industrial clustering and the British motor sport industry', *Regional Studies*, 815–827.

Pinder, J. (1982). 'Causes and kinds of industrial policy', in *National Strategies and the World Economy* (ed. J. Pinder). London: Croom Helm, pp. 41–52.

Pinder, J., T. Hosomi and W. Diebold (1979). *Industrial Policy and International Economy*. New York: The Trilateral Commission.

Plasschaert, S. (1994). 'Introduction: transfer pricing and taxation', in *Transnational Corporations: Transfer Pricing and Taxation* (ed. S. Plasschaert). London: Routledge, pp. 1–21.

Pomfret, R. (1997). *The Economics of Regional Trading Arrangements*. Oxford: Clarendon Press.

Porter, M. (1990a). *The Competitive Advantage of Nations*. New York: The Free Press.

Porter, M. (1990b). 'The competitive advantage of nations', *Harvard Business Review*, 73–93.

Porter, M. (1994). 'The role of location in competition', *Journal of the Economics of Business*, 35–39.

Porter, M. (1996). 'Competitive advantage, agglomeration economies, and regional policy', *International Regional Science Review*, 85–94.

Porter, M. (1998a). 'Clusters and the new economics of competition', *Harvard Business Review*, 77–90.

Porter, M. (1998b). 'Location, clusters, and the "new" microeconomics of competition', *Business Economics*, 7–13.

Porter, M. and Ö. Sölvell (1998). 'The role of geography in the process of innovation and the sustainable competitive advantage of firms', in *The Dynamic Firm* (A. Chandler *et al.*, eds). Oxford: Oxford University Press, pp. 440–457.

Posner, M. (1961). 'International trade and technical change', *Oxford Economic Papers*, 323–341.

Prais, S. (1981). *Productivity and Industrial Structure*. Cambridge: Cambridge University Press.

Pratten, C. (1971). *Economies of Scale and Manufacturing Industry*. Cambridge: Cambridge University Press.

Pratten, C. (1988). 'A survey of the economies of scale', in *Studies on the Economics of Integration*, Research on the Costs of Non-Europe, Vol. 2, Brussels: European Communities, pp. 11–165.

Predöhl, A. (1929). 'The theory of location in its relation to general economics', *Journal of Political Economy*, 371–390.

Puga, D. and A. Venables (1997). 'Preferential trading arrangements and industrial location', *Journal of International Economics*, 347–368.

Puga, D. and A. Venables (1999). 'Agglomeration and economic development: import substitution vs. trade liberalisation', *Economic Journal*, 292–311.

Purvis. D. (1972). 'Technology, trade and factor mobility', *Economic Journal*, 991–999.

Pyke, F. and W. Sengenberger (eds) (1992). *Industrial Districts and local Economic Regeneration*. Geneva: ILO.

Pyke, F., G. Becattini and W. Sengenberger (eds) (1990). *Industrial Districts and Inter-firm Co-operation in Italy*. Geneva: ILO.

Quah, D. (1996a). 'Empirics for economic growth and convergence', *European Economic Review*, 1353–1375.

Quah, D. (1996b). 'Regional convergence clusters across Europe', *CEPR Discussion Paper* No. 1286.

Rauch, J. (1993). 'Does history matter only when it matters little? The case of city-industry location', *CEPR Discussion Paper* No. 4312.

Reich, R. (1990). 'Who is us?', *Harvard Business Review*, 53–64.

Reich, R. (1982). 'Why the U.S. needs an industrial policy', *Harvard Business Review* (January/February), 74–81.

Reuber, G. (1973). *Private Foreign Investment in Development*. Oxford: Clarendon Press.

Robson, P. (1983). *Integration, Development and Equity*. London: George Allen & Unwin.

Robson, P. (1987). *The Economics of International Integration*. London: George Allen and Unwin.

Robson, P. (1998). *The Economics of International Integration*. London: Routledge.

Rodas-Martini, P. (1998). 'Intra-industry trade and revealed comparative advantage in the Central American Common Market', *World Development*, 337–344.

Romer, P. (1994). 'New goods, old theory and the welfare costs of trade restrictions', *Journal of Development Economics*, 5–38.

Rubin, S. (1970). 'The International Firm and the National Jurisdiction', in *The International Corporation* (ed. C. Kindleberger). Cambridge, MA: The MIT Press, pp. 179–204.

Rugman, A. (1985). 'The behaviour of US subsidiaries in Canada: implications for trade and investment', in *Canada/United States Trade and Investments Issues* (eds D. Fretz, R. Stern and J. Whalley). Toronto: Ontario Economic Council, pp. 460–473.

Rugman, A. and A. Verbeke (1998). 'Multinational enterprise and public policy', *Journal of International Business Studies*, 115–136.

Sala-i-Martin, X. (1996). 'Regional cohesion: evidence and theories of regional growth and convergence', *European Economic Review*, 1325–1352.

Santangelo, G. (1999). 'The geography of corporate research activity in ICT across Europe', Discussion Paper No. 276, Department of Economics, University of Reading.

Sapir, A. (1992). 'Regional integration in Europe', *Economic Journal*, 1491–1506.

Sapir, A. (1993). 'Structural dimension', *European Economy Social Europe*, No. 3, 23–39.

Sapir, A. (1996). 'The effects of Europe's Internal Market Program on production and trade: a first assessment', *Weltwirscaftliches Archiv*, 456–475.

Scaperlanda, A. (1967). 'The EEC and US foreign investment: some empirical evidence', *Economic Journal*, 22–26.

Scaperlanda, A. and E. Reiling (1971). 'A comment on a note on customs unions and direct foreign investment', *Economic Journal*, 355–357.

Scaperlanda, A. and R. Balough (1983). 'Determinants of US direct investment in Europe', *European Economic Journal*, 381–390.

Schatz, K. and F. Wolter (1987). *Structural Adjustment in the Federal Republic of Germany*. Geneva: ILO.

Schmalensee, R. (1988). 'Industrial economics: an overview', *Economic Journal*, 643–681.

Schmitz, H. (1998). 'Fostering collective efficiency', *Small Enterprise Development*, 4–11.

Schmitz, H. (1999). 'Collective efficiency and increasing returns', *Cambridge Journal of Economics*, 465–483.

Schmitz, H. and K. Nadvi (1999). 'Clustering and industrialization: introduction', *World Development*, 1503–1514.

Servan-Schreiber, J. (1969). *The American Challenge*. New York: Atheneum.

Sharp, M. and K. Pavitt (1993). 'Technology policy in the 1990s: old trends and new realities', *Journal of Common Market Studies*, 129–151.

Sharp, M. and G. Shepherd (1987). *Managing Change in British Industry*. Geneva: ILO.

Siebert, H. (ed.)(1995). *Locational Competition in the World Economy*. Tübingen: J.C.B. Mohr.

Sleuwaegen, L. (1998). 'Cross-border mergers and EC competition policy', *World Economy*, 1077–1093.

Smith, A. and A. Venables (1988). 'Completing the internal market in the European Community', *European Economic Review*, 1501–1525.

Smith, D. (1981). *Industrial Location – An Economic Geographical Analysis*. New York: John Wiley.

Smith, D. and R. Florida (1994). 'Agglomeration and industrial location: an econometric analysis of Japanese-affiliated manufacturing establishments in automotive-related industries', *Journal of Urban Economics*, 23–41.

Stahl, K. (1987). 'Theories of urban business location', in *Handbook of Regional and Urban Economics* (ed. E. Mills). Amsterdam: Elsevier, pp. 759–820.

Steiner, M. (ed.)(1998). *Clusters and Regional Specialisation*. London: Pion.

Sternberg, R. and C. Tamásy (1999). 'Munich as Germany's no. 1 high technology region: empirical evidence, theoretical explanations and the role of small firm/large firm relations', *Regional Studies*, 367–377.

Swann P., M. Prevezer and D. Stout (eds)(1998). *The Dynamics of Industrial Clustering*. Oxford: Oxford University Press.

Tharakan, M., D. Greenaway and J. Tharakan (1998). 'Cumulation and injury determination of the European Community in antidumping cases', *Weltwirtschaftlicher Archiv*, 320–339.

Tharakan, M. and P. Lloyd (1998). 'Competition policy in a changing international economic environment: an overview', *World Economy*, 997–1002.

Thompson, G. (1999). 'Introduction: situating globalization', *International Social Science Journal*, 139–152.

Thomsen, S. and P. Nicolaides (1991). *The Evolution of Japanese Direct Investment in Europe*. New York: Harvester Wheatsheaf.

Tiebout, C. (1957). 'Location theory, empirical evidence and economic evolution', *Papers and Proceedings of the Regional Science Association*, 74–86.

Tironi, E. (1982). 'Customs union theory in the presence of foreign firms', *Oxford Economic Papers*, 150–171.

Tödtling, F. (1983). 'Organizational characteristics of plants in core and peripheral regions of Austria', *Regional Studies*, 397–412.

Tondl, G. (1998). 'EU regional policy in the southern periphery: lessons for the future', *South European Society and Politics*, 93–129.

Trebilcock, M. (1986). *The Political Economy of Economic Adjustment*. Toronto: University of Toronto Press.

Tyson, L. (1987). 'Comments on Brander's 'shaping comparative advantage': creating advantage, an industrial policy perspective', in *Shaping Comparative Advantage* (eds R.G. Lipsey and W. Dobson). Toronto: C.D. Howe Institute, pp. 65–82.

Tyson, L. (1991). 'They are not us. Why American ownership still matters', *The American Prospect*, (Winter), 37–49.

Tyson, L. (1992). *Who's Bashing Whom?* Washington: Institute for International Economics.

Tyson, L. and J. Zysman (1987a). 'American industry in International Competition', in *American industry in International Competition* (eds J. Zysman and L. Tyson). Ithaca: Cornell University Press, pp. 15–59.

Tyson, L. and J. Zysman (1987b). 'Conclusion: what to do now?', in *American Industry in International Competition* (eds J. Zysman and L. Tyson). Ithaca: Cornell University Press, pp. 422–427.

UNCTAD, (1983). *The Role of Transnational Enterprises in Latin American Economic Integration Efforts: Who Integrates with Whom, How and for Whose Benefit?* New York: United Nations.

UNCTAD (1993). *World Investment Report: Transnational Corporations and Integrated International Production*. New York: United Nations.

UNCTAD (1995). 'Incentives and foreign direct investment', TD/B/ITNC/Misc. 1, 6 April 1995.

UNCTAD (1996). *Sharing Asia's Dynamism: Asian Direct Investment in the European Union*. New York: United Nations.

UNCTAD (1997). *World Investment Report: Transnational Corporations, Market Structure and Competition Policy*. United Nations: New York.

UNCTAD (1998). *World Investment Report: Trends and Determinants*. United Nations: New York.

UNCTAD (1999a). *World Investment Report: Foreign Direct Investment and the Challenge of Development*. United Nations: New York.

UNCTAD (1999b). *Investment-Related Trade Measures*. New York: United Nations.

UNCTAD (2000). *World Investment Report: Cross-border Mergers and Acquisitions and Development*. New York: United Nations.

UNCTC (1991a). *The Impact of Trade-related Investment Measures on Trade and Development*. New York: United Nations.

UNCTC (1991b). *World Investment Report: The Triad in Foreign Direct Investment*. New York: United Nations.

Vaitsos, K. (1978). 'Crisis in regional economic cooperation (integration) among developing countries: a survey', *World Development*, 719–769.

Valaskakis, K. (1999). 'Globalization as theatre', *International Social Science Journal*, 153–164.

van Aarle, B. (1996). 'The impact of the Single Market on trade and foreign direct investment in the European Union', *Journal of World Trade*, 121–138.

van Geenhuizen, M. and P. Nijkamp (1996). 'Progress in regional science: a European Perspective', *International Regional Science Review*, 223–245.

Vanhove, N. and L. Klaasen (1987). *Regional Policy: A European Approach*. Aldershot: Avebury.

Venables, A. (1985). 'Trade and trade policy with imperfect competition: the case of identical products and free entry', *Journal of International Economics*, 1–19.

Venables, A. (1994). 'Economic integration and industrial agglomeration', *Economic and Social Review*, 1–17.

Venables, A. (1996a). 'Equilibrium locations of vertically linked industries', *International Economic Review*, 341–359.

Venables, A. (1996b). 'Localization of industry and trade performance', *Oxford Review of Economic Policy*, 52–60.

Venables, A. (1998). 'The assessment: trade and location', *Oxford Review of Economic Policy*, 1–6.

Venables, A. (1999). 'The international division of industries: clustering and comparative advantage in a multi-industry model', *Scandinavian Journal of Economics*, 495–513.

Vernon, R. (1966). 'International investment and international trade in the product cycle', *Quarterly Journal of Economics*, 190–207.

Vernon, R. (1974). 'The location of economic activity', in *Economic Analysis and the Multinational Enterprise* (ed. J. Dunning). London: George Allen and Unwin, pp. 89–114.

Veugelers, R. (1991). 'Locational determinants and ranking of host countries: an empirical assessment' *Kyklos*, 363–382.

von Thünen, J. (1826). *Der Isolierte Staat in Beziehung auf Landtschaft und Nationalökonomie*. Hamburg: Perthes. [Translated from German by C. Wartenberg, *von Thünen's Isolated State* (1966), Oxford: Pergamon Press].

Vosgerau, H. (1989). 'International capital movements and trade in an intertemporal setting', in *European Factor Mobility* (eds I. Gordon and A. Thirlwall). New York: St. Martin's Press, pp. 215–232.

Wallis, K. (1968). 'The EEC and United States foreign investment: some empirical evidence re-examined', *Economic Journal*, 717–719.

Wasylenko, M. (1991). 'Empirical evidence on interregional business location decisions and the role of fiscal incentives in economic development', in *Industry Location and Public Policy* (eds H. Herzog and A. Schlottmann). Knoxville: The University of Tennessee Press, pp. 13–30.

Weber, A. (1909). *Über den Standort der Industrien*, Tübingen: J.C.B. Mohr [Translated from German by C. Friedrich, *Theory of the Location of Industries* (1962), Chicago: University of Chicago Press].

Weder, R. (1995). 'The Swiss dyestuff industry', in *Studies in Swiss Competitive Advantage* (eds M. Enright and R. Weder). Bern: Peter Lang, pp. 24–60.

Wever, E. and E. Stam (1999). 'Clusters of high technology SMEs: the Dutch case', *Regional Studies*, pp. 391–400.

Whalley, J. (1987). 'Brander's 'Shaping comparative advantage': remarks', in *Shaping Comparative Advantage* (eds R.G. Lipsey and W. Dobson). Toronto: C.D. Howe Institute, pp. 83–89.

Wheeler, D. and A. Mody (1992). 'International investment location decisions: the case of U.S. firms', *Journal of International Economics*, 57–76.

Wilkinson, B. (1985). 'Canada/US free trade and Canadian economic, cultural and political sovereignty', in *Canadian Trade at Crossroads: Options for New International Agreements* (eds D. Conklin and T. Chourchene). Toronto: Ontario Economic Council, pp. 291–307.

Woodward, D. (1992). 'Locational determinants of Japanese manufacturing start-ups in the United States', *Southern Economic Journal*, 690–708.

World Bank (1993). *The East Asian Miracle*. New York: Oxford University Press.

Wren, C. (1990). 'Regional policy in the 1980s', *National Westminster Bank Quarterly Review*, 52–64.

Yamada, T. and T. Yamada (1996). 'EC integration and Japanese foreign direct investment in the EC', *Contemporary Economic Policy*, 48–57.

Yamawaki, H. (1993). 'Location decisions of Japanese multinational firms in European manufacturing industries', in *European Competitiveness* (ed. K. Hughes), Cambridge: Cambridge University Press, pp. 11–28.

Yannopoulos, G. (1990). 'Foreign direct investment and European integration: the evidence from the formative years of the European Community', *Journal of Common Market Studies*, 235–259.

Yuill, D., K. Allen, J. Bachtler, K. Clement and F. Wishdale (1994). *European Regional Incentives, 1994–95*. London: Bowker.

Zysman, J. (1983). *Governments, Markets and Growth*. Ithaca: Cornell University Press.

Zysman, J. and A. Schwartz (1998). 'Reunifying Europe in an emerging world economy: economic heterogeneity, new industrial options, and political choices', *Journal of Common Market Studies*, 405–429.

Index

For Product Safety Concerns and Information please contact our EU
representative GPSR@taylorandfrancis.com Taylor & Francis Verlag GmbH,
Kaufingerstraße 24, 80331 München, Germany

Printed and bound by CPI Group (UK) Ltd, Croydon, CR0 4YY
08/05/2025
01864506-0001